Rio Grande Narrow Gauge
By John B. Norwood

Edited by Donald J. Heimburger
Layout by Marilyn M. Heimburger

Library of Congress Catalog Card Number: 82-84384
ISBN 0-911581-00-6

First Edition
Printed in the United States of America

Heimburger House Publishing Company
310 Lathrop Ave.
River Forest, IL 60305

©1983 by Heimburger House Publishing Company, River Forest, Illinois. All rights reserved. Nothing may be reprinted or copied in whole or part without express written permission from the Publisher.

DEDICATION

One of the great disappointments of my life is that I was not around to have helped build and operate the original Denver & Rio Grande-Rio Grande Western railroad.

This book is dedicated to those who did—the ghosts of General William J. Palmer and his contemporaries in this great building of a transportation system that opened the Rocky Mountain Empire. No less, it is dedicated to all of those later generations of men and women who have kept the General's dream alive and the Rio Grande viable.

I sincerely and humbly also dedicate it to the women who followed the railroad, birthed and raised the following generations, comforted and pleasured the men of the early and following generations of Rio Grande railroaders. They have never been given their just dues for, without them, the Rio Grande would not have been completed, nor have become the great system it now is.

And, to the finest example of these women, a special commendation and thanks to my wife. A railroader's life being what it was, and is, she had the chore of rearing our children and in packing and unpacking our belongings twenty-nine times while I was being moved from assignment to assignment about the line, from one end to the other, and back and forth across it with numerous intermediate stops.

Chris Burritt

Contents

Prologue **6**

Chapter 1—Man comes to Narrow Gauge Land **10**

Chapter 2—General Palmer dreams of a railroad **14**

Chapter 3—The railroad becomes incorporated—
Chronology and accomplishments **21**

Chapter 4—Building the Narrow Gauge—Alamosa to Chama **34**

Chapter 5—Over the Continental Divide—Chama-Durango **54**

Chapter 6—On to Silverton—Durango to Silverton **62**

Chapter 7—The Chili Line—Down the Rio Grande to Santa Fe **78**

Chapter 8—Land of the Navajo—Farmington Branch **90**

Chapter 9—The San Juan Basin and the railroad **98**

Chapter 10—New towns and their names—Alamosa to Santa Fe and
the San Juan Extension **108**

Chapter 11—Main towns of Rio Grande river drainage—Alamosa,
Antonito and Santa Fe **118**

Chapter 12—Lumber industry along the Narrow Gauge **148**

Color Section **153**

Chapter 13—Rio Grande steam **164**

Chapter 14—The *San Juan* **202**

Chapter 15—Derailments **218**

Chapter 16—Snowstorms on Cumbres **224**

Chapter 17—Forewarnings of abandonment **234**

Chapter 18—Local color on the Narrow Gauge **248**

Appendix **254**

Index **310**

Prologue

The men who make history, have not time to write it. — **Metternich**

The men and the boy-men who conceived, built, maintained and operated a 3-foot gauge railroad that hastened the opening and development of the Rocky Mountain Empire—Colorado, New Mexico and Utah—were busy men. Each day as they drove spikes and laid iron from the plains to the passes on the Narrow Gauge, they added a bit more to the history of the winning of the West.

These men were too busy to write of the history they were making. Only by word of mouth in the long, cold nights around the cannon heaters of outfit cars and flat-topped stoves of cabooses has their saga come down to us.

STORY OF A DREAM

This is the story of the dream of a man and those who worked with him to make it come true. It is a story of their struggles, aspirations and accomplishments. In the telling we cannot overlook the women who made homes for them, nursed and consoled them, pleasured them and made their hard lives a little easier.

This is the story of the memories, the heartaches, the joys, the failures and the successes that make up the building of the Narrow Gauge . . . the railroad that started in a small way to fulfill the desire of one man to own and control his own railroad—one that just kept growing until it became the dominant factor in the development of a new frontier.

From its beginning this rail system was to be a rebel in its engineering, its concept and its financing. The gauge chosen was the first of many later innovations. Because of economic and engineering factors, the rails were laid to a gauge of 36 inches, and the descriptive term of "narrow gauge" was early applied to the line to distinguish it from the more commonly accepted "standard gauge." The line, named the *Denver & Rio Grande*, proved that narrow gauge could be built faster and less expensively across mountainous terrain. The volume of earthwork was minimized and auxiliary structures, such as bridges, in turn required less material. Thus, the Narrow Gauge was able to rapidly build railroads into each of the new communities springing up within the Rocky Mountain Empire as required to serve the needs of the recently-started mining, lumbering and agricultural projects.

Broadly speaking, the frontier stage of development of this empire lasted from the close of the Civil War to the last decade of the 19th Century. During this period the Denver & Rio Grande Narrow Gauge built a web of rail lines across the face of the Rocky Mountain Empire. The web was spun of ribbons of iron rail weighing 30 pounds to the yard, running parallel 36 inches apart, spiked to ties hewed from native timber.

Speed, and more speed, was the battle cry of the engineering and construction forces on each new segment started. To answer that demand the Narrow Gauge laid rail in twisting, curving and climbing patterns (often contradictory to generally accepted engineering rules) to tie together the miles and miles of mountains, plains, valleys, and desert of Colorado, Utah and northern New Mexico—the Rocky Mountain Empire.

CENTURIES OF EXPLORATION

More than four centuries of exploration and colonization preceded the opening of this frontier and the building of the narrow gauge Denver & Rio Grande Railroad. Coronado must be credited with providing the first information concerning the nature of this land. Near the middle of the 16th Century the Spaniards, in their avid search for gold, dispatched Coronado on a long and fruitless search for the Seven Cities of Cibolla. For the ensuing 250 years Spain dominated the area. Spanish names, Spanish ways and Spanish cultures all became an inseparable part of the land the Narrow Gauge would later operate in.

In 1803, President Thomas Jefferson signed the agreement for the purchase of the Louisiana Territory. Little was known of the vast western regions which the young nation had acquired. The Lewis and Clark expedition was organized to explore the Northwest. Shortly after, a similar expedition, under Lt. Zebulon Pike, was mounted to do the same in the central and southwestern portions of the Purchase. Both of these were government expeditions. Other expeditions, some private and some government, followed at intervals, but the reports from the Pike Expedition had the greatest influence on the eventual opening of the Rocky Mountain region. This was especially true of the area along the Front Range, up the Arkansas River, the San Luis Valley and southward down the Rio Grande River to Santa Fe, New Mexico.

Pike's travels were not without difficulties, including being taken captive by the Spaniards at the lower end of the San Luis Valley to be conducted as a prisoner, along with his party, to Mexico City. He was also frustrated in his not being able to reach the top of a high peak, later named for him, near what is now Colorado Springs. In 1810, after returning from Mexico City, Pike prepared and published an account of his journey. His data was influential in starting and promoting trade over a route that would become known as the Santa Fe Trail. His descriptions and observations formed the first extensive and authoritative report of the land south of the Platte to the Spanish territory. In this report is found the first mention of the possibility of gold to be found in the area he covered. The mention did not attract any special attention.

FUR TRADERS REACH ROCKIES

But Pike's report, along with other information trickling back to the States from various sources, stirred the imagination of those in the fur trade. Mountain men, trappers and fur traders were not long in reaching the Rocky Mountains. Soon, from them, stories began reaching civilization—stories of the presence of gold, silver, red iron ore, coal, good grass and timber, as well as springs that seeped oil that would burn, and gas above the oil seeps that could be set afire.

Denver & Rio Grande locomotive No. 1 was put in service July 3, 1871. She's a product of Baldwin.

Prospectors, many with farming backgrounds, headed for the mountains and creeks of the Rockies. They were primarily after gold, but when they failed to find it, they stayed in the land to farm and raise livestock. Thus, in the early years, the influx to the Rocky Mountain Empire from the East was confined to the hardy mountain men and fur traders who were followed by the gold seekers. It was not until near the end of the Civil War that more permanent settlers and developers started to arrive.

The state of the economy and society in the East and the South in the aftermath of the Civil War encouraged people to move from these areas to a new and more promising land. Each man and woman of the resulting migration came to the West with the hope of being able to start new lives and to escape postwar pressures in their old homes. They came not with the high expectations of the Fifty-Niners, the gold seekers who believed that each would be able to shovel up a wagon load of gold on the slopes of Pike's mountain and return home. Rather, they came believing that development of the new frontier would afford them opportunities to work and stay, to find a place for their skills and muscles.

They did find need for their skills and muscles, but it soon became apparent to the settlers that better means of transportation to bring in supplies and export new wealth were required; railroads were needed to complete the civilization of the new lands. One of the more prominent newcomers, General William Larimer, spoke for all when he stated: "We are satisfied with our prospects here. There is wealth here not only in the mines, but in the soil. We have innumerable treasures, sufficient to justify immigration to the fullest extent.

William Jackson Palmer

A railroad is coming. The Pacific Railroad is planning to build through the West. The West is demanding it. Denver City demands it. For this country is bound to settle. Manifest Destiny has shaped its end. We have laid the foundation for a city, an outlet for this gold bonanza, and for the Rocky Mountain region."

THE GENERAL HAD A DREAM

Soon another general with the given name of William came to Denver City. That man was William Jackson Palmer. With him he brought a dream that would inspire the building of the Narrow Gauge. His railroad would be only 3 feet wide between the rails, but it would be long enough to reach from Denver and the Front Range in Colorado, to Salt Lake City and the great Salt Lake in Utah; not as wide as other railroads of the period, but tough and hardy enough to challenge and conquer the high passes of the Rockies and the hot, dry deserts of Utah. He envisioned an obstacle-defying railroad possessed of a derring-do that could put a roadbed and rails into each major new mining camp as quickly as the ink dried on the claim notices of new strikes.

To build and own his own railroad was not the General's only dream. Back East there was a small, demurely elegant, snubnosed girl with a musical voice. Her christened name was Mary Lincoln Mellen, but she preferred the nickname "Queen." So, besides seeing himself as the Railroad King of the West, the General also spent some time building air castles in which Mary Ellen was his Queen.

On January 17, 1870, the General wrote what he called a love letter to Mary Ellen. In essence, however, the letter was written by a lonely man pouring out his aspirations to a girl he hoped would understand:

"I had a dream last evening while sitting in the gloaming at the car window. I mean a wide-awake dream. Shall I tell it to you? I thought how fine it would be to have a little railroad a few hundred miles in length, all under one's own control with one's friends, to have no jealousies and contests and differing opinions."

The letter went on to outline how he would fill all the necessary jobs, how each employee would profit, and how the railroad would affect the social and cultural aspects of the area through which he would build.

THE RAILROAD GREW

In the years ahead, the "little railroad a few hundred miles in length" expanded circumstance by circumstance until the major city at the east end of the line, Denver, was tied to its sister city on the west end, Salt Lake City, and to the capitol of New Mexico, Santa Fe. What resulted were two parallel ribbons of steel 3 feet apart uniting the three principal cities of three states to make the Rocky Mountain Empire for all practical purposes one community.

Not many years after they were joined, competitive pressures made it necessary for portions of the original narrow gauge to be converted to standard gauge. However, it was quickly apparent that other portions of the system could not, economically or geographically, be converted to the wider gauge.

Those sections that remained narrow gauge were located on the Marshall Pass-Montrose route and the Cumbres Pass-Durango route. Branches from these main stems also retained the original gauge, including Montrose to Ouray; Mears Junction to Alamosa; the Chili Line between Antonito, Colorado and Santa Fe; and the Farmington Branch between Durango and Farmington. The latter originally built standard gauge and then converted to narrow gauge.

Of the portions that remained narrow gauge until the end only that segment over Cumbres Pass—between Alamosa, Durango and Silverton—kept the spicy flavor and aura of romance associated with the Denver & Rio Grande during its first two decades of building and expansion.

The standard gauge lines of the Rio Grande remain a viable and active transportation system, but spicy flavor, romance and historical sentiment was not justification enough for the narrow gauge vestigal remains of the original routes to be kept in service. The Depression was the beginning of the end for

William Palmer and his associates; Zebulon Pike Centennial Celebration, 1906.

them, and in following years, segment after segment ceased to operate and services were abandoned. Just a few years prior to World War II, abandonment proceedings aimed at closing the Chili Line between Antonito, Colorado, and Santa Fe, New Mexico, met with little more than token resistance from the public.

Later, following WWII, application was made to abandon the lines between Salida and Montrose, including the Mears Junction to Alamosa branch. Again, inexplicably and illogically, neither the people living along these lines, nor any other group, offered any significant or organized opposition.

LAST RAILS CHALLENGED

But in the early 1960's when it became apparent that the balance of the remaining narrow gauge trackage, the San Juan route between Antonito and Durango, would be facing abandonment, the situation changed. The railroad was challenged by organized, entrenched opposition, with battle lines sharply defined, and the public committed to a no-retreat stand. Some intrinsic factor about the last remnants of the narrow gauge led the few remaining first-generation veterans, and almost all second-generation residents, along the line to go to war in an effort to save *their* railroad. Other organizations, railroad fans, government agencies and historical societies joined the resistance group.

The 3-foot gauge railroad over Cumbres Pass and along the San Juan River represented intensely-felt values for these people.

They would have been hard put to define these feelings in words, but to lose the railroad was like losing a part of their hard won and beloved heritage. The narrow gauge had served and been a part of them for three-quarters of a century.

To each and all of these, the San Juan Line was the last relic of a proud time when a new land was being opened and made livable and productive. It was *The Narrow Gauge*.

This, then, is the story of the opening of their frontier, the building of a railroad in it, and the people who built it and left an unforgettable, proud legacy.

In the beginning there were only the mountains and plains. From them came a plea best put into words by the American poet, Sam Foss:

> *Bring me men to match my mountains,*
> *Bring me men to match my plains,*
> *Men with empires in their purpose*
> *And new eras in their brains.*

The men came. They built a railroad, and they left behind the story, the glory and the nostalgia of the Narrow Gauge.

Chapter 1
Man comes to Narrow Gauge Land

To completely savor and appreciate the land of the Narrow Gauge it would be necessary to read and study many lengthy and learned volumes, or to spend many days touring the country in order to properly grasp its immensity of physical roughness that makes any construction of roadways so difficult. A story such as this one is hardly the place for a long treatise on the history and geography of Narrow Gauge Land, but some knowledge is required, or we cannot be sufficiently sympathetic, or in empathy with General Palmer and his people as they built the Narrow Gauge.

The geography and climate of the land has changed many times through the ages and was not always as we find it today. Although in the essentials, the appearance and nature of the terrain and its plant cover has changed but little from that first seen by the nomadic hordes coming down from the north some 25,000 years ago. Coronado, if he were to come back, might be puzzled to find a different type of cattle grazing on the plains, canals for irrigating where he remembered watercourses, and blacktop roadways where he had followed game and Indian trails.

The water would be smelly and make him and his men sick and the air would smell as bad and make their eyes and nostrils burn, nor could they see as far because of a disconcerting haze. But, all these things aside, Coronado would see no changes in the land and its cover as he had known it.

LAND THROUGH THE AGES

Colorado and its sister states, Utah and New Mexico, developed through the geologic ages by several great uplifts of the surface of the earth, erosion, subsidences and inundations. Their history can be read in the pages of the rock layers on the earth's surface. Some pages are almost illegible, some are missing, and the story is not easily read or perfect, but it is the only document from which we can gain knowledge of the earth's past. Back in the earliest geologic ages, the forms of animal and plant life were simple and primitive. Millions of years slowly passed by and the processes of evolution produced more complex forms, died and their skeletons and remains became fossils from whose forms we can deduce their forms and structures.

The most important of these early periods of narrow gauge land was the Cretaceous. Plant growth flourished, died and sunk into the marsh areas to become great coal beds. Toward the end of this period the earth had a severe stomach ache and in its agonies produced the Rocky Mountains that made a high plateau and mountainous region appear where the low plains and swamps had been. The rising of lava and igneous rock from the interior of the earth was accompanied by vapors, gases and highly heated mineral-charged waters. The earth's stomach pains continued, and the newly-intruded rock material was subjected to violent movements during the throes of suffering. The emerged mountain range of rock faulted, folded, slid, was crushed and tumbled. In the course of these actions, channels were formed, both on and under the surface, by means of which the mineralized solutions

The year is 1858 at the junction of Cherry Creek and the Platte rivers. Twelve years later the first spike was driven in this vicinity.

could flow and come in contact with other solutions, gases and solids and to form combinations which in cooling or being precipitated became the ore bodies that would later form the first wealth of the land and bring people to it about the middle of the 19th Century.

Nature, following the uplifting of the mass of rough rock, started the long process of smoothing the range to a more esthetic contour, until it is now as we know it. The agents used were ice, water, wind and chemicals. Water and ice accumulated or fell on the high mountain tops and by gravity moved downward. As they moved, surfaces were ground finer and carried along to be redeposited. Where there were no channels, they were cut. Strong winds blew and aided in the process of erosion and redisposition. To the east of the mountains, the face of a high plain began to form and in the mountains large, flat surfaced parks appeared. Canyons, basins, cirques and smooth hill sides became new features of the mountains.

Colorado State Historical Society

FAUNA AND FLORA

New forms of fauna and flora evolved—some still exist, others ceased to exist, leaving only fossils behind for us to know they were once here. By the time Coronado came, the species had become fixed about as we know them now. There were wild fruits and berries, a few types of nuts—and the buffalo, along with deer, antelope, elk, sheep and small game.

Some 25,000 years ago a horde of shaggy, nomadic hunters crossed the Bering Strait, either on an earth or ice bridge and moved southward, following the land where it was being released slowly from the last glacial period. Game was doing the same, and these nomads followed the game. Eventually their wanderings brought them to the high plains and the Front Range. Here they found buffalo and other game in abundance and quantities of wild fruits and berries. We have a meager knowledge of these people—only the little evidence archaeologists have been able to find. We do know a newer people who may or may not have evolved from the first nomadic Asiatic Horde appeared. These were the Indians who, at the coming of the Mountain Men are estimated to have been about 15,000 strong in Narrow Gauge Land.

Coronado started his journey from Mexico that would bring him to the plains and mountains of Colorado in 1540. It would be almost 250 years later before Americans came to the same area. So the earliest explorers of Narrow Gauge Land were Spaniards. They were also the first colonizers and settlers.

Colonization of the New World began with the second expedition of Columbus in 1493. From bases in the West Indies the Spaniards kept reaching out. By 1513, Balboa had looked at the Pacific Ocean. That year, also, Ponce de Leon discovered and named Florida. Four years later Yucutan had been explored. Then, in 1519, Cortez led his Conquistadores to Mexico City, the largest and most powerful city of Indians in North America. After conquest, this city became the base from which following expeditions and expansion would start. It became the capital of New Spain, in the minds of the Spaniards, all of North America.

Remains of the old tollgate house, hostelry and midway between Chama and Antonito, located a quarter mile from the Osier water tank.

From this base the Spaniards quickly pushed their frontiers northward and developed some rich mines. They used the native Indians as slaves to work these mines. The virile, prolific invaders did not spend all their time mining and a new race of people, the Mexicans, resulted. To provide food for the new mining camps, farming was engaged in and cattle ranches grew.

GOLDEN CITIES

As the Spaniards became more proficient in native languages, they listened to stories of wonders and golden cities far to the north of any place they had so far been. Mexico and Peru were still pouring out wealth but, if the stories were true, even greater wealth could be found beyond the northern horizon. An attempt to colonize Florida and find pearls and gold failed. The leader became discouraged and started westward along the coasts of the Gulf of Mexico. The vessels used were crude and they were shipwrecked somewhere on the Texas shore. One of the survivors, Cabeza de Vaca, arrived back in Mexico after six long years of wandering among Indian tribes of the southwestern United States. He learned much about the land and more stories of cities and wealth—always just a little farther north. All this information was made available to the officials of New Spain and a fever to find the rumored cities and wealth grew.

Expeditions under Friar Marcos de Niza, Coronado and others struggled northward trying to find the fabled Seven Cities of Cibolla. No golden cities were found, only mudwalled Indian towns, and their inhabitants were only poor tillers of the soil. There was no gold or other form of wealth. But always they told more stories of riches to be found—always just over the northern horizons.

The discouraging news brought back to Mexico City by the returning expeditions dampened the enthusiasm of official New Spain and interest in the northern areas was at a low point. Decades passed, and the riches of Mexico and Peru were no longer flowing so freely. But Spanish churchmen envisioned a second wealth, so far as they were concerned, in the tribes of Indians who could be converted to Christianity and while being converted could be used to build missions and work farms and tend herds of cattle and flocks of sheep. In 1581 a Father Rodriquez and two companions went north to make such a beginning among the Pueblos. The following year another expedition under Espejo set out to explore and with a secondary purpose of trying to find Rodriquez. Espejo returned with several thousand native-made cotton blankets and a confirmed discovery of mines in Arizona. Again New Spain was fired with ambitions for conquest and settlement in the northern areas.

To give impetus to the new drive toward the north was the factor of Sir Francis Drake's voyage and his looting along the Pacific Coast. Spain became convinced that the only way to forestall English settlement of North America was to accelerate its own conquest and settlement of the New Mexican lands and the California coast. The project for colonizing New Mexico was entrusted to Juan de Onate, a prominent citizen of northern Mexico, who was married to a granddaughter of Cortez and a great-granddaughter of Montezuma. Onate was to handle the agricultural duties and the missionary order of Franciscans the ecclesiastical.

DEPART FOR NEW MEXICO

In 1598 the colonizing party of 400 men including 130 soldier-settlers, some having their families with them, departed for the New Mexico lands. Eight missionaries accompanied the party. Indian and Negro slaves drove the 83 wagons and carts carrying colonizing equipment and supplies and herded the 7,000 head of livestock that would be used to start herds and flocks in the proposed colony. The party started in February, crossed the Rio Grande River near present-day El Paso, and arrived at what is now the San Juan community in New Mexico in mid-August. Work was immediately started on the building of an irrigation system and the building of a church. Members of surrounding Indian tribes were quickly being converted, or more truthfully, were enslaved. Other missions and established farms and communities followed the one at San Juan.

San Juan and the New Mexico colony thus became the second colony in North America. Florida was the first. This Spanish project was nine years earlier than the Virginia colony and 22 years before the Pilgrims landed. Parties from the New Mexico colony explored in all directions looking for more land, gold and slaves, but until the end of the 17th Century, further development of colonies and missions north or west of San Juan was slow. Without doubt these parties wandered over Colorado, Utah and Arizona, but the records to confirm this are almost non-existent. By 1630, the year of Boston's founding, there were 25 missions in New Mexico and 60,000 Indian converts in 90 pueblos. Fifty missionaries were working diligently to convert the natives and teach them. The males of the colonists and their second generation offspring were working just as diligently with the Indian women to increase the numbers of the new breed resulting from the mixing of Indian and Spanish blood. Men being men even though frocked, the soldier-settler Spaniards received assistance from the missionaries in this endeavor to populate the new land with a new breed.

In return for the privilege of being converted, the natives were expected to contribute labor and produce. Indians occasionally fled the pueblos and missions to tribes in the mountains and plains of Colorado. About the middle of the century, a large group fled from Taos and was pursued by a force under Juan Archuleta. This expedition captured the fugitives at a point named El Cuartelejo, supposed to have been about 100 miles east of Pueblo, Colorado. The account of this expedition is thought to be the earliest written record of Spaniards well into Colorado since it is very difficult to relate Coronado's journey to specific locations in Colorado. Although a number of parties without doubt had been active in the San Luis Valley and the Durango area, none of them wrote records of their journeys. However, there had been enough journeys made so that by word of mouth there was in existence considerable knowledge of the area and the better known rivers, and prominent areas had received and were spoken of by definite Spanish names.

REVOLT OF 1680

For about 50 years nothing significant occurred in the New Mexico colonies and missions until in 1680 the Pueblo Indians revolted. A medicine man, Pope, was the leader in this uprising which resulted in the slaughter of about 400 Spanish settlers and forced the balance to flee down the Rio Grande. The colony areas were reoccupied 12 years later to some extent by Spanish forces under Don Diego de Vargas. Santa Fe was reoccupied but food became short so de Vargas started raiding Indian pueblos for corn and other foods. He got as far as Taos when, for safety reasons on his return trip to Santa Fe, he had to take a circuitous route which took him into Costilla County's present location in the San Luis Valley. A supply of meat was obtained in a meadow on the Culebra River while another party was busy hunting elk on San Antone Mountain, south of today's Antonito, Colorado. This party had a skirmish with a band of Ute Indians, but it ended

The San Luis Valley looked like this when General Palmer conceived his new railroad; it took a real dreamer to see farms and homes where sagebrush grew. *Courtesy D&RGW*

with peace being made when the Utes found they were attacking Spaniards rather than Pueblo Indians. De Vargas completed his journey and carried large supplies of food to Santa Fe and the colonists. His return journey was down the west side of the Rio Grande along a route much later to be used by the Narrow Gauge's Chili Line.

So by the end of the 17th Century the Spaniards were again in control of New Mexico, but now they had another worry. There was equipment and stories brought to New Mexico by wandering Indians, especially the Navajo, that gave evidence the French were coming in from the north and east. To better determine what the situation was, and to try to recapture some fugitive Indians, it was decided to send a party to the plains of eastern Colorado. This expedition was the charge of Juan de Ulibarri. The force consisting of 40 soldiers and 100 Indian allies got under way in 1706 and its journeyings passed present-day Trinidad and Walsenburg. It reached the Arkansas River at about Pueblo. From Pueblo, Ulibarri moved on in a northeastward direction until he reached the vicinity of the area the Spaniards referred to as El Cuartelejo. He found the fugitive Indians he was in pursuit of at this point living with the Apaches. Ulibarri took possession of the area as prescribed by the tenets of earlier discoverers of new lands.

Ulibarri returned to New Mexico. His diary described the areas he had traversed in great detail, and it gives us our best early description of the land east of the Rockies. He also gave a name to this area, the Province of San Luis. It also introduces the first rivalry for the region between the French and the Spanish.

It was almost another 100 years before France sold the portion they claimed as theirs to the young nation that was developing along the Atlantic. The Spaniards did not know what trouble really was until America bought the Louisiana Territory and started out to see what it had bought and to make use of its new acquisition.

Chapter 2

General Palmer dreams of a railroad

During World War I one of the small Class C locomotives rushes a trainload of livestock East to feed the troops. *Author's collection*

The trappers and fur traders came as the first Americans to exploit the Rockies. The Indians were already there. None of these were ever numerous, and their wants and needs were of a nature that transportation to supply them was not hard to provide such as crude boats, pack trains, wagons and carts. But the demand and price for beaver pelts declined in the 1830's. The mountain men and traders moved to the plains and turned to the buffalo robe trade. Trading posts of fixed locations and considerable size were established to more effectively accommodate the new trade. More wagon trains were required to haul the heavy robes to market, and the buffalo hunters and Indians who engaged in the robe trade had to have more and heavier supplies than the beaver trappers. A few military posts such as Fort Garland in the San Luis Valley had to be supplied.

Gold seekers were appearing more frequently in the Rocky Mountains, and the New Mexicans finally started moving from the old colonies in the Santa Fe-Taos area to the San Luis Valley, Trinidad and Walsenburg-Pueblo lands. Beyond the mountains, in Utah, the first settlement of followers of Brigham Young, members of the Church of Jesus Christ of Latter-Day Saints, nicknamed Mormons, was started in the Great Salt Lake Valley in July, 1847. The vanguard consisted of 143 men, three women and two children. Hundreds more were to follow close behind so that, by the time Denver began to grow, there was a thriving community of industrious people who had come to stay on the western perimeter of the Rocky Mountain Empire. The Mormons had products to sell and need for things they could not provide themselves. They needed transportation more efficient than wagon trains. To the south was Santa Fe, the earliest established major trading center of the Rockies. The movement of goods to, from and through Santa Fe was substantial for California and Mexico and especially Chihuahua and Mexico City interchanged trade at Santa Fe.

GOLD IS DISCOVERED

The die was cast when gold was discovered near the junction of the South Platte River with Cherry Creek, about where Denver would eventually be located. The Pikes Peak gold rush of 1859 was a bust, but many who made this rush stayed along the Front Range and founded several small, rough communities. That same year in May, John H. Gregory discovered the Gregory Lode, a vein of gold-bearing quartz near Central City. This was followed by other lode and placer discoveries that justified development and working.

Less than two years later, on February 28, 1861, a law was signed that created Colorado Territory from the territories of Kansas, Nebraska, Utah and New Mexico. For the first 10 years development was slow. The Civil War and its aftermath contributed to this slowness, and the ores being mined were refractory ores and difficult to extract, process and transport. Indian resistance around the settlements and along the travel routes threatened the very existence of the new territory.

Above all, the lack of suitable means of transportation from trade and manufacturing centers of the East and Midwest retarded development. The need was there and was answered by a railroad, the Kansas Pacific, which reached Denver on August 15, 1870. Colorado became the "Centennial State" in August, 1876 and the needs of communities in the mountains would soon be served by the narrow gauge.

REACHES FULL STRIDE

It was not until the 1880's that Colorado and the Narrow Gauge reached full stride, although the remaining years of the 1870's following statehood were far from idle ones. Social life

Artist's sketch of Fort Garland in 1868. *Colorado State Historical Society*

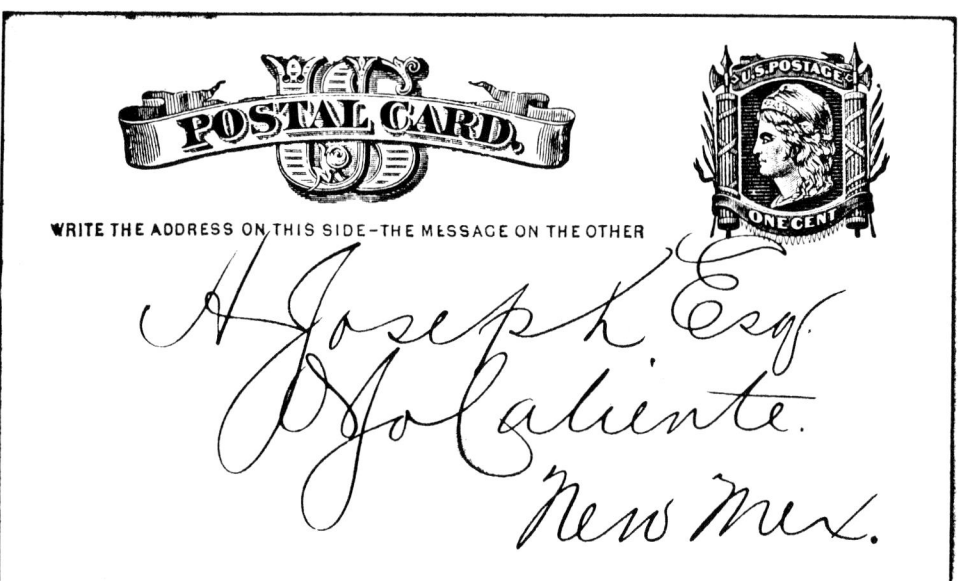

In the cottonwood trees along the San Juan River, settlers built their homes.

was improving in ratio to the availability of money; mining centers were beginning to pour out wealth in gold and silver. Aspen, Leadville, Silverton and others were crying for rail transportation. Coal and steel industries were beginning—irrigation systems and a cycle of wet weather caused an influx of farmers, and dry farming was being mastered. Smelters were built and the smoke rose constantly from their smokestacks. The Panic of 1893 hurt the mining and smelting industry, but the discovery and development of Cripple Creek started a revival. Farming, including new crops such as sugar beets, continued growing and produced more new wealth. The livestock industry, with wool production, thrived. All in all, the health, wealth and expansion of all these never really

Up the draw from the old line across La Veta Pass was this settler's simple home.

stopped after the 1870's, and Colorado became the commercial center of the Rocky Mountain West.

Railroads, and in particular the Denver and Rio Grande narrow gauge, played a major role in the development of lands bought sight unseen, a portion of the Louisiana Purchase. The Narrow Gauge, the three foot gauge railroad that started out as a dream of General William Jackson Palmer, kept on growing until it connected Denver, east of the mountains, with Salt Lake City, on the Great Salt Lake. The connection made commerce between the Rockies' sister cities possible, and made the dreams of a great new commonwealth in the West come true.

Three railroad systems, later to become transcontinental giants, were first to the Rocky Mountains. Each of them more or less followed established wagon train routes westward from the Mississippi and Missouri Rivers. The Union Pacific-Central Pacific line skirted the main Rocky Mountain range to the north through Wyoming to Ogden, Utah, thence to California. A branch, the Denver Pacific, that left the main line at Cheyenne, Wyoming, entered Denver on June 22, 1870. The Kansas Pacific that had been stalling at Sheridan, Kansas, was spurred by the Denver Pacific's action and reached Denver on August 15, 1870. A route aimed first at the Santa Fe trade detoured the rough terrain and mountains of Colorado and was built over Raton Pass through New Mexico. It was called the Atchison, Topeka and Santa Fe.

Railroad building, rather railroad projections on paper, became a mania of the West. New railroads were announced so frequently that newspapers and local records could not keep up. Most of the projects died quiet deaths as quickly as the promoters had milked the gullible of their cash.

RAILROADS TO DENVER

The first railroads to Colorado logically came to Denver. The Denver Pacific provided a link with the Union Pacific, a transcontinental route. Arrival of the Kansas Pacific was important as a more direct route to points that at that time were more closely bound by mutual ties to Colorado. But the coming of the Kansas Pacific to Denver was to mean even more to Colorado than the mere arrival of the railroad. With the railroad came a man who would have great impact on Rocky Mountain Empire railroad building and industrial development.

That man, General William Jackson Palmer, was destined to leave a lasting impression on the economical and cultural development of the Rocky Mountain Empire, as well as to become involved in Old Mexico. Those who make history and should be most remembered do not always receive the attention due them. In Colorado there are only three monuments to General Palmer. There is a small lake, almost a pond, at the summit of the divide about midway between Denver and Colorado Springs named Palmer Lake. In the Denver Union Station is a bronze plaque that reads:

**Union Cavalry general
Pioneer railroad builder
Prophet of Colorado's greatness. He mapped the routes of three transcontinental railways, supervised the building of the first road to Denver, organized and constructed the Denver and Rio Grande Railroad, stimulated the state's industries, cherished its beauties, founded Colorado Springs, fostered Colorado College and served our sister republic of Mexico with sympathy and wisdom in developing its national railways.**

Cover page of a D&RG public timetable issued in 1886.
Courtesy Colorado State Historical Society

There is also a bronze equestrian statue in Colorado Springs at an intersection near the college in the middle of the intersection.

The third monument is a similar plaque in Union Station at Salt Lake City and one in Mexico. A few books and articles have been written about the General and his accomplishments but none have been widely distributed. The man deserved more than this to commemorate him for in the final analysis he was responsible. He lacked the spark that is vital to becoming a popular historical figure, and he was too busy making history to write it.

PALMER IN HISTORY

Judge Wilson McCarthy, then president of the Denver and Rio Grande Western Railroad Company, on May 27, 1954, made a speech before the Newcomen Society in North America that best places General Palmer in history. Judge McCarthy had a special ability to relate to Palmer because the Judge was in a very real sense reorganizing and revitalizing that which the General had started over 80 years before.

"It is my privilege to bring you an improbable story. It is the story of William Jackson Palmer.... It is the story of a man imbued with Quaker faith in peace and universal brotherhood. Yet in time of national peril, this man became a daring cavalry leader in the War Between the States.

"Before he was 20, he was an expert in the utilization of coal, then a new fuel. While still in his 20's, he won the star of a brigadier general. At 34, he owned his own railroad. He raised millions to lay track through unpeopled country.

"He founded the Denver and Rio Grande Western Railroad, Mexican National Railways, organized the Colorado Fuel and Iron Company. He created Colorado Springs . . .

"Someone has said men are products of the times into which they are born. Certainly that was true of William Palmer."

Judge McCarthy told of the General's sojourn to England at the age of 19 to study railroads and coal mining and the use of coal as fuel in locomotives. He returned home at age 20 and became private secretary to President John Edgar Thomson of the Pennsylvania Railroad. He sat in on many discussions concerning the possibility of building a line to California and the Pacific. His railroad career was interrupted by the Civil War. Palmer, in spite of his Quaker upbringing, entered the conflict and emerged as a General. Thereafter a position with the Pennsylvania Railroad in the quiet state of the same name no longer interested him. The West was drawing him to it.

In August, 1865, Palmer moved to St. Louis. The Union Pacific was starting to build westward from Omaha and the Central Pacific was moving east from California. General Palmer was employed as treasurer of the Kansas Pacific, which was moving west from Lawrence, Kansas. As the name implies, this route was projected across Kansas to the Pacific with the actual line not too clearly defined. The consensus was that towns and farms would follow the advancing rails. Colorado Territory—Denver and the mining camps— were waiting, and ox carts moved too slowly to supply the demands and needs of people in the new territory.

While he was in charge of financing for the Kansas Pacific, General Palmer became well acquainted with bankers, brokers, financiers and politicians interested in railroad and land development. This was later to prove to be of value when he started to build his own railroad.

In 1867, Palmer headed a survey party to find a practical route to the Pacific for the Kansas Pacific. He was accompanied by a young Englishman of an influential family, Dr. William A. Bell. The association and friendship continued through both their lives.

ROUTE IS SURVEYED

By January, 1868, the party had mapped and surveyed a route to San Francisco between the 32nd and 35th parallels. Palmer returned to work with the Kansas Pacific and was placed in charge of construction. The Kansas Pacific never made use of the survey to the Pacific because it ended its westward building upon entry into Denver on August 15, 1870. The Union Pacific later took over the Kansas Pacific.

While engaged in his duties in charge of construction on the Kansas Pacific, Palmer did not forget the two surveys he had made for westward routes. From his recollections of what he had seen he began to weave a dream. He revealed this dream to the girl he was courting and was destined to be his wife: "I had a dream last evening while sitting in the gloaming of the car window . . . Shall I tell it to you?"

Judge McCarthy summarized this dream for his listeners: "The road of his own, that General Palmer dreamed about, was incorporated October 27, 1870, as the Denver & Rio Grande with an authorized capital stock of $2.5 million dollars. He conceived of it as running from Denver to Mexico City with branch lines extending into the mountains.

"It was a bold plan. Denver was no metropolis. The 1870 United States Census gave it 4,759 people. It was a town of wooden sidewalks and dirt paths. It had no water system. In the entire territory of Colorado south of Denver there were only 10,000 persons living in small settlements . . .

"Having gotten his plan under way, Palmer married Queen Mellen on November 7, 1870, and they immediately sailed for England . . ."

Of course, we do not know what Queen (Mary Lincoln) thought of this honeymoon for it was in reality a busman's holiday. Palmer visited the Festiniog narrow gauge railroad line in Wales and talked with railroad engineers who had built such lines in India. From his discussions, he decided that only a narrow gauge railroad would be practical in mountain country where standard gauge costs would be prohibitive. Disregarding the many reasons to be given later as to why a gauge of three feet was chosen, the fact is Palmer based his decision on reasons of economy and speedy construction. Not long after the line was completed to Ogden, Utah, competitive pressure would force him to abandon his reasoning on the main line and bring about conversion to standard gauge on the miles of tracks involved in competition for transcontinental and interchange traffic. In the mountainous regions of southwest Colorado and northern New Mexico, narrow gauge was retained.

Another unique feature of the Denver & Rio Grande for that period was that Palmer neither sought nor received any land grants from the federal or state governments. He wanted this railroad to be his; the only concession he ever requested was for a 200-foot right-of-way through public land and an allocation of 20 acres every 10 miles for station grounds.

Understandably, Judge McCarthy, in 1954 speaking as the trustee and president of the railroad Palmer had started more than 80 years earlier, spoke mostly of the man and the best qualities of that man. But there were other facets—many of them—to Palmer's personality. He was a combination of many complexities. So few of his associates or his wife fully understood him. It is even likely at times he did not understand himself. However, the many unusual characteristics of Palmer provided exactly the combination required to dream of, start, engineer and complete the railroad that was a major factor in the opening of Colorado, northern New Mexico and Utah. The complex, rugged and stubborn nature of the General was in all ways transferred to and reflected in the nature of the road he built.

In fact, neither the lake at the top of the divide between Plum Creek and Fountain River, the equestrian statue in Colorado Springs, the bronze plaque in Denver Union Station, nor the speech by Judge McCarthy were the most appropriate tributes to the General. In the 1960's the most tangible reminder of the General existed in the remaining miles of narrow gauge railroad still operating. True, what remained of the many miles of narrow gauge had become uneconomic because of high operating costs and lack of traffic opportunities, but they did remain as a monument to the builder.

PRECEDENTS BROKEN

In the history of railroad building and operation Palmer set and broke many precedents. The D&RG was built using available local resources. To provide rail and fittings faster than England and the East could supply them, he developed iron-ore and coal deposits, and also quarried limestone. He organized and brought to production Colorado's only steel mill, The Colorado Fuel and Iron Corporation. He started and operated many logging and lumber enterprises. A great number of Colorado's cities and towns were built because of the railroad, some were promotions of the D&RG subsidiary land companies. Colonies involved in the opening of thousands of acres of new agricultural land and the irrigation systems to water them were either sponsored by or financed by Palmer and his associates. And where he pointed the way with agricultural developments, others took lessons from these pilot projects and completed the jobs Palmer was frequently too involved or too impatient to finish.

As a railroad construction engineer, the General more often than not made this own rules and not always in conformity with contemporary ideas. He apparently worked by two precepts: Take the shortest path between two points and follow a water course if possible. Students of his original lines are often led to the conclusions that he laid out and built the Narrow Gauge just to prove that no natural obstacle could stand in the way, or defeat, his construction gangs. People in new mining camps, lumber camps, or farming communities wanted a railroad, and he was determined to get one to them by the shortest and quickest way.

Many passengers who rode the varnish through the Royal Gorge and Black Canyon (of the Gunnison River), across Marshall, La Veta, and Cumbres Passes, down Embudo Hill on the Chili Line, along the Navajo and San Juan Rivers to Durango, and up the Animas River to Silverton often exclaimed: "Incredible, fantastic. What a great engineering feat." If results are the criteria, they were great engineering *accomplishments,* but whether the stiff grades and tight curvatures made engineering *sense* was another question entirely, particularly where in many cases better, more feasible routes were available.

At the time the Narrow Gauge was being built some factors existed that today would not be of consideration. Rails and rail fittings were in short supply, a situation that dictated that a route be as short as possible, irrespective of grades. Sawed, treated ties were unheard of; they could best be cut and hewed along, or close to, the projected line. Likewise, strategically-located water supplies for locomotives and fuel availability were questions facing the builders. All the time, the new communities and industries were clamoring for an early arrival of the railroad.

Customers who before the railroads were used to the slow

Public timetable of 1887 shows Curecanti Needle on the original main line along the Gunnison River west of Gunnison, Colorado. *Colorado Historical Society*

gait of oxen and horses did not complain about the only relatively faster speed of trains dragging over four per cent grades and around tortuous curves.

One of the D&RG early engineers, Arthur Ridgway, who worked for the railroad from 1892 to 1941, summarized the attitude of the earlier builders. On the flyleaf of one of his field notebooks Ridgway wrote: "A great engineer is not so overburdened with education he cannot use his own brain and ingenuity to solve any problem facing him, using only the resources available to him." Based on this definition General Palmer and his associates were engineers. Arthur Ridgway's father, Robert Matlick Ridgway, a Civil War buddy of Palmer, was one of the engineers who laid out and constructed much of the original route.

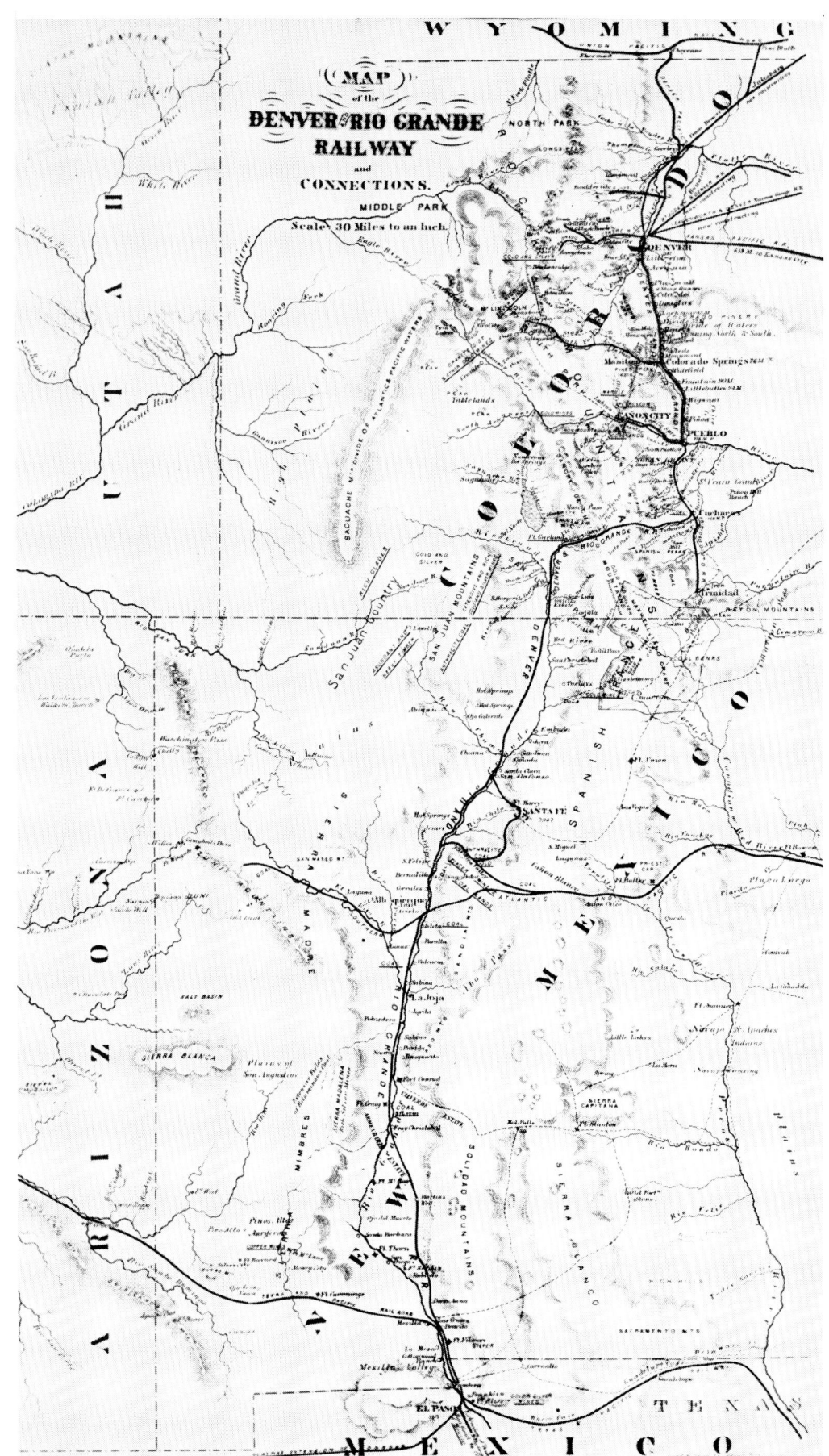

From First Annual Report to the Stockholders dated April 1, 1873. *Colorado State Historical Society*

A photographic enlargement from a large wood-engraving of a view of Denver's Larimer Street, eastward from Cherry Creek, published in Frank Leslie's Illustrated Newspaper, New York, on August 20, 1859.

Colorado State Historical Society

Chapter 3

The railroad becomes incorporated
Chronology and accomplishments

General William Jackson Palmer's dream of a "little railroad a few hundred miles in length" as he pictured it was a bit more substantial than a vision. Palmer had been thinking of a Colorado railroad all during his employment with the Kansas Pacific.

Only two weeks after writing to Queen, Palmer took a preliminary step toward bringing his dream to actuality. He filed articles of incorporation for the Rio Grande Rail Road and Telegraph Company with the Secretary of the Territory of New Mexico. Incorporation was followed by Governor Hunt, acting for Palmer, purchasing 9,312 acres of land at a location that later became Colorado Springs. Most of the land was bought from the United States government at $1.25 per acre.

Action accelerated when rumors spread that a group of Denver promoters were to form a railroad company to build a line closely approximating Palmer's planned route. To counter the rumored action, articles of incorporation of a railroad, the Rocky Mountain Railway Company were filed in Denver by Governor Hunt for General Palmer.

Upon the arrival of the Kansas Pacific at Denver, Palmer resigned from its employ. Two months later, in October, Palmer wrote Queen's father: "We are determined to put through the N. and S. Line immediately." The same evening he wrote this letter, Wilson Waddingham, a New Mexico land-grant speculator and co-purchaser of the Maxwell Land grant in northern New Mexico, invested $50,000 in the north-south project and authorized Palmer to sell his Maxwell Grant stock and invest it in the proposed railroad. It became evident that Palmer was not intent on only building a railroad to the Rio Grande and Mexico City. An entry in a letter written to Waddingham at the time stated that Waddingham's subscription was just what was needed and "I feel very confident of having the I.P. (the Imperial Pacific) completed to our colony and Colorado City, before the spring is over."

On October 27 the president of Palmer's competitor railroad, the Denver and New Mexico Southern Railway Company, filed a formal notice of the dissolution of that corporation. That afternoon Palmer filed the articles of incorporation of the Denver and Rio Grande Railway Company. Just before appearing to file these articles, Palmer had held a meeting at which the New Mexico corporation, the Rio Grande Rail Road and Telegraph Company, was consolidated with the new Colorado company.

PLAN FOR NEW ROAD

The plan for the new road was a lot more than "a few hundred miles in length." It called for a main line to extend southward from Denver to the junction of the Monument and Fountain Creeks (Colorado Springs), then to a point at or near Pueblo. From there the line would head west up the Arkansas River and through the "big canyon" (Royal Gorge) to the mouth of the South Arkansas, and up this stream for a few miles. Leaving the South Arkansas the line would surmount Poncha Pass and descend into the San Luis Valley to meet the waters of the Rio Grande at Rio Bravo (Alamosa). The railroad would then proceed generally down the Rio Grande River and the Rio Grande Valley to El Paso where a connection with a Mexican railway was anticipated.

Seven branches off the main line were described as possibilities. One branch was to extend south from Pueblo to cross Raton Pass and then connect with the main line in the Rio Grande Valley. Another closely approximated a route later used in the building of the Denver & South Park. A third branch was projected from the mouth of the South Arkansas to Utah via Tennessee Pass. Fourth was a spur running eastward from the lower San Luis Valley to the Sangre de Cristo Range and the Maxwell Grant. A fifth one would have pre-empted a Cumbres Pass route, for it was projected to start from the main line at a point "near or accessible to the Valley of the Chama" and continue to the San Juan Valley. This

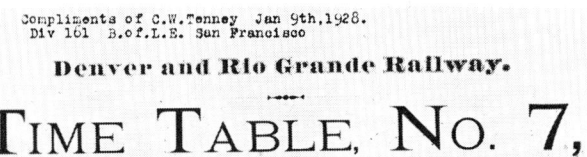

Rio Grande Western RR roster of officers apparently soon after Palmer resigned as president of the D&RG on August 9, 1883 and kept control of the RGW. *Colorado State Historical Society*

OFFICERS.

W. J. PALMER, President,		New York.
GEO. FOSTER PEABODY, Vice-President,		"
D. C. DODGE,	2nd Vice-Prest. and Gen'l Manager,	Denver.
C. W. DRAKE,	Secretary and Treasurer,	New York
A. E. WELBY,	Superintendent,	Salt Lake City.
J. H. BENNETT,	Gen'l Fr't and Pass. Agent,	"
THERON GEDDES,	Auditor,	"
G. W. KRAMER,	Manager Express,	Denver.
W. F. COLTON,	Cashier and Ass't Sec'y,	Salt Lake City.
N. W. SAMPLE,	Consult'g Supt. M. & R. S.,	Denver.
W. BROWN,	Ass't Gen'l Fr't Agent,	Salt Lake City.
W. P. McELROY,	Purchasing Agent,	"

MACHINERY DEPARTMENT.

J. B. DAILEY,	Master Mechanic,	Salt Lake.
A. STRUTHERS,	" "	Grand Junction.

BRIDGES, BUILDINGS AND ROADWAY DEP'TS.

J. L. THOMSON,	Supt. B. & B. & W. S.	
THOS. LEE,	Gen'l Roadmaster.	
C. SELBY,	Roadmaster Western Division.	
T. BYRNE,	" Eastern "	
J. O. CONNELL,	Asst. " San Pete Branch.	

TRANSPORTATION DEPARTMENT.

S. O. SNYDER,	Trainmaster.
A. T. MILLER,	Chief Dispatcher.
J. C. BOSCHA,	Car Accountant.

route would logically have been up the Vallecito River or from Espanola and over Horse Lake Pass, in northern New Mexico. The coal fields at Cerillos, New Mexico, were recognized as a sixth possible branch and the seventh one was aimed at the silver mines at Pinos Altos (Silver City, N. Mex.) from a point described as near Albuquerque.

This preliminary description of the route of the D&RG made no mention of routes over Marshall Pass, Cumbres Pass nor, specifically, as via Trinidad and Raton Pass. Neither was La Veta Pass included. Critics have said, with some justification, that Palmer was a promoter and speculator—an opportunist, who never knew from one day to the next where he would point the next segment of railroad line. In honesty, it must be admitted, the D&RG as it looked upon its arrival at Ogden bore only a slight resemblance to the original project. More sympathetic students of the history of the D&RG can point out, however, that there was never any doubt in the General's mind where he was going—he was going to every new mining camp as quickly as its location became known, and he was going to create townships as he went. If humanly possible, those townships were going to be built on land he owned and could sell for money to build his next piece of railroad. Too, he was building into areas largely unsettled, and surely undeveloped . . . into areas only partly mapped and explored well enough to make any definitive or permanent plans.

The D&RG had optimistically announced that its rails would reach Colorado Springs before the end of spring 1871. This did not prove to be true. Delivery of rail from Great Britain was delayed and the first spike, at Denver, was not driven until July 28, 1871. The last spike of the Denver-Colorado Springs segment was pounded in on October 21. Five days later, on the morning of October 26, the first passenger train left Denver headed for the three-month old city of Colorado Springs . . . one year, minus a day, after the papers of incorporation had been filed.

The line was not officially opened for business until January 1, 1872. Grading was already started beyond Colorado Springs toward Pueblo. This second segment was completed June 15. On November 1, construction had been completed westward from Pueblo to Labran (Florence), Colorado. Then came the Panic of 1873, followed by a post-panic period during which money was not available for further extension. Between November, 1872, when the road reached Florence, and February, 1876, the only trackage completed was 8 miles from Florence to Canon City. These were galling, frustrating years for Palmer and his associates . . . and for communities begging for a railroad.

FINANCING A PROBLEM

Somehow during this period of depression Palmer managed to continue making interest payments on his mortgage bonds. Nevertheless financing was a problem, and company archives indicate that between 1870 and 1886 construction money was obtained from several sources by using a great number of stratagems. Again, critics say not all of them could bear the light of day. Perhaps not today, but during that period speculation was rife and everyone with money was looking for a way to invest, especially in western projects. About 50 per cent of Palmer's financing came from the Dutch; 40 per cent from the English; and from the United States and others, the remaining 10 per cent.

In reality the D&RG was more like one of today's conglomerates than it was a railroad company. The railroad was, in effect, the parent company, with land companies, coal companies, iron mining enterprises, sawmills, timber and town companies stemming from it. Financing of the subsidiaries hinged on the position of the railroad as the parent. In turn, when necessary, some of the subsidiaries bolstered the credit of the railroad. Palmer's consistent interest payments and good financial contacts during the period of depression enabled him and his associates to form the Southern Colorado Coal and Town Company in 1874 when good coking coal was discovered near Trinidad. However, to receive returns from any investments in the Trinidad coal fields it was imperative that the railroad be extended from Pueblo to Trinidad.

Financing was finally arranged so that construction could be started toward the coal fields. The project started in January, 1876, and on April 6 the rails reached El Moro, a company town almost within sight of Trinidad. The citizens of Trinidad had been enthusiastically awaiting the arrival of the railroad and believed its coming would bring new money and activity. When Palmer stopped at El Moro and built his own town, these people reacted just as those at Pueblo, Canon City and Florence had. They felt they had been betrayed by the D&RG and later would cooperate with the Santa Fe to the disadvantage of the D&RG. Later this pattern would be repeated at Conejos, in the San Luis Valley, where Palmer created Antonito as a company town . . . at Animas City where Durango was built nearby as the railroad town. Many of the criticisms and antipathies directed at the General in the future originated with his town building policies and pressures.

About midway between Pueblo and Trinidad a branch line was started westward toward the San Luis Valley. The junction was named Cucharas and Walsenburg grew up near this. In July, 1876, the iron reached Francisco's Ranch (La Veta) 22 miles from Cucharas. The now usual company town was built here and the construction was halted while a satisfactory route was being scouted out across the Sange de Cristo range.

Disappointed and chagrined at the failure of both the El Moro routes to divert much of the San Juan and New Mexico traffic to the Denver & Rio Grande Railway, Palmer decided the only solution was to proceed over the Sangre de Cristo

An early Rio Grande passenger train at the summit of the original La Veta Pass route. *Courtesy D&RGW*

Francisco's Plaza, renamed LaVeta, now has a telegraph office. *Colorado State Historical Society*

range to the San Luis Valley quickly. The route he chose projected a 4 per cent grade and a maximum curvature of 30 degrees over La Veta Pass.

In spite of snow, winds and freezing temperatures, grading was completed to the summit late in March, 1877. By early June rails had reached the same point. On July 1 construction had advanced as far as Wagon Creek (Russell). Thirty days later the railroad established a railhead at a point named Garland (shortly after renamed Garland City). Palmer's expansionist policy and an overburdened financial structure made it necessary to halt any construction west of Garland City until February, 1878.

SANTA FE'S SURPRISE

Early in 1878 Palmer discovered the Santa Fe's financial situation to be worse than his and permitted himself to be lured into a false sense of security. As a result he was caught napping when the Santa Fe gained possession of the route into New Mexico over Raton Pass by a surprise move.

Loss of this strategic pass into New Mexico discouraged Palmer but did not cause him to abandon his plan to secure New Mexico traffic. He merely changed his tactics and decided to press completion of the La Veta Pass route to the Rio Grande River and then go south from the San Luis Valley to Santa Fe, N. Mex.

A full-fledged silver rush to a new strike in California Gulch on the Upper Arkansas dictated in addition that construction should forge ahead through the Royal Gorge to Leadville. D&RG forces started working just below the mouth of the Royal Gorge on April 19, 1878, but the Santa Fe seized the actual mouth. The second round of the battle with the Atchison road was on. This confrontation soon became known as the "Royal Gorge War", the bloody war, according to contemporary accounts . . . but the only blood shed was by one warrior who accidentally shot himself in the rump as he was crawling out of a window in Pueblo.

Days of "warfare" followed during which both sides maintained noisy, threatening tactical positions in the field. While railroad lawyers surveyed the situation, there were threats of mayhem, conflict—conferences were held and the hired warriors spent most of their time drinking, poker playing, girling, changing sides to get better pay, and in general confusion. The newspapers had a heyday.

While all this was going on, D&RG affairs took a turn for the worse. Its bondholders insisted that the odds against winning a clear-cut decision against the Atchison road were too great. In October, Palmer yielded to their pressure. He had fought a good fight in the face of depression and opposition from another major railroad, but with his resources exhausted to a dangerous point, Colorado's "Baby Road" was up for grabs. On October 19 Sebastian B. Achlesinger and James D. Potts, D&RG bondholder representatives, signed an agreement with the AT&SF to lease the narrow gauge for a period of 30 years.

The lease stipulated that the Rio Grande would turn over all completed trackage, 357 miles, its rolling stock, and other equipment at a rental rate starting at 43 per cent of gross receipts and gradually scaling down to a final rate of 36 per cent. AT&SF agreed not to build or encourage any parallel or competing lines and that any construction beyond existing D&RG terminals would be of three-foot gauge. It further promised not to discriminate against the Denver company in matters of freight or other charges and to pay the rent each month.

Fortunately, Santa Fe did not honor these commitments, and for once Palmer had the State of Colorado solidly behind him. In June, 1879, he secured a court order restoring the D&RG to his control. On June 9 he booted all employees of the Atchison off the property without any apologies. Leadville was reached July 20, 1880.

From the feuding between the Santa Fe and D&RG came an agreement that was to have far-reaching results on future plans of Palmer and his road. This was the "Boston Treaty" or Tripartite Agreement drawn up at a meeting between the two parties held in Boston in February, 1880.

The first portion of the treaty stipulated conditions for settling the Royal Gorge matter. The agreement then outlined commitments the two lines would be bound by for the next 10 years. The Santa Fe agreed not to build north or west of Pueblo except for a line to the Florence/Canon City coal fields. The D&RG agreed not to extend its lines east of Pueblo or below a point 75 miles south of Conejos in the San Luis Valley.

CHARACTER CHANGES

The battle for the passes and the Royal Gorge War was over, and the character of the narrow gauge, north to south railroad projected by Palmer 10 years earlier underwent drastic alteration. It was no longer a cozy little homegrown, home-ruled railroad being built for the good of a territory and the profit of one man and his associates. As a north-south railroad between Denver and Mexico City it offered no threat to any of the east to west transcontinental railroads. But when

Corner of Blake and "F" streets, Denver, in 1870. *Colorado State Historical Society*

Denver at "F" and Larimer streets looking east the year the Denver & Rio Grande was chartered and 12 years after the first semi-permanent encampment at the junction of Cherry Creek and the Platte. *Colorado State Historical Society*

The railroad replaced transportation such as this D&B Powers wagon train of Leavenworth shown at Denver between 14 and 15th streets on June 20, 1868. This is Holladay Street (later re-named Market Street). The mules? They were later lost in an Indian raid south of Denver. *Colorado State Historical Society*

it became apparent that the D&RG was changing course and would eventually connect Denver and Front Range communities with Salt Lake City and Ogden, thus placing it in a position to vie for a portion of the transcontinental traffic, Jay Gould and his ilk were perturbed.

Financial manipulators such as these quickly perceived that besides being a threat transcontinentally, the D&RG could be used effectively as another piece in the great chess game being played for control of transcontinental railroads. The signing of the Boston Treaty took sole control of the Rio Grande out of Palmer's hands and placed it in command of financiers with goals and attitudes far different from Palmer's.

While negotiations that culminated in the Boston Treaty were under way, other activities were going forward. West of La Veta rail was again being laid with urgency to reach the Rio Grande River at Alamosa so further extension to Santa Fe and the San Juan could get going. As early as September 9, 1877, one more financing gimmick had been accomplished with the incorporation of the Alamosa Railway Company. This incorporation provided means for financing the few miles of railroad needed to move from Garland City to Alamosa. However, it was not until February, 1878, that contractors and track men could be assembled to start laying rail. Terrain on this segment was favorable for fast progress. There is some uncertainty as to the exact date the D&RG did reach Alamosa. Palmer says it was July 10, but J.A. McMur-

trie, chief engineer, in a report to the stockholders, says that the date was July 6 when "track was laid and road opened for business to Alamosa." The gateway to the section of railroad later to become the mecca for railfans and called *The Narrow Gauge* had been reached.

In New Mexico descendants of Coronado, Onate, Father Rodriquez, Espejo and their Indian wives and consorts—the Nuevo Mejicanos—were clamoring for the railroad to hurry down to their country. Palmer was just as anxious to get there and his thoughts went further . . . as far as Mexico City. He found time in all his other activities to become feverishly engaged in negotiations with Porfirio Diaz of Mexico to secure concessions for building two narrow gauge lines south of the border. One was to go from Laredo, Texas, to Mexico City; the other from Mexico City to the Pacific Coast. Success achieved, the General was now in a position that, should he be able to build to Santa Fe and on to the border, he would fulfill the clause in the original articles of incorporation . . . "down the Rio Grande Valley to El Paso where a connection with a Mexican railway is anticipated."

To the west another community was clamoring just as loudly as the Nuevo Mejicanos. The prospering Mormons of Utah's Salt Lake region wanted a railroad too. Gold and silver had been discovered on the west side of Marshall Pass in west central Colorado, and coal was found in abundance at Crested Butte. Ouray was becoming important as a staging

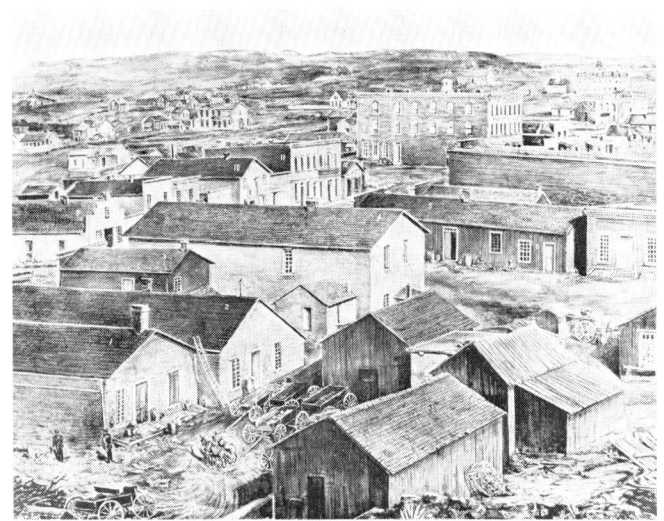

Pueblo in 1872 looking northwest from a hill east of Santa Fe Avenue. Colorado State Historical Society

point for equipment and supplies going to new mines opening over the mountains west of Silverton. The great valley of the Gunnison had enough lush grass and water to fatten a hundred thousand beeves.

OVER MARSHALL PASS

In September, 1880, contracts were let for grading a line from South Arkansas (Salida) to Gunnison City over Marshall Pass. Having experienced the snow, wind and low temperatures on La Veta Pass, the route over Marshall Pass held no new terrors. Gunnison City was reached in August, 1881. Construction was halted just long enough to throw a celebration party and then it was on into the Black Canyon to continue construction westward toward Montrose, Grand Junction and the Utah state line.

The three-foot gauge railroad reached the eastern border of Mormon country on December 20, 1882, and kept right on laying rail. Meanwhile a sister railroad, the Rio Grande Western Railway (usually called the "Western") was building eastward from Salt Lake City. The two railroads met a few miles west of Green River, Utah, on March 30, 1883.

Another last spike was driven and the link between the two capital cities, Denver and Salt Lake City, was completed. Six weeks later an extension was finished between Salt Lake City and Ogden, Utah's second largest city. At Ogden a connection was made with the Union Pacific.

At the same time Palmer was marshalling his forces and equipment for the assault on Marshall Pass—February, 1880—he was beginning to lay rail south from Alamosa and earlier than he had hoped to be able to. In less than a year, Cumbres Pass was whipped and there was a railroad into Chama, New Mexico on the San Juan Extension. On the last day of 1880, the Narrow Gauge was at Espanola, New Mexico, 91 miles from Antonito, and 16 miles *south* of the deadline prescribed by the Boston Treaty.

The year of 1881 was one of frenzied building of tracks. The Annual Report of 1881 opens with an understatement: "The year 1881 has been one of great activity."

The following completions were reported to the stockholders of the Rio Grande:

- **Poncha to Maysville, April 25**
- **Canon City to Westcliffe, April 25**
- **Chama to Durango (San Juan Extension), July 27**
- **Poncha to Gunnison City, August 6**
- **Blue River Extension, September 18**
- **Mears to Hot Springs Iron Mine (Orient), October 28 (Extended to Alamosa in 1890)**
- **Tennessee Pass route completed to Red Cliff, November 20**
- **Alamosa to Wagon Wheel Gap, November 20**
- **Gunnison to Crested Butte, November 24**
- **Calumet and Hecla Iron Mine, November 28**
- **Silverton Branch, 19.1 miles of it, December 31**

Palmer was riding high on glory, accepting all challenges to build a railroad to each new strike or community, especially if there was consensus by others that it couldn't be done. He set two goals for 1882—to reach Silverton and to build to the

At right is the roundhouse at Pueblo in spring of 1873. It's here in Pueblo that adherents of the Santa Fe tried to hold off adherents of the Rio Grande, but were smoked out—or bought off. *Colorado State Historical Society*

Fremont came over the Pass to the right of the snow-covered peak and followed the line of willows in front of the sand dunes of the San Luis Valley looking for a railroad route. General Palmer wasn't the first to dream of a railroad across the Valley. *Courtesy D&RGW*

Salida circa 1883. *Colorado State Historical Society*

Utah border. Both were attained. Silverton had a railroad on July 8, and the Utah State line was reached 10 days before the year's end.

The General's early decision to build narrow gauge was proving his point that 3-foot gauge was the fastest and most economical one for mountainous terrain. The completion of so many miles of railroad in mountainous terrain would not have been possible had standard gauge been used.

Palmer's own words were: "The Denver and Rio Grande Railway, while traversing the Rocky Mountain plateau at the base of the mountains for most of its length, required to cross one mountain chain, and would inevitably have many branches frequently running up through narrow and tortuous canons (or valleys) to the gold and silver mines, parks, forests of lumber, coal, etc., in the adjoining mountains. These side lines would in time be numbered by hundreds between Denver and El Paso, and still more in Mexico. They would of necessity require to be of narrow gauge, as their construction of a broad gauge would involve tunneling, rock cutting, bridging, etc., so expensive as to be impracticable, and it was desirable that the gauge of these would be consistent with efficiency, for these branches would have passengers to carry, with machinery and mixed freight, as on the main line, although a less proportionate amount of light and bulky goods."

Expense was probably the governing factor, but another great consideration was that a 3-foot gauge railroad required a roadbed and structure on a smaller scale than standard gauge and consequently could be built faster.

Had the General not been so wrapped up in his successes and accomplishments of 1881, he would have taken time to reflect on the impact of D&RG actions and given more thought to what lay ahead.

WHAT FUTURE HELD

Palmer should have reviewed the morality and ethics abused in his numerous financial subterfuges. The account juggling that went on between the railroad and the land companies, construction and town site companies, coal mines and iron pits, and steel mills had not previously been questioned by investors. But there was resistance growing from these money sources to his hell-bent-for-leather policies of expansionism. Above all, Palmer did not recognize the fact that upon signing the Tripartite Agreement he no longer enjoyed autonomous control of the D&RG.

More likely, in his stubborn and egotistical manner, he simply disregarded the storm clouds that were boiling up from financial circles to the east. British, European and Eastern financial groups did not hold with Palmer's philosophy that, to exist, the entire length and breadth of the Narrow Gauge must have branches to support the trunk. These financiers overlooked the fact that a decade earlier, they were begging to invest in the West and Palmer's railroad. What they would not overlook was that all the money was being used for building branches and none was going for dividends.

Leading the opposition to Palmer was Jay Gould, for Gould had plans of his own for railroad building in the Rockies. There was also dissension in Palmer's own camp. Dr. Bell, vice-president of the D&RG, resigned and others followed, including three members of the board of directors.

Palmer was given a directive by the controlling financial interests to quit spending time on his Mexican adventure and other personal activities that at times took priority over railroad affairs. He was ordered to devote full time to railroad company matters or to resign as its president.

By 1883 it had become apparent that the basic interest of the British investors was to obtain regular returns at a high rate of interest. Many meetings ensued to decide what could be done about Palmer and his policies.

An excerpt from a review of what occurred in one of these meetings appeared in the *Investor's Review* in 1894: "We all agreed that whatever else happened he (Palmer) must have nothing more to do with the road, nor could we under any circumstances seek his advice. 'Put the knife in deep,' was the phrase used by one of our members who had acquired a semi-professional reputation in such work as ours."

Palmer fought back, and was re-elected president amidst quarrels over policy. But he tired of these quarrels for "the knife" was deep in him and his railroad. He resigned as president on August 9, 1883.

He did retain control of the western portion of the road, the "Western"; and he maintained his interest in and contributed significantly to the building of the Mexican narrow gauge lines.

His plans and a dream of a "little railroad a few hundred miles in length, all under one's own control with one's friends" had outgrown its original concept; indeed, the railroad had come a cropper in the financial steeplechase. In the years to follow, each segment of the D&RG would develop its own individual characteristics, history and atmosphere. Much of the original 3-foot gauge would shortly be either three-rail track or standard gauge.

One of the considerations in having opted for 3-foot gauge in the beginning had been a hope to isolate the D&RG from competitive intruders, thereby avoiding its inclusion into a more complex trans-continental system. One writer, Marshall Sprague, has referred to Palmer's choice of a narrow gauge as being a desire to lock a chastity belt on the Rocky Mountain Empire with the only key held by him. His desire was not to be realized.

The Chili Line, Antonito to Santa Fe, Salida to Montrose, Poncha Pass and Cumbres Pass routes would remain narrow gauge up to final abandonment because of geographical and economic circumstances. The balance was converted to standard gauge. Parts that remained narrow gauge evolved into microcosms of the standard gauged segments, with exception of the railroad west and south of Antonito—at the south end of the San Luis Valley—to Santa Fe, Durango and Silverton.

On these sections the essence of Palmer's original concept would remain. On them an aura of what-had-been, romance, adventure, accomplishment and derring-do remained.

The beginning of another of Palmer's new towns. *Colorado State Historical Society*

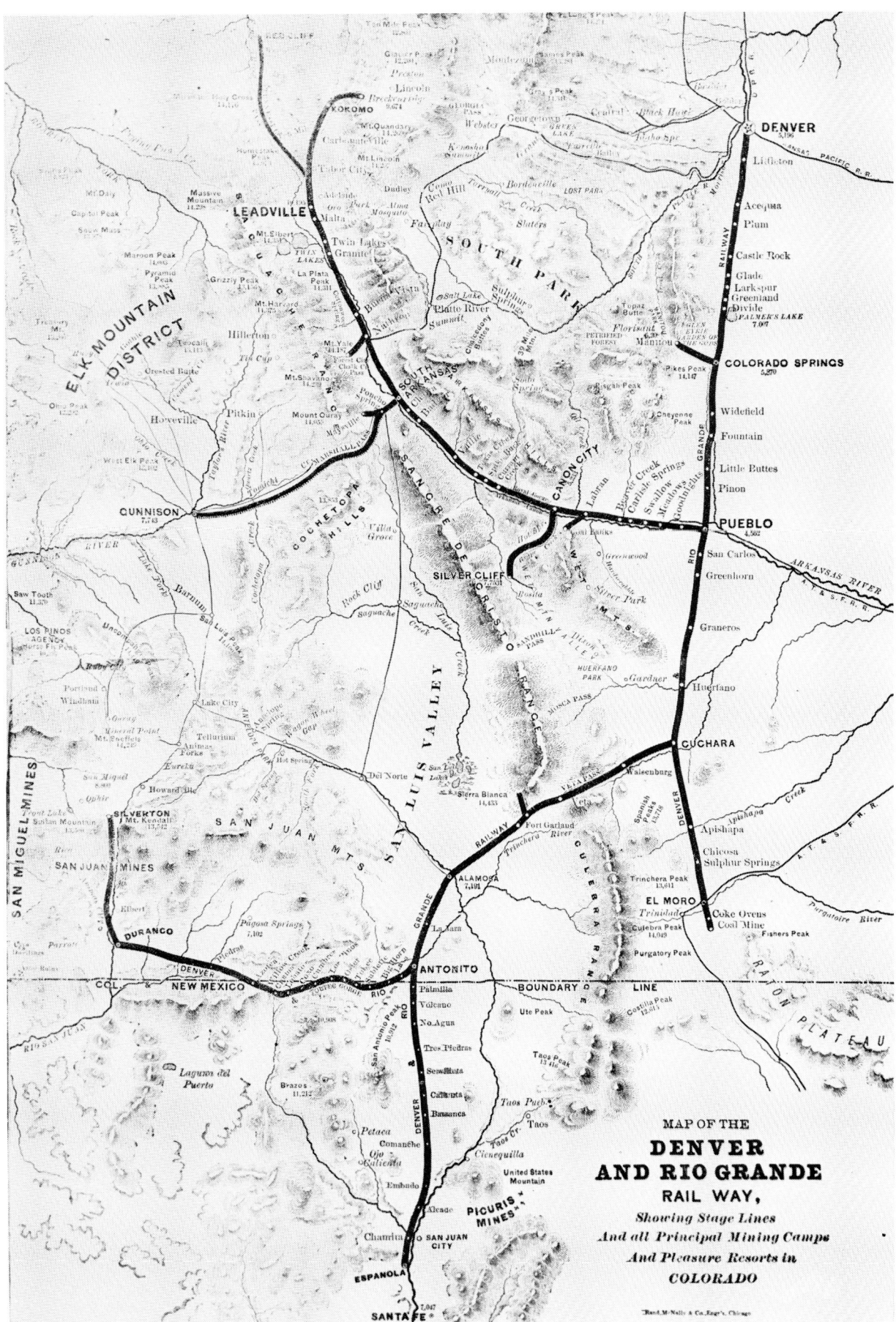

By the end of 1879, the General's dream had changed some. The map is from the Report to Stockholders of the D&RG, 1880. *Colorado State Historical Society*

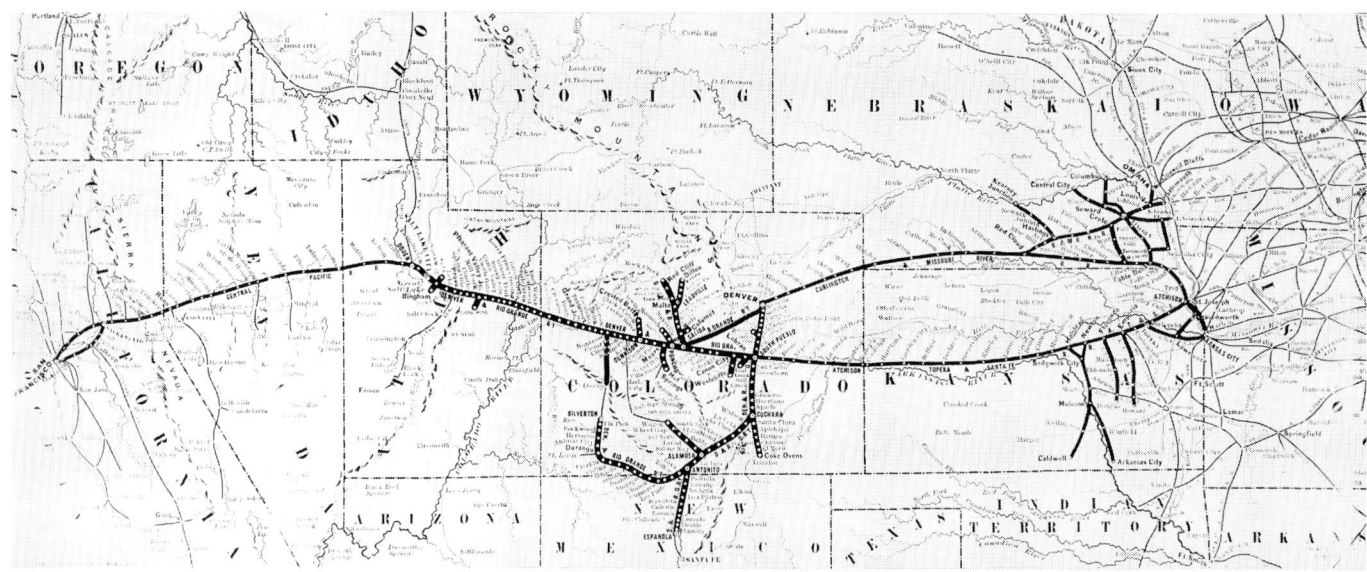

At the time of Palmer's resignation, the railroad was being built according to his general plan. Map is from Annual Report to the Stockholders for 1883. *Colorado State Historical Society*

Memoranda regarding construction of the Denver & Rio Grande Railroad

(Copied from an old undated and unsigned paper in the Rio Grande archives.)

What is supposed to have been the first narrow gauge railroad in America was the plan of the parties who organized the Denver and Rio Grande Railway Company. The official incorporation was effected on the 27th day of November, 1870, under the laws of the then Territory of Colorado. The object of the Company was to construct and operate certain railways and telegraph lines and to promote any associated interests.

The routes of the various railways and telegraph lines are designated as follows:
1. The Denver and Rio Grande Railway.
2. The Denver and Southern Railway.
3. The South Park Railway.
4. The Western Colorado Railway.
5. The Moreno Valley Railway.
6. The San Juan Railway.
7. The Gallisteo Railway.
8. The Santa Rita Railway.

The organization of the Company and procuring of capital is described by the following excerpt from a letter dated January 23rd, 1872, to D.C. Brooks, Editor, Railway Review, Chicago, written by Howard Schuyler, Assistant General Manager of D&RG.

"The officers of the Company are as follows:

Gen'l Wm. J. Palmer, President.

Rob't H. Lamborn, Vice-President, Philadelphia

Wm. S. Jackson, Sec'y & Treas., Colo. Springs

Wm. H. Greenwood, Gen'l Mgr. of Const. & Genl Supt., Denver.

J.P. Mercereau, Chief Engineer, Denver

Howard Schuyler, Asst Gen'l Mgr., Denver

W.W. Borst, Superintendent, Denver

D.C. Dodge, Gen'l Fr. & Tkt. Agent, Denver

"The enterprise was originated in the fall of 1870 by Gen'l Wm. J. Palmer and Col. W.H. Greenwood after the completion of the Kansas Pacific Railway, with which they were connected as Managing Director and Chief Engineer respectively, to Denver. They were cordially assisted by Dr. W. A. Bell, Ex.-Gov. A.C. Hunt and others of Colorado, and on the 27th of October, 1870, a final organization was effected, a considerable sum of money pledged and the work put in hand at once under the direction of Col. Greenwood. In the east the enterprise met the encouragement of John Edgar Thomson, President, Pennsylvania RR, Thomas A. Scott, S.M. Feltwich and many other prominent Railway men who lent it substantial aid. Gen'l Palmer and Dr. Bell presented the plan in Europe with such success that the whole sum necessary to build and equip the first section of the road from Denver to Colorado Springs, 76 miles, was pledged before March, 1871."

Surveys had apparently been carried on in connection with the Kansas Pacific Railway surveys for a considerable time before any definite idea of the D&RG project was formed, but the field notes, or at least what is left of them now, are in such miserable shape that hardly any definite information can be elicited from them. The absence of date of final location is particularly conspicuous, although in one place there occurs the following notation: 'Location of line finished to Lake at 2:15 p.m., Feb'y 22nd, '70.' The station numbers at this point correspond with numbers at Palmer Lake, as shown on map of line, Denver to Colorado Springs, subsequently filed in U.S. Land Office.

Final location reached Fountain City (Colo. Springs) March 10th, 1871, and North Pueblo (about Dundee Section House) in October, 1871. Reconnaissances and preliminary locations were, of course, made simultaneously in other directions, particularly south and west. What looks as being the first survey (no date given) into North Pueblo appears to

To illustrate their locomotive sales brochure, Baldwin Locomotive Works used a Rio Grande engine, No. 13, the Mosca. The Mosca was twice as heavy as the earlier Montezuma.

have followed closely along the first alley east of Grand Avenue in Barndollar & Co's. Second Addition, and may account for the purchase of the property still held by the Railroad Company in Block 13 of said Addition between said alley and Grand Avenue.

J.P. Mercereau, J.D. Schuyler, N.P. Reynolds, Harry King, J.A. McMurtrie, J.R. DeRemer and others appear to have been the Locating Engineers engaged on the various surveys.

The Union Contract Company and the National Land and Improvement Company were organized to aid the construction of the Railway and to promote the development of tributary lands.

J.K. Brewster was Right-of-Way Agent and secured most of the original right-of-way between Denver and Pueblo, partly by deeds and partly by options, not yet taken up.

Ordinance granting the right-of-way through Denver was applied for on May 1st, 1871. This was passed and approved on June 1st. Deed No. 1872.

Special Act of Congress granting 200 feet wide right-of-way across all vacant government land was passed June 8th, 1872.

CONSTRUCTION OF LINE
DENVER TO COLORADO SPRINGS

N.P. Reynolds, was Div. Eng'r for first 20 miles south from Denver.

Harry King was Div. Eng'r next 23 miles to North Pine (Larkspur).

J.A. McMurtrie had charge of next 33 miles to "Mouth of Monument" (Colorado Springs).

Grading seems to have started about March 1st, 1871, south of Monument by Moore & Carlile, who had contract for Sections 55, 56, 57, 58, 59, 67 and 68.

T.M. Field had contract for grading most, if not all, from Mile Post 4 to 49, near present Greenland.

S.A. Hutchins had contract for Sections 53, 54, part of 55, also all of 70 and 71.

No other contracts are mentioned in the old records.

Roadbed was made 10 feet wide on embankments and 12 feet in excavations for 3 ft. gage of track.

The following prices were paid for grading:

Hard Rock
  Exc. . . . . . $2.25 per c.y.
Soft Rock
  Exc. . . . . . $1.25 per c.y.
Earth
  Exc. . . $.30 to .40 per c.y.
Borrow . . . . . . $.20 per c.y.
Waste . . . . $.25 per c.y.
Hard Pan . . . $0.60 per c.y.
Haul per
  100 ft. . . . . . $.02 per c.y
Box Cul
  Masonry . . $5.00 per c.y.
Clear'g & Grub'g
  . . . . $50.00 per acre

Cross ties cost 50 cents each from M.P. 0 at Denver to M.P. 12, thence 40 cents from M.P. 12 to 25, and 69 to 76, and 30 cents each for the balance with 7 cents for hauling to line.

Ties were 6" face, 6" thick and 6½ feet long, laid 2,640 to a mile.

Piles were paid for at $4.00 to $4.50 each delivered 12' to 28' in length with 65¢ per foot for driving. H.R. Holbrook had contract for driving piles.

Sawed bridge lumber cost $28.00 to $30.00 per M.

Undressed building lumber $35.00 per M.

Dressed lumber $40.00 per M (Chicago clear $60.00).

Lumber for Cherry Creek bridge was ordered to be delivered on or before June 27th, 1871.

It may be of interest to note that in those days 100 lbs. of Sugar cost $17.00, and that the Railway paid $10.00 for printing 4,000 election tickets for Fremont County of March 15th, 1871.

Track laying was started at Denver July 1st and completed to Colorado Springs about October 20th, 1871.

Track was laid with 30 lb. iron rail, purchased in England and shipped by boats over New Orleans to Kansas City, thence by K.P.Ry. to Denver. The cost at New Orleans was $46.00 plus import duties at 70¢ per 100 lbs., or a total of $61.68 per gross ton.

At least a portion of this rail was considered very poor and breaks under the light trains then operated were frequent during the first year, but it is also indicated that they were only 80% full spiked and being laid on ties 2 feet apart on a narrow, unsettled roadbed, a better result could not be expected. We are inclined to believe that we still have some of the original 30-lb rails in service on our light traffic tracks.

A track laying gang of 55 men ordinarily laid 2 miles of this kind of track per day (probably 10 hours) at a cost of $209.00 for wages and incidentals. It is stated they could lay four miles if crowded for 15 hours.

After the track was laid into the Rockies, snowslides became commonplace and each one was a setback for the Rio Grande. Each one was also full of potential dangers. This one is at MP 491.75.

An early photo of Engine No. 206. Courtesy D&RGW

Chapter 4
Building the Narrow Gauge
Alamosa to Chama portion

Early in 1878, the year the Rio Grande reached Leadville and was pushing westward to Utah from Gunnison, track crews were approaching the Rio Grande River at Alamosa on the La Veta Pass segment. In accordance with Palmer's original wishes, plans called for the railroad to push south from Alamosa to Antonito and beyond toward Santa Fe and the Mexican border—plans that two years later would be aborted by the Treaty of Boston and would leave the railroad that was started as Mexico-bound only a branch line terminating as Española, N. Mex.

APRIL 1, 1894
FOURTH DIVISION—2nd and 3rd Districts.

Station No	Miles from Denver, via La Veta	Local Mileage	Telegraph Calls	STATIONS.	AGENTS.
Y0	250.4		As	Alamosa*	Roper, Jas. ... F, T & E
Y5	255.6	5.2		Henry	
Y14	264.7	14.3	Jr	La Jara	Smith, W. H. ... F, T & E
Y22	272.8	22.4		Manassa	
Y29	279.0	28.6	Na	Antonito*	Hatfield, F. B. ... F, T & E
Y39	289.5	39.1		Lava	
	294.9	44.5		Big Horn Sec. House	
Y48	298.1	47.7		Big Horn	
Y54	304.8	54.4		Sublette	
Y59	309.2	58.8		Toltec	
Y62	312.2	61.8		" Section House	
Y67	317.1	66.7	Bc	Osier	Bennett, J. B. ... Teleg'h
Y70	320.8	70.4		Los Pinos	
	324.2	73.8		" " Sec. House	
Y79	329.3	78.9	Br	Cumbres	Aderhold, H.H. Teleg'h
	331.0	80.6		Coxo	
Y84	334.2	83.8		Cresco	
Y88	338.7	88.3		Lobato	
Y92	342.8	92.4	Ch	Chama*	Pollard, C. L. ... F, T & E
	343.6	93.2		Biggs Junction	
	346.8	3.2		Chama Mill	
Y98	347.9	97.5		Willow Creek	
	349.6	99.2		Biggs Mill	
Y102	352.7	102.3		Azotea	
	354.5	104.1		Sullenbergers Spur 2	
Y107	357.5	107.1		Sullenbergers Spur 3	
Y112	362.2	111.8	Ro	Monero	Hatfield, D. O. F, T & E
	363.9	113.5		Verona	
Y115	365.5	115.1	Fc	Amargo	Hinton, J. W. ... F, T & E
Y118	368.4	118.0		Lumbertown Spur	
Y122	372.0	121.6		Dulce	
Y135	376.4	126.0	Jo	Navajo (Tel. Box)	
	385.4	135.0		Juanita	
	389.0	138.6		Gato Water Tank	
	392.9	142.5		Rip Rap Spur	
Y143	393.8	143.4		Carracas	
Y152	402.3	151.9		Arboles	
Y159	409.5	159.1		Vallejo	
Y167	417.7	167.3		La Boca	
Y174	424.4	174.0	Ig	Ignacio	Ryerson, W. R. ... F, T & E
Y186	436.0	185.6		Florida	
Y190	440.3	189.9		" Mesa	
Y192	441.7	191.3	Pt	La Plata June (T. Bx)	
Y194	444.6	194.2	Bz	Bocea (Tel. Box)	
	449.4	199.0		Slaughter House	
	450.0	199.6		San Juan Sm. Junct.	
	450.4	200.0		Southern Junction	

*Coupon Stations.

Part of Annual Roster, April 1, 1894, showing stations Alamosa to Southern Junction (Durango).

— 17 —

The silver and gold discoveries in southwest Colorado at Silverton and the vicinity brought about some new plans that called for the railroad to be extended west from the San Luis Valley to the San Juan River. The new project was given the name of the San Juan Extension.

The stockholders of the D&RG were presented with an annual report on April 15, 1881. The reports, written by Palmer and official members of his staff, did not agree in all instances where dates of completion and some mileages were given, and there were a few other minor conflicts of facts. However, it did definitely inform the stockholders the Rio Grande River had been reached. Whether it was on July 6, 1878, as reported by Chief Engineer J.A. McMurtrie, or July 10 as stated by Palmer, is immaterial. McMurtie added that contracts had been let in the middle of June of that year and 40 miles of grade completed by October 1, when the engineering corps was called in for the winter. It is only 28 miles from Alamosa to Antonito, so 12 miles of grade had been completed either toward Santa Fe or Chama, McMurtrie does not say which. Neither does he clearly define how far west of Antonito, nor on which route or routes, contracts had been let.

A casualty of this era was the town of Conejos, which the railroad should have, and intended to build through. But, as had occurred at other established towns, the Rio Grande made the usual demands on the town for financial assistance, free station grounds and right-of-way, plus freedom from taxation, and as had happened before, a monetary disagreement ensued. As a result, the railroad laid out a townsite of its own about one mile from Conejos and named it Antonito. The new town became the junction for the San Juan Extension to the west and the Santa Fe Branch. Antonito immediately became relatively prosperous and active so many of the people of the area moved to the new community, while Conejos was reduced to village status although it remained the county seat.

Naming the site of Antonito and selling lots turned out to be far easier than reaching it with track, because no rail was laid south of Alamosa during 1879. The reasons were many, and the solution was to result in a change of character for the entire D&RG narrow gauge domain.

Although there was an urgency in pushing the line from Alamosa to Santa Fe and over Cumbres Pass to the San Juan, the drain on money, labor and supplies, and effects of the many controversies with the Santa Fe seriously hampered plans to push the Santa Fe Branch and the San Juan Extension. When track laying south of Alamosa finally resumed on February 20, 1880, progress was slow. It took until March 30 to reach Antonito, or an average of just a little over one mile a day over favorable terrain and a grade ready and waiting.

SECURING GOOD LABOR

Recognizing this was below D&RG standards, R.F. Weitbrec, manager of construction, reported: "The most serious difficulty we have had to encounter has been and is still the securing of sufficient quantity of good labor." Since November, 1879, there have been an average of at least

THE SCENIC LINE OF AMERICA,
THE DENVER & RIO GRANDE RAILWAY,

With its numerous branches and extensions penetrating all sections of Colorado and northern New Mexico, forms the greatest system of Narrow Gauge Railway in the world, and affords Tourists, Invalids, and Business Travel

THE BEST, AND IN MANY INSTANCES THE ONLY ROUTE

To the leading Health and Pleasure Resorts of the Rocky Mountains, and to the Richest Mining Regions and most Important Cities of the Mid-Continent.

FOR BUSINESS:

DENVER, COLORADO SPRINGS, PUEBLO,

Cañon City, South Arkansas, Alpine, Buena Vista, Leadville, Kokomo, Red Cliff, Gunnison City, Silver Cliff, El Moro; Alamosa, Antonito, Durango, Silverton, Taos, Espanola, Santa Fe, and the marvelous San Juan and Gunnison Countries.

FOR HEALTH AND PLEASURE:

Manitou, Garden of the Gods, Pike's Peak, Royal Gorge, Poncho Springs, Brown's Cañon, Cottonwood Springs, Twin Lakes, Veta Pass, Wagon Wheel Gap, Toltec Gorge, Phantom Curve, Los Pinos Valley, Pagosa Springs, Ojo Caliente, Comanche Cañon, Cave Dwellings, Aztec Ruins, &c.

THE MOUNTAIN SCENERY

Of this Line is unequaled in variety and grandeur by that of any other railway on either hemisphere, and the hotels at the attractive points are the best west of the Missouri River.

Two daily Express Trains, equipped with Pullman Palace Sleepers, Horton Reclining Chair Cars, Elegant Regular Coaches, Model Open Observation Cars, Westinghouse Air-Brakes, and running over Steel Rails, Iron Bridges and Rock Ballast, insure the highest type of rapid, safe, and luxurious railway travel.

The Denver & Rio Grande Railway, with its eastern connections at Pueblo and Denver, forms the shortest route by many miles, and the quickest by over ten hours' time, between all points East, and the interior of Colorado.

NEARLY 800 MILES IN OPERATION, AND THE ONLY LINE UNDER COLORADO MANAGEMENT

D. C. DODGE,
General Manager.

F. C. NIMS,
General Passenger and Ticket Agent.

DENVER, COLO.

In 1888, the Denver & Rio Grande advertised in *Crofutt's Grip-Sack Guide*

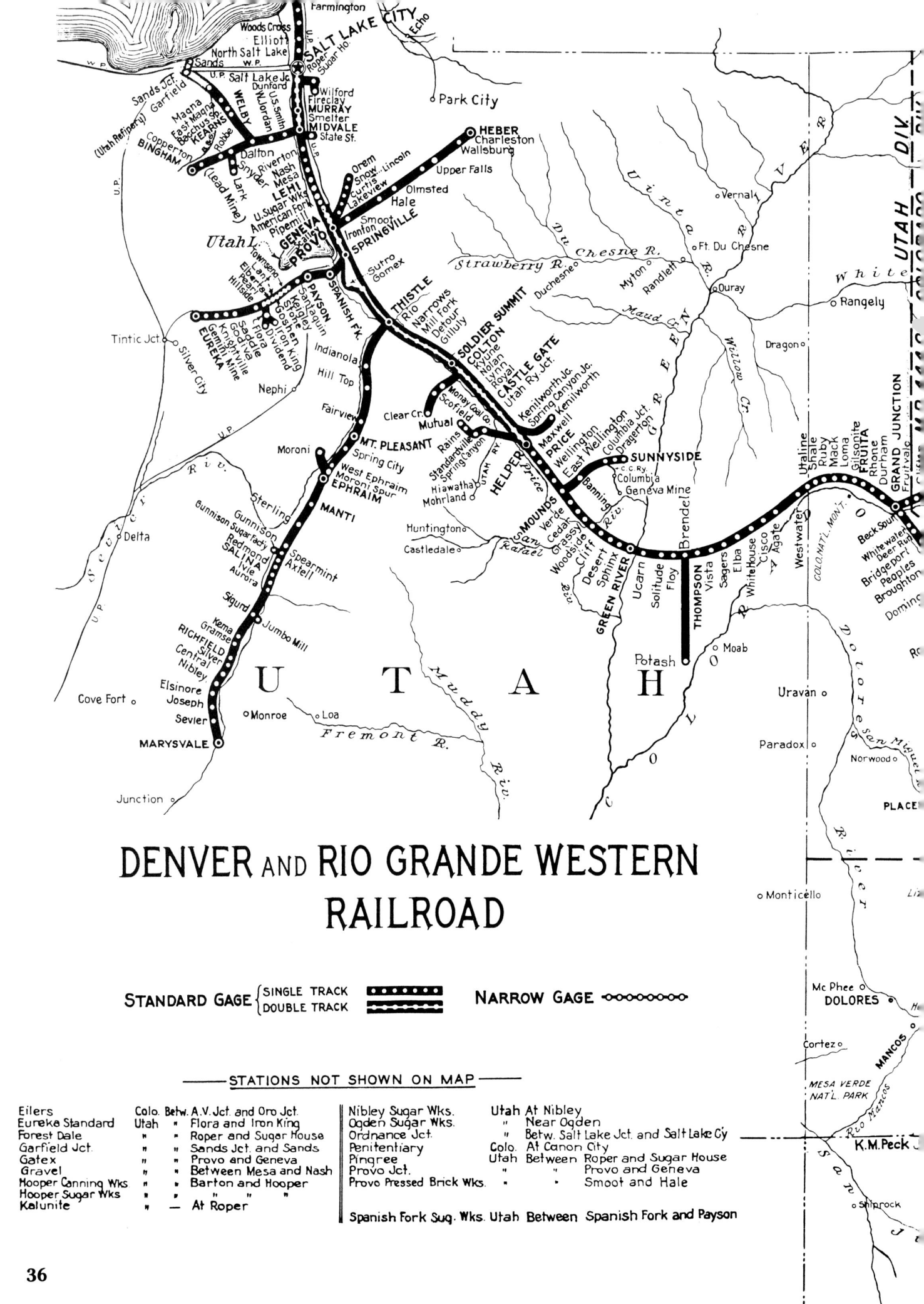

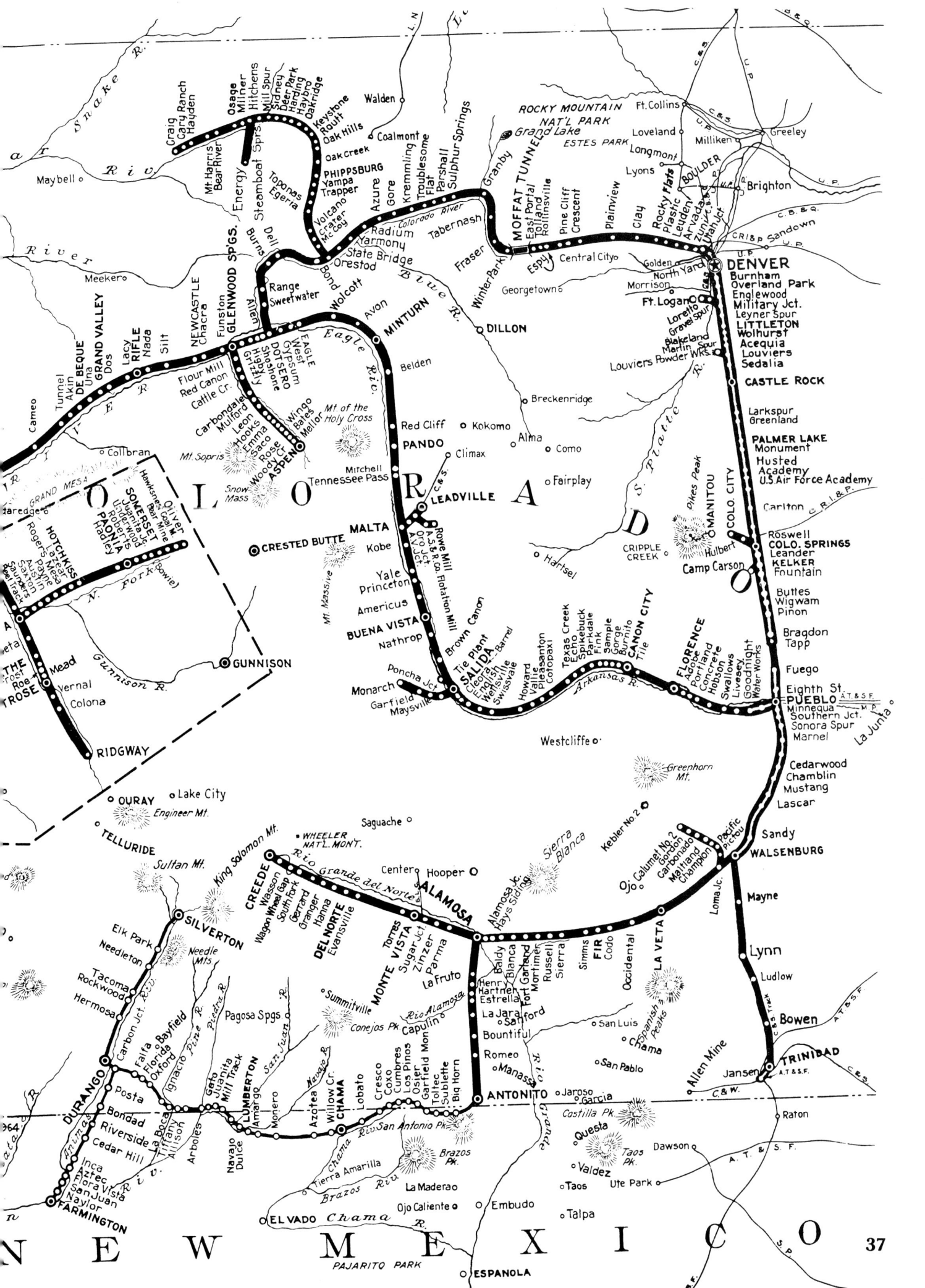

TOP. Extra East with a consist of livestock, lumber and pipe empties approaching Highway 17 between Lobato and Cresco. BOTTOM. Engine 480 pulls away from the coal chute at Alamosa in the winter of 1940. *Both photos, R.W. Richardson/Colorado RR Museum*

Winter on the Rio Grande could be fierce. Here work trains meet at Big Horn Siding between Sublette and Antonito. Lead engine is No. 492, a K-37 2-8-2 built by Baldwin, rebuilt from #1021 in 1928. The locomotive went to the Toltec Scenic Railway in 1970.

Two Rio Grande steamers team up through the Rockies heading for Cumbres. *John Krause/Dr. Richard Severance collection*

RIGHT. At Cumbres Pass where mountain soil gave way.

LEFT. Stockyards at Osier.

1,000 laborers per month shipped from Denver and Pueblo to the various grading camps."

Apparently most of these recruits deserted to the mines, returned home or continued on to other parts. Weitbrec stated that the cost of this one item, labor recruiting and transportation of recruits, had amounted to $33,350 for the year. He lost his patience and put a stop to the ticket and traveling expense loss: "Our expense in this line clearly demonstrated that the class of labor secured was the least desirable. Any number of worthless fellows were anxious to get a free ride to Colorado, and I made up my mind that unless a man could raise enough money to pay his railroad fare and expenses that the chances were he was an undesirable man to have."

Out of this problem of recruiting labor grew an important decision: The Rio Grande began recruiting local help, which meant the brown, lean and ever-enduring Nuevo Mejicano. Indeed, as the Rio Grande headed toward Santa Fe and the San Juan, it was advancing into the heart of the New Mexican country and culture. From that time forward, the Nuevo Mejicano would assume a dominant role in the building of, and later, the maintenance of the roadway and tracks of the narrow gauge.

Arrival of tracks at Antonito presented a bit of a quandary to Palmer. He knew he was limited by the Boston Treaty as to how far into New Mexico he could build, and those limits would not permit him to go all the way to Santa Fe until the Treaty expired. In the end he decided to go as far as he could, and a bit farther, at least to Espanola. The San Juan Extension had no such limitations and Silverton was beckoning. Construction went forward on both routes with the Extension receiving some priority. So, in a sense, the Chili Line at that period became somewhat an entity in itself and thus merits its own story.

Although the go ahead had been given to build over Cumbres Pass, it was known there were better routes to the San Juan but speed in reaching the new silver camps gave Cumbres the edge and so the choice was made. Reconnaissance-type surveys were made of other passes through the San Juan Mountains that divided the Rio Grande from the waters of the San Juan, with the view of securing the best and fastest route to the town of Silverton. One was over Cunningham Pass, earlier named Stony Pass by Dr. F.V. Hayden, an earlier explorer; South Fork Pass, which generally followed what later became known as the Wolf Creek Pass route; and a third pass called Alamosa Pass by Manager of Construction Robert F. Weitbrec. The latter probably ran up Alamosa Creek and over the divide before descending to the San Juan by way of the East Fork. This would approximate today's Elwood Pass.

In the D&RG engineering files is a faded, undated map that titles it as the route of a 'fly-line' survey possible between Antonito and Chama up the west side of the San Antone River to Hopewell (New Mexico), thence to the Chama River near the Canones Creek confluence and up the Chama River valley to a point where the Little Chama joins the main river. From there the line would continue westward as it was finally located. Except for the time factor involving a longer construction period, this would have been the best route of all and relatively snow free. It would have had better grades and could have been run due west to cross the Continental Divide by the ancient Horse Lake Pass of the Padres as hinted at in the very earliest projections Palmer made for a line to leave the Rio Grande River near Espanola thence to Durango and Silverton.

CUMBRES PASS

Cumbres Pass was not one of the historic passes. It was not a short cut between any major settlements, and other routes

Westbound #483 with a mixed narrow gauge-standard gauge consist has just met an eastbound narrow gauge train at Romeo. *R.W. Richardson/Colorado RR Museum*

Nos. 495 and 486 lead the charge on the Narrow Gauge with this freight train, shown in both photos at different locations. *John Krause/Dr. Richard Severance collection*

The K Class, a 36 (486) and a 37 (491) provide the entertainment in this beautiful view on the Chama to Cumbres line. *John Krause/Dr. Richard Severance collection*

In the winter, taking on water — like here at Needleton Water Tank — was a cold job, but it had to be done.

were more favorable. Neither Spaniards, prospectors or bull-team wagoners had any special reason to use it. Wild game did not favor the area so the Indians only infrequently made visits.

The area's most substantial encounter with history had come in July, 1848, when the Second Regiment of Missouri Volunteers shot it out with a mixed band of Jicarilla Apaches and Muache Utes in a cluster of rocks on a grassy hillside about halfway between Cumbres and Chama. Two soldiers and 36 Indians were killed in the skirmish. Legend and speculation also say that somewhere on Cumbres Pass is where Indians caught up with and killed Doctor Benjamin Kerns and Old Bill Williams as they were returning from a mission to retrieve belongings left behind at Embargo Creek when it became necessary for the survivors of John Charles Fremont's ill-fated fourth expedition to locate a transcontinental railroad route to retreat to Taos.

The Cumbres Pass route decided on, contracts had been let late in 1879 for grading and bridge building on the San Juan Extension all the way to Durango, 200.3 miles from Alamosa. A severe winter set in and drastically retarded that work until the end of April, 1880. Surveying Cumbres Pass during the summer had been one thing, but grading the line during the winter was another, and a foretaste of the conditions that railroaders on the Narrow Gauge would face each winter on Cumbres in the future.

For some meteorological reason, Cumbres Pass was directly in the path of a snow course that received deep snowfall accompanied by high winds. Palmer did know that most of the land on the route between Antonito and Chama was almost treeless and that the greater part consisted of alpine meadows and gentle slopes. A forest fire, known as the Osier Mountain fire, had raged unchecked over the broad top of Cumbres Pass in 1879, wiping out thousands of acres of evergreens and increasing the barrenness. He did not know, and there were no records to show, that the snowfall on Cumbres could be as much as 500 inches during the winter, compounded by severe drifting.

When grading and tracklaying resumed at the end of April, a great deal of heavy rock work was encountered, and mainly on account of the difficulty in securing efficient labor the work dragged on through the summer and autumn. By the early snows of winter the end of track was still 15 to 20 miles east of the Los Pinos-Chama Divide. A few detractors of the engineering of the Cumbres Pass Route have implied that when Weitbrec and McMurtrie were instructed to start building over Cumbres to the San Juan, in a fit of pique they laid some ties on the ground at Antonito in a generally westerly direction, spiked two rails to them, and told the track boss to just keep adding panels until he got to Chama.

In order to obtain anything nearly approaching acceptable grades on the east side of Cumbres Pass a lot of surveying was required. This, in conjunction with the necessity of heading the many deep canyons along the route on the segment between Big Horn and Los Pinos — eliminating as many bridges as possible — no doubt resulted in some improvisations that substituted for good engineering design. Maximum grades of one per cent and alignment that will produce two or three degree curves are the standard on modern railroads. The Cumbres line had maximum grades of 211.2 feet to the mile, or 4 per cent, and maximum curvature of 25 degrees. Sixty-four miles of railroad were required to link Antonito and Chama, two points only 34 miles apart by air.

On March 16, 1881, Weitbrec submitted a report to

You're seeing one of the last passenger trains between Alamosa and Durango before the trains were discontinued. The *San Juan* made its last trip in Colorado in February, 1951. *D&RGW photo*

You're at trackside on June 1, 1958, near Romeo and the soothing sounds of steam still exist as Extra 480 and 490 westbound head a 74-car standard gauge and narrow gauge freight train. An idler is between the 490 and the standard gauge cars; a second idler is between the standard gauge cars and the narrow gauge ones. The idlers and the standard gauge cars will be left at Antonito, and the narrow gauge cars will go on west. *Richard Kindig*

TOP. The contrast in size between standard gauge and narrow gauge is shown with these cabooses at Alamosa in January, 1949. *R.W. Richardson/Colorado RR Museum*

The difference between standard gauge cars and narrow gauge cars is shown in this April, 1953 photo at Alamosa. An idler car separates the cars. BOTTOM, LEFT. Narrow gauge stock cars at Hartner on December 31, 1952. *Both photos, R.W. Richardson/Colorado RR Museum*

Idlers feature two couplers to accommodate either standard or narrow gauge cars.

Palmer: "The winter of 1880-1881 proved to be even more severe than the previous one, and the track which was completed to Chama, January 18, 1881, was laid in the face of almost continuous storms, and under extraordinary difficulties."

Company records show that in February 1881, 1102 men and 393 teams were employed on the San Juan Extension. The severe winter produced numerous cases of frozen hands and feet, plus several deaths. There were loud complaints against the company, whose recruiters had assured new recruits they could expect to work in a mild climate. The recruiters, like the locating engineers, had never seen Cumbres when she was buried under snow and being torn by high altitude winds.

In his report, Weitbrec, in addition to describing the line between Antonito and Chama, described the proposed route beyond to Durango and Silverton: "Commencing at Alamosa and running south to Antonito, a distance of 28.7 miles; thence westerly along the slopes of San Antonio (more commonly called the San Antone) Conejos and Los Pinos Creeks to the Divide between the waters of the Los Pinos and the Chama, thence westerly to the junction of the Little Chama with the Chama, thence westerly to the Continental Divide, thence down El Amargo Canyon, Navajo Creek and the San Juan River to the mouth of the Piedra, thence in a westerly direction to Durango, in the Animas Valley, thence north to Silverton, the total distance of 245.3 miles."

Another report, dated April 1881, was made by Weitbrec to Palmer in regard to the San Juan Extension, and his reference to the Antonito-Chama segment was even more pointed, notwithstanding the fact that the later report gave a date of completion to Chama different than his earlier report: "This portion of the Extension is the wildest as well as the most costly piece of railroad work in this country, and was completed December 31, 1880, although not turned over to the operating department until February 1, 1881."

CROSSES STATES 11 TIMES

After the rail was laid and its location drawn on a map, it

An eastbound freight heads for Lava during the cold winter season on the Narrow Gauge.

was discovered that the line crossed the boundary separating New Mexico and Colorado 11 times between Antonito and Chama. Trainmen always told passengers there were 13 crossings, but 11 is correct. There was one more state line crossing 39 miles west of Chama at Milepost 378.20.

The crossings east of Chama were located at the following mileposts, using the later identified mileposts, or 'joint line' mileages rather than the original designations:

    283.75 - Colorado to New Mexico
    284.68 - New Mexico to Colorado
    284.91 - Colorado to New Mexico
    290.28 - New Mexico to Colorado
    291.04 - Colorado to New Mexico
    291.18 - New Mexico to Colorado
    294.29 - Colorado to New Mexico
    307.30 - New Mexico to Colorado
    309.52 - Colorado to New Mexico
    311.79 - New Mexico to Colorado
    330.47 - Colorado to New Mexico

Engineering reports and lines drawn on a map, however, gave but a hint of the involved engineering problems and rugged natural obstacles it was necessary to overcome in building the Antonito-Chama portion of the San Juan Extension.

Leaving Antonito at an elevation of 7888 feet, the line ran westerly up a wide, shallow valley. Approximately nine miles from Antonito a sweeping curve to the south enabled the track to climb a grade that carried the roadbed over the lava escarpment of an ancient volcanic flow. A short distance across the level of the flow the line was built on a circle of sufficient perimeter to attain grade to cross a second flow. The west end of the loop of track on this circle was only a few yards away from the beginning of the loop. A water tank was built in this area and given the name of Lava. Water was pumped several miles from San Antone Creek, being raised some 500 feet in the process. Although the elevation at Lava was 8468 feet, the tableland was dust dry (the snow-and-water country began a few miles farther west).

Five miles beyond Lava, a double loop was built to gain grade. A section house, named Big Horn, was situated in the center of the first loop so that a train in either direction passed it three times. Three miles beyond the Big Horn section house, a siding was located at the base of a prominent peaklet called Big Horn. There also was a wye at Big Horn Siding and, in the early years, a train order telegraph office. A short run brought westbound trains to Sublette, where there was a good supply of spring water. Freight trains in both directions stopped at Sublette so that locomotives could take water and fires could be cleaned. The crews broke out their "thousand-mile lunches", an institution on Cumbres Pass because a man never knew how long the trip over the pass would take. The firemen, especially, carried a lot of eating supplies because it took a lot of shovels of coal to make enough steam to whip Cumbres grades.

Sublette, at an elevation of 9,022 feet, in addition to being a watering point for the locomotives, was the point where the terrain changed from that associated with the Foothills Zone to vegetation and climate conditions of the Montane Zone. From the water tank at Sublette to a point just east of Chama, the ground cover consisted of grasses, low willows, alders and many varieties of wild flowers in season. Heavier cover was made up of spruce, balsam, aspens and some fir. These trees grew sometimes in copses, groves or singly, sometimes separated as single species, sometimes commingled. Small, swift streams bordered by willows and alders ran from the hillsides to join the Los Pinos on the east side of the Pass; on the west side more streams drained into Wolf Creek. Both of the main drainages eventually flowed to the Gulf of Mexico via the Rio Grande and Chama rivers, which came together as one near Espanola.

CUMBRES SCENERY

Only a short time passed after passenger service was established over Cumbres Pass before the D&RG realized they had a valuable attraction in the scenery of Cumbres Pass. The traveling public felt the same way and word of the rugged, soul-satisfying beauty of Cumbres Pass was widely publicized by word of mouth and print.

George A. Crofutt, one of the first recognized rail and travel fans, man of mystery, and writer of guidebooks about the West, rode the Narrow Gauge varnish over Cumbres shortly after service was available. In 1885 he published his *Grip-Sack Guide of Colorado*. (Note: In 1966, Francis B. Rizzari, Richard A. Ronzio, and Charles S. Ryland—Cubar

Associates, Golden, Colorado—reprinted and distributed this book as originally published, adding a fine collection of contemporary photographs. This is a gold mine of information for the student of Colorado history.)

Crofutt tells what the viewer sees and feels in words of the period, and of special interest is his account of Cumbres Pass route between the upper Big Horn loop and Osier, the most spectacular part of Cumbres scenery:

"The view from this point (Big Horn loop) is most grand. Beyond the valley to the south rise the mountains, timbered in places, in others covered with a mantle of evergreens, the ground bespangled with beds of flowers of every tint and hue; to the east appears the great dome of San Antonio mountain; beyond, the San Luis valley, with its green and gold; and still farther to the left Mount Blanca and the Sangre de Cristo mountains. Take a long look for it will be the last at this time.

"Proceeding north, and west, and south, and west again, we are *far up* on the side of a rugged canyon, beside which the mountains rise to a towering height, throwing out great rocky ribs, as though to bar our further progress. The valley is crowded out, and the rugged surroundings are grand and exciting; at times in a tunnel, then on the edge of frightful precipices, beneath castellated heights and natural monuments; following around the head of yawning chasms, with an occasional ray of sunlight sifting through the overhanging crags, such are portions of the scenery of "Phantom Curve," in Toltec Canyon, just before reaching Toltec Tunnel, 35 miles west of Antonito. At this point the canyon narrows to a frightful gorge, the granite walls rising to nearly 1,000 feet above the roaring waters, and apparently only a few feet apart.

"Looking down the canyon from the eastern entrance to the tunnel, the view is charming. The lofty precipices, the castellated summits, the distant heights, the fantastic monuments, the contrast of the rugged craigs, and the graceful curves of the silvery streams beneath them, the dark green pines and cedars, interspersed with groves of aspen quaking in their green, yellow and silvery foliage, and which are to be seen in the gorges and crowning the heights, combine to constitute a landscape that is destined to have a worldwide notoriety, and to be visited, described and painted by people from all parts of Christendom.

"Passing through the tunnel which is cut through the solid rock for a distance of 366 feet, the scenery is also very grand, but quite different from that viewed below. The gorge is very narrow and deep, the opposite cliffs, 2,000 feet in height, and where the eye takes in the greatest depth the train runs upon a solid bridge of trestle-work, set in the rocks, as if it were a balcony, purposely attached to one of nature's most imposing mansions, so that the very finest possible view of the wonderful scenes everywhere around could be most advantageously obtained."

Crofutt was like most passengers who rode the Narrow Gauge westward. The view after leaving Toltec Tunnel was anticlimactic. The alpine meadows, the shelf road just west of Osier, and the spine-chilling high bridge built on a curve over Cascade Creek could not compare with the spectacular countryside viewed from Sublette to the west end of Toltec Tunnel. Even the final climb to the top of Cumbres Pass and the shock of the initial descent on the west side of Windy Point to the first crossing of Wolf Creek did not arouse the senses in the manner the best part of the earlier westward climb did. The passage a second time over Wolf Creek on the high spider web of the bridge at Lobato, about five miles east of Chama, often went unnoticed.

Chama, the town at the foot of the westward Cumbres grade, deserves more than passing mention, for it has a history, a culture and an atmosphere of the Old West that merits better handling later.

No. 497 is on the point this day to pull a 19-car freight with the help of a sister locomotive. *John Krause/Dr. Richard Severance collection*

ABOVE. It's a beautiful day in the Rockies as No. 494, a K-37, takes the tight curves the track throws her. Not far behind in the train another Rio Grande locomotive follows this one, helping to lift today's tonnage up over the mountain barriers between Chama and Alamosa. *John Krause/Dr. Richard Severance collection*

TOP, RIGHT. Engine No. 481 on the west leg of the wye at Cumbres has just come out of the covered wye after turning on this March 6, 1958. And the snow isn't over yet this year! *Richard Kindig*

BOTTOM, RIGHT. Extra West, with No. 476, is wasting coal and fogging it up in the lower (south) end of the San Luis Valley heading for Chama. *R.W. Richardson/Colorado RR Museum*

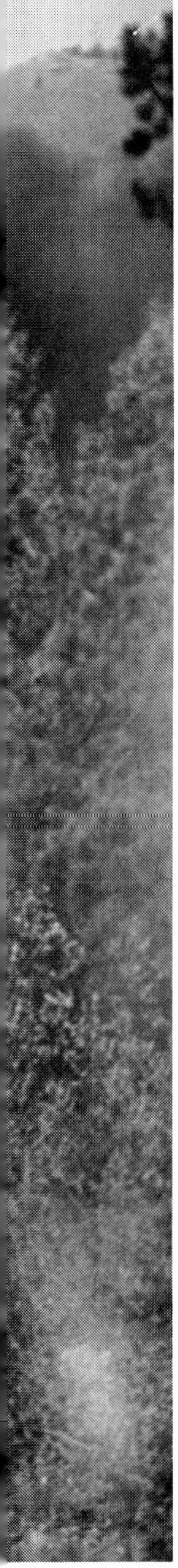

51

TOP. No. 494 assists with a freight movement. The fireman peers down over the trestle and the doghouse door swings open. This is railroading on the Narrow Gauge!

FAR RIGHT, BOTTOM. No. 498 with caboose snug behind drifts over the trestle. *Both photos, John Krause/Dr. Richard Severance collection*

RIGHT. Road engine 493 smokes it up on the Chama-Cumbres Turn with a consist of crude oil from Chama, Gramps Field, and lumber. The train—with a helper on the rear—starts across the high steel trestle over Wolf Creek at Lobato on July 18, 1952. *R.W. Richardson/Colorado RR Museum*

The D&RGW signal man standing in the doorway of the depot is watching history for one of the last times. Progress is coming—the narrow rails will be scrapped and the shrill steam whistle won't echo again in the desert territory in and around Dulce. It seems a short time ago they were just building the line into Dulce... *John Krause/Dr. Richard Severance collection*

Chapter 5

Over the Continental Divide
The Chama-Durango portion

The bad weather of the winter of 1880-1881 that made construction over Cumbres Pass so difficult continued to plague the railroad builders west of Chama. By March 16, 1881, the end of track was only a little more than 15 miles beyond Chama. Nevertheless, this placed the track laying some five miles west of the Continental Divide, approaching the upper end of a canyon that Robert F. Weitbrec, manager of construction, called El Amargo Canyon, later and better known as Monero Canyon. Thus the San Juan Extension was the first Rio Grande track to cross the Continental Divide, for it was to be about a month later before the Salida-Gunnison line did so.

Of course, crossing the Divide on the San Juan Extension was not a major event. The crossing is at MP 354.45, just 10.33 miles west of Chama. The elevation of Chama is 7,863 feet and at the Divide 7,723 feet, so in effect the railroad ran downhill to cross the Divide. (Water on the east side flows to Willow Creek and thence to the Chama River. On the west side it flows to Monero Creek to flow into the Sea of Cortez. The Chama River water goes to the Gulf of Mexico.)

As construction passed out of the area of hard rock and steep mountain grades of the Cumbres Pass segment of the line into sedimentaries and relatively level terrain, progress should have quickened, but problems continued as the engineers chose to follow the waterways of the route west of Chama earlier described by Weitbrec. Grading was slowed as the roadbed followed meanders of these rivers and tributaries, all of which flowed through canyons that were cut in soft sandstones and shales.

Additional delay resulted from having to blast shelves along the steeply faced sandstone cliffs for the roadbed and in building bridges across drainages when there were no other alternatives for building grades. But generally speaking, progress while somewhat slow, went without any significant incident through the settlement of Monero and down the canyon of many names.

At the west end of the 3-mile-long Monero canyon one of the very level areas to be found in the Rockies began. This was the Amargo Park that was about 8 miles long from the outlet of Monero Canyon to the beginning of Navajo Canyon. The railroad broke out of Monero Canyon toward the end of March and the town of Amargo was established as a temporary railhead.

On April 1, Chief Engineer McMurtrie reported to Palmer summarizing the route from Chama. He stated the line ran from Chama over the Continental Divide, down Amargo (Monero) Creek and through the canyon of this drainage for 3 miles on a 2 per cent descending grade to Amargo Station, 365.67 miles from Denver. This report was conspicuous for its brevity.

Amargo was a typical end-of-rail conglomeration of tents, shacks and piles of construction material. It was occupied as a staging point for the drive to Durango for too short a period to

Pagosa Jct. Oct 4 - 1911

Pagosa Jct. During Flood Oct...

have left much of a mark in the history books. It did live through one short afternoon of clouds of black powder smoke, whining ricochets of bullets and war whoops of a small band of drunken Apaches. There is nothing to show that they were any of Geronimo's braves or even that they had serious intentions. Neither is there any record that any blood was shed—either by the ferocious Indians or by the deadeye marksmen among the defenders.

At Amargo, the Rio Grande construction forces poised for the final drive to Durango. Now the silvery San Juan was in sight! The term silvery San Juan had two connotations. The obvious reference was to the wealth of silver ore found in the San Juan district. But to those privileged to ride parallel to the San Juan, seated in the cupola of a caboose on a night when the moon was full and riding high, the term had another, more esthetic meaning—the water flowing along beside the railroad became a river of silver when the moon was reflected from its surface.

BUILDING TO DURANGO

Soon after April 1, the builders of the Narrow Gauge were ready to start the last stage of building to Durango. After the grading and track gangs left Amargo, it seemed as if the gods of the canyons and mountains had relented. From Amargo to Durango there were some slight delays incidental to construction but no difficulties. Too, by now, railroad building to these men had become old hat to the point they hardly needed a location crew out ahead to set grade stakes, or overseers to tell them how and where to lay the ties and rails. Pushing the 3-foot gauge westward was just a matter of starting with the sun and laying the last rail of the day when it went down—just a matter of so many ties placed and so many rails spiked to them each day.

Amargo Park was rapidly crossed. Construction began on a few shacks at a point where Rito de la Nutria Ciega (Blind Beaver Creek) flowed into Amargo Creek. These were the beginning of the town of Lumberton, N. Mex. A timber trestle was built over Blind Beaver Creek. Just east of the beginning of Navajo Canyon another town was beginning, its outlines being marked and subdivided by plowed furrows, the Jicarilla Apache Indian Agency town of Dulce.

Nobody knew for sure who owned the land—Jicarillas, Utes, Emmet Wirt, the Gomez family, the Sanchez family, or whether it was public domain. At the time no one cared much—the Rio Grande was in a hurry and the people wanted a railroad. When land ownership later was defined everybody got a little, even the Apaches. In the settlement, the Jicarilla Apaches formally received land that they had occupied as a reservation since an unratified treaty of 1855. The Gomez and Sanchez families retained title to a choice little valley south of Dulce that became an enclave within the reservation. Emmet Wirt was appointed as the sole licensed Indian trader with the Jicarillas. From the profits resulting from this appointment he accumulated title to considerable land in the general area—and a lot of money.

Even a few newcomers got a taste of the pie, including sawmill operators. A few hardscrabble homesteaders in addition to filing for homesteads filed on timber claims and later sold them to the lumber barons.

PREVIOUS PAGE. What a difference one day can make! Pagosa Junction (Gato), Colorado, is dry on October, 1911 (top), but 24 hours later the San Juan River had swollen its banks and caused havoc on the Rio Grande.

Leaving Amargo Park and entering Navajo Canyon, Palmer's railroad builders, smug with the awareness of their technical accomplishments and their ability to bridge cultures and history with 30-pound rails, followed a route that was at least two centuries old. Although it was an easy route, a good and safe route, and well known, it had never been heavily used or gained historical significance. The first recorded use was made during the travels of two young Franciscan priests, Silvestre de Escalante and Francisco Atanasio Dominguez, who in July 1776 left Santa Fe and one month later left the Chama River watershed and crossed the Continental Divide by way of the Horse Lake Pass and then followed old Indian trails to reach Amargo Park and then down the San Juan River to the vicinity of Durango.

Rail laying had to pause at the Navajo River long enough for a bridge to be completed. Taking advantage of this delay at the same time, the carpenter gangs went to work building a water tank. They also threw together some dwellings for a section maintenance gang and the man who ran the pump to keep the tank filled. Although rail laying was delayed, grading did not stop, for the grading crews swam the river with their teams and rafted enough equipment across to continue grading. The bridge completed, rail was rapidly laid to the junction of the Navajo and San Juan where a bridge over the San Juan was built.

Again, as at Navajo, rail laying was delayed while the bridge was building, but grade crews swam the San Juan and kept on working. In addition to the bridge, other facilities were built, including a section house, bunkhouses, a depot and stockyards. A small town named Juanita grew from these first buildings and stayed alive for almost half a century.

For about 40 miles after leaving Dulce, the railroad builders found most of the country uninhabited except for a few temporary camps of Indians in Navajo Canyon, although along both the Navajo and the San Juan were numerous small pieces of fertile soil that had been deposited by the rivers. Most were at the mouth of cross canyons or other protected places near the main streams. All were protected from the wind and snow and could be irrigated. The lean brown men, the paisanos, now forming the bulk of Palmer's track gangs, had come to work on the railroad from small farms. A number of them preempted choice locations to return to after work on the D&RG was no longer available. Many sent for their families to start ranchitos while they were still working. In not too many years after the first passage of the railroad builders through this section, there was a string of green fields and brown adobe homes paralleling the Narrow Gauge.

STEADY PROGRESS

Track-laying progress was steady after the San Juan was bridged and crossed. A few miles west of Juanita, where Gato (Cat) Creek entered the San Juan, a site was selected for one more station and water tank. A carpenter gang was left here to build section houses and a water tank. A pumping facility was also built and a home for the pumper. Later a refueling facility would be added. The location was first named Gato Watertank, then Gato, Pagosa Junction and finally again was renamed Gato.

Cat Creek was bridged and beyond the Rio Grande followed the course of the San Juan generally, bridging cross drainages of tributaries as necessary. The principal ones, in succession, were the Piedra, Los Pinos, and Florida Rivers. For five miles west of Gato the railroad was built above the high water marks along sandstone and shale hillsides. A valley followed this section, characterized by fertile deltas and filled-in oxbows that the San Juan had left behind in its constant search for

The San Luis Valley with drifting snow, uninhabited and unmarked by three-foot rails, is beautifully lonely. The Rio Grande didn't seek or receive any state or federal land grants to build its empire. *Courtesy D&RGW*

new channels. Ute land began at about this point. With 40 miles of uninhabited land behind them, the builders now found themselves in an area of established small farms and farm settlements—occupied by Ute Indians, Spanish Americans and a few Americans. The clusters of houses and camps hardly could be called towns, but at least the area was developing along lines that, with the coming of the railroad, would attain permanence. The American settlers who had become discouraged by a lack of luck in prospecting around Silverton had returned to their basic trade by settling on open land to establish farms.

The Rio Grande laid down ties and spiked rails to them, 36 inches apart, without any more delays, and rolled into Durango on the 27th day of July 1881. Or did it?

July 27 was the date given for completion of 107.8 miles of track between Chama and Durango by Palmer in his report to the stockholders of April 1, 1982, and is the completion date used by historians. However, contemporary records cite with bravado the fact that Durango had been connected to the rest of the world by a telegraph line completed on July 30, 1881. In the first message sent over this line to the press of the country on that date, Durango sent greetings to the nation and boasted that the Denver and Rio Grande would reach Durango on August 1.

Durango would grow to become a micro-metropolis and the key to activity in the southwest corner of the Narrow Gauge world, with main lines and major branches leading to the four cardinal points of the compass. It was named Durango because the terrain of the area very much resembles that surrounding Durango, Mexico, for which it was named. Durango, Colorado, is surrounded by mountains rich in minerals and coal, picturesque mesas, plateaus, high peaks and valleys.

Durango's first inhabitants consisted mainly of former residents of the older nearby Animas City. When the Rio Grande prepared to renew building toward the San Juan in 1879, its town builder and chief negotiator in real estate, Dr. William A. Bell, went to the Animas Valley to arrange for land for the Durango terminal. He first went to Animas City, just up the Animas River from the location of present-day Durango. His proposals to the residents of Animas City followed established D&RG lines and the reception of these proposals was the usual refusal. Bell then arranged for several loyal Rio Grande employees to homestead claims along the Animas downstream from Animas City. Soon after filing on these claims, the psuedo-homesteaders sold to the Durango Land and Coal Company. Durango was laid out on these plots and land sales began. Railroad facilities were plotted also and some construction got under way. So, by the time the Narrow Gauge rolled into Durango it had a going town and some facilities to receive it.

Like Conejos which was superseded by Antonito, Animas

City, a booming town of 2,000 population, felt secure in its permanence. Its newspaper, the *Southwest* expressed the confidence of most of the residents when on May 1, 1880, it said:

"The Bank of San Juan has issued a circular in which it is stated that a branch office will be opened at the 'new town of Durango on the Rio Animas.' Where the 'new town of Durango' is to be or not to be God and the D. and R. G. Railroad only know. If they are in 'cahoots' we ask for a special dispensation."

Two days before the end of the year, however, Durango's new newspaper, Durango *Daily Record,* in its first issue reported:

"All of Animas City is coming to Durango as fast as accommodations can be secured. Even the *Southwest* is coming, despite its small opinion of our dimensions. It will move down some day next week."

Again, as at Conejos, Animas City did not become a ghost town, but it was relegated to the status of a suburb of Durango.

BIG CELEBRATION

The citizens warmly embraced the new town and the new railroad, if the celebration held on August 5 was any indication. Quibblers about details may argue as to whether the Narrow Gauge reached Durango on July 27 or August 1, 1881—but there can be no doubt about the fact that on August 5 one big celebration was held to herald the arrival of the railroad at the new town of Durango. Because all the dignitaries were not present for the scheduled celebration on August 5, Durango residents staged a rerun on August 6.

The celebration to welcome Palmer's Narrow Gauge to Durango was not just the event of the year, it was the event of the century so far as Colorado was concerned. Music and noise were made by a cornet band, a French horn band, drum corps, fiddles, guitars, shotguns, pistols and anvil cannon—most of them making noise simultaneously. As long as vocal cords were physically able to do so, there was a lot of whooping and hollering. Any celebrant who felt his voice failing took steps to strengthen and lubricate it by making frequent visits to several locations where the necessary elixirs and lubricants were being dispensed in copious quantities.

One participant tried to climb into the barrel of San Juan Sangaree the committee had provided. He got one leg in before he was pulled out. To show the difference between ordinary sangaree and San Juan Sangaree (a mixture of wine and *ranch* whiskey) it was reliably reported that the rescued celebrant lost the sole of his boot and part of his toes due to the corrosive potency of the brew. His misfortune was his own fault for it was a well known fact that *ranch* whiskey (Taos Lightning) only corroded externally. Taken internally all it did was to tan the innards of the drinker, burn out ulcers, atrophy the kidneys and destroy the liver. A few heavy drinkers of ranch whiskey were known to have been relieved of all their pains and worries by steady application to the brew.

The news of the Durango celebration had been widely spread and on such a grand occasion no politician worthy of the name could stay away. Governor Frederick W. Pitkin arrived ahead of the day of celebration. Three ex-governors, William Gilpin, John Evans and A. Cameron Hunt, along with sundry other prominent persons, elected to ride from Denver to Durango with General Palmer on the special celebration train.

The day of the celebration arrived right on schedule—the Celebration Special did not. Some sinking track between Alamosa and Antonito, rocks falling in Navajo Canyon and a few other things delayed the train, not the least being that a few apprehensive passengers insisted at some of the more

It's February 20, 1953, as a westward extra nears Azotea, New Mexico, with 487 and 492 in charge of a 57-car train at 20 miles an hour. Richard Kindig captured the scene for us to enjoy.

dangerous places on Cumbres Pass that the trains be stopped so they could get off and walk until they considered it safe to board again.

But Durango was cocked and primed for its celebration and was not going to wait for the delayed Celebration Special. The proceedings, short a number of distinguished guests, got under way at 10 o'clock with a big parade to the Fairgrounds, where a race track had been laid out. Mayor J.L. Pennington opened the ceremonies and introduced Governor Pitkin. A lot of races were run, and the ladies of Durango fed the crowd a grand free barbecue. Among the viands were five whole oxen, a dozen sheep, two wagon loads of bread and biscuit and four barrels of coffee.

This was Celebration No. 1—the Celebration Special finally reached Durango about 11:40 the evening of August 5. A second celebration was organized for the following day—more barrels of Sangaree were mixed, bread baked and animals killed for the barbecue. There was not a single dissenting voice against the holding of Celebration No. 2.

Governor Pitkin availed himself of the opportunity to make a second speech and the tardy three ex-Governors and General Palmer made short speeches. Otherwise, Celebration No. 2 did not differ a great deal from Celebration No. 1 except participants did build up a heavier head of steam as time passed, and no one tried to immerse himself in the sangaree.

At the conclusion of Celebration No. 2, a Grand Ball was held in the new smelter building which was still awaiting installation of machinery and the only building large enough to accommodate the 500 people who attended the ball. Durango bands furnished music for dancing. Some critics said the music showed the influence of too many trips to the sangaree barrel, but then some of the dancers were less than coordinated on the dance floor. A late supper was served in relays, 100 people were served in each relay, and it took from 11 p.m. until 3 a.m. to serve everyone.

To this day there is still controversy about whether Celebration No. 1 or Celebration No. 2 was the biggest or the best. One old-timer was emphatic that No. 2 was the celebration to end all celebrations. He solemnly swore that the spirit of the festivities reached such heights that he personally heard one *macquereaux*, or *Mac*, tell his stable of *fillies de joie* to get up off their backs, put on their clothes and join the fun.

There is no arguing with that kind of criteria.

Caboose 0503 trails a freight which also has a U.S. Army box car in tow. *John Krause/Dr. Richard Severance collection*

It's 10 a.m. on a bright August morning in Chama, and No. 492 and her sisters await their train orders. *Chris Burritt*

Chapter 6

On to Silverton
Durango to Silverton

The two celebrations that greeted the coming of the Narrow Gauge to Durango were hardly over before Palmer was ready to start building up the Animas River to the silver boom town of Silverton. A terminal town achieved at Durango and a railroad built to it, the General was now set to move north up the Animas and through its canyon to reach the traffic represented by the mineral wealth of Baker's Park and its surrounding rich peaks and gulches.

Before that old nemesis, Winter, stopped track laying, the Silverton Branch had reached Rockwood and slightly beyond to where a sheer cliff fell off into the Animas. The shelf road, today called the High Line, had to be blasted and built before the construction of the railroad could continue. Work was suspended on December 11 because of severe winter conditions, heavy rock work, and the inability of the Colorado Coal and Iron Company to keep ahead of the demand for rails and fittings.

Work continued during the winter on building the High Line and a bridge over the Animas River a short distance beyond the sheer cliff. The bridge is located at today's Milepost 471.23. Other activities ceased, awaiting more favorable weather. However, in the spring, good progress was anticipated, for taking a leaf from precedents set at the crossings of the Navajo and San Juan rivers, grading crews had swum the Animas and graded as far as the junction of Cascade Creek with the Animas before shutdown.

The winter-plagued work at the High Line and on the bridge over the Animas was slow, and progress was made at the cost of many frozen fingers, feet and ears, but the blasting of rock and the forming of bridge timbers did not cease. Workmen and supervisors alike shivered at night in their blankets in the bunkcars at Rockwood until they could no longer stand the cold, then built dugouts in the hillsides that were warmer than the thin-walled outfit cars.

With the first sign of better weather, the Rio Grande shifted into high gear. On July 8, 1882, the railroad entered Silverton. Regardless of whether Silverton wooed Palmer or Palmer wooed Silverton, the Rio Grande had to enter the town on Silverton's term. For once Dr. Bell and Palmer were unable to pose the threat of a competing town if their demands for concessions were not met. Baker's Park, the small alpine valley in which Silverton was located, was so situated geographically that it was impossible to lay out a new town owned and controlled by the railroad. Property values were boom-high in 1882 in Silverton, and land for station grounds and a wye did not come cheap.

As badly as the silver mines needed a railroad, not all of the residents of Silverton viewed the coming of the Narrow Gauge to their town with joy. In fact, Silverton newspapers took less than a bright view of the eminent arrival, although between the two papers there was not complete accord on this. *La Plata Miner,* Silverton's first newspaper, made outspoken gestures of hostility to the coming, but the *Herald,* Silverton's second paper, took a more restrained stand, at times even championing the road's cause. Words fell thick

This is the Silverton train ready to depart the station at Silverton before it became such a tourist encampment. No. 463 looks primed for the trip back to Durango in this picture. Note the painted running boards, the spark arrester, the white flags and the weathering beneath the cab. It even appears the car stoves are lit.

Crib work is evident here on the High Line trackage; only one key was used.

and mean between the two editors. An especially biting editorial against the railroad appeared in the *Miner*. In rebuttal, and to take the opposite side, the *Herald* said: "The impression prevails, and it is the correct one, that Silverton is only awaiting for railroad facilities for the camp to boom, and now that we are on the eve, as it were of enjoying these privileges, a newspaper claiming to be the representative organ of southwestern Colorado, and withal the 'pioneer journal' of this section, assumes to voice the sentiments of this region by coming out in a four or five column tirade against the railroad arriving in Silverton, on general principles, and denouncing individually and collectively the directors of the D. & R. G. road as a band of thieves and pick-pockets, and the whole corporation as rotten to the core and gigantic swindle *in toto*."

DUEL OF WORDS

All of this was in strict accord with the historical battling that went on in the mountain towns of Colorado when there was more than one newspaper. The people of Silverton reacted to the duel of words as they would to any good contest. Teamsters and stage drivers took sides with the editor of the *Miner*. Their headquarters were in Anesies' bar. Mine owners, cattle ranchers and the editor of the *Herald* used the Imperial Cafe, across the way on Green Street, for their command post. Legend says that the *Herald's* editor often became so fatigued from the evening strategy meetings he had to be carried home on a shutter. Fortunately, the railroad arrived before the two enemy camps got down to shooting, cutting or stomping each other.

While the two editors exchanged verbal blows, the General and his powder-monkeys were cussing the hard granite of the High Line. Black powder was still in use as the explosive—many drill holes were needed, and the hard rock dulled drill steel very rapidly. In order to *pull* a significant amount of rock with each round of shots it was necessary to resort to a method of blasting known as *springing,* or locally as *spragging*. Holes were drilled in a pattern along the top surface of the rock using drill steel struck by hammer men swinging a double-jack hammer. When the series of holes had been drilled to the desired depth, each hole was loaded at the bottom with a charge of black powder and all fired. After one, or sometimes more charges, a cavity was formed at the bottom of the holes. These were then filled with as much powder as they could hold and fired. Often, after a lot of preparatory work, the amount of rock pulled was disappointing.

It was slow, tedious work—and hazardous, and during winter it was cold. Reminders of this monumental rock work remain today. On the face of the wall of the High Line can be seen numerous patterns like a many-rayed sun etched in the rock. These are the fracture marks where the drill holes were sprung for the final rock pulling blast.

There was no alternative route, and the High Line had to be built. Fortunately grade coincided with a slight shelf that sloped toward the edge of the precipice that somewhat minimized the amount of blasting required, but to utilize this favorable condition it was necessary to level and supplement the shelf with a great deal of crib work. This cribbing could not be done until the manmade shelf was completed, for to secure the cribbed walls, it was necessary to drill deep holes in the floor of the new grade in which anchor rods were placed. After the anchors were in place, molten lead was poured in the holes to lock the anchors in place and stop corrosion. A series of these anchor rods were set vertically as the cribs were built up. When the desired height was reached, retaining rods were placed down through the protruding eyes on the ends of the anchors to form a retaining key for the walls.

There was a large number of anchors and keys used. Each of these was hand-formed by blacksmiths of wrought iron and testifying to their craftsmanship, and the expertise of the masons who placed the rock cribs, these original cribs and their associated iron work are intact and in good condition almost 100 years after being built.

Just beyond the High Line a microcosm of a valley was situated. Its dimensions did not justify a bridge, and there was not enough fill material immediately available to make a fill. So, while work was going ahead on the High Line and the Animas bridge, a long curving trestle was constructed across the swale to carry the track. This trestle was eventually left in place when the fill was made and for a number of years caused track subsidence as the buried tree trunks rotted away.

At the bridge it was first necessary to build abutments on each side of the chasm, but fortunately the chasm at this point had sheer, solid rock walls that minimized this factor. The greatest amount of work consisted of framing the timbers of the bridge after heavy sawed timbers were delivered at the site from newly-opened sawmills in the Chama area. A great number of timbers were required and each had to be framed to the correct dimensions after arriving at the site—mortise and tenon joints cut and holes drilled for spiking. Before the bridge had been completed, a lot of strokes of the two-man crosscut saws had been made, as many or more blows struck on chisels and many rotations of the augers made. It was all hand work—and in the middle of a cold winter.

NARROW CANYON

The High Line anchored and the Animas bridge completed, rail could be laid on line already graded although, at many points after Animas Canyon was entered until Silverton was reached, grading was a misnomer. The canyon was narrow and at many places there was barely room for the roadbed between sheer rock walls and the rushing Animas. Many thousands of feet of cribbing were built of freshly-cut pine logs and filled with rubble to make a roadbed to support the ties and rails.

It was necessary to cross the Animas three more times after leaving Animas bridge. Thus, including a major bridge at a crossing just north of Durango, a total of five bridges were built on the Silverton Branch.

NEXT PAGE. No. 476 pounds the rails between Durango and Silverton with a short freight in September, 1952. *John Krause/Dr. Richard Severance collection.*

From this aerial view of Animas Canyon, you can see the railroad paralleling the river. *D&RGW photo*

The final two miles into Silverton across the floor of Baker's Park went like a breeze compared to the trials of building in the canyon. When the railroad did arrive, the miners were too busy digging ore, the railroad builders were worn down to a frazzle, and Palmer was in a hurry to start hauling ore. There was not much of a celebration to mark the coming of the Narrow Gauge—not even any reference to the driving of the traditional last spike.

Building the line across Cumbres Pass was tough, but in building the portion of the Silverton Branch between Hermosa and Silverton, Palmer's track and bridge men had achieved a special niche in the history of mountain railroad building.

Denver and Rio Grande Time Table No. 19, issued two weeks after completion of the Silverton Branch, listed eight stations between Durango and Silverton, including Animas City. The latter was the first town planted on the upper Animas. It almost became a ghost town several times but finally settled down to being a suburb of Durango. The first station above Animas City was Home Ranch, 6.6 miles from Durango. Little is known of this station except that, in the railroad records it shows the first revenue earned on the Silverton Branch was for a shipment that originated at Home Ranch for which the customer paid a bill for $456.24.

Next beyond Home Ranch was Trimble Springs. This was a passenger stop for a spa that was built around a hot medicinal spring discovered by one of the early arrivals on the Animas, a man named Trimble. With rail passenger service available, affluent health seekers from Denver and points east flocked to Trimble Springs in search of cures for everything

PREVIOUS PAGE. It was still railroad practice to carry a caboose on the Silverton Train when this photograph was taken. This is one of the earlier trains. *D&RGW photo*

from corns to arthritis to ingrown toenails to impotency. The curative powers of the waters become so well known that a fine hotel, the Hermosa, was built. By 1885 the establishment was valued at $100,000, but records fail to say whether or not old man Trimble profited. The springs became so overworked that many of the curative powers were lost and today will only perform a few of the original miracles.

Two miles above Trimble Springs a farming community, aptly named Hermosa, Spanish for beautiful, grew up. Hermosa had a population of about 150 people, all engaged in farming. Livestock and vegetables were raised and found ready markets in Durango, Animas City and Silverton. Orchards were planted and when the trees blossomed in the spring and the meadows turned green, Hermosa was a breath-taking picture framed against the high cliffs and snow-clad mountain ranges. A water tank, still in use, was built of redwood lumber on the banks of Hermosa Creek.

At Hermosa the grade of the Silverton line abruptly changed from 1 per cent grade to 2.5 per cent. This heavy grade was constant to Rockwood, 6.6 miles from Hermosa. From the crest at Rockwood there was descending grade to the river at a point where Crazy Woman Creek emptied into the Animas. At a much later date a hydroelectric plant was built here and a siding and passenger flag stop called Tacoma were established.

At the time the rails first reached Rockwood the town's population was of a transient nature that did not stay constant long enough for a head count. There were good grazing lands, timber, and several tie-cutting camps in the vicinity.

A devastating washout about a mile up the river from Tacoma. Nature has spoken.

The trackage called the "High Line" between Durango and Silverton is located between Rockwood and Tacoma. In early days hundreds of freight trains made this journey.

Old No. 463, a K-27 built by Baldwin in 1903, leads a freight train on the High Line. In 1955, the engine was sold to Gene Autrey and later donated to the town of Antonito. *John Krause/Dr. Richard Severance collection*

The town was chiefly important as a major staging point for freight wagons and stage coaches operating between the San Juan area and Rico, Colorado, 35 miles by road from Rockwood.

Rockwood remained active and prosperous until Otto Mears built the Rio Grande Southern, another narrow gauge railroad, into Rico. In its heyday the town had seven large warehouses, a number of saloons, a dance hall, a railroad station and a blacksmith shop that worked 24 hours a day shoeing oxen, horses and mules.

The Ute Indians considered Rockwood a source of irritation because the town was built on one of their favored camping grounds. Also, just over the hill toward Durango, there was a jewel of a lake named Shalano. Game and fish abounded in the area and only by the friendly actions of Chief Ouray were Rockwood and Shalano kept from becoming historic battlegrounds.

The ore loading track at Silverton looks pretty loaded with snow on this day. The Fourth of July looks like it's a long way off.

Although the grade descended at Milepost 470, just beyond Rockwood, to reach water level of the Animas, this did not mean there was a lighter grade the balance of the way to Silverton. From Crazy Woman Creek on to Silverton the grade was classed as being 2.5 per cent *ruling* ascending Nine miles from Rockwood, at the junction of Cascade Creek with the main river, a siding was built and named Cascade Siding. A section headquarters was built in the small existing settlement. The community of Cascade came into being because the old stage and wagon road from Silverton more or less followed the Animas for 20 rugged miles and then swung west and south over Cascade Hill to a stage stop on top of the hill, and thence southward to Durango and Animas City.

Needleton, at Milepost 480.3, was established four miles above Cascade Siding where several good mineral prospects had started a small settlement. The prospects never became mines and the residents all moved away. The Rio Grande moved the siding to a more favorable location at Milepost 482.31. Needle Creek enters the Animas on the east side here. Needleton Tank was built at Milepost 484.4 where a small unnamed creek supplied water by gravity.

In a small park where Elk Creek pours into the Animas, and six miles from Needleton Tank, a wye and loading facilities for cattle and ore were built. Elk Park was the railhead for passengers and ore originating at the head of Elk Creek. In a short while cattle and ore, with some lumber, were being shipped regularly from Elk Park. The wye was built to enable trains to be turned to return to Durango when snowslides or washouts prevented continuing to Silverton, and the wye saw rather frequent use.

Here's Animas Canyon fighting back. This Rio Grande train was hit by a snow slide; no one was hurt, but there was plenty of snow to shovel.

The Silverton tourist train stops for a drink amid Nature's pure beauty.

The Silverton train runs besides the sparkling Animas River. *D&RGW photo*

NEXT PAGE. The Silverton train is westbound approaching Rockwood with Lake Shalano below. The Lake was a favorite Ute Indian campground. *D&RGW photo*

SILVERTON TANK

No water tank was ever built in Silverton, but there was one provided about 2.5 miles out of Silverton and called Silverton Water Tank. This tank later was destroyed by the vortex action of a giant snowslide. Just beyond the tank was a bridge over the Animas, the last one on the branch, and after the crossing, the balance of the run to the Silverton depot was across the flat floor of Baker's Park. This bridge was often threatened but never damaged by an immense snowslide that ran at least once each year off a spur of Kendall Mountain. The slide was quickly given the name Jumping Jenny because just about 500 feet above the track was a rock outcropping that acted much like a ski jump. The mass of snow, by the time it reached the jump was moving very rapidly and soared in a parabola above and across the track to come to rest on the far bank of the river.

Silverton was built in one of those numerous open flat areas high in the Rockies and called 'parks'. Prominent peaks around Baker's Park were Kendall, Anvil, Boulder and Sultan. The area is very rugged, upheaved and disordered. Four million acres of Animas River drainage encompassed peaks, canyons and many watercourses. There is no single area in the United States as highly mineralized as the Silverton one. There are 40 prominent gulches, each of which at one time earned classification as a mining district in its own right. The entire country is interwoven with a vast web of veins of low grade ore interspersed with enough high grade occurrences to keep prospectors and miners dreaming and hoping that the next shot will open another bonanza.

Charles Baker and his six companions first wandered into the park, later to bear his name, in 1860. Before winter drove them out, they had found enough color to determine them to return the following summer. In 1861, more gold was found and news of its discovery reached the Cherry Creek Settlements. Almost forgotten stories of gold found by earlier Spanish explorers were resurrected and grew with each telling. However, activity in the San Juans was limited by the hostility of the Ute Indians until 1873 when the Brunot Treaty was signed. This treaty opened the Silverton area for a white invasion and soon many prospectors came in. The discoveries came fast and in numbers, each better than the last. It quickly became evident that the reports were valid and that at the head of the Animas was a great treasure chest. Palmer was just getting started with his railroad and there is no doubt his active mind began working on the possibility of going to the source of the promising area with his railroad.

As more reports came in about Silverton and the whole San Juan district, Palmer became more and more certain he must build to it. The fever was not cooled until he finally laid steel into the park Charles Baker had discovered.

It is only fitting that the last operating miles of the Narrow Gauge should be the Silverton Line that runs up the Animas to Silverton—The Mining Camp That Never Quit.

As an outcome of the abundance of ore in so many places in the vicinity of Silverton, the town became a railroad terminal in miniature. At one period before the boom died in the first decade of this century, there were four railroads operating with Silverton as a terminal, including the Narrow Gauge.

Otto Mears came to America from Russia as a 9-year-old orphan, shuffled off to relatives in New York who subsequently sent him to an uncle in San Francisco. On arrival there the potential guardian was either dead or missing. Otto was on his own among the surging goldseekers on San Francisco's streets at the age of twelve. He was hollow-cheeked

The Silverton train is now on a segment of the High Line, a spectacular portion where the tracks seem to cling desperately to the side of the mountains. *D&RGW photo*

and small and spoke barely a word of English, but he was tough.

Before he died in 1931, he had earned a reputation for capability in many lines. He was a soldier, including service

No. 478 works its way across the high trestle on the Durango-Silverton portion of the Rio Grande with the daily consist of passengers.

under Kit Carson in the Navajo campaign, a successful agriculturist, a builder and operator of sawmills and gristmills, owner and operator of stores, teamster and packer, publisher of newspapers, builder of telegraph lines and other things. But he is best remembered as being a builder of toll roads in the mountains of Colorado, the short line Silverton railroads, and the Rio Grande Southern, a narrow gauge road that ran from Durango to Ridgway, Colorado, through Rico and Telluride mining districts.

The other Silverton-based lines were the Silverton Northern, Silverton Railway, and, built about 1899, the Silverton, Gladstone and Northern (sometimes the latter road used the word Northerly instead of Northern). These roads served the mines toward Howardsville, Green Mountain, Astor, Animas Forks, Gladstone, Red Mountain and over the crest of this mountain to Joker. Freight and passengers were carried on routes that a self-respecting mule would balk at traveling. Mears issued silver, and a few gold, passes to all and sundry for use on his roads. He did on these lines what was an almost impossible bit of railroading, admitting to only one completely impossible thing which he could not accomplish. He could not find a route that he could carry a railroad on over Red Mountain to Ouray—and the Western Slope of the Rockies haunted him with its nearness and potential.

When even he had to accept the impossibility of a railroad from Silverton to Ouray, he examined other alternatives. The result was the building of the Rio Grande Southern from Durango to Ridgway, 163 miles of railroad that posed construction and operating problems as great as any Palmer had to contend with. Completion of the Rio Grande Southern in a sense permitted Silverton and Durango to say they were on a transcontinental route—a circuitous one—but you could travel across the country via Denver, Durango, Ridgway, Grand Junction and Ogden with a short side trip to Silverton.

If the Creede branch had been extended further northwest, it would have no doubt run right into Ouray, Colorado, a town built around the silver, gold and lead mines. The Montrose to Ouray branch—36 miles long—was built in 1887 following the Uncompahgre River. In 1953, the rails were torn up. On March 21, 1953, the last run was made over the line with No. 318 and caboose 0584. No. 318, a lightweight locomotive, originally came from the Florence & Cripple Creek. *R.W. Richardson/Colorado RR Museum*

Mears' RGS also furnished the link that provided a perimeter railroad completely around the Colorado mineral belt.

Silverton-The Mining Camp That Never Quit-was never a wild town or a tough town as mining camps are supposed to be. It never reached the heights of notoriety such as Leadville, Creede, Tombstone and others, although it did have its Blair Street and was on the circuit the soiled doves traveled from camp to camp in Colorado. It did have the makings of another rowdy mining camp but never quite made the grade. Basically what kept it from doing so was that the Narrow Gauge arrived too quickly after the first big strikes. Good women rode the passenger trains to town—some with their children—and the miners found wives, homes were built and made comfortable with furnishings the railroad hauled in. Churches and schools came early and were active in bettering the morals and education of both young and old. Silverton was basically a family town and the bad element never had a chance.

Silverton knew more about the love knot than it did about the hangman's knot. It was a fine town to live in and to rear a family in. It still is.

NEXT PAGE. The sheer rock cliffs distinguish the High Line from other parts of the Durango-Silverton train journey. *D&RGW photo*

Chapter 7

The Chili Line

Down the Rio Grande to Santa Fe

Eastbound freight on Barranca Hill on the Santa Fe branch with Engine No. 77. *D&RGW photo*

In a documentary sense, the history of the Chili Line can be traced back to February 1, 1870. On that date the Articles of Incorporation for the Rio Grande Rail Road and Telegraph Company, forerunner of the Denver and Rio Grande, were filed with the Secretary of the Territory of New Mexico. The stated objective was to build a railway and telegraph line from a point on the northern border of New Mexico through the valley of the Rio Grande to El Paso.

Maps, dated 1871 and 1872, project a route from Denver to the Cucharas River and turning west there to cross a mountain pass designated as the Sangre de Cristo Pass to Fort Garland, thence south. The route south of Fort Garland is shown as being on the east side of the Rio Grande to a point where Rio Costilla enters the Rio Grande, which is also the Colorado-New Mexico border. Crossing the Rio Grande on a bridge here the line was to remain on high tableland to the mouth of the Chama River and down the river to Santa Clara and San Ildefonso, two Indian pueblos.

About midway between these two pueblos a loop railroad was to start, going through Ft. Marcy to Santa Fe and return to the main El Paso route through the Galisteo Valley. This loop was called the Gallisteo (sic) Railway in the certificate of incorporation. The projection continued the railroad on southward to Bernalillo and Albuquerque, generally following the Rio Grande River to El Paso.

In October, 1879, Chief Engineer McMutrie and Construction Engineer Robert F. Weitbrec met to plan for continuing the advance beyond Alamosa. Management had handed the two men a package in its decision to build toward Durango and Santa Fe simultaneously. Complete surveys had not been finished and there were other problems to consider. There was no timber for ties close to the right-of-way from Alamosa to Antonito, nor was there any easily accessible on most of the Chili Line. A labor supply was doubtful. The D&RG started recruitment of native New Mexicans. This practice proved then and in the future to be a policy that was fortuitous.

PUBLISHED BIDS

Weitbrec and McMurtrie prepared and published bids for ties, rail, and grading. Since some 40 miles of grade had already been completed south of Alamosa and only waited ties and rails, their chore was lightened by this much. The bids contemplated that the first segment of the Santa Fe line would be from Antonito to White Rock Canyon, down river a few miles from where Espanola was later established. Specifications for ties read, "to be of good sound spruce or pine, the dimensions to be six inches thick, not less than six inches face, and six and one half feet long." Closing date for the bid was to be up to noon November 15. All orders were to be processed and placed not later than January 1, 1880. Construction was scheduled to start from Alamosa March 1. However, it actually started February 20 and by March 30 rails reached the new town of Antonito. Start of building on the Chili Line immediately followed.

An annual report to the stockholders issued in April, 1881, shows the advance of the Chili Line during the previous year had experienced problems not associated with actual construction. Palmer was off in Mexico a good part of the year and ex-Governor A.C. Hunt, who had come to fancy himself a topnotch railroad locating engineer (he was also a large shareholder), made a nuisance of himself trying to tell the survey parties what they should do and what routes they should select. Because he was a heavy investor in the venture, Palmer hesitated to antagonize him when Hunt fired a barrage of complaints to the General that Chief Engineer McMurtrie was ignoring Hunt and all of his suggestions. To placate Hunt, Palmer had McMurtrie waste $10,000 and valuable time to run a survey based on Hunt's ideas. The survey conclusively proved it could cost $300,000 more to follow Hunt's suggestions.

McMurtrie's own plan was that construction on the Chili Line would be segmented. The first segment, about 30 miles, was from Antonito to a supply of sweet water at a small settlement at Tres Piedras, N. Mex. The first bridge work on the way to Santa Fe was at a crossing of the San Antonio River, about one mile from the depot at Antonito. Beyond the bridge the line progressed across the lava flow of San Antonio Mountain generally following around the base of the inactive volcano.

The second segment, one of 27 miles, stayed on the high mesa land from Tres Piedras to a point designated as Caliente—some 35 years later to be renamed Taos Junction. McMurtrie wanted to carry the line from here to the Rio Grande River, bridging to the east side then follow the river south. But the Rio Grande flows in a very deep canyon for miles along here and the walls are sheer. McMurtrie had to abandon this plan and instead established a route that dropped off the mesa down Barranca Hill on steep grades of four per cent with many tortuous curves through Comanche Canyon. Thirty-pound iron rails were specified between Antonito and the start of the descent of Barranca Hill, but for the descending grade, McMurtrie ordered steel rails to be supplied by the Colorado Coal and Iron steel mills.

THIRD SEGMENT

The third segment was defined as being from Caliente to White Rock Canyon, a distance of about 38 miles. The fourth and fifth segments were to be the Galisteo Railway into Santa Fe and on to Albuquerque. McMurtrie did not make it to White Rock Canyon, nor to Albuquerque. Provisions and restrictions of the Boston Treaty resulted in a decision to stay on the west side of the river and build to the demarcation line specified by the Treaty—and some miles beyond to a logical place for an end-of-track town to be built.

On Christmas Day, 1880, rail reached a point in the vicinity of San Juan Pueblo. This pueblo was one of the first Spanish settlements and had been used or occupied by Indians and Spaniards since about the beginning of the 17th century.

Building continued on down the river and crossed the Rio Chama. Palmer did not think he could go further without causing the AT&SF to charge breaking of the Boston Treaty. The last spike to be driven by the Rio Grande on the Chili Line went into a tie at Milepost 371.62 from Denver, 91.3 miles from Antonito and 34.29 miles short of Santa Fe. Building of station facilities and buildings started for the terminal and the beginning of a town to be named Espanola.

Chief Engineer McMurtrie and Manager of Construction R.F. Weitbrec gave conflicting completion dates. Weitbrec reported to Palmer: "Soon after letting of contracts for the San Juan line, contracts for the grading and for building bridges on the New Mexican line, extending from Antonito southerly to Espanola (91 miles) were let, and the work pushed with as much vigor as the scarcity of labor would permit, until its completion February 4, 1881."

McMurtrie's report two weeks later said: "Tracklaying started at Alamosa on February 20, and was completed as follows:

> To Antonito, 28.7 miles south of Alamosa, Mch 30, '80.
> To Las (sic) Piedras, 34½ miles south of Antonito, July 18, '80.
> To head of Comanche Canyon, 64½ miles south of Antonito, Nov. 19, '80.
> To Espanola, 91 miles south of Antonito, Dec. 31, '80.

Some of the stockholders were beginning to question the quality of Palmer's railroad building and, in November, 1882, at the behest of five members of the Board of Trustees, the Rio Grande commissioned T.E. Sickels, consulting engineer of the Union Pacific, to "make a thorough inspection of the property and at your earliest convenience submit your professional opinion upon the condition of the road and its location."

For the Santa Fe line portion, Sickels reported: "From Espanola the line extends up the Valley of the Rio Grande twenty-three miles to the southern end of Commanche Canyon, where it diverges and ascends to the western tablelands. These lands are followed nearly to Alamosa. Of this line, ninety miles are prairie grading, twenty-four miles are average grading and six miles canyon grading. The canyon grading consists of numerous cuttings in cemented gravel, from ten to forty feet in depth; the materials being almost as difficult as rock to excavate."

CONNECTION BEGINS

Rail laying on the Chili Line being ended at Espanola,

Actually the roads were not very good and the hotels were few and far between. Even the Rio Grande didn't reach all these places. *Colorado State Historical Society*

A 1887 timetable shows the Royal Gorge of the Arkansas River.
Colorado State Historical Society

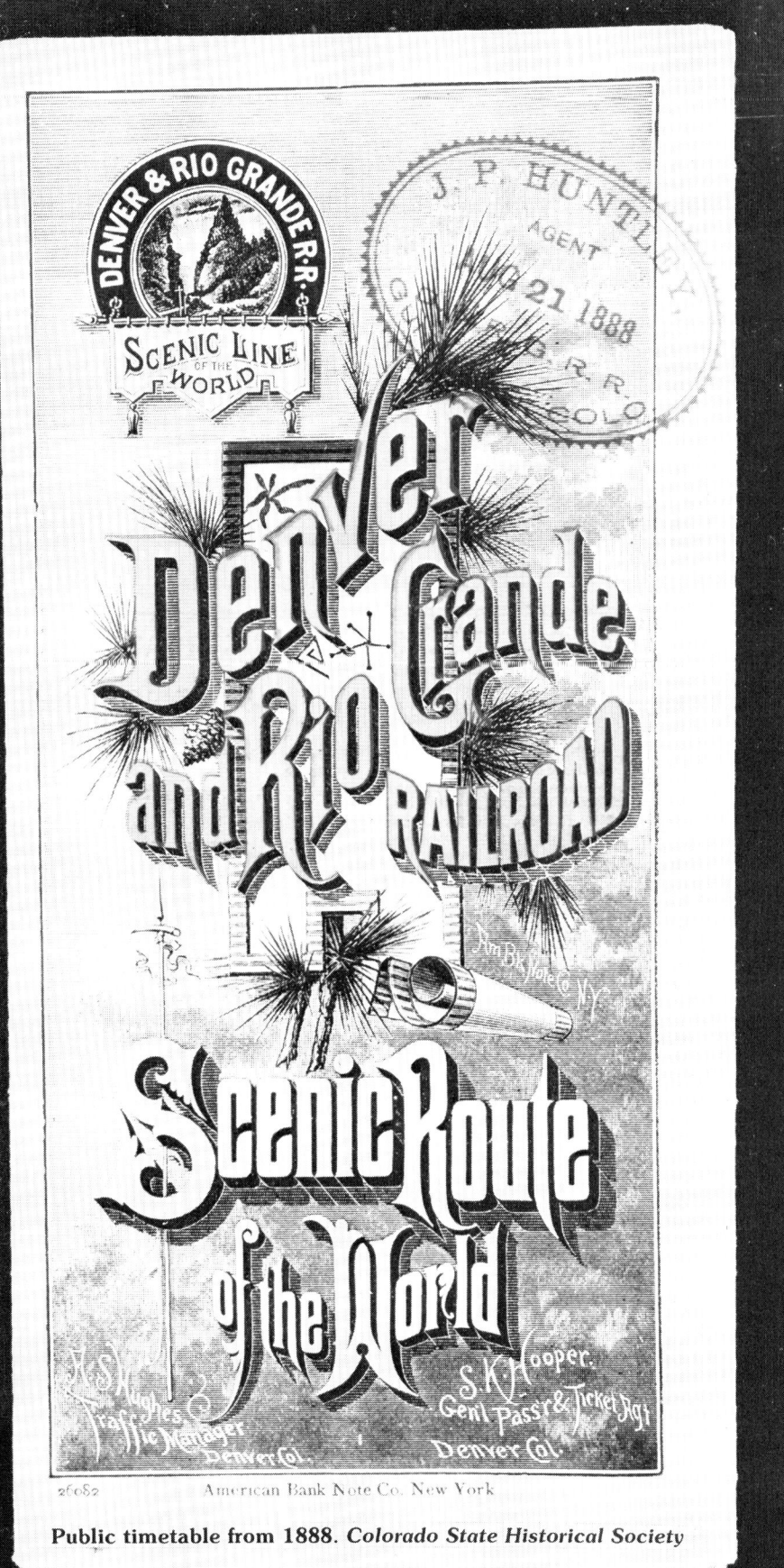

Public timetable from 1888. *Colorado State Historical Society*

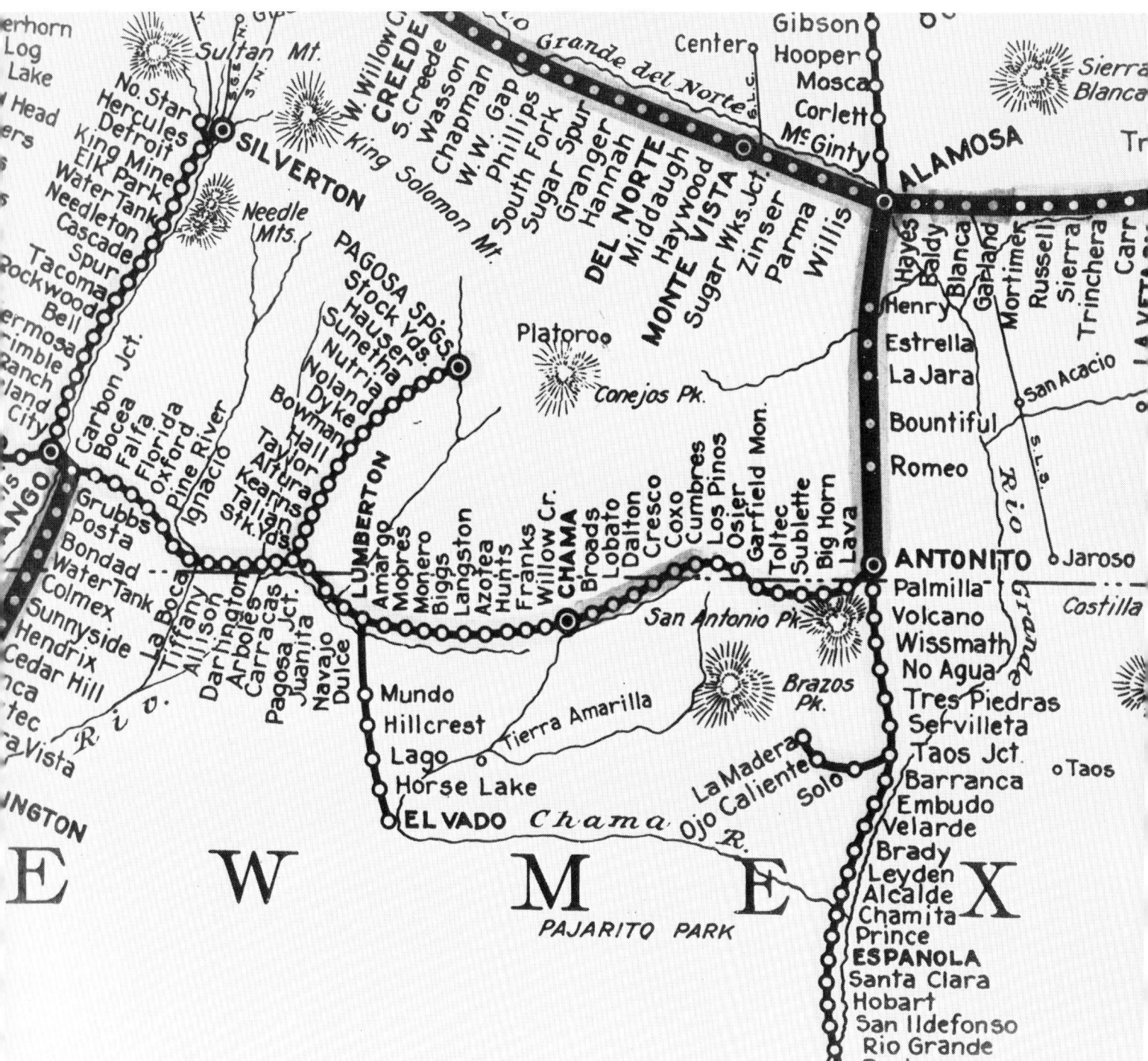

Taos Junction and the La Madera Branch; map dates from 1918-1920. Note El Vado Branch is listed.

Palmer looked in another direction. Steps were taken to start building a connection from Espanola to the San Juan Extension at Chama, following the Chama River. At Chamita, 4.9 miles up river from Espanola, construction of this connection was actually started. During the spring and summer of 1881, a survey of the first 23 miles was made and some grading done. Winter stopped the work on November 21, and it was never resumed. The Board of Directors ordered Palmer to lessen his preoccupation with his railroad building in Mexico and other personal activities and to devote his time and energies to Rio Grande business, including pushing completion of the railroad to Salt Lake City.

All of the corporate energy of the Rio Grande was thrown into the project of reaching Salt Lake City. Payments of dividends to stockholders ceased. The company was forced into receivership and in the financial donnybrook that ensued Palmer resigned as president. Leaving the presidency of the D&RG did not mean he had left railroading. He was still president of the western half of the Denver-Salt Lake City route, the Rio Grande Western, and he was actively engaged in two Mexican railroad ventures. Promoter, planner, dreamer and manipulator that he was, it is impossible to accept that he was not involved in the next phase of the history of the Chili Line, the extension of the line from Espanola to Santa Fe.

Rio Grande management had reconciled itself to the fact that until the Boston Treaty expired, the end-of-track of the Chili Line must remain at Espanola. Waiting 10 years for a

Lead locomotive No. 499 has two helpers between Chama and Alamosa. *John Krause/Dr. Richard Severance collection*

The mountains are quiet except for the slight whistling wind and the mountain birds. Then No. 493, a K-27 rebuilt in 1928 and retired in 1970, brings its train of clanging and bumping cars into view, but what a sound! *John Krause/Dr. Richard Severance collection*

Refrigerator cars No. 52 and 169 sit in Alamosa on Christmas Eve, 1948. Refrigerator cars on the Narrow Gauge came in two sizes — long and short, seeing much use on the Farmington Branch and Chili Line. Potatoes were a money crop around Tres Piedras and Taos Junction. Train No. 451 was the main distributing agency of merchandise and perishables west of Antonito. *R.W. Richardson/ Colorado RR Museum*

railroad simply because of a piece of paper was a bitter pill for the people of Santa Fe to swallow. The AT&SF promised them a branch line from the east, but the residents of the city of Holy Faith wanted more. They wanted a road that would tie them together with the earlier New Mexican settlements, San Juan, Velarde, Embudo, and north to Costilla, Conejos and San Luis Valley. When it was assured that Palmer and the Rio Grande would not willingly break the Treaty and build on into Santa Fe, the New Mexicans took matters into their own hands to provide a railroad from Santa Fe to Espanola.

TS&NRR INCORPORATES

A group of these people incorporated the Texas, Santa Fe and Northern Railroad Company on December 9, 1880. The purpose of the new corporation, as stated in the certificate, was grandiose. The TS&N declared it was to build, maintain and operate a railroad and telegraph line in New Mexico Territory and to eventually expand to Utah, Colorado and Texas, as well as to extend into the Republic of Mexico. Neither Palmer or any of his recognized co-workers were listed among the organizers, but the language of the corporation papers and the plans had a familiar ring.

Capital stock of the new company was 120,000 shares with a par value per share of $100. C.J. Lowry was elected president and Charles H. Gildersleeve, an attorney of Santa Fe, secretary. Charles H. Irvin, who had helped survey the D&RG route to Espanola was the chief engineer.

Irvin's first move was an effort to obtain the right-of-way and partially completed grade of the Rio Grande south of Espanola. His letter, written to McMurtrie, was referred to Palmer. Rio Grande General Counsel L.K. Bass advised Palmer that he had best keep "hands off." In a letter to Palmer, Bass quoted an excerpt from the second article of the Boston Treaty to the effect that the Rio Grande would not "directly or indirectly construct or promote the construction of any railroad or voluntarily connect with, or take business from or give business to any railroad which may be hereafter constructed in New Mexico south of the parallel of latitude seventy five miles south of the village of Conejos."

Bass further advised Palmer he should proceed with the necessary condemnation proceedings to insure ownership of the unused right of way and grade to the D&RG. Palmer agreed and instructed Bass to "hold all rights & go on quietly with condemnation."

It was not until May, 1882, that the TS&N let contracts for ties, track and bridge material, grading and construction. The firm of Orman and Crook, builders of much of the Antonito-Espanola line, was successful bidder for construction contracts. The contract specified completion of construction by November 1, 1882. With the beginning of work by the TS&N to obviate any legal accusations or actions against the Rio Grande by the AT&SF charging violation of the Treaty, General Counsel Bass filed a telegram to the TS&N warning it that there must be no trespassing on the right-of-way claimed by the Rio Grande, and, further, that the D&RG would not countenance the TS&N.

D&RGW's 40-foot refrigerator car No. 167 appears to have a warp in its frame. It was part of a series Nos. 150-169. The car now rests at the Colorado Railroad Museum. *Don Heimburger, Fall, 1982*

No. 492 brings up the rear on a freight. *John Krause/Dr. Richard Severance collection*

The TS&N chief engineer, and ex-Rio Grande surveyor, responded promptly and properly—right on cue—that the D&RG had no rights on the east side of the river and could not keep the TS&N from building there and that he did not intend to use even 100 feet of the D&RG's partially-completed grade. The Rio Grande was on public notice it would not voluntarily assist the TS&N, nor would it countenance it; the latter railroad had taken just as strong stand that it would not use anything owned or claimed by the D&RG. The AT&SF could scream and accuse all it wanted to about the Boston Treaty being violated—but that's about all it could do!

This little strategic by-play out of the way, the Texas and Santa Fe had more pressing worries, namely where to find the funds for building. Three years after the contracts were let, Santa Fe newspapers and the populace were mutually agreed that, at the rate the project was going, the Treaty of Boston would expire before the TS&N had rails laid and trains running between Santa Fe and Espanola.

In the autumn of 1885, Bernardo Seligman, vice president of the TS&N, went to New York prospecting for money. He was partly successful in that a syndicate sent a representative, Luther M. Meily, to Santa Fe in January, 1886, to explore the proposition. Meily personally inspected the now weather-eroded grading and made an offer by which the railroad would receive about $50,000 in bonds of other railroads in lieu of cash. The offer also provided that all TS&N bonds issued up to that time would be placed in trusteeship and held for Meily, and that all old debts must be paid. Last, he stipulated that a new board of directors representing Meily and the syndicate would be appointed.

The offer at first was not acceptable to the New Mexico group. A counter proposal was made to Meily, but he refused to modify his offer, although he did agree to an extension of time for the TS&N directors to consider his more thoroughly.

Following numerous meetings, pledges were made, outstanding debts reviewed and arrangements with creditors, including Orman & Crook, the grading contractors, made. J.B. Orman came out strongly in favor of Meily's offer. By mid-June it appeared that all the conditions of Meily's proposal could be met. He then threw the New Mexicans a curve and requested that the Santa Fe county bonds for railroad use voted in August, 1885, with a one year deadline for use, be extended through January, 1887. The voters finally approved a six months extension and the deal was on. Meily came to Santa Fe and took charge of construction. There had never been any doubt in his mind the offer would be met, and he had a contracting firm, E.R. Chapman & Company, all organized and ready to start restoring the old grade and building additional. The same firm was also to lay the rail.

RAIL ORDER GIVEN

Tie camps were established, a sawmill began sawing bridge timbers, and Meily signed a contract with the Colorado Coal and Iron Company for the rail which was to be 40 pound per yard steel. Another contract was let for building a steel bridge over the Rio Grande and second hand rolling stock obtained.

It looked like Meily and the TS&N were ready to start rolling. Then occurred one of those things that made working with New Mexican labor so frustrating. The Nuevo Mejicano was convinced some things were more important than working for money. One of them being that when it came time to harvest the winter food supply of squash, beans, corn and chilis, nothing could take precedence. That time came just as Meily was ready to start construction, and he found himself without laborers. Progress slowed almost to a standstill in September while the track workers and locally-owned horses were harvesting. The last week of September there was a force of less than 200 men working on the TS&N—Meily needed 1,000 to do all he had started.

Further complication was injected by the AT&SF, which

The rails bend and twist in the Rockies as No. 497 follows the railed path to the next station. *John Krause/Dr. Richard Severance collection*

now had its branch into Santa Fe, quoting a freight rate for hauling the rail from Pueblo to Santa Fe so much lower than the Rio Grande's rate to Espanola that it had to be taken advantage of. Construction that was under progress based on starting at Espanola was reprogrammed to work out of Santa Fe. Chief Engineer Irvin moved his survey crews and work forces to Santa Fe and started building northward.

All of the TS&N plans at Santa Fe were based on the assumption that the Santa Fe railroad would build a three-rail connection into the AT&SF depot. This was assuming too much, for the Atchison line was just as scared of the Boston Treaty as the Rio Grande was and refused a connection with the TS&N. The County Commissioners then granted the home railroad a right-of-way through the city of Santa Fe along Rosario and Guadalupe streets to the vicinity of the AT&SF depot. The owners of the depot agreed to build a narrow gauge line that would permit the local line to come to the depot parallel to the Atchison tracks but specifically stated there must be no physical connection.

Every man and good-sized boy that showed up and asked for work was hired, but Meily still did not have enough. Teams of horses were in even more demand. Meily, the Easterner, could not understand the natives—"Everything seems to hold back and haggle and drag."

To aggravate the situation more, bridge and track material was arriving in good supply and ties were available as needed—only men and horses were holding up progress. The first engine of the TS&N arrived and was fired up on October 21. It had no place to go, but its shrill whistle was a joy to the people of Santa Fe. They felt that engine No. 3,

Baldwin Class 56, a 2-8-0 emblazoned *General Meily* belonged to them. Fifteen days after the arrival of the engine the bridge and rail were in place across the Rito Santa Fe and the following day eight 30-foot narrow gauge flat cars arrived and were unloaded. Early November 6, 1886, the first northward train from Santa Fe, bells ringing and whistle blowing, moved proudly up Rosario and Guadalupe Streets, crossed Rito Santa Fe on the new bridge all the way to the end of the line, almost three miles out of town.

The maiden voyage finished, the *General Meily* was put to work hauling track building materials to the working face. Rail, fittings and all necessary material were arriving in fine shape. The crops harvested for the year, more teams and laborers showed up daily. Two large contingents of Mormons arrived from the San Luis Valley bringing horses and other equipment with them. Meily was laying one mile of track per day and telling the world he was laying two.

Right after Christmas the TS&N passenger cars arrived, were unloaded and polished to a shine. The railroad was as far north as Diablo Canyon and an exuberant citizen sponsored an excursion and picnic to the end of the line. January 1, 1887, was the date the TS&N put the last rivet in the bridge over the Rio Grande River. Eight days later the connecting link with the Rio Grande Railroad was an accomplished fact.

RAILROAD FINISHED

A couple of hours before midnight, January 8, by the light of tallow-pot torches and bonfires, President Luther Meily gave a public demonstration of his expertise with a spike maul and set the last spike into an ordinary tie. It was not a golden spike, and it was not a teak tie, but the New Mexicans could care less as they raised a mighty shout of exultation that *their* railroad was finished.

The morning of January 9, 200 people crowded on the first passenger train to run all the way from Santa Fe to Espanola. The trip took five hours but, braving charges of violating the Boston Treaty, the D&RG beanery served a "splendid dinner" to all, gratis. When all the food and liquor in Espanola had been consumed, the celebrants boarded the cars for a moonlight ride back to Santa Fe. It has been quietly admitted by some old-timers who were present that more than a few of the 200 had to be carried on the train.

Regular passenger service was inaugurated January 13, 1887, and nine days later the first carload of freight was interchanged at Espanola. The Rio Grande was no longer concerned about violating the Boston Treaty, for there was strong evidence the Santa Fe Road was going to break it by building north from Pueblo. On the same day regular passenger service began, Meily traded $50,000 in railroad stock for an equivalent amount of county bonds voted as a bonus for completing the line to Espanola. The Santa Fe Board of Trade set aside 11 acres of land to be used for building a TS&N terminal and yard.

For all the high hopes of the persistent New Mexicans, the Chili Line did not prove profitable. Mining was almost nonexistent. Sheep did well on the high mesa lands but cattle did not, so livestock contributed but little. All of the farms between Santa Fe and Antonito were small ranchitos, primarily subsistence farms. Coal, lumber, and consumers' goods from Denver, Pueblo and the San Juan Extension, then and later, were what the Chili Line had to survive on. Originated traffic never was important. It was one of the first branch lines of the Palmer empire to demonstrate that the passenger, express and mail business could not alone support a railroad operation.

Timber, close enough to the railroad for profitable marketing, did not exist all along the line. In 1888, a short lumber spur was built off the Chili Line to a sawmill operated by R.W. Stewart & Co. It was 2.15 miles long and called the Tres Piedras Lumber Spur. It was listed through 1892 then disappears from the records. There is some evidence it was moved about three miles north of Tres Piedras but still served the Stewart Company. Except for tie hacking and some small roving sawmills, this was the extent of lumber operations on the Chili Line for the first third of a century of operations.

At the start of WWI, 1914, the only important branch ever built off the Chili Line was constructed. It was a lumber branch called the La Madera Branch and ran from Taos Junction (Caliente) to La Madera, New Mexico, a distance of 16.43 miles. The line was built under a special refund arrangement by the Rio Grande for the Halleck & Howard Lumber Company based on a life expectancy of 25 years. The lumber company was over optimistic by 15 years due to much of the timber being damaged by dry rot. Lumbering ceased in 1927, the railroad maintained one-day-a-week service on the branch for awhile then applied for abandonment. The first application was denied in August, 1928. A second application made about mid-year of 1930 was successful. The La Madera Branch was dismantled in 1932 and the Pinon trees and junipers grew up and erased the marks of the short-lived attempt to lumber on the Chili Line.

There was never a prosperous period on the Santa Fe Branch. From 1934 to 1939 total revenue for the period was just a bit over $700,000. Operating costs were about $75,000 more than income and there was a matter of $100,000 in taxes. Under these circumstances the Rio Grande filed application for abandonment on November 14, 1939. The company was in receivership at that time. A verdict was rendered by Judge Foster J. Symes permitting the railroad to abandon. A certificate of public necessity and convenience was filed with the Interstate Commerce Commission requesting authority to abandon on April 8, 1940. This was granted January 22, 1941, but in March, U.S. Senator Edward Johnson asked for a Senate investigation of the abandonment.

After hearings were held, the State Corporation Commission of New Mexico petitioned for and received a rehearing before the I.C.C. Once more the Commission ruled in favor of the Rio Grande and the company received authority to abandon the Chili Line effective September 1, 1941. The last southward train from Antonito ran August 30. The following day was a Sunday with no train scheduled from Santa Fe northward. Monday, September 1, the last scheduled revenue train departed for Antonito from Santa Fe.

So ended the Chili Line, built to Santa Fe on the route to Mexico City by way of El Paso, built of dreams into a land and a heritage of a people who came to the land long before the Narrow Gauge, seeking a second treasure of Montezuma, into a land of reputed golden-walled cities that, when reality had to be accepted, proved to be only mud-walled villages in a land of sand and brown adobe mud.

General Palmer was not at the head of the Rio Grande Railroad when Santa Fe was finally reached. His dreams of his own little railroad that would run from the "Mile High City" at the junction of Cherry Creek and the Platte to the ancient seat of the Aztecs at Tenochtitlan, Mexico City, ended short of Santa Fe, El Paso and the floating gardens of Mexico's capitol. The dream ended 34.29 miles short of the City of Holy Faith, and a lot shorter of Mexico City.

No. 499 smokes it up between Chama and Alamosa with a load of mostly gons and flats. *John Krause/Dr. Richard Severance collection*

Chapter 8

Land of the Navajo
Farmington Branch

In many respects the Farmington Branch was not part of the Narrow Gauge. Rather, it could be likened to a foundling left on a doorstep. It was built not with any hope of being a contributor to Rio Grande profits, but as a countermove in a battle of railroad giants. Definitely, it was not part of the plans for a railroad as originally contemplated by General Palmer—he had no part in its planning or building. At the time of building of the Farmington Branch, Palmer had been disassociated with the D&RG more than 20 years and was entirely out of the railroad picture for three years.

The Farmington Branch was built 23 years after the Silverton Branch and was the last major construction by the Rio Grande west of Antonito. (The La Madera Branch on the Chili Line came later and was only a timber spur.) This branch, built from Durango into the Land of the Navajo, was built in an effort to keep a major potential competitor out of the San Juan country. The Southern Pacific ran surveys and

made plans for a standard gauge railroad into the San Juan basin, primarily as a threat in a battle for territory between George Gould, son of Jay Gould, and Edward H. Harriman, and secondarily to enter the southwest Colorado coal fields. Consequently, when the Farmington Branch was built by the Rio Grande, it was built standard gauge, so in the beginning it could not be classed as narrow gauge. At the time of the building, the home railroad was not sure it could retain possession and thought it might have to sell to the SP, another reason for building standard gauge.

This is the Land of the Navajo. Engine No. 478 crosses the trestle at Inca on the Farmington Branch with a trainload of pipe and casing for the gasfields at Farmington. *A.M. Payne*

The 20th Century arrived on a wave of buoyant optimism. Wall Street was running the country and investment bankers were in the saddle. These capitalists went crazy over consolidations and railroads were the main pawns; local control of railroads went by the board and rapacious financiers took over.

The railroad 'battle of the giants' that involved the Rio Grande most closely was the vendetta between Edward H. Harriman and George Gould. George, the son of Jay Gould, was dedicated to accomplishing his father's lifelong ambition for putting together a transcontinental railroad controlled entirely by him. In 1900, George made his first bid to do this. Using the Missouri Pacific, a Gould property, George started buying Rio Grande stock heavily; in turn the DRG started buying all the Rio Grande Western paper it could. At the time the D&RG and RGW were still separate entities and not yet consolidated as the Denver and Rio Grande Western Railroad Company.

About the same period, Collis P. Huntington, one of the SP founders, died. This permitted Edward H. Harriman to make a series of moves that, as a final result, gave him control of the Southern Pacific. It cost the Harriman interests $102 million, but they were able to announce: "We have bought not only a railroad but an empire." George Gould's aspirations for a family controlled transcontinental line, it became apparent, faced a struggle with Harriman interests.

During the year of 1900 Gould made every effort to cloak his manipulations in secrecy and to some extent was successful. However in February, 1901, when a contract was signed for the D&RG to purchase the Rio Grande Western, the cat was out of the bag. Harriman was astute enough to perceive that Gould's next move would be one aimed at reaching the Pacific. The gauntlet had been thrown. To protect the SP domain, Harriman had no choice but to accept the challenge.

George Gould, the son, was far from being the man his father was. Among other weaknesses he held an almost childlike faith in Harriman's charitable nature and was friendly with his enemy almost to the point of being "rather intimate." Harriman had no such hangups. He challenged Gould to a showdown on his suspicions that Gould planned to build to the coast. Gould was evasive, and the meeting ended with Harriman telling Gould: "I will kill you if you build that railroad."

Harriman drew first blood by closing the Ogden gateway. His second attack was aimed at Gould's rear defenses, in a totally unlikely area, the San Juan basin of the Narrow Gauge. From this move came the incentive that caused the Farmington Branch to be built, a line without rhyme or reason built a distance of 47 miles.

SAN JUAN RAID

Harriman announced his plans and intentions for the San Juan raid to the world in great detail. He left no doubt that he was going to attack Gould where it would hurt. In turn, Gould in his ignorance of the kind of enemy he faced, went ahead with surveys and plans for building the Western Pacific from par value of the $5,600,000 of preferred capital stock heretofore authorized was issued."

To keep Gould uncomfortable, Harriman did bring suit. The court actions came to a head in early 1909 when a decision in favor of Harriman was handed down with the proviso that he must build the Arizona and Colorado in a reasonable time. However, Harriman died before construction started and the Arizona and Colorado died with him. The Rio Grande was unhappily left with 47 miles of standard gauge railroad appended to 200 miles of narrow gauge tracks. Harriman's efforts to bedevil Gould and the Rio Grande lived on after his death. The Farmington Branch was like an inflamed appendix and caused about as much misery. Until it was converted to narrow gauge it caused the Rio Grande a lot of pains. The more recurring one was the transfer of lading at Durango, after one transfer had already been made at Alamosa; special problems in maintaining standard gauge power and cars at shops set up, as Durango was, for narrow gauge equipment, and providing yard facilities in the narrow gauge Durango terminal to also take care of standard gauge.

The agricultural and industrial potentials Gould described to his stockholders did not develop. The first 15 miles of the branch was through terrain too high above the Animas River to permit irrigation. Beginning at about Cedar Hill it was possible to bring water by gravity from the river, and the land was fertile, but there was not enough for large-scale farming. Timber growth was essentially pinon and juniper on the hills and soft woods, such as cottonwood and willow, along the river. Orchards were planted and brought to maturity, but they did not produce enough to have significant impact on gross branch revenue. Grazing land was scarce and the only livestock shipping of note was the seasonal movement of the scrawny sheep coming off the Navajo reservation. The income from this movement each year was as lean and thin as the Indian raised sheep.

There was a short period of profitable operation during World War II when the San Juan farmers found pinto beans produced like mad in the sandy soil around Aztec. Train loads of the spotted beans moved from the branch to a hungry world. Then the war was over and people were tired of their bean diet. Again the Farmington Branch became a nonprofitable operation.

UNEXPECTED DEVELOPMENT

Not for long though. In 1951 an unexpected development occurred and prosperity came to all of the Narrow Gauge west of Alamosa. For a number of years there had been crude oil activity of an unexciting nature around Farmington. Then a drilling company put down a well to the oil sand—and kept on drilling. The probe went into strata bearing natural gas and blew the lid off the sleeping land of the Navajo. Building of

Another trainload of pipe arrives from the east at Durango.

Gondola No. 9351 has ends removed for use in pipe carrying. The lettering indicates the car was built in 1925. *A.M. Payne*

the Farmington Branch, at long last, was justified.

The company that punched the first hole into the treasure of gas had kept the secret of its activities better than George Gould had. No hint of what was brewing leaked out until the discovering company was ready to announce its find.

At the start of the business day of September 12, 1951, the Southern Union Gas Company, at Farmington, notified the Rio Grande it was shipping 235 standard gauge carloads of line pipe from a west coast point to Farmington by rail. The announcement had the devastating effect of a block-buster. A quick inventory of open top cars on the Narrow Gauge, at Alamosa and west, showed a total of 75 available. Just barely enough to make one narrow gauge train with a few spares for, in transferring, it would require 30 narrow gauge load-bearing cars to handle 20 standard gauge loads. Then,

because the pipe was longer than the narrow gauge cars, an additional 29 three-foot gauge cars would be required as idlers between the loaded cars. The maximum number of cars that could be safely braked down grade from Cumbres to Chama was 60.

It did not take a mathematical genius to figure that the 75 narrow gauge cars readily available could not begin to handle the movement. The situation was made worse when Southern Union advised that the 235 carloads were only the initial shipment and many more would follow. Besides line pipe there would be much well casing, drilling machinery, drilling mud and other supplies. The gas company would not even venture a guess as to the ultimate volume or period of time the movement would last.

The Rio Grande immediately started gathering open-

This open-end gondola was used in pipe movement. It was converted to narrow gauge from a standard gauge box car. Photo was taken in November, 1953 at Alamosa. *R.W. Richardson/Colorado RR Museum*

This narrow gauge flat car was reinforced with rail to carry oil field equipment from Alamosa to the Farmington field. Photo was taken January, 1955. *R.W. Richardson/Colorado RR Museum*

topped cars in the Salida-Gunnison district for movement to Alamosa. The total to be moved was a discouraging 110 cars. These, plus the 75 on the San Juan end, had to have the ends removed before they could be used. The Mechanical Department was beefed up for a 24-hour-day operation in order to convert the open-tops to open-ends and to take all stored power out of white lead. A more detailed inventory and evaluation of narrow gauge cars was made to determine what could be converted for the pipe trade. A number of standard gauge box cars, and some flats, were also sent to Alamosa to be equipped with narrow gauge trucks and made into pipe cars. Roadway gangs got into gear with a program to get the line ready for a density of movement it had never previously carried. All furloughed employees were called back and new ones recruited. Cranes and other transfer machinery and supplies were ordered on an emergency basis.

When 1952 rolled around there were 400 cars in service moving pipe with more standard gauge cars being converted to narrow gauge. Two mobile cranes and a gantry crane were working on the pipe and a gang of about 100 transfer laborers was working daylight to dark on boxcar transfer of other drilling supplies. To add to the tonnage, all kinds of building material for new homes and business buildings for Farmington began to arrive in volume. The total gross ton-miles reached figures unprecedented on the Narrow Gauge and demonstrated that the three-foot line could haul a lot of tons. Then the cost figures started to become available and the weakness and fallacy of a narrow gauge railroad concept became apparent.

A cost study in depth was made to substantiate current figures to determine how much the great increase in business was converting to net. The analysis developed a cost of $85.00 per narrow gauge car from the start of transfer at Alamosa to the return of the empty for another load. Or, on a standard gauge carload basis, it was costing $127.50 for a 250-mile narrow gauge haul compared to a cost per car of $65.00 to haul the standard gauge load from Ogden, Utah, to Alamosa, 800 miles.

Southern Union's warning that the first 235 carloads was just the beginning proved true. Records were not kept to show how many carloads, or line-miles of pipe or how many carloads of drilling mud, machinery, and building material were hauled over Cumbres during the development of the Farmington gas field. There was a study, made in July, 1956, that shows that during the previous month, 550 standard gauge carloads of pipe were transferred to narrow gauge and moved. An additional 175 carloads were unloaded and stored on the ground at Alamosa. The narrow gauge cost had increased to $89.70 per carload.

POPULATION SWELLS

The year before Southern Union announced the discovery of gas, Farmington had a population of 3,637; its sister city, Aztec, had 885 residents. Ten years later Farmington had 23,786 and Aztec 4,137 people in their communities. The year 1956 was the peak year of the boom and, true to boom town tradition, activity and growth fell off rapidly.

The gas boom woke up the Narrow Gauge people, but it also woke up another ethnic group even more. The lives of the Navajo Indians, changed from an essentially pastoral life of herdsmen following their flocks of sheep and horses from water hole to water hole, constantly searching for grass, to a people made relatively rich by royalties. Wagons and old pickup trucks gave way to Cadillacs and new pickups; radios and television sets became common on the reservation. Many of the Navajo men worked in the gas fields while the younger men and women moved to town and were absorbed in the American town life. They could be distinguished from the Anglos by ethnic characteristics, but they were better behaved and more courteous. Matriarchy remained the form

Newly-converted to a narrow gauge flat car from a standard gauge box. Alamosa rip track, October, 1955. *R.W. Richardson/Colorado RR Museum*

This flat car had the brake staff removed so car could be used between two cars of pipe with overhanging load. Alamosa, December, 1951. *R.W. Richardson/Colorado RR Museum*

of social organization in the tribe, with the *singer*, the wise man and keeper of legends and tribal history, still the boss. The Navajo had one belief that contributed to happy family life—no man could look directly at, or stay in the same room, with his mother-in-law.

The Navajo was an enigma to both whites and other Indians. Ethnologically he could not be classified. His tenets and his religion were complicated, and only a Navajo was in tune with the vast and remote land he lived in. That rough, wild land was a sensitive one easily destroyed when nature was out of balance. The Navajo believed that from the earth man came and from the mother gains life, so the earth must never be injured or mistreated. The land in itself can never be owned by an individual. He may use it, but if he abuses it, he will suffer. As an individual, the Navajo may possess horses, sheep, cattle, blankets, jewelry, household utensils—he may even own a song, especially if it is his song and leads others to respond to the beauty of the land and the joy of life. Ceremonial songs belong to the tribe in the same sense that the guardianship of Navajo Land was a tribal responsibility.

Thus, when wealth represented by natural gas began to flow from the land, the framework for sensible control for the good of all Navajos was already a way of life in the tribe. Tribal committees organized ways and means to establish funds and projects for the benefit of all tribal members. The individuals on the whole accepted this—just so each family had a new pickup. What more would you expect from a people smart enough to keep a son-in-law and a mother-in-law apart?

The Farmington Branch went into decline after 1956 but was not abandoned until the rest of the Narrow Gauge was also.

Chapter 9
The San Juan Basin and the railroad

The *San Juan* was a proud pair of trains that held onto their style, elan and exclusiveness right up to the time of discontinuance. With six cars, today's *San Juan* (June 13, 1947) is pulled by engine No. 473. It's traveling east of Durango along the Animas River. *Richard Kindig*

Starting about 1870 the influx of settlers and businessmen from the East brought about a rapid change in Colorado, both along the Front Range and in the mountains. At the time Palmer first started planning his railroad, it could be said with truthfulness that the D&RG was going into an area almost in the wilderness state. By the time the Rio Grande was first reached at Alamosa, this was no longer true and especially the San Juan Basin part of Narrow Gauge Land.

There was little activity or settling in the country drained by the Animas and San Juan rivers immediately following discovery of gold near Silverton by the Baker expedition of 1860-61, although prospecting parties continued penetrating the district and made discoveries. These parties brought back information that familiarized the state with the geography and potential of the San Juan. Small farmers and stock raisers began to trickle in and establish holdings along the two rivers and their tributaries. The Ute Indians, occupying this land under treaty, were perturbed and in opposition, to the point that rapid settlement was delayed. The Brunot Treaty was signed in 1873 opening the area to whites, and the rate of settlement and mine development accelerated.

By the end of 1874 there were enough newly-arrived people to justify creating the original La Plata County comprising almost the entire southwest quadrant of Colorado. Thus, by the time Palmer had rail through the Royal Gorge and over the Sangre de Cristo Range, the San Juan district was no longer wilderness.

Fields had been cleared for farming, irrigation systems started and orchards planted. Pasture land was claimed and flocks of sheep and herds of cattle were grazing on them. Some hogs had been brought in. Timber was being cut and rock quarries opened. In the mining field, the precious metals of Baker's Park were being actively sought and mines opened—there was knowledge of a plentiful supply of good coal around Durango and development of this only awaited demand.

At the headwaters of the Animas in the last half of 1872, even prior to the signing of the Brunot Treaty, and through 1873, over 3,000 mining claims were staked out and recorded. The southern portion of the Colorado Rockies gave evidence it was a vast storehouse of mineral wealth. As more and more prospectors came in, discovered and developed mines, the broader the horizons of opportunity grew. News of each new major discovery filtered back to Denver. By the time the information filtered back to the older communities, every discovery had become a bigger bonanza than the last.

Silverton fever was rampant, and miners, prospectors and adventurers hurried there, driven by visions of quick and great wealth. The more solid citizens, tradesmen, craftsmen, suppliers and teamsters moved slower, but they moved. They realized there would be demand for the services and goods they had to offer.

The army of miners, settlers and their supporting troops continued to arrive on the San Juan. By the time the Narrow Gauge reached Durango, built by the railroad to be ready for the arrival, it was a going community.

Mrs. Romney, editor of the *Durango Record,* bragged that Durango had six stores carrying dry goods and general stocks; three drug stores; four hardware stores; three wholesale and retail groceries; one furniture store; one bank and one smelter; five lumber companies; four brickyards; 12 firms dealing in real estate and mines; four livery stables; six

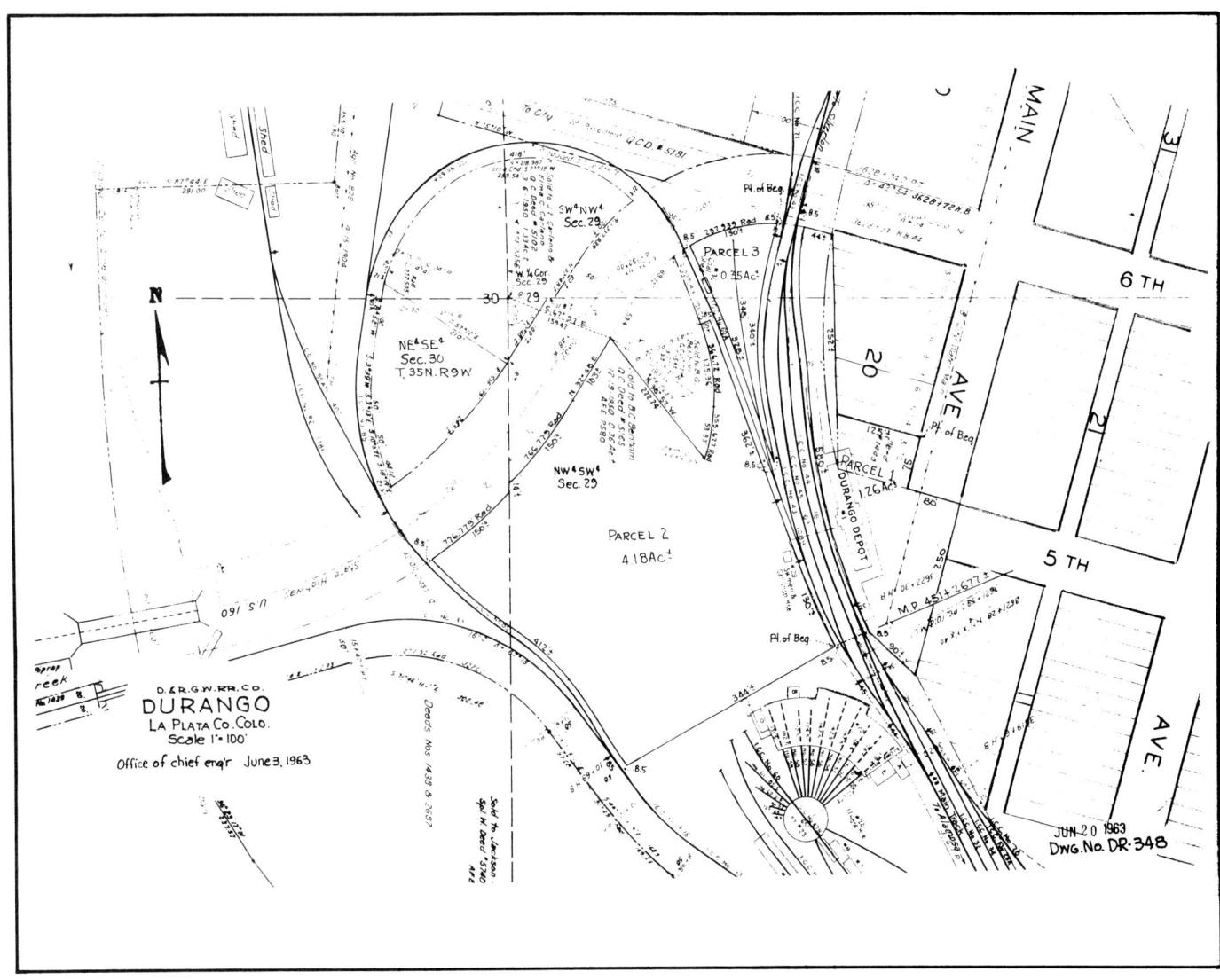

hotels; 12 restaurants; six lodging houses; four bakeries; six meat markets; three fruit and confectionary stores; three saddlery and harness shops; four new depots and cigar stands; three barber shops; three stage and express companies; two wholesale liquor dealers; and 25 saloons. In addition, for the fair sex, there were one millinery store, four jewelry stores, and one dressmaker. A man on the town could escort his damsel to either of two theaters for the evening—the Coliseum or the Clipper. Mrs. Romney was a lady so she refrained from bragging about a number of cribs, a few parlor houses and more young ladies' rooming houses catering to the libidinous appetites of the male population.

FIRST SETTLEMENTS

It was an impressive array of services and establishments in an area virtually unknown and virtually wilderness until Charles Baker found color at the head of the Animas in 1860. The first settlements were at Animas City and Animas Forks made by about 100 people who came with Baker when he returned in the spring of 1861 after wintering in Taos. Between 1862 and the big rush in 1873, the area was sparsely settled. No one would have predicted the growth that exploded upon signing of the Brunot Treaty, for no parties wintered in Baker's Park during the winters of 1870, 71 and 72. Federal troops had cleared the entire area during the last of the 1860's due to Indian troubles brought on by violations of the original treaty. Charles Baker was killed by Indians in the Park bearing his name in 1871. While negotiations were under way pending the Brunot Treaty in 1872 the area was again cleared. This was a bitter pill to prospectors and miners since a party sent out by Governor Pile of New Mexico had located the first lode mine, the Little Giant, on the north side of Arrastra Gulch in Baker's Park. The Pile party, after locating the lode, built a crude Mexican-style arrastra, rock crusher and processed 27 tons of ore which yielded $150.00 per ton—rich stuff considering possibly half of the values were lost in the crude processing.

After the signing of the Treaty, which opened the San Juan mountains to the whites, it was a race to see who could move onto previously-staked claims first, or find new ones. The peaks and valleys, gulches and streams came alive with activity; mines, lodes and placers—some rich, some not—opened faster than the recorder could keep claims filed. Gold was there, but nothing like the great veins of silver-bearing rock.

Not all of the new strikes were high grade, and even high grade lode minerals must be smelted. The first smelter was not built at Silverton until 1876 by Greene and Company. Prior to that, the closest smelters were at Black Hawk, Colorado, and other points along the Front Range. Haulage rates from Silverton varied from $30 to $60 per ton, depending upon distance and the time of the year. Because of this, to pay a mine had to have very rich ore, or hand-selected (high-graded) if of lower value.

The potential wealth of the Silverton District, in the final analysis, was transportation sensitive. The mineral treasures

Continues on page 103

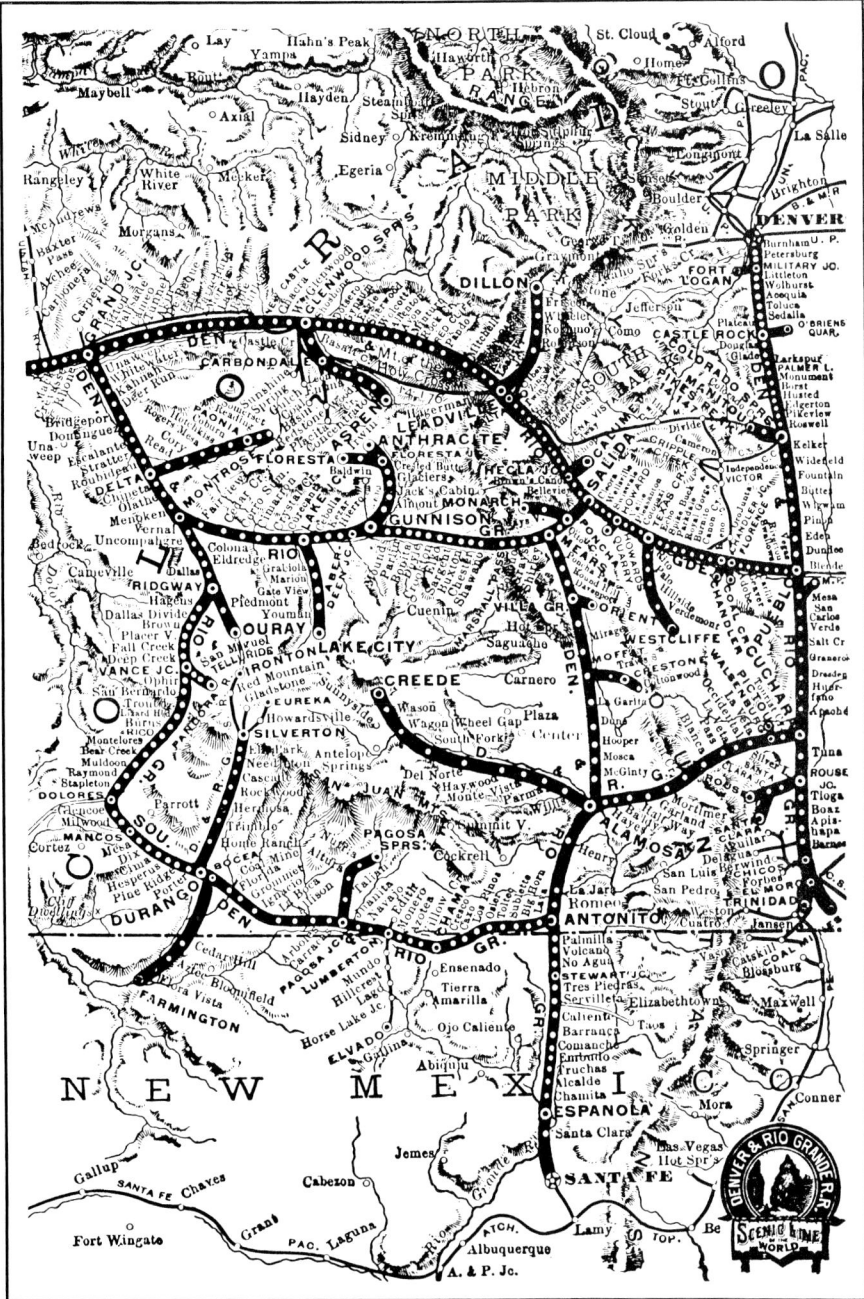

In 1962, the Rocky Mountain RR Club held a Narrow Gauge Excursion and printed a small booklet in conjunction with the trip. The map and descriptive information which came from a 1903 tourist guide, are re-printed from it. *Courtesy Rocky Mountain RR Club.*

DURANGO.
Metropolis of the San Juan.
Population, 8,000.
Distance from Denver,
via Veta Pass 450 miles.
Via Salida, 502 miles.
Via Ridgway, 540 miles.
Elevation, 6,520 feet.

This thriving city is the county seat of La Plata County, Colorado, and is the commercial centre of southwestern Colorado. It is the market for the agricultural region of Farmington and Bloomfield, New Mexico, and the valleys of the Rio de las Animas, the Rio Florida, etc.

Two miles below Durango is the wonderful "ninety-two feet thick" vein of coal, one of the largest in the State, and here are also great coke ovens. All the surrounding hills are more heavily timbered than in any other part of Colorado. In addition to its many other resources Durango boasts of two of the largest smelters in the State, reducing from their native state the precious ores of the wonderfully rich mines of the entire San Juan.

With two railroads in operation, and several in contemplation, and with its natural resources Durango will in time, and a very short time too, prove to be the metropolis of the Great Southwest.

The famous Cliff Ruins, a description of which will be found further

101

on, are reached from Durango, by the Rio Grande Southern Railroad to Mancos Station, thence by saddle horses or wagons.

In a word, Durango is one of the most progressive towns in Colorado, and is surrounded by a country of unexampled richness. Mining, agricultural and pastoral pursuits all contribute to her success; but best of all her business men are alive, and by their liberality, generosity and push insure a good future for the city.

Farmington, Bloomfield and Aztec are growing towns in New Mexico, just over the southern line of La Plata County. They are in the heart of a large agricultural and stock growing district, and near many ruins of the homes of the ancient Cliff Dwellers.

Trimble Hot Springs are reached nine miles above Durango. The spacious hotel stands within a hundred yards of the road to the left of the track. Here are medicinal hot springs of great curative value, and here, in the season, gather invalids and pleasure seekers to drink the waters and enjoy the delights of this charming resort. The water as it pours out of the rock is at a temperature of 120 degrees, and runs constantly in a stream three inches in diameter. Within two feet of it is another spring flowing as much more in a stream of cold water. Bath houses have been erected, and the hot and cold water can be mixed. The medicinal properties of these springs are beyond question. Four miles further up the Animas valley are the Pinkerton springs of warm water, closely resembling in properties those at Trimble's. Leaving the springs behind, the train speeds up the valley, which gradually narrows as the advance is made, the ascending grade becomes steeper, the hills close in, and soon the view is restricted to the rocky gorge within whose depths the raging waters of the Animas sway and swirl.

Magnificent Scenery. From Durango, the metropolis of the San Juan, to Silverton, the scenery is of surpassing grandeur and beauty. The railroad follows up the course of the Animas River (to which the Spaniards gave the musical but melancholy title of "Rio de las Animas Perdidas," or River of Lost Souls) until the picturesque mining town of Silverton is reached. The valley of the Animas is traversed before the cañon is entered, and the traveler's eyes are delighted with succeeding scenes of sylvan beauty. To the right is the river, beyond which rise the hills; to the left are mountains, increasing in rugged contour as the advance is made; between the track and the river are cultivated fields and cosy farm-houses, while evidences of peace, prosperity and plenty are to be seen on every hand.

Durango — Narrow Gauge Capital of the World — is the main jumping off point for the new Durango & Silverton Railroad, formerly owned and operated by the D&RGW. Under D&RGW control, the narrow gauge operated two sections of the passenger train to Silverton, 45 miles away. Note open observation cars at rear of trains — the *Silver Vista* revisited?

could not be exploited until better, cheaper transportation was available or if smelters of greater capacity were built near the mines. It is easy to understand why the arrival of the Narrow Gauge was so anxiously awaited. A wagon, whether pulled by oxen, horses or mules, is definitely limited in the weight it can carry. It also moves slowly, especially in mountainous terrain and over rudimentary roads. Bad weather can delay or even stop movement. The total tonnage of freight handled by wagon is limited at best.

The second smelter built in the San Juan area was not fully in operation when the Narrow Gauge reached Durango. A smelter had been built at Rico two years previously, the Grand View, but its capacity was pressed to keep up with Rico ore. Thus, growth was dependent upon money, and money was dependent upon getting ore out of the ground and converted to bullion. It was a vicious circle that only a railroad could break.

The railroad did arrive to open the treasure chest at Silverton in July, 1882. By the end of the year it hauled 13,754,352 pounds of freight out of Silverton and 11,190,098 pounds in. Statistics were kept by pounds instead of tons to make them more impressive. These pounds reduced to tons come to only 12,472 tons, by today's standard no great achievement but in 1882, most impressive. For comparison, at a maximum of two tons per wagon load, this is about 6,500 wagon loads. At an average of $45 per ton by wagon, the customers at Silverton would have paid a freight bill of about one-half million dollars. The D&RG records show they collected not quite $125,000.

One resident of Silverton who could cipher started a short-lived furor when he figured out that Palmer was charging an average of $7.50 per ton outbound, including the short haul tonnage going to Durango, and $12.50 per ton coming in, including traffic originating in Denver and Pueblo. Cooler heads

No. 494 leads a train load of freshly-sawed wood through the mountains on the Alamosa-Chama line. *John Krause/Dr. Richard Severance collection*

At Durango, the Rio Grande Southern, incorporated in 1889, made connections. To serve passengers, the road used Galloping Geese such as No. 5. Clayton Tanner shot this photo of a Goose on the turntable at Durango in 1950.

with more business acumen stopped the uprising by pointing out to all that they were paying only about a fourth of what they had been paying in wagon rates—and getting faster, more reliable service. Housewives were able to have items and luxuries brought in that they could not afford by wagon. Owners of low grade ores were finally able to make a profit on their holdings.

OLD RECORDS GONE

All the old records of the first few years of operation of trains on the Silverton Branch are gone. It is anyone's guess as to how many trains made a daily round trip, but the Rio Grande ran extra passenger trains when required. Freight trains operated as frequently as power was made ready; there was no dearth of tonnage. Train and engine crews did not work under a 16-hour law. They were paid monthly wages and when called for a trip, they finished it—16 hours, 24 hours or whatever it took. At the end of a trip they tied up to get what rest they could while the engine was being serviced for another trip. Each locomotive was assigned to an engineer and his tallow-pot (fireman). Train crews, by natural rotation, usually had the same engine crews.

At Durango there was always a train for Silverton ready to go and when the engine was released by the roundhouse foreman, the engine crew was called, and the caboose was coupled on and another train headed for Silverton. Cabooses were assigned to train crews, and each crew over a period of time turned their caboose into a second home, complete with cooking facilities and a food supply as well as bunks.

Over the entire Narrow Gauge, the business hauled train by train was of a uniform sameness. Eastward there was ore, coal, coke, lumber, livestock, and some farm products, especially hay. Westward, tonnage consisted of foodstuffs, household goods, furniture, construction materials and mining supplies and equipment. When the San Juan and New York Smelter first started in Durango, it was rated as a 40-ton per day installation. Thus, on any given day, at least 40 tons of ore coming out of Silverton would be consigned to Durango, and more than that would be moved east to Blackhawk, Leadville, Denver or Pueblo. With some seasonal exceptions, during the first half century of operation on the Narrow Gauge, the eastward tonnage was predominantly ore, coal and lumber.

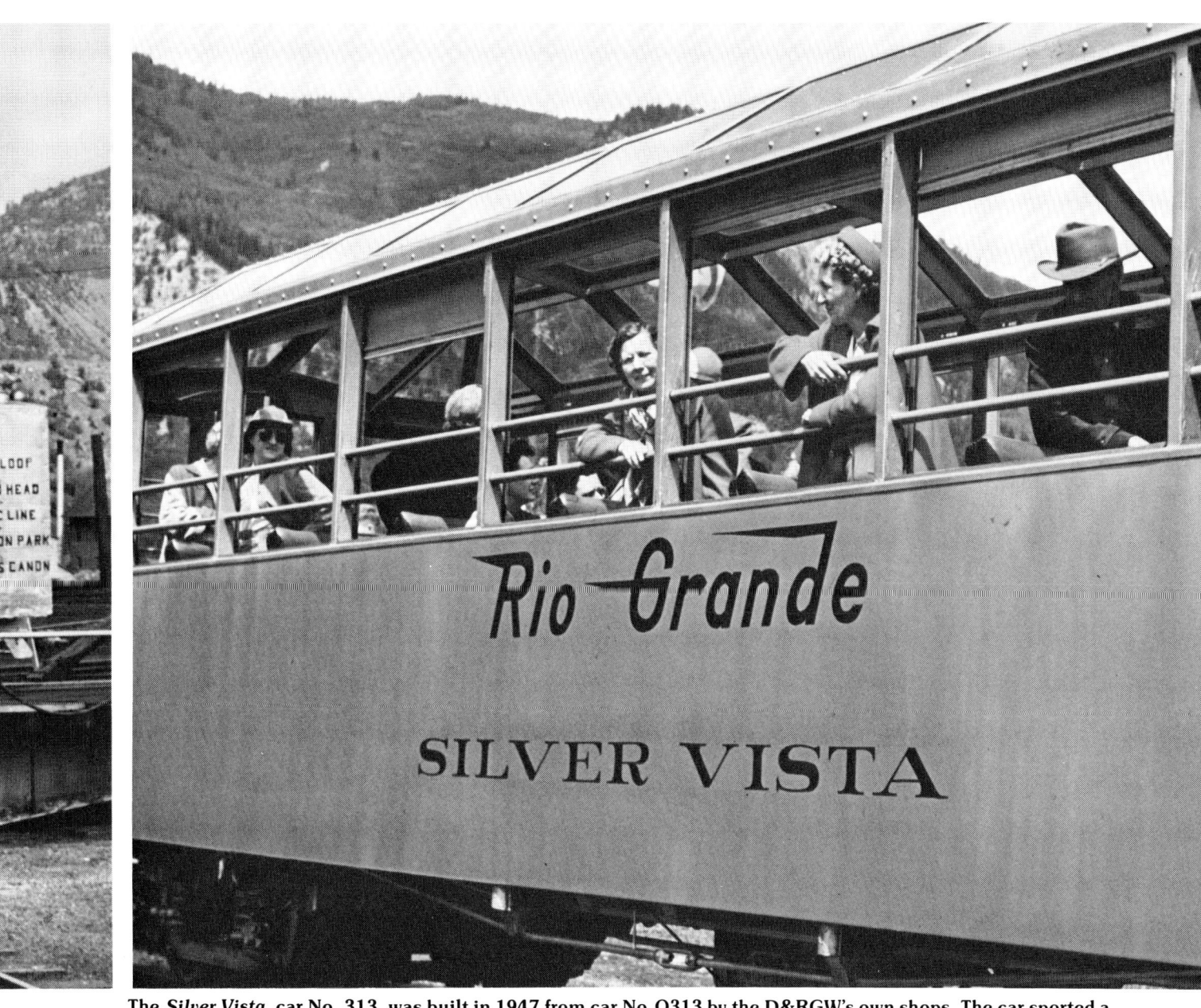

The *Silver Vista*, car No. 313, was built in 1947 from car No. O313 by the D&RGW's own shops. The car sported a steel-and-glass roof for viewing. *C.H. Tanner*

During the same period, the Rio Grande seldom had to worry about empty car hauls. Every car was in demand, including stock cars used for loading hay and lumber when not in use for livestock. Especially between Durango and Silverton, cars arriving Silverton loaded with the many items required at the mines and in the town were quickly unloaded, then spotted for loading outbound ore.

Smelting capacity at the Durango smelter was increased again and again, but so did the output of the Silverton mines. In the lumber industry there was heavy and constant production for the first 20 years of Narrow Gauge operation. Tractive effort of the locomotives used did not increase much, and there were no grade reductions. It took a lot of engines and a lot of trains to move all the tons there were to be moved.

Major crew terminals were maintained at Alamosa, Chama and Durango. At the junction points of branch lines with the main line, small subterminals were operated, such as Antonito for the Chili Line. In the period that can best be called early Narrow Gauge, before the advent of the 16-hour law, crews went where the engine went, especially the engineer and fireman. There was no assurance when a train left Durango for Chama that its crew would turn at Chama. Their engine might be called to go on to Alamosa when ready, and they went with it. A train of solid business for Santa Fe out of Chama might be run around the west leg of the wye at Antonito and kept going instead of the crews continuing through to Alamosa. If there was no Hours-of-Service Law, neither was there any first-in-first-out handling of crews at terminals; when the engine was ready the crews went to work.

On the Narrow Gauge, men in road service more or less established homes for their families based on the fact that Alamosa, Chama and Durango were the major operating points that they would be working out of most of the time. In later years the contracts were signed setting up home terminals, hours of service, seniority, first-in-first-out, and similar rules to make train service more attractive. Prior to this, crewmen were pretty much on their own to find sleeping and eating accommodations. Narrow Gauge rails looked out for themselves and carried their "1000-miler" lunches.

Train crews slept and ate in the cabooses; enginemen learned to cook ham or bacon and eggs on a scoop heated in the firebox. Enginemen also had a problem of sleeping quarters. They went to rooming houses or hotels, sometimes curled up and slept on the warm sand in the sandhouse or the journal box waste bins in the roundhouse. All of the Narrow Gauge train service men were a breed apart and proud of their toughness and expertise.

It is difficult to determine in retrospect whether the railroad made the country of Narrow Gauge Land or the country made the Narrow Gauge what it was. Without the railroad the mining industry would have been lost; without the mine products to haul, the railroad would not have remained viable. A second industry, almost a sibling of the railroad, was the smelting industry. Neither could live without the other. This was true especially during the period when silver mining and lead production far outpaced the importance of gold mining. The first productive smelter was built at Black Hawk, Colorado. With the discovery of the rich silver-lead carbonates at Leadville, the smelting industry there quickly took the lead. At one time there were about 30 smelter or reduction works in operation. In addition, there were other smelters in the mining towns of Colorado. The Rio Grande hauled in the material to build them, then carried the crude ore that was to be smelted.

OTHER SMELTERS

However, Denver and Pueblo smelters were not put out of business by Leadville or local smelters. In 1880, the Boston and Colorado Smelter had moved from Blackhawk to a location near Denver where fuel and labor were more available. The big Grant Smelter burned at Leadville, and the owners relocated at Denver. In 1886 the Globe Smelter opened in the Denver area and between 1882 and 1888, three major smelters started up at Pueblo, including the great Eilers operation and Meyer Guggenheim's Philadelphia Smelter. The fuel and other supplies for these and the ore to keep them working formed the major portion of Rio Grande tonnage and operating patterns developed from the smelter service demands.

The Panic of 1893 did not hit the smelters as hard as it did the mines, and in 1899, eighteen of the largest smelting concerns of the country organized the American Smelting and Refining Company. Seven of the major plants in Colorado were included in the new organization and the Durango smelter was one of them. In 1903 the Guggenheims attained control of the AS&R, and a policy of shutting down small, local smelters started. Durango smelters were kept operating. The impact on these localities was adverse but beneficial to the D&RG. Crude ore, over and above the capabilities of the Durango smelter, moved the long haul to Denver, Pueblo and Leadville.

The smelters had another effect that meant more business for the Narrow Gauge. At first, smelters used charcoal made of wood cut in the vicinity of the smelters, but timber for making charcoal was soon depleted. Coal and coke took the place of charcoal. Trinidad, Gunnison, Monero and Durango-area coal mines were quickly put in production, and the Rio Grande was there ready to haul the product.

Colorado's first coal is believed to have been mined about 1864. Available records indicate a production of about 5,000 tons per year until 1870 when 13,500 tons were mined. By 1880 the production was up to a half-million tons per year, and two years later passed the million ton mark. Except for a small portion used in the Denver area, the Rio Grande hauled most of this coal. In 1888, Colorado had 63 operating coal mines with production approaching three million tons. By 1910 this figure had climbed to 10 million tons per year.

Hauling of black diamonds was big business on the Rio Grande, especially the Narrow Gauge.

Not all the coal mined was shipped as raw coal. Coke ovens were built and operated at Durango and Monero, and much of this production was used at Durango. Any above local needs went to Leadville, Denver, Pueblo or other remaining smelters. The glow, smoke and smell from the beehive coke ovens was an accepted part of life of residents of these two towns. God had not yet invented ecologists and environmentalists.

Then there were other commodities to move, but the transportation demands of the coal and metal mines were the mainstay of the Narrow Gauge. Lumber contributed heavily, however, and there were seasonal movements of sheep, cat-

tle and a few pigs. A minor item was fruit, mostly apples, from the Hermosa and lower Animas Valley. The Rio Grande Southern, after Otto Mears built it to link Durango and Ridgway, poured more tons of the same commodities into the connecting terminals to swell the volume the Narrow Gauge had to haul.

The little railroad the General had dreamed of, in the gloaming on the Kansas prairies, and resigned from when it no longer was under the sole control of himself and his friends, fulfilled all his expectations for opening and building an empire in the Rocky Mountains. It remained viable, prosperous and active until the changes wrought by World War I began to change the lives and needs of the mountain people.

This is the Durango yards, with No. 486 and the first "Black Panther" No. 3000 that the Rio Grande tested for the U.S. Army.

It's June, 1952, and No. 494 and 496 earn their keep. *John Krause/Dr. Richard Severance collection*

Chapter 10

New towns and their names
Towns along the Narrow Gauge—Alamosa to Santa Fe and the San Juan Extension

A few settlements in the areas into which the General and his men built the Narrow Gauge existed already on a near-frontier basis and had names. More settlements resulted from the railroad's progress and had to be named. Some of the old names of existing communities were retained, some were changed.

Using the 1915 D&RGW roster, the year the Narrow Gauge peaked, for reference we can gain an inkling of the task it was to name all these rail locations. Some, but not many, of the old station names had been deleted, though most of them still had references in some form. Some names were Indian or Mexican-derived. Other names were drawn from famous people, and a few names resulted from typographical errors or a misunderstanding of the local pronunciations.

On the entire Narrow Gauge, including that west of Salida, there were approximately 350 individual place names for stations. On the Narrow Gauge, Alamosa to Silverton and Santa Fe, there were 136 station names, including sidings, spurs and towns.

On the Salida and Montrose district there was not the same originality in choosing names there was on the Narrow Gauge. In Palmer's original descriptions he referred to a *Punche* or *Puncha* Pass. Eventually this became Poncha Pass. This is a good example of how the early railroad builders misused the Mexican language. In Spanish, the closest you can come to Punche is *punches*, popcorn; Puncha is a thorn or sharp point; Poncho is either a saddle blanket or cape or, ended with an *a*, could mean easy-going. In trying to reconcile Mexican or Indian names as used by Palmer to physical or other characteristics, you can place almost any interpretation you want on the name. Mears Junction was named for a soldier, not for Otto Mears. Marshall Pass was named for a soldier who first traversed it enroute from an outpost in the Uncompahgre Valley to civilization to find a dentist to remove an impacted wisdom tooth. Shawano was named for an Indian. Bonita was named because the Mexican track laborers as they first came in sight of the location exclaimed, "Ah! Que bonita!! (Ah, how pretty). Gunnison was named for the army officer who explored and wrote of the area and made a railroad survey down the Colorado River. On the Crested Butte branch there was a hunter-fisherman outfitter who had a complex of cabins near the railroad where the train would stop to let off clients of Jack Howe. The point was first named

PRECEDING PAGE. No. 495 shoves freight between Chama and Alamosa. *John Krause/Dr. Richard Severance*

Howeville, but was so often referred to as Jack's Cabin that the name was changed to Jack's Cabin.

So it went, all over the Narrow Gauge as its rails were pushed from point to point. Alamosa, the easternmost terminal of the Narrow Gauge, derived its name from the heavy stand of cottonwood trees along the Rio Grande River (in Spanish, *alamos,* and anglicized it became *Alamosa*). There were two stations called Henry. The first was 17 miles from Alamosa on the Creede Branch, named for the father of irrigation in the San Luis Valley. Later this Henry became Monte Vista, and a station five miles south of Alamosa was given the name Henry.

La Jara, one of the major farm communities in the Valley, was named for La Jara Creek. In Spanish you have a wide choice of why this name or word was used. *Jaro,* or *jara,* can mean a carroty color, or in the masculine can mean thickets of small oak shrubs; *jara blanca* is for the small wild rose, or *jara* can mean a sharp pointed arrow (a deadly thing given the feminine gender by clear thinking Spaniards).

Palmer's men probably did not give much thought to meaning—they just wanted a name for a station on the banks of La Jara Creek. A few miles farther on they built a station near the ranch of a prominent family of early settlers named Romero. Because of poor writing or cartography the station name ended up as Romeo, and that is what it still is. Antonito was supposed to be named San Antonio for the San Antonio River at the west edge of the new town. Some timid soul thought the General might think this was sarcasm aimed at his failure to get to Mexico, so the town was named Antonito.

It is on the Chili Line that Spanish-derived names became most apparent. Palmilla was named for a coarse blue cloth of wool dyed and woven by local women. No Agua was named because of there being no water. Tres Piedras, for the three stones that form a landmark near the town. Servilleta, a little jewel of a park laid out like a napkin; Barranca, the Gorge; Embudo, the funnel (where the Rio Grande River comes out of the Rio Grande Gorge like the throat of a funnel). On down the line from Embudo it was more convenient to use the names of Indian pueblos—Alcalde, Santa Clara, Pajarita, San Ildefonso and Jacona.

Narrow gauge locomotive No. 494, a set of idlers and two standard gauge loads, head to Antonito from Alamosa on three-rail track. *R.W. Richardson/Colorado RR Museum*

The contrast between standard gauge and narrow gauge box cars is striking. *R.W. Richardson/Colorado RR Museum*

When the La Madera branch was built, the practice continued—la madera can mean either timber or lumber; Solo, a siding, means lonesome—and it was—and Ojo Caliente for a hot spring.

Going west on the San Juan Extension, Lava was named for the lava flow it was built on; Big Horn was easier to spell than the descriptive Mexican words for the sharp little peak at the station, El Cuerno Grande. The old mountain man, Sublette, was commemorated by having the station of Sublette named for him. The gorge of Los Pinos Creek was an imperial sight, so it was named for the greatest of Mexican Indian cultures, Toltec. Station names changed frequently in the first few years of the Narrow Gauge operation, an example being that Sublette was first named Boydsville.

One station name designated a location that never had a siding or any other station facilities. On September 26, 1881, members of the National Association of General Passenger and Ticket Agents held memorial burial services for James Abram Garfield, President of the United States, who had died one week before from the results of an assassination attempt on July 2, 1881. These services were held at the west end of Toltec Tunnel and a granite memorial was erected there in commemoration. The site was named Garfield Monument, and for many years passenger trains made a stop here so passengers could view the Toltec Gorge and the monument.

Osier was named for the abundant growth of willows along nearby Los Pinos Creek. The next station west was Los Pinos, The Pines, which were actually spruce trees. Cumbres was easy to name; when the last rail was laid ascending westward, the New Mexican track gangs raised a shout, "A la Cumbre", at the top. At the foot of the first pitch off Cumbres, where the line crossed Wolf Creek, a siding was built and named Coxo. There is a big curve here and the word in Spanish should have been *codo*, meaning elbow.

A water tank and siding were built at about the present Archuleta-Conejos county line and named Cresco. The railroad builders were still having trouble understanding Spanish pronunciation. Across Wolf Creek Gorge and to the east a few miles, is a prominent, high-crested ridge of mountains—the New Mexicans called it *El Creston*, the D&RG made it Cresco.

CHAMA

Chama, at the foot of the hill, already had a name which was retained. There are three possible Spanish interpretations for Chama. Chamada means a stand of abundant brushwood, which there was; chamarra refers to clothing made of sheepskin and the early Mexican sheep herders did dress in chamarra; or, chama which is Mexican slang for a swap, i.e., horse trade. No legends or records clarify the question of which is correct.

Just after crossing the Continental Divide, in an open park through which the road was built, was a large old adobe ranchhouse that had a flat earthen roof and a great porch across one side. Mexican natives used the word azotea to mean either a flat roof or a porch. The siding and section quarters built near the old ranchhouse thus became Azotea. Monero was a Rio Grande misspelling of minero, meaning miners, or a mine operation. About halfway through Monero Canyon a spur was built for a logging operation. It was variously called El Mopre, El Magre and Moore. Neither of the Mexican words have any meaning; maybe they were just local cuss words.

Amargo was for bitter (alkali) water; Dulce for sweet, or good water. Navajo and Juanita got their names for the rivers

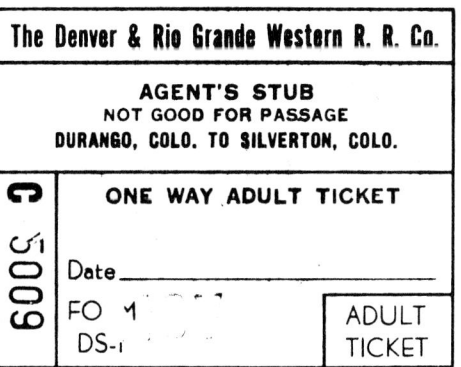

crossed at their locations. Gato took its name from being located where Rito Gato (Cat Creek) enters the San Juan.

Carracas could have been another misspelling or, in the singular carraca, was correctly used. Carrascas means scrub oak trees and many were on the hillsides. Carraca has many meanings—a piece of junk, something old, a ratchet or auger, or as a verb it can mean rattle. The one who named Carracas never left any explanation. Maybe the natives around Carracas used the word carraca as an allusion to the rattle of the cars on the less-than-smooth track—a rattler—and Palmer used the word without realizing his railroad was being ridiculed.

Of course, all the errors in the usage of Spanish terms were made by D&RG men other than the boss, for Palmer personally was fluent in Spanish.

A siding and water tank built west of Carracas was named Arboles for the large grove of cottonwood trees at the site. At MP 414.34 some Yankee, lonesome for Broadway, named a station Tiffany. The station built to serve the Ute Indian Agency was appropriately named Ignacio for the Ute chieftain. Oxford, no doubt, was named by a homesick remittance man. The water tank and siding just east of Ignacio, La Boca, maybe was correctly named. It was located at the mouth of a shallow canyon—Spanish for such a place is boca, but there was an old irrigation flume, unused and in disrepair here, and the word in Spanish for a flume is *la bocal*. Falfa was not a contraction for alfalfa but another misuse of a Spanish word, *falda*, meaning the beginning of a hill. Bocea, west of Falfa,

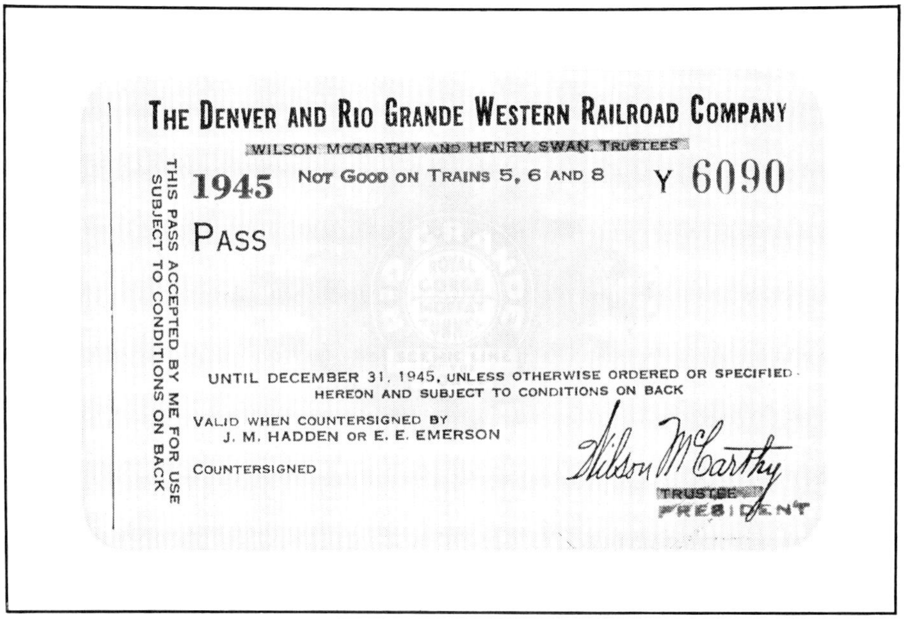

THE DENVER AND RIO GRANDE WESTERN RAILROAD COMPANY
WILSON McCARTHY AND HENRY SWAN, TRUSTEES

1945   NOT GOOD ON TRAINS 5, 6 AND 8   **Y 6090**

PASS

UNTIL DECEMBER 31, 1945, UNLESS OTHERWISE ORDERED OR SPECIFIED HEREON AND SUBJECT TO CONDITIONS ON BACK

VALID WHEN COUNTERSIGNED BY
J. M. HADDEN OR E. E. EMERSON

COUNTERSIGNED

Wilson McCarthy
TRUSTEE
PRESIDENT

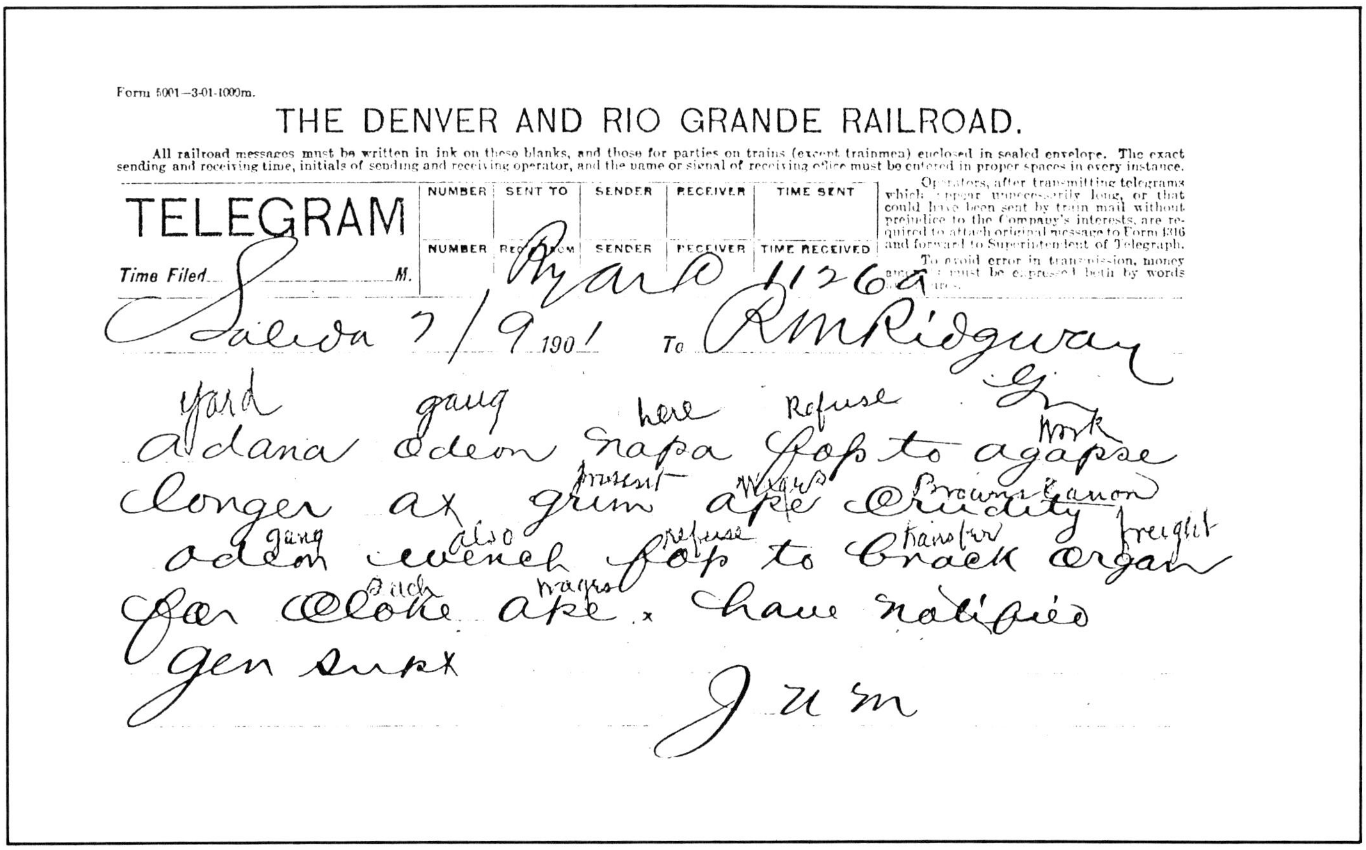

THIS PASS ACCEPTED BY ME FOR USE SUBJECT TO CONDITIONS ON BACK

Form 5001—3-01-1000m.

THE DENVER AND RIO GRANDE RAILROAD.

All railroad messages must be written in ink on these blanks, and those for parties on trains (except trainmen) enclosed in sealed envelope. The exact sending and receiving time, initials of sending and receiving operator, and the name or signal of receiving office must be entered in proper spaces in every instance.

TELEGRAM

Time Filed_____ M.

Salida 7/9 1901 To R M Ridgway

Ryan 1126a

Yard gang here refuse
Adana Odeon Napa fop to agapse work
longer ax grim ape Brown Canon
Odeon evench also fop to Crack Organ
for Aloke ape have notified
gen supt

J U M

The Denver and Rio Grande Western Railroad Company
NOT GOOD ON CALIFORNIA ZEPHYR TRAINS

1952-1953   Y 363

Pass J.R. Lopez and Wife,
Crane Tractor Operator and Wife
Purchasing Dept.,

BETWEEN ALL STATIONS UNTIL DECEMBER 31, 1953, UNLESS OTHERWISE ORDERED OR SPECIFIED HEREON AND SUBJECT TO CONDITIONS ON BACK

VALID WHEN COUNTERSIGNED BY
J. M. HADDEN or E. E. EMERSON

COUNTERSIGNED   *Wilson McCarthy*
                                      PRESIDENT

The Denver and Rio Grande Western Railroad Company
NOT GOOD ON CALIFORNIA ZEPHYR TRAINS

1957-1958   Y 1797

Pass Mrs. Lucile Evans
PBX Operator
Bet. Stas. East of Grand Junction

BETWEEN ALL STATIONS UNTIL DECEMBER 31, 1958 UNLESS OTHERWISE ORDERED OR SPECIFIED HEREON AND SUBJECT TO CONDITIONS ON BACK

VALID WHEN COUNTERSIGNED BY
E. E. EMERSON or

COUNTERSIGNED   *G B Aydelott*
                                      PRESIDENT

The Denver and Rio Grande Western Railroad Company
NOT GOOD ON CALIFORNIA ZEPHYR TRAINS

1959-1960   Y 2628

Pass Mrs. Charlotte Wilkinson
PBX Operator

BETWEEN ALL STATIONS UNTIL DECEMBER 31, 1960 UNLESS OTHERWISE ORDERED OR SPECIFIED HEREON AND SUBJECT TO CONDITIONS ON BACK

VALID WHEN COUNTERSIGNED BY
J. C. METZ JR. OR

COUNTERSIGNED
                                      PRESIDENT

The Denver and Rio Grande Western Railroad Company
NOT GOOD ON CALIFORNIA ZEPHYR TRAINS

1961-1962   Y 22

Pass C. W. Brown and Wife
Coach Porter and Wife

BETWEEN ALL STATIONS UNTIL DECEMBER 31, 1962 UNLESS OTHERWISE ORDERED OR SPECIFIED HEREON AND SUBJECT TO CONDITIONS ON BACK

VALID WHEN COUNTERSIGNED BY
J. C. METZ JR. OR

COUNTERSIGNED   *G B Aydelott*
                                      PRESIDENT

THE PULLMAN COMPANY
FOR COMPANY BUSINESS TRAVEL ONLY

1966-67-68   E 8786

THIS PASS ENTITLES   J. M. Sloan
ACCOUNT   Assistant Trainmaster, D&RGW RR.
TO OCCUPY   BERTH OR SEAT

IN CARS OPERATED BY THE PULLMAN COMPANY ON THE

DENVER AND RIO GRANDE WESTERN RAILROAD

CANCELLED

UNTIL DECEMBER 31, 1966
                                      Vice-President

The Denver and Rio Grande Western Railroad Company

1965-1969   T 234

Pass   Miss Frances Dodds
Daughter of Mr. W. M. Dodds
General Agent

Expires July 2, 1968

VICE PRESIDENT

The Denver and Rio Grande Western Railroad Company

8298

Pass Mrs. R. G. Webb, Sons Rocky and
Scott, Daughters Kerry and Wendy
Wife and dependent sons and
daughters of T&T Maintainer

Good Until March 18, 1973

                                      G B Aydelott
                                      PRESIDENT

LIFE TIME PASS
Rio Grande Railroad

For   Mr. and Mrs. E. H. Parker   No. 286
      Machinist and Wife

IN RECOGNITION OF 50 YEARS OF SERVICE

                                      G B Aydelott
                                      PRESIDENT

was a locally used Mexican term for a hill; it is not recognized as such in Spanish or away from the communities of New Mexicans west of Chama.

Palmer named the end of the line on the banks of the Animas Durango because he thought the surroundings and the mineral richness very much resembled Durango, Mexico.

The only station on the Silverton Branch with a native name was Hermosa. The scenery and physical aspects at the water tank and siding located where Hermosa Creek was crossed could only be described as beautiful. You can't very well name a railroad station Beautiful, but you can use the Mexican word that says the same thing.

The Farmington Branch, built much later than the Narrow Gauge, had a number of stations with Mexican or Indian names, but they were not given by the early builders. Besides the purely Americanized names for stations on the branch, there were Aztec, Lodo, Posta, Bondad and Flora Vista.

Names for the new stations on the Narrow Gauge just sort of seemed to happen, and the builders were too busy and uncaring to waste time recording explanations for their choices. Some were appropriate, some did not fit at all—and it hardly mattered—although some of them later nearly drove Morse telegraphers and train dispatchers up the wall trying to make the proper dot-and-dash combinations for some of the Mexican derived names.

Place Names and Mileposts, West and South of Alamosa —1915

ALAMOSA TO SANTA FE

Milepost	Place	
	(S-denotes siding only or flag stop)	
246.10	Alamosa	
252.24	Henry	S
255.15	Estrella	S
261.36	La Jara	
264.31	Bountiful	S
268.47	Romeo	
275.52	Antonito	
286.95	Palmilla	S
293.88	Volcano	S
295.16	Wissmath	S
296.68	Lawton	S
303.07	No Agua	S
310.25	Tres Piedras	
317.37	Connell Tank (Water)	
319.88	Servilleta	S
331.72	Taos Jct.	
333.95	Carson	S
340.33	Barranca	S
347.78	Embudo	
350.80	Velarde	S
352.37	Brady	S
353.70	Leyden	S
355.76	Alcalde	S
361.96	Chamita	S
364.87	Prince	S
366.82	Espanola	
369.80	Santa Clara	S
371.50	Hobart	S
372.69	Pajarita	S
373.75	San Ildefonso	S
376.13	Rio Grande	
379.34	Buckman	
383.21	Jacona Sec House	S
389.02	Jacona	
400.55	Santa Fe (Old Depot)	
401.10	Santa Fe (Union Depot)	

CALIENTE (LA MADERA) BRANCH

331.72	Taos Jct.	
338.90	Solo	S
344.03	Ojo Caliente	
348.02	La Madera (Mill)	

(Note - The mileposts used in these lists are the 1915 mileages which were those from Denver via Colorado & Southern-Joint double track. Later they were changed by an average of plus 4.80 miles. Any mileposts used in the book are the later established mileposts.)

ANTONITO TO DURANGO

Milepost	Place	
	(S-denotes siding only or flag stop)	
275.52	Antonito	
285.97	Lava	S
291.35	Big Horn Sec. House	S
294.61	Big Horn	S
301.26	Sublette	S
305.66	Toltec	S
308.64	Toltec Sec House	S
310.52	Garfield Monument	S
313.60	Osier	S
317.32	Los Pinos	S
320.70	Los Pinos Sec. House	S
325.80	Cumbres	
327.40	Coxo	S
330.70	Cresco	S
334.11	Dalton	S
335.19	Lobato	S
338.20	Broad	S
339.32	Chama	
344.40	Willow Creek	S
349.21	Azotea	S
352.73	Azotea Sec House	S
354.76	Biggs	S
358.67	Monero	
361.00	Moore	S
362.11	Amargo	S
364.75	Lumberton	
364.96	RG&SW Jct.	
368.53	Dulce	
372.86	Navajo	
381.93	Juanita	S
385.56	Pagosa Jct.	
390.43	Carracas	S
398.53	Arboles	S
401.50	Darlington	S
406.01	Allison	S
409.54	Tiffany	S
414.06	La Boca	S
420.94	Ignacio	
424.22	Pine River	S
428.10	Oxford	S
432.49	Florida	S
436.79	Falfa	S
441.07	Bocea	
444.11	Carbon Jct. Sec. House	S
444.23	Carbon Jct.	S
446.72	R.G.S. Jct.	S
446.72	Durango	

RIO GRANDE & SOUTHWESTERN R.R.

Milepost	Place	
0.00	Lumberton	
7.36	Mundo	
12.00	Hillcrest	

19.00	Lago
27.22	Horse Lake Jct.
32.21	Gallina Jct.
33.16	El Vado

PAGOSA SPRINGS BRANCH
(Trains stopped on flag at all places)

385.56	Pagosa Jct.
386.68	Stock Yards
390.33	Talian
393.33	Kearns
396.20	Lone Tree
398.04	Altura
400.78	Hall
402.20	Bowman
402.67	Dyke
403.38	Tank
406.54	Nutria
408.35	Smith
410.11	Lake
411.51	Sunetha
411.62	Hauser
415.88	Stockyards
416.33	Pagosa Springs

(The close distances between place names illustrate how active the Pagosa Springs Branch was in 1915—and that the area was heavier populated, at least along the line, than today.)

SILVERTON BRANCH

Milepost	Place
	(All named places, sidings or flag stops)
446.72	Durango
449.15	Animas City
449.52	Ireland
453.06	Home Ranch
455.89	Trimble
457.72	Hermosa
463.35	Bell
464.29	Rockwood
467.48	Tacoma
469.81	Cascade Tank
473.22	Tefft
473.64	Cascade
477.51	Needleton
479.60	Needleton Tank
485.67	Elk Park
489.36	Silverton Tank
489.99	King Mine
490.56	Ross
491.20	Hercules
491.51	Silverton Smelter Jct.
492.06	Silverton Ry. Jct.
492.46	North Star Mill
491.90	Silverton
492.13	Silverton Northern R.R. Jct.
492.33	End of Track

FARMINGTON BRANCH

444.33	Carbon Jct.
445.34	Grubbs
448.20	Lodo
452.58	Posta
454.26	Sunnyside
457.78	Bondad
459.90	Bondad Tank
462.24	Colmex
464.13	Hendrix
466.86	Cedar Hill
468.95	Perry
471.06	Inca
477.00	Aztec (Depot and agent)
482.73	Flora Vista
486.59	Hood
491.40	Farmington (Depot and agent)

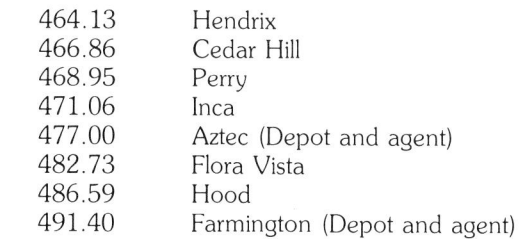

The Chama to Alamosa line finds No. 494 and 490 smoking it up. *John Krause/Dr. Richard Severance collection*

A K-37 Class locomotive, No. 493, leads the charge with another helper following. *John Krause/Dr. Richard Severance collection*

No. 486 has a mixed consist as she takes her train around the Cumbres Horseshoe. *John Krause/Dr. Richard Severance collection*

Sixteen cars of freight, preceded by No. 492 and followed by No. 488 and a caboose, move over the rails between Chama and Cumbres. *John Krause/Dr. Richard Severance collection*

Extra West with No. 484 on the point is about two miles west of Antonito, heading for the summit and Chama on February 5, 1956. *R.W. Richardson/Colorado RR Museum*

Chapter 11

Main towns of Rio Grande river drainage
Alamosa, Antonito and Santa Fe

The first permanent settlements in Colorado were in the San Luis Valley, with most of them being located on the lower reaches of the Conejos River at the south end of the Valley, or east of the Rio Grande River on the Costilla Creek drainage. All of these were small farming communities inhabited by people from lower down the Rio Grande of New Mexican ancestry and lineage. With the exception of a few luxuries freighted in from Taos or Santa Fe, they were sustained from and by the land, and the land was not all fertile or easy to farm. Only the small acreage near the source of water to provide irrigation could be brought under cultivation to the point a small community had enough to eat and cloth it.

Although there had been a healthy and active culture of the New Mexicans from Taos south down the Rio Grande Valley for over two centuries, development of the San Luis Valley on the upper Rio Grande did not get under way until well into the 19th Century. Progress and population increases once it began was slow and erratic until the coming of the railroad in 1878.

There was apparently one of these small New Mexican family farm communities among the cottonwood trees of the Rio Grande called Bravo, either by the inhabitants or the railroaders. It could not have been large or active and at its location a new town and railroad center grew to become Alamosa. Railroad records merely state it acquired the land without saying how or from whom. In May, 1878, a plat of the planned town was filed and on July 4th, or one of the other dates shown in railroad files, two months after the plat was recorded, the D&RG reached the Rio Grande River.

The first business buildings of Alamosa can be said to have come to town on this first train as well. The Occidental Hotel and the Broadwell Hotel served an early breakfast to their patrons in Garland City, were loaded on flatcars and moved bodily to Alamosa, unloaded and set up in time to serve a late evening meal to customers. The Gem Saloon served eye-openers to those needing them in Garland City and was moved to Alamosa on the first train and was ready to serve nightcaps before bedtime at its new location. These three buildings and businesses were landmarks in Alamosa for a number of years.

Back on the railroad Palmer realized, at least privately, that further construction for a year or more in any direction out of Alamosa would have to be held in abeyance. He also realized that Alamosa was the logical point at which to establish a terminal for lines that eventually would extend on up the Rio Grande River toward present day Creede, planned Santa Fe and San Juan lines and a connection from the Marshall Pass line over Poncha Pass. Yard trackage was laid down, a large frame depot built and the building of locomotive and car repair facilities started. The locations of the railroad structures determined the ultimate shape of the town of Alamosa more than the carefully drawn town plat.

A stock train heads for the snow-peaked Cumbres mountains.
John Krause/Dr. Richard Severance collection

Alamosa in 1882. *Colorado State Historical Society*

The Alamosa Division headquarters and passenger station were built after the old frame building burned. Note the three-rail tracks. *D&RGW photo*

The D&RG and Palmer have been accorded recognition as town-makers. "Makers" they may have been—town planners they certainly were not. Alamosa is a good example. The streets were straight but too narrow, even for that time; State Street ran north and south, Main Street east and west. Worst of all, with miles of flat land available, the blocks were undersize, resulting in small lots for residences. Through the town, or influencing the way the town grew, the rails ran east to west. The first street north of and paralleling the track was called, with reason, Crib Street. Of course, wives and preachers objected to this but the street was not misnamed. The two hotels and the Gem Saloon may have been the first businesses into Alamosa to feed the hungry and quench the thirsts of the railroaders but these men had other appetites to cater to so it did not take long for the row of cribs to be built and opened for business. For some reason Alamosa never did rate or support a parlor house.

During the first 10 years of Alamosa's history it was not only a terminal for the railroad but also the base for freighting operations to mining camps the railroad had not yet reached or did not serve. Two such forwarding companies were Field and Hill and F.S. Struby and Company. In addition to their freighting business both conducted large general stores. Contemporary records indicate they kept over 500 teams of horses, mules and oxen working. Based on this, Alamosa must have had a heavy population of teamsters, blacksmiths and farriers, wagon repairmen and a large investment in supporting stables, corrals and warehouses.

Barlow and Sanderson operated stage lines in and out of Alamosa and had their own layout of facilities and complement of employees. The boom was on and people just kept coming and building homes. The homes and the businesses tended to build as close to the tracks as possible and once more it was demonstrated that Palmer was fallible. After the the road was in operation to Silverton, Espanola, Wagon Wheel Gap and over Poncha Pass and the tremendous flow of traffic developed, the D&RG sadly woke up to the fact it did not have proper land available to build an operative yard. The town it had caused to come into existence was throttling the rail operation and causing extra expense, delays and difficulty in freight handling.

BUILT LOCOMOTIVE SHOP

Using Main Street and State Street as the lines dividing Alamosa into quadrants, in the southeast quadrant the railroad built its locomotive shop and roundhouse and car repair facilities. To be closer to work, those employed in these functions built homes nearby. They were not imposing homes, being mostly small square or oblong boxes nailed together of rough-sawed pine boards so much alike they looked almost like rowhouses. In the southwest quadrant, along the Narrow Gauge going south, the stockyards were built, and in this area the people of New Mexican ancestry built a community touching the parent community but almost completely culturally and otherwise separated. The homes here were mostly of adobe, small, but truthfully better kept, cleaner and more practical than the pine board homes in the southeast quadrant.

In the northwest quadrant the first homes were also of pine board construction but better built and as money and material was available, rooms were rapidly added and the exteriors were covered with shiplap and painted white. The schools and churches, as they were established, were in this quadrant. The more affluent rail and town people took up residence in this area.

For a number of years in the early history of Alamosa the northeast quadrant was largely without homes because much of it was so low the annual spring run-off flowing in the Rio Grande inundated much of the section. A levy was later built and homes began to appear.

By the end of the 1880's brick and stone replaced pine as building material and stucco or shiplap concealed the original drab rough pine exteriors of homes built during the early years of Alamosa's establishment. Cottonwood slips were cut along the river banks and planted along with some evergreens brought from the mountains and a few varieties of hardy imported shade trees. Some lawns, flower and vegetable gardens began to appear and gradually Alamosa lost its stark look of newness.

Near the depot area, hotels and restaurants with a sprinkling of assorted small businesses replaced the disreputable and unsightly cribs. On Main Street the banks and other major buildings were soon built, but the streets were all still sand and gravel and moved with the winds. Somewhere in the back of each home or building stood a Chic Sale that, during the heat of summer, added aroma to the effluvia emanating from the stockyards, coal burning boilers at the roundhouse and steam locomotives.

So, for the first 50 years of its existence, Alamosa was neither a pretty town, nor a picturesque one. It never even had the distinction of being a rowdy town or one where there was any of the normal frontier time hellraising. As an example, the cribs and their tenants were almost all gone by 1900.

Alamosa, up until World War I, just remained and looked like a rail's end town, which in a sense it was.

Essentially Alamosa was a town of people of the American culture and this was true going south for the first 20 miles. At Romeo, six miles east of Antonito, there was a sharp dividing line where the culture became New Mexican. This line of delineation extended from the Sangre de Cristo range on the east to the San Juan range on the west, making the south end of the San Luis Valley an enclave of New Mexicans in a predominantly white American community. This resulted in great part because of the existence of Mexican land grants.

There is a common misconception that the communities of New Mexicans at Conejos and the surrounding south end of the San Luis Valley were old communities when the railroad entered their domains, but this is not true. The San Luis Valley was well known by the New Mexicans settled along the Rio Grande River below Taos but not settled until after the land grants. Most of this knowledge was gained by expeditions coming to the area for the purpose of capturing Indian slaves, for it was not only in the south that slavery existed in the United States in the early 1800's. The Mexicans and New Mexicans enslaved great numbers of Indians and the traffic in slaves was a regular and well organized business. Boy slaves brought a price of about $100 and girls sold for $100 to $200. Mexican slave traders sold Indian slaves to the Mormons up until Governor Brigham Young of Utah issued a proclamation against the practice on January 31, 1852.

EARLIEST LAND GRANT

The earliest land grant, and the largest and most valuable confirmed one, over a million acres in the San Luis Valley, was the Sangre de Cristo Grant, often called the Costilla Grant. This grant was east of the Rio Grande River and extended from this river eastward to the summit of the Sangre de Cristo range taking in the valleys of the Costilla, Culebra and Trinchera rivers in the San Luis Valley. This land was granted to Stephen Luis Lee and Narciso Beaubien of Taos, on December 30, 1843 by Governor Don Manuel Armijo. There is no record of actual settlements on this grant until

At the Alamosa transfer stockyards, Rio Grande, RGS, UP, Clinchfield and CB&Q stock cars are seen. Note the old railroad car in the stockyards themselves.

sometime in 1846 and development of communities and farms on it was slow.

The second large land grant involving the San Luis Valley, the Conejos Grant, often called the Guadalupe Grant, was never confirmed. The boundaries were the Rio Grande River on the east and the San Juan Mountains to their crests on the west. This put the southern boundary about latter day Cumbres station and the northern one at a line running east to west from near the D&RG station of Villa Grove almost to South Fork. Thus, for all practical purposes the entire San Luis Valley was land grant territory. The existence of the Conejos Grant and its litigious nature kept a cloud hovering over the railroad and settlers in the San Luis Valley for many years. The grant dated back to some time in 1833 originally; reinstated in 1842, and was in various courts until about 1903 when the Court of Private Land Claims rendered a decision adverse to the claimants. It could not very well do otherwise because a large part of the land was taken up and improved under the regular land laws of the United States and towns grown and peopled on it. Antonito was one of these.

It appears that the first efforts to settle on the Conejos Grant was at the junction of the Conejos and Antonio (San Antonio) rivers. Some farming and irrigation started but the pressure of Indians and other factors made it impossible to successfully complete the project. In 1846 the newly appointed United States Governor, Charles Bent, authorized a Julian Gallegos and his associates to settle on the Conejos and assured them they would at least "be considered as privileged should their title be declared not valid." No significant action was taken to settle on the Conejos immediately but by the early 1850's towns were founded.

The first colony of any size to locate on the Conejos Grant was led by Major Lafayette Head, later to become Colorado's first Lieutenant Governor. His co-leader was Jose Maria Jacques. Early in 1854 these two men brought some prominent New Mexico leaders and a colony of 50 families to settle on the north bank of the Conejos River opposite the present town of Conejos. This was the first permanent and continuous settlement west of the Rio Grande river and was named Guadalupe. A church was built in 1857 across the Conejos from Guadalupe and named the Church of Nuestra Senora de Guadalupe. The Conejos River flooded frequently at Guadalupe so the people began to move from the older town to land close to the church. Conejos, as the new town was called, then dates only from about 1857, and was only a bit more than 20 years old when the railroad arrived and established Antonito.

Other small communities in the vicinity of Conejos were contemporary. San Jose and San Rafael were founded in 1856; Rincones in 1857; San Juan, 1861; Las Sauces, at the junction of the Conejos and Rio Grande rivers, 1867; Capulin, Mogotes, Ortiz, San Miguel and a plaza town built about two miles south of Conejos was given the name of the original settlement, Guadalupe. In the spring of the same year, the D&RG reached Alamosa, 1878, a colony of Latter-Day Saints (Mormons) settled in the San Luis Valley and in 1879 founded the town of Manassa about 10 miles northeast of Conejos. Other Mormon towns, Ephraim and Sanford followed, and some of the Saints settled near La Jara. The land at Ephraim was too marshy and its residents soon moved to Manassa.

REPLICAS OF TOWNS

All of the new settlements at the south end of the Valley (until the railroad and the Mormons arrived to change the patterns) were replicas of towns and villages the New Mexican settlers had come from farther down the Rio Grande. The homes were built predominantly of adobe bricks, although there were some of jacale construction, upright poles set close together in a trench and then plastered over with adobe mortar. By our standards they were small, consisting of two to four rooms that created a boxlike shape under a flat earthen roof.

ANTONITO

As young as the community of Conejos was, it was not about to accede to Palmer's demands upon it and the conditions to be imposed for bringing the railroad into Conejos. As a result, Antonito, about a mile from Conejos, was born as a D&RG town. Trackage necessary for a junction point for the two lines—one aimed at Santa Fe, the other the San Juan Extension—was laid down. A station built of lava rock quarried on the Extension about 15 miles west of Antonito was shortly raised, as well as a coal chute and water tank of timber just east of the station. Shortly after, a large wooden freight house and an agent's living quarters were added. The latter were of rough sawed pine lumber concealed under coats of bilious yellow or railroad red paint, depending upon what color was currently in favor on the railroad.

The Alamosa Division inspection car, MW-02, provided a bumpy ride for employees.

Another cattle train unloads at Alamosa. Yesterday the cattle were on the open range, today they're headed for the butcher shop.

In March, 1949, at Alamosa, this box car got a new stencil job including the streamlined Rio Grande logo. *R.W. Richardson/Colorado RR Museum*

No. 169 — a retired veteran of the road — rests in glory in the city park at Alamosa.

Antonito Station—and its inhabitants—looked like this in 1885. *Colorado State Historical Society*

In 1880 George Reidel opened a general store and shortly after the Colston House on the east side of the tracks provided the first hotel accommodations in Antonito. These were frame structures. A schoolhouse of sorts was built and slowly more frame houses appeared. The first church was not opened until 1887 when the Presbyterians built their house of worship. This was a matter of jubilation for the Protestants as it was one of the few instances in Colorado that they had an active church going ahead of the Catholics. The people of the latter faith did not have a church until the St. Augustine Catholic Church was established in 1889. The first bank was opened in 1881 by H.L. McMullen. It did not get much patronage from the Mexican population for those people believed in keeping family funds in gold or silver coins buried under a loose brick of the fireplace.

Eventually, most of the people of Conejos moved to Antonito so they could be closer to the excitement of the railroad and almost without exception they brought their adobe Mexican style architecture ideas for home building with them. By this time there were enough frame or brick homes or businesses to keep Antonito from resembling a typical New Mexico type town but just barely. For some reason for many years Antonito had two Main Streets; one east of the tracks and one west and both faced the railroad. Rooming houses and restaurants were on the east Main Street; the stores and saloons on West Main Street. The town was incorporated in 1889 and J.J. Corlett was elected the first mayor in November of that year. The two Main streets were later done away with and a new single Main Street was located on the west side about a block and a half from the railroad and paralleling it using an alley that was the back yard of the buildings along the original western Main Street. Along this new street more businesses opened, constructed mostly of brick or large adobe structures that were stuccoed. All streets were of native soil—dust blew and mud puddles formed in

This rail arrangement called a draw-rail allowed 3-ft. cars to be turned on a 3-rail wye.

them—and they were heavily enriched by the leavings of horse-drawn traffic, flocks of sheep and herds of cattle being driven down Main Street to the stockyards at the west end of town.

From the beginning, Antonito numbered about three persons of New Mexican ancestry to one white American. Eventually the ratio climbed even higher until about 90 per cent of its residents could claim Mexican descent.

Maybe this is the reason that Antonito was such a law-

The *San Juan*, with a *Shavano* tailgate sign, is ready to depart Antonito on one of its last regular Alamosa-Durango runs.

abiding community. It was never bothered by prostitution, heavy drinking, gambling or gun fighters.

Antonito did have one distinction, however. It had larger than usual outhouses and they were located close to the backdoor of each residence, for Antonito for a long time had a real problem. That was its domestic water supply. In winter all the wells went dry and water had to be hauled from the river. The going price was 25¢ if filtered; 15¢, if not. Filtering did not help a lot, but people hoped it would and paid the 25¢ rate considering the extra dime was worth gambling that the water when filtered just might keep them from being afflicted with the discomfort of "Montezuma's Revenge" (amoebic dysentery). There was something about the Conejos River water that kept the users of it traveling frequently from their backdoors to their large-size three and four holer outhouses.

All of the south end of the San Luis Valley prospered and

Three-rail track and idler at Antonito help demonstrate the difference. The higher coupler was in the center of the standard gauge; lower one in the center of the 3-ft. gauge cars.

in 1901 the Rio Grande laid a third rail from Alamosa to Antontio so it could use standard gauge equipment. The people of Antonito sort of lost interest in the railroad station as a meeting point after that. Antonito was a Narrow Gauge town and the people just did not take to the big stuff like they did the 3-foot equipment that was a tie with their own early origins.

SANTA FE

Santa Fe, the capitol of New Mexico Territory, had the honor of having filed the first corporation papers of the railroad that would eventually become the Denver and Rio Grande Western. So Santa Fe first began its acquaintance with the Rio Grande on February 1, 1870. But Santa Fe was to wait a long time for the Rio Grande to reach it under its own name. Its first railroad north, the Texas, Santa Fe and Northern Railroad Company, was built and owned locally. The first regular passenger train to operate between Santa Fe and a connection with the D&RG at Espanola was inaugurated January 13, 1887, and it would be a T&SN operation until the AT&SF broke the Boston Treaty permitting the D&RG

Engine Nos. 488 and 483 with a mixed consist arrive Antonito to take on coal and water for the climb to Cumbres. *R.W. Richardson/Colorado RR Museum*

Here's the draw-rail on the east leg of the wye at Antonito that allowed narrow gauge equipment to turn.

to take over the T&SN and operate into Santa Fe under its own identity.

Unfortunately, during the period from February, 1870, until the D&RG officially and legally began running into Santa Fe, the town and its people had undergone some changes, as had its culture to some extent. By 1890 Santa Fe was no longer a city of churches, government and trade caravans. While retaining the flavor and color of its earlier history, it had moved into the more modern, swifter paced present.

We are indebted to Susan Shelby Magoffin and her daily journal kept on a journey between Independence, Missouri, and Santa Fe. The journey began in June, 1846, and ended at Santa Fe on the evening of August 30. At that time Santa Fe was under the Star Spangled Banner but still very much Mexican, except for traders and mountain men, or American merchants and military personnel. It did not change much until after the Civil War ended.

Mrs. Magoffin describes walking down a long hill into the valley in which Santa Fe was located. She touches on the nature of this street and its squares (blocks) few of which were occupied solely by homes, but that on one square might be a home, a church, or other types of buildings. Interspersed among the squares were to be found corn patches, and running through the town was a river. This was more a creek than a river, the Rito Santa Fe which the T&SN would have to bridge before it continued laying rail toward Espanola. She writes of one aspect that distinguishes the City of Holy Faith—the frequent, melodious chiming of church bells. She also comments that General Kearney, occupying the former Governor's chair and holding Santa Fe as part of the United States, had not molested the habits and religion of the inhabitants. It would have done him little good to have tried anyway, for the New Mexicans do not change their ways easily or rapidly.

Mrs. Magoffin moved into an adobe home hear the church that was a prototype of most of the homes in Santa Fe then and for years to come. Even today Santa Fe has successfully tried to maintain the typical New Mexican form of architecture in its homes and business houses.

Santa Fe was founded by the Spanish in 1609 on the site of an Indian village. It was the first permanent settlement of whites in the Southwest, and one of the oldest in the United States, and has been a center of government since 1610. The Governor's Palace, built of adobe, dates from 1610.

When the rails of the Narrow Gauge were pulled out of Santa Fe, the event created hardly a ripple in the lives of a people who for over three centuries had been part of or seen a lot of history in the making.

CHAMA

There was never at any time anything soft or effete about Chama, but neither was it ever a bad town in the tradition of most towns at the end of the rails. The people of Chama breathed coal smoke, rubbed cinders from their eyes, and learned to sleep through whistles blowing, bells ringing, engines popping off and cars being switched hitting together. Chama took paydays in stride, drinking, gambling and girling a little, then settled down to await the next arrival of the paycar and paymaster.

There was no historian among the railroaders that came to the location where Chama was to grow. Apparently there was some kind of small community there but there is no early description to tell us what it was like. We can surmise it was a small New Mexican patriarchy hid away in the forest of pine and based on an economy of wool and sheep and self-sufficient. Railroad records and railroaders' stories all described Chama as a *new* town.

There were two levels at Chama, the river level where the railroad built its tracks and facilities, and the upper level where eventually the town was established. The first *town* was a town of tents and temporary shacks. It is also apparent that neither level was surveyed for a town site nor was there any evidence of the area being claimed by anyone as their property. So, when anyone got ready to build a home on the upper level they just preempted a piece of ground and started building. The railroad did the same when it built stockyards later and the early sawmills, stores, stables and other enterprises followed.

Chama was a railroad town and an Anglo one. The people

who were already there and the New Mexicans who came with the railroad established their own community a mile or more from the Anglo town. It was a closely knit enclave of New Mexicans, a few Indians and a few blacks. It was referred to almost from the beginning as *Chihuahua*. The residents of the two communities did not fraternize to any extent and the occasional white railroader who strayed into Chihuahua looking for female companionship soon returned to Anglo town much wiser and in poorer physical condition than he went in.

Chama supposedly was part of the Tierra Amarilla land grant, but there were two or three more contiguous grants and this contributed to the uncertainty of ownership. Too, in 1872 the Superintendent of Indian Affairs in New Mexico, during the winter had moved the Muache Utes to an agency located at Tierra Amarilla and more or less turned them loose in the general area. There were two bands of Apaches, including the Jicarillas, that lived on the same land as the Muaches.

President U.S. Grant abrogated any treaties with the Jicarilla Apaches on August 1, 1876, and opened any land they claimed to citizens of the United States. The Apaches did not take kindly to this and there was sporadic restlessness and a few minor raids. Geronimo eventually became the leader of the unhappy Apaches but almost all of his forays were away from Chama and the railroad to Durango. Of course, everything of a criminal or violent nature was blamed on the Apaches or Utes. None of the accusations ever were confirmed and rumors of impending raids to be made on Chama or the railroad were always proven as nothing but bar room talk.

A K-37, No. 491, arrives Chama on a very cold morning.

It's late December and Train No. 115 arrives Chama after following the flanger.

DURANGO

The first recorded description of the location that would become Durango is in *Escalante's Journal*. Late in July, 1776, Fray Silvestre Velez de Escalante, was accompanied by Fray Francisco Atanasio Dominguez and eight lay companions, including Don Bernardo Miera y Pacheco, a captain of militia, who was a surveyor and map maker.

The journey began at Santa Fe and followed a northwestward course by way of the Chama River and Horse Lake Pass, thence down the Navajo and San Juan rivers to about where Gato station was built by Palmer. The party continued down river, westward, crossed the Piedra and reached Los Pinos River near present day Ignacio. Continuing, it forded the Florida and reached the Animas River, near the site of Durango.

A delay was necessary here due to the cold and dampness and Father Dominguez "running a temperature because of his rheumatism." Escalante also wrote that, for this reason, they were unable to go to see some veins and metal-bearing rocks in the mountains that they had reports of. Rumors of these would continue to crop up later at various times and from many sources, but none would become a factor in the opening of the Durango-Silverton area until Baker's discovery almost a century later.

The founding of Durango by the Rio Grande was the same old story. Dr. William A. Bell showed up on the Animas in the vicinity of Animas City to provide a terminal town for the advancing Narrow Gauge. Landowners of the established community and the Rio Grande's land scout could not come to agreement on the terms.

Westbound extra 487-492 is nearing the Continental Divide near Azotea, New Mexico, west of Chama, with 57 cars at 20 miles an hour. The Divide here is lower than the elevation at Chama, but it divides waters that run to the gulfs of California and Mexico. *Richard Kindig*

What followed was SOP to Dr. Bell. He picked another site, now Durango, and had a number of Rio Grande employees homestead the area. Shortly after filing, the homesteaders sold their rights to the Durango Land and Coal Company, a quickly arranged subsidiary of the Palmer conglomerate. Building of railroad facilities got under way and some homes started to be raised. Many of the Animas City citizens saw the handwriting on the wall and moved homes and businesses to the new location.

An official post office, with W.M. Keightley as postmaster, opened its doors January 3, 1881. Four weeks later John and Ella Pearson recorded the first baby born in Durango, their daughter, Mary Isabelle. The community held a party for her and among the many presents given her were two building lots and a horse and saddle. The celebration merited a story in the *Police Gazette*.

On February 27, the Episcopalian Reverend C.M. Hoge opened the doors of the first church. This building served as both church and schoolhouse until the following February when the first school building was completed.

The growing community, destined to be the key to activity in southwestern Colorado, needed a name, and because the locale reminded him of Durango, Mexico, Palmer named the town Durango. It would rapidly become the trading center of the region and be the Narrow Gauge capital of the world with main lines and major branches leading to the four cardinal points of the compass. It would later become a smelting and coal mining center, a movie-making center and a mecca for hundreds of thousands of tourists and railfans.

There was plenty of good, clean water in the Animas, but Durango was too busy building to carry water from the river. A pipe was run from the springs that now furnish water for the fish hatchery. At the discharge end the pipe line entrepreneur delivered water to the homes and businesses at two bits per barrel. On the river bank two large cisterns were built and a pump installed to provide water for fire fighting.

But the provision for fire fighting was inadequate when the big fire of '81 broke out. Many blocks of wooden buildings, including the courthouse and city hall burned. The fire fighting engine burned before it could be used. Rebuilding was under

Engine No. 498 and a sister are lined up on the outbound track at Chama, called for a Chama-Cumbres turn.

In the early days, Navajo Indians came to town to trade their wool. This is downtown Durango. *Colorado State Historical Society*

Early day general store at Durango, complete with vinegar barrel, pickle barrel, cracker barrel and airtights — cans. *Colorado State Historical Society*

way almost before the ashes cooled and this time brick and stone was the predominant material used. In fact, owners and purchasers of lots within the burned out area were required to use either stone or brick. No doubt the operators of three brick yards had a hand in setting the building code. It was a good provision, however, for the new buildings were more fire resistant and flying bullets did not penetrate them.

ORE SMELTING

After railroading, the smelting of ore soon became one of the important enterprises. The first smelter was a small one-furnace deal that could handle about 40 tons per day. It kept growing until finally it was big enough to be included as one of the smelters in the combine that became the American Smelter and Refining Company. Such a large smelter requires more fuel than locally produced charcoal can provide. So Durango soon had a coking industry using locally mined coal. There was soon a surplus of coke being produced and this surplus moved to Palmer's steel mill at Pueblo. Some went to Leadville, but the Trinidad field took care of most of the Leadville and Denver area smelters.

Durango was not satisfied with just having a railroad; it also soon had a street car system. At first this was a light rail line running from the Rio Grande depot to Whitter, near present-day fairground. It was a two-car operation with one car traveling up and the other down at the same time. A few turnouts were provided so the cars could meet and, depending how heavy the "up" car was loaded and how the horse drawing the Toonerville car felt, some of the meets were not very close. Business was not heavy enough to justify the installation of a centralized traffic control system.

The two cars were short, with a standup capacity of about 20 people if they were not too heavily dressed. There were two hard benches, one on each side of the car that would accommodate 10 people; any over that had to stand. The cars were enclosed but unheated. The driver was also the conductor and controlled the one-horse-power propulsion unit.

In the autumn of 1892 Old Dobbin and the two small cars were retired and operation of an electric line began. The electrified line ran over the old horsecar line and soon after electrification, the line was extended to Animas City. Two cars operated regularly, making the trip in about 15 minutes, one way. A passing track was located at about 19th Street. Electricity was provided by a steam-powered plant erected on the site where the Ball Machine shops were later built. Incidentally, this was the first electric plant in Durango. The first interurban cars were light, with two wheels under each end and anything but smooth riding. These later were replaced by two heavy-duty cars which were continued in operation until the farewell trips on October 10, 1920.

The Silver Panic of 1893 hurt Durango but not irreparably. Durango came back stronger than ever after this Panic. Just before silver went into a slump, the last spike was driven on

In mid-foreground is the new Rio Grande roundhouse and depot at Durango in 1883. *Colorado State Historical Society*

The Rio Grande Narrow Gauge runs to the left of the Animas River through the bushes and trees.

the 162-mile-long Rio Grande Southern to give Durango a direct route to the Western Slope. Telluride and Rico metal mine production, Hesperus-Perrin's Peak coal and Dolores lumber began to funnel through Durango. In 1905 the Farmington Branch was built, although this branch produced more headaches than profit and added little to Durango's activities.

Silverton and the Silverton Branch continued to prosper and remain active as did the Rio Grande Southern. Southwest Colorado continued to grow and mature. Lumber, livestock, coal and metal mining, agriculture and orchards all produced freight for the slim-gauge railroad. Continued building in the area resulted in good tonnage to haul westbound. The smelter was operating and was converted to the processing of vanadium ore during WWII to obtain the material for the atomic bomb that knocked Japan out of the war.

Oil was found at Farmington and a refinery built to make the Farmington Branch a bit more profitable. Then one of the wells at Farmington was drilled deeper and natural gas discovered. Durango was the center of all this oil-gas activity, and the Narrow Gauge hauled practically all the casing, pipe, drilling mud and other supplies used to develop the Farmington field. Lights burned at the railroad all night and there was a constant bang of couplers in the train yard. Drilling and pipe line activity slacked off in the early 1950's.

Then Hollywood discovered Durango and things were never to be quite the same anymore. Films made in the Durango area did more to advertise the scenery than all of Palmer's and Colorado's efforts in the past. Background shots of Animas Canyon, the Grenadier and Needle Mountains and the Silverton train brought tourists and railfans—not just in small parties but in hordes. Building of accommodations for these multitudes boomed. The Rio Grande dressed up the Silverton train and later added a second section. If you were a railfan or tourist it became a must that you go to Durango and ride the Silverton train.

Durango, the goal Palmer drove toward in 1881, had seen many changes and undergone more. The year-round residents found they were no longer living in a microcosmic metropolis but had become cosmopolites rubbing elbows with people from all over the world. After a few summers of being in daily contact with tourists, railfans, movie people and other gungho types nothing surprised or shocked them.

In fact, they became so blase that when one of the movie starlets paddled out to a rock in the middle of the Animas, clad only in her birthday suit to do the little mermaid stunt au naturel, only her press agent and photographer paid any at-

This is a view of Durango from Smelter Hill. In the foreground is the Durango roundhouse with in-and outbound tracks. The station is behind the roundhouse along the tracks. *A.M. Payne*

The next snowstorm covered the sign.

This is a reproduction of a hand painting made in 1875 or 1876 by Emil Fischer showing Baker's Park (later Silverton) in 1874. *Colorado State Historical Society*

tention to her. The natives just kept on walking across the bridge without bothering to look or ask questions. The local papers did not even give the gal the publicity she was after.

SILVERTON

Silverton—The Mining Camp That Never Quits. On Anvil Mountain, overlooking Silverton and the alpine beauty of Baker's Park is the "Christ of the Mines Shrine." Carved in Italy of Cararra marble, it stands as a symbol of the faith Silverton has in the present and the future.

For over 100 years, Silverton has had faith in itself and in the mineral-rich mountains around it. Palmer had faith in Silverton's promise. So did Otto Mears, who built hundreds of miles of toll roads and railroads to the heads of valleys, over Red Mountain Pass to the Joker Tunnel near Ironton.

Rumors and stories of riches to be found in the rough mountains surrounding Silverton had been told for almost a century by the Spanish, Mexicans and Indians before Charles Baker and his six companions gave body to these rumors with their discoveries in 1860.

Baker's party of prospectors panned down the Arkansas, crossed Poncha Pass to the San Luis Valley to strike the Loring military road over Cochetopa Pass. They then traveled to the Lake Fork of the Gunnison. The party reached Lake San Cristobal having walked right over the riches of the Lake City gold and silver deposits—but then, they were placer miners and rocks meant nothing to them.

Panning the Lake Fork as they went they came to the head of the stream and a land of many hued cliffs with the stream boiling through a deep canyon that seemed without end. For days they climbed through spray and over rocks to a high mountain meadow between the later site of Edith and Whitecross Mountain. Leaving the meadow they struggled over Cinnamon Pass to enter the heart of the San Juan Range.

What they viewed was an upheaved, disordered array of high snow-capped peaks unlike any other mountain range. It was as if the Mineral Belt of the Rockies had been flowing from the north to strike an impassable obstruction that the moving stream piled up against chaotically. The peaks, can-

Donkeys carried supplies into the mountains around Silverton. *Colorado State Historical Society*

This was one of the early mines around Silverton that was served by the Denver & Rio Grande Narrow Gauge. Note how the mine structure projects out over the railroad tracks below. *Colorado State Historical Society*

This is an early day view of Silverton with Kendall Mountain in the background. *Colorado State Historical Society*

LEFT. Raging water and falling rocks unearthed this track on the Silverton Branch.

yons and watercourses in the four million acres of the Animas River drainage form a picture of a giant, violent maelstrom that has frozen in place. Silverton is at the heart of this frozen maelstrom.

Baker's party did find gold near Silverton, but the season was far advanced and it could not winter at the discovery. They left by way of Molas Pass, thence to the site of Durango and backtracked Escalante's trail over the Horse Lake Trail to Abiquiu, New Mexico. The winter was spent in this Mexican settlement and at sometime during the winter either Baker or one of his companions leaked news of their discovery. This news reached Denver and Leadville area diggings.

Several parties outfitted and headed into the San Juan Mountains. It is highly improbable they made it into Baker's Park so early in the year, at least to do any prospecting. No news came out of the mountains announcing other discoveries, but Baker had stirred up a hornet's nest with his original discovery of gold.

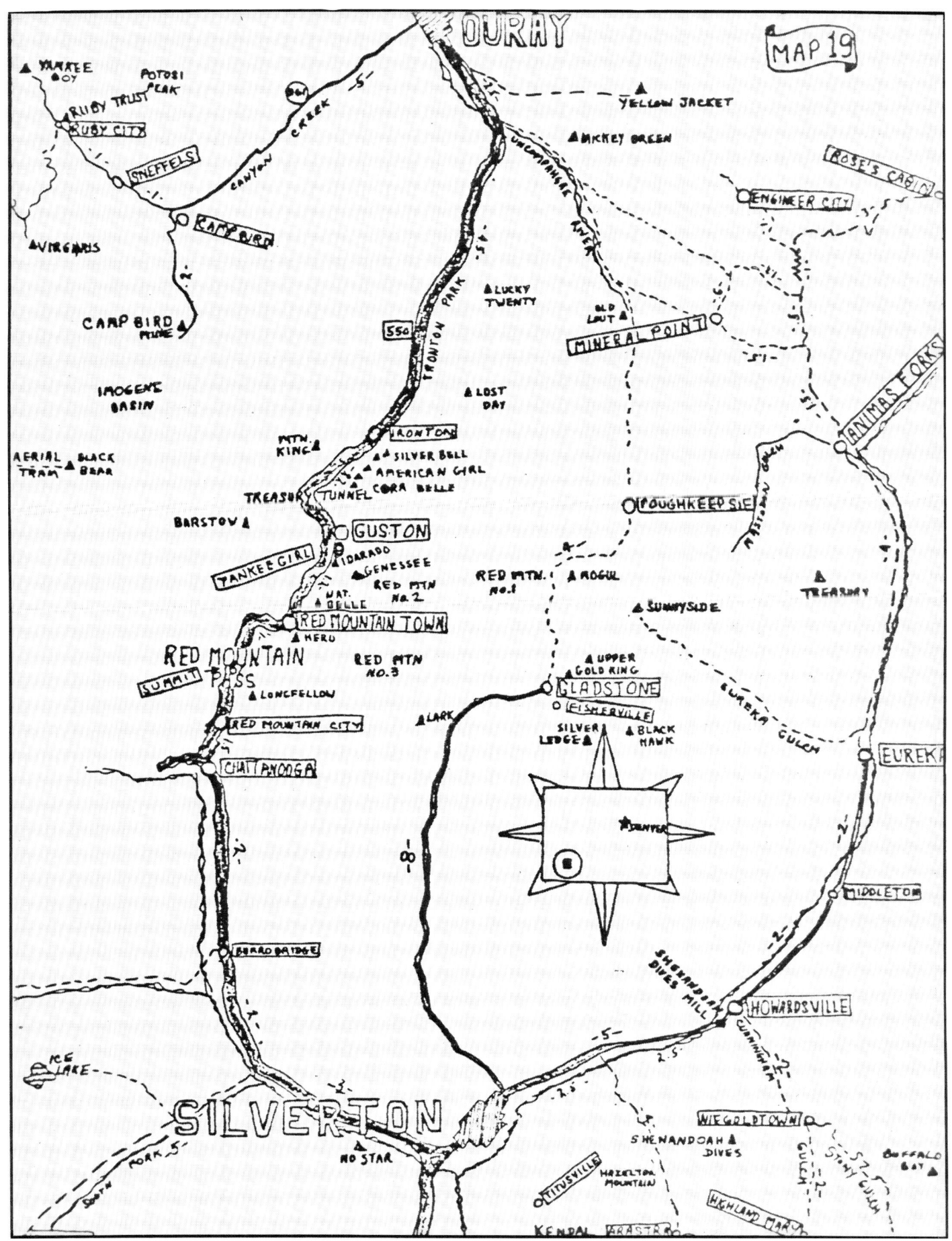

This old map came from Perry Eberhart's *Guide to the Colorado Ghost Towns and Mining Camps* **of 1959.**

Early day Silverton. *Colorado State Historical Society*

A spring washout on the Silverton Branch, right outside of Silverton.

Silverton gets her annual winter white dress.

William Newton Byers, editor of the *Rocky Mountain News* was the hornet with the deadliest sting. The population of Denver was not very large and Byers had visions of it becoming a ghost town if too many took off for the new Eldorado. His editorializing was an overkill and kept enthusiasm for the San Juan strike at a high pitch. Had he kept quiet, the rumors of gold to be found in Baker's Park may have received but little attention and Silverton's development delayed a long time.

In spite of Byer's efforts, Baker was able to organize a company of 100 men, women and children. The party was at the junction of Hermosa Creek and the Animas in the spring of 1861. Their route was from Santa Fe and over the Horse Lake Trail. Before proceeding on to the final destination on the headwaters of the Animas in the vicinity of latter-day Eureka, Baker paused long enough enroute to plat the town of Animas City.

The high hopes, kindled by first results in the new diggings, waned. By late July the discouraged gold seekers, spurred by the news that the war between the states had started, packed out. Baker's Park and partly built Animas City were abandoned. And here the record becomes confused. There is no doubt that Baker was in Missouri and signed on as a captain in the Confederate Army. The question is whether he went direct to Missouri in 1861 or later. There are some references to indicate he was back on the Animas in 1862 with a party that became mutinous and tried to hang Baker. He escaped the rope and left the diggings. However, it is more likely that it was the 1861 party that, becoming disgruntled and disappointed, was the one that tried to hang Baker. At least the Park was abandoned in 1861, and after the Civil War ended, Baker made several more trips to the Silverton area but how many is uncertain. We know he was there in 1871, for he was killed somewhere in the Park that year by Indians.

In the late sixties, other prospectors from Colorado, Nevada and Arizona camps began penetrating the area to prospect. In doing so they were trespassing on land set aside by the treaty as the Ute Reservation. But treaties could not stop the influx and it was necessary in order to keep peace for federal troops to clear them out. No one wintered in Baker's Park in 1870-'71 or '72, this in spite of the fact that a party sent out by Governor Pile of New Mexico had located and mined the first lode which was found on the north side of Arrastra Gulch and named the Little Giant. This party built an arrastra and crushed about 27 tons of ore which yielded $150 per ton. But this party was moved out and apparently did not return later.

The federal troops kept the area cleared until the Brunot Treaty was signed by the Utes and the United States. Signing of this paper blasted the Silverton treasure chest wide open.

Before the end of 1873, over 3,000 claims had been recorded. Stories that grew bigger the farther they went from Silverton kept reaching Denver. One of the men that listened and began thinking about the significance of these stories, if true, was General Palmer.

The noise of the celebration in honor of the Narrow Gauge reaching Durango had hardly quieted before rail was being laid toward Silverton.

REPORT HAS ERROR

The Report to the Board of Directors dated April 1, 1882 contains an error, or misprint, as it shows 19.1 miles of track constructed on the Silverton Branch by January 1, **1881**. This is one year too early. Construction was halted on December 11, 1881, just west of Rockwood, 19.1 miles from Durango, because the blasting of the shelf along which the High Line runs was going to take at least until spring to finish. Also, the Colorado Coal and Iron Company was unable to keep up with demand. Rail laying stopped then because of these reasons and severe winter conditions. However, work continued on cutting the shelf out of the cliff and in building the bridge over the Animas at Milepost 471.23. Grading had been completed before the shutdown to the junction of Cascade Creek with the Animas.

Workers on the High Line and bridge construction suffered mightily from the low temperatures. There were many cases of frozen feet, fingers and ears, but the work continued. At night these men shivered through the nights in the construction cars at Rockwood until they could no longer endure. Then dugouts were built in the hillsides. They were crude but at least were warm. Periodically three or four of the girls off the Line at Durango came to Rockwood to help warm up the dugouts. These visits never occurred except at times when the paycar had just been to Rockwood and paid off the workers.

With the first sign of better weather, the Rio Grande shifted into high gear and on July 8, 1882, Silverton had its railroad. Miners were digging too hard and Palmer wanted to start hauling ore so there was no celebration.

Between the arrival at Silverton and the end of the year, 13,754,352 pounds of freight had been hauled out of Silverton and 11,190,098 pounds in. Palmer was the most popular man in Colorado so far as Silverton was concerned, until someone looked at his freight bill. The average rate for hauling ore the short distance to Durango was $7.50 per ton. Most of the inbound business came from Pueblo or Denver at $12.50 per ton. When people at Silverton began to think about these figures there arose a squall like a scalded cat makes. Memories were short. They forgot how previous to the arrival of the railroad they had been paying wagon rates of $30-$60 per ton for the haul over Stony Pass between Silverton and Del Norte, then some more to get to Pueblo or Denver.

Excluding Animas City, which had become almost a suburb of Durango, in 1882 there were more small communities and more people living along the Animas and through the canyon to Silverton than there are today, or at any time after the railroad went through. Time-Table No. 19 was issued by the Rio Grande two weeks after the railroad reached Silverton. It listed eight stations between Durango and Silverton, including Animas City.

Home Ranch, first station above Animas City, forwarded $456.24 in freight the last half of 1882. The next station was Trimble Springs, a passenger stop serving a medicinal hot spring spa, built and operated by a man named Trimble. He paid $100 for the land the spring flowed from because he suffered from chilbains and corns on his feet and thought the water would cure them. After the railroad was available, the spring was made the central attraction for a large spa. By 1885 the establishment was valued at $100,000, but records fail to show whether Trimble still was the owner. The establishment included a fine hotel, the Hermosa, and comfortable bathhouses.

Patronage was excellent, and it was claimed that the waters would cure corns, arthritis, rheumatism and ingrown toenails. As more people visited and used the springs, even more fantastic claims were made, among them being that the waters would cure dandruff, restore hair to bald pates, make the impotent potent, make the barren fertile, and soak away all the miseries brought on by mountain living. However, so many people used the waters in the early years they lost much of their curative qualities, and today will only perform part of these miracles.

Hermosa, Spanish for beautiful, was built in a picture setting. About 150 people farmed and tended orchards here. The railroad built a water tank to supply full tanks before the trains started upgrade. In the spring, with newly-greened fields and orchards in blossom, Hermosa lived up to its name to the utmost.

Leaving Hermosa the grade changes from 1 percent to 2.5 percent to Rockwood, 6.6 miles from Hermosa, then it is descending to the river at Tacoma. From that point it is almost a constant 1 percent ascending to Silverton. Until the hydroelectric plant was built, it was nine miles to the next station. When the plant was built a siding and station named Tacoma resulted. Until then after leaving Rockwood there were no stops until Cascade Siding at the junction of Cascade Creek and the Animas where a section headquarters was built. There was already a small community without name as a kind of hostelry for wagons and stages on the old road that more or less followed the Animas for 20 rugged miles before it swung west and south over Cascade Hill to a stage stop named Cascade. From Cascade the road continued through Rockwood to Durango. Cascade may have at times been called Murnane. It was such a small community, and all descriptions and distances where Murnane is involved, fit those for Cascade also.

Murnane or Cascade, the place gained negative renown for three things: it served absolutely the lousiest food in Colorado; the only beds available were shake-downs on the earthen floor and they were bad; and the price of hay was 5ᶜ per pound (which holdup price you were not informed of until after your animals had consumed the hay).

On the railroad, Cascade Siding, now called Tefft, is at Milepost 478. At Milepost 480.3 a small insecure settlement had sprung up because of some prospects that never quite became mines. The railroad had a stop here and named it Needleton. When it became apparent the prospects would not be producers, the railroad moved the siding and station to a more favorable location at Milepost 484 but kept the name Needleton.

In the small park where Elk Creek enters the Animas, a wye, stock loading facilities, ore loading tracks and depot were built and called Elk Park. A lot of lumber, good ore and livestock moved out of Elk Park in the early years. The wye was used to turn trains that could not make it through to Silverton because of snowslides or other natural obstacles and therefore the train could turn back to Durango. The worst snowslide area of Animas Canyon is between Elk Park and the point where it opens into Baker's Park. Some of the slides in this section piled snow as much as 50 feet deep, mixed with rocks and trees. Several years they could not be cleared without seriously delaying Durango-Silverton trains so tunnels were driven through them. Passengers and foodstuffs were portaged around the slides at times and Otto Mears in a few cases used his engine and cars to back from Silverton to the slides to relay the portaged traffic.

The suction of a fast-running snowslide must be observed to be believed. A water tank about three miles below Silverton named the Silverton Water Tank was pulled over and destroyed by one such action. Trees as much as 10 inches in diameter growing on cliffs along the slide path, and many limbs, were sucked into slides and made removal more difficult. Slides did run at about the same locations. One just beyond the last bridge over the Animas was called the Jumping Jenny because it struck an outcropping above the tracks and becoming airborne, went into the air above the tracks and landed across the river.

Silverton was one town where Palmer had to enter on the town's terms. Property sold dear, but there was no place else to go to build a company town. Palmer paid the high prices demanded for land he needed, but he took steps to recover the expense when he began hauling into and out of Silverton by charging exorbitant rates.

Silverton had two newspapers, the *La Plata Miner* and the *Herald*. The *Miner* opposed letting the Narrow Gauge come to Silverton. The *Herald* championed the road's coming. A duel of words developed between the two editors and the populace naturally took sides. Teamsters and stage drivers sided with the *Miner;* mine owners and cattle ranchers, the *Herald*. Adherents of the *Miner* headquartered in Anesie's Bar; the opposition in the Imperial Cafe. Tradition says the editor of the *Herald* often became so fatigued from the strenuous and well-libated strategy sessions he had to be carried home on a shutter. Fortunately, the railroad arrived before the two enemy camps got down to shooting, cutting or stomping each other.

OTTO MEARS BUILDS

Otto Mears got into the railroad building game in June of '89 and started construction of the Silverton Railroad that eventually reached the Joker Tunnel, 16.06 miles from Silverton. Most of this line operated until 1926. After 1905 it was known as the Silverton Railway. In 1899, Mears built the Silverton Northern to serve Eureka and the Animas Forks. This operated until 1939, the same time the Sunnyside mine closed. The Silverton, Gladstone and Northerly, built in 1896 to Gladstone, 7.5 miles, for the Gold King Mining Company was bought by the Silverton Northern in 1915. The Gold King had ceased operations in 1910.

The Silverton Northern ran the swankiest, most profitable passenger trains. There were four scheduled trains daily, each grossing about $20 per mile. At the same time freight trains were carrying ore so rich, armed guards rode from the mines, through the interchange to the Rio Grande at Silverton and on to the smelter at Durango.

Silverton residents usually say there are seven ghost towns in the area. These are: Howardsville, Middleton, Eureka, Animas Forks, Mineral Point, Gladstone and Chattanooga. But that expert on Colorado ghost towns, Perry Eberhart, recognizes 26 more. Around Silverton there are 40 prominent gulches, all with some mineralization. Each new discovery brought a camp into being, and each in its time held dreams of wealth for the inhabitants. Some of the dreams lasted as little as a week, some a few months and a very few for several years. The mountains do not bury ghost towns as rapidly as the jungles, but they are as effective. Most of the evidence that a location once was a ghost town has disappeared so completely that even ghosts returning to look for their old homes cannot find them.

Every mining boom town has its notorious "gaming" street. Silverton's sporting street was named Blair Street for an 1870 pioneer. Like all such streets, the unruly element went too far and the city fathers and good women decided to clean it up. Bat Masterson was hired to do the job and came to Silverton with his cronies. They did quiet Blair Street down a bit but failed to wipe it out, or clean it up. Maybe they did not want to anyway. Bat and his followers were all veterans of the Western scene and fully realized there was a need for such an escape valve consisting of wine, women and song among the kind of men it took to open a new wild country.

Silverton was often visited by three classes of "circuit riders." The good women of the town objected to the first of the three. These were the prostitutes who traveled a circuit leaving Denver and reaching Silverton by way of Pueblo, Leadville, Creede and short stops at other camps enroute.

The "portable prostitutes" stopped in Leadville for a month or so, then, as their drawing power waned, moved to Summitville or Creede, thence to Silverton. From Silverton the circuit breaks were Rico, Telluride, Ouray, Lake City and the Gunnison area. By the time Gunnison was played out, the girls were getting sort of fatigued, so used part of their earnings for a sojourn at Glenwood Springs where they took the baths and recuperated enough to start the circuit all over. While in Glenwood they dressed and acted the part of ladies of leisure and did not perform professionally. Some were able to snag husbands and left the trade completely.

The circuit riding revivalists and preachers arrived in each of the towns the girls were sojourning in, almost at the same time. The men of God had driving ambitions to convert the hell-raising men of the mining camps. They also enjoyed the food and sympathy given them by the good women and could always hope to save one of the fallen sisters.

Not too far behind the first two groups came the circuit-riding judges. Unlike the perambulatory ladies of pleasure, the judges did not offer pleasure, nor did they preach salvation. They did not plead or exhort, but simply listened to evidence, then dispensed justice as they saw it—but not always according to the law. To conclusively settle a case, all they had to do was buy a new rope, find someone to tie the hangman's knot and a convenient tree. There was never any reprieve from a case settled in this manner.

What really cooled off and almost wiped out Blair Street and the circuit rider was that the Rio Grande made it easily possible for good women to come to town. They had no difficulty in finding husbands who were anxious to settle down. The unions resulted in homes and children. Schools were built for the children and churches were built and patronized. It was not very long after the good women came that the love knot was better known than the hangman's knot. Silverton turned into a fine family type town and was a good place to live.

Silverton—The Mining Camp That Never Quits. It has lived through fire, epidemics, flood, panics, Blair Streets, Bat Mastersons, depressed metal prices and Depression. The Symbol of Faith on Anvil Mountain holds its hands high in blessing, and Silverton holds the faith.

NEXT FOUR PAGES. Mixed freight with #484 on the point and #492 as a helper moves over the rails from Chama to Alamosa in August of 1965. *Both photos, Chris Burritt*

Chapter 12
Lumber industry along the Narrow Gauge

More lumber is being shipped over the Rio Grande in this scene by John Krause. *Dr. Richard Severance collection*

On the Narrow Gauge, from beginning to end, revenue was produced from hauling crude ore, concentrates, coal, lumber, and, of course, consumer goods. Livestock for the most part was never a profitable source of revenue. In the final analysis, had there been a program for keeping totals over the years, it is probable that timber products would show as the greatest producer.

The first record of a revenue shipment on the D&RG is one of 10 cars of lumber hauled September 8, 1871, from Plum Station to Denver, a distance of 25 miles. During the first full year of operation after the line reached Colorado Springs, by far the heaviest tonnage hauled was lumber. By the 1873 Panic, 20 sawmills were producing and shipping lumber. Demand was so low during the Panic they all shut down and the D&RG lost valuable business.

With the end of the Panic all along the expanding D&RG there was a revitalized need for lumber, and lumber again was the one single product that could be depended on for income. This continued well up to the Great Depression, especially on the Narrow Gauge. Up until the start of WWI there were many mills west of Chama, and they were extremely active and productive. However, forests are not limitless or inexhaustible and the truth of this became apparent rather early.

Before the land could be completely ravished, a few thoughtful persons called attention to the wastefulness of the pioneer methods of logging to depletion. These thinkers preached that nature's gifts were exhaustible, and that the people who were to follow them had just claims to a share of the timber.

Their efforts and crusades were successful. In 1886 a division of forestry was created in the Department of Agriculture. Five years later Congress authorized the President to set aside forest reserves to protect timber remaining on public domain. In 1892, four of these reserves were established in Colorado. The same year the term "Timber Land" was changed to "Forest." Then Theodore Roosevelt set aside 148,000,000 acres in 150 reserves, many along the route of the Narrow Gauge, since the reserves established in Colorado comprised one-fifth of the entire state.

The lumbering industry along the D&RG, especially on the Santa Fe Branch and west of Chama, began to feel the pinch. From a dependable 8 to 10 per cent figure of revenue produced on the entire system, lumber dropped in 1910 to only 4 per cent. The impact on the Narrow Gauge was even more severe. The entire pattern of development changed almost overnight. Branch lines built solely because of the logging and lumber industry did not cease operating immediately, but the practice of building spurs into the timber to serve every new mill stopped.

Although the D&RG was not a land grant railroad such as the Union Pacific or Santa Fe, Congress did enact a piece of legislation, "Granting the Right of Way through the Public Lands to the Denver and Rio Grande Railway Company." The Act specifically stated the width of the right of way, 100 feet on each side of the track. It also provided for "such public lands adjacent thereto as may be needed for depots, shops, and other buildings for railroad purposes and for yard room, and side tracks, not exceeding twenty acres at any one station, and not more than one station in every ten miles."

Then the Act quit being specific and opened the gates for abuses and eventual lawsuits when it said: "and the rights to take from the public lands adjacent thereto, timber, earth, water, and other material required for the construction and repair of its railway and telegraph line, be, and the same hereby granted and confirmed unto the Denver and Rio Grande Railway Company."

Even Webster is ambigious in defining "adjacent." There is little wonder then that later one judge would render a decision that for the purpose of the Act, "adjacent" meant not to exceed 15 miles from the right of way—but he did not specify whether the distance set applied from the main line or a branch line. A second judge ruled the distance could be as much as 100 miles if that was the closest line and the railroad needed timber. Besides not defining what was meant by "adjacent", it did not set any limit on amounts to be taken or under what conditions. Neither did it establish policing powers or penalties.

In Colorado, San Isabel Forest was created in 1902; Gunnison, Leadville, San Juan, Park Range and Wet Mountains in 1905; Cochetopa, Fruita and Ouray the same year. The D&RG believed the Act permitted them to take timber from the one of those closest to the piece of railroad that needed material for the "construction and repair of its railway and telegraph line." The newly-created Forest Service thought it was taking more than it needed and that the New Mexico Lumber Company and the D&RG were devising a scheme to profit at public expense. To collect evidence, arrangements were made to cruise the timber (along the Narrow Gauge west of Chama) to determine what had been cut. At the same time an injunction was served against a number of lumbering organizations pending settlement of suits charging timber piracy.

FEDERAL INVESTIGATION

An investigation by the government, lasting three years, was launched by the government in areas served by the Narrow Gauge. Near the end of 1909, proceedings began when charges were filed against the D&RG and the New Mexico Lumber Company for alleged piracy of a million and a half dollars worth of timber. The question to be decided was what was meant by "adjacent". The government based its case on an interpretation that the materials had to be "adjacent" to a main line and that the authority could not be extended to resources and materials adjacent to branch lines or spurs built, essentially, to harvest stands of timber. It also wanted an answer as to whether the New Mexico Lumber Company was a bona fide private corporation or a child of the D&RG.

The question of ownership was one that neither of the companies was prone to discuss. At least they joined forces and collaborated in disputing the claim of timber piracy.

(The name of the Rio Grande, and abbreviation commonly used at this period was "D&RG". There had been an operating arrangement between the Rio Grande Western and the Denver and Grande since 1901, but the relationship was not formally fixed [by bond and stock consolidations] until 1908. Chartering as the Denver and Rio Grande Western Railroad Company came even later.)

As part of the government's early investigation, it had cruised the stumpage of the timber in question to determine how much had been cut. The two defenders disagreed with the figures projected. In the spring of 1910 a joint party that consisted of representatives of the government, D&RG and New Mexico Lumber began checking the original cruise. Trouble quickly brewed when the party was denied access to records of the original cruise.

John Veaver, government representative, tried to get the other representatives to double cruise, that is, measure and estimate the stumpage twice. He took the stand that their

An early sawmill town in northern New Mexico — simple living.

cruise had to be at least within 50 per cent of the original or the re-check would be thrown out of court. Welsh Nossman, the New Mexico Lumber cruiser, refused to accept this. He was adamant that he must cruise on a basis of a true, one-time cruise—if the defendants were at fault, so be it, but the cruise was going to be honest.

To resolve the matter, after a lawyers' conference, it was agreed that the D&RG-New Mexico Lumber party and the government party would cruise alternate sections. Strangely enough, when the final results were in, Nossman's figures confirmed the accuracy of 32 per cent of the original cruise; Veaver's results showed the original was only 30 per cent accurate. A compromise figure of 31 per cent was agreed to for court purposes.

In the court proceedings, Attorney E.N. Clark represented the D&RG and attorney Clyde Dawson the New Mexico Lumber Company.

FIGURES ACCEPTED

Numerous reference were made to the original cruise by government attorneys. Attorney Dawson requested Federal Judge Robert E. Lewis to have the books referred to entered in evidence. Government attorneys objected strenuously, but the judge ordered that they be entered. With the entry of this evidence, the case of the government went to pieces. Ex-

Pound Brothers planing mill at Chama; lumber was the backbone of Chama's economy.

amination of the books developed there was no doubt that much of the timber had been cruised as much as three times for some sections. The figures of the joint cruise were accepted as basis for settlement by arbitration.

The two companies, D&RG and New Mexico Lumber, paid the government $90,000 and the case was closed. The word "adjacent" never was defined, and actual ownership of the New Mexico Lumber Company was not disclosed, but all injunctions were lifted and all pending timber-claim patents were issued.

Lumbering again became active on the Narrow Gauge, but it quickly became apparent the frontier-type harvesting was finished.

Fundamentally, charges of timber piracy stemmed from the way timberclaims could be made. Unlike mineral claims that had to have assessment work done on them to be valid, timberclaims could be made sight unseen. All that was required was to file claim to a section not previously claimed, pay $2.50 an acre and hold for 10 weeks. Claimants then received a receipt and acknowledgement of claim. Naturally, the claim was then sold to the highest bidder—a large timber-lumber operator. This caused the government to charge collusion, but the law was so wide open collusion was not necessary. Under the law, what the claimant did with the timber after 10 weeks was nobody's affair.

TIMBER!!!

By the time the Narrow Gauge had reached Durango, lumber mills were being built trackside. West of Chama began a wild, feverish, thoughtless slaughter of the frontier stands of pine. Logging spread up the slopes, across flats and into valleys and canyons and great timber chutes brought logs by gravity from the mesa tops. No thought was given to leaving seed-trees, and every tree was cut and run through the sawmill. When no timber was left the mill was dismantled and moved to another location. Often the moves were made between sundown and sunup and the day was awakened there by saws already whining. Very shortly after, rail would be laid as a spur to the new location, the track material coming from the spur that served the previous location.

The butts of many logs bore a stamped "G.T." to indicate they came from government land "adjacent" to the D&RG and was to be made into lumber to be used "for the construction and repair of its railway and telegraph line." One aged,

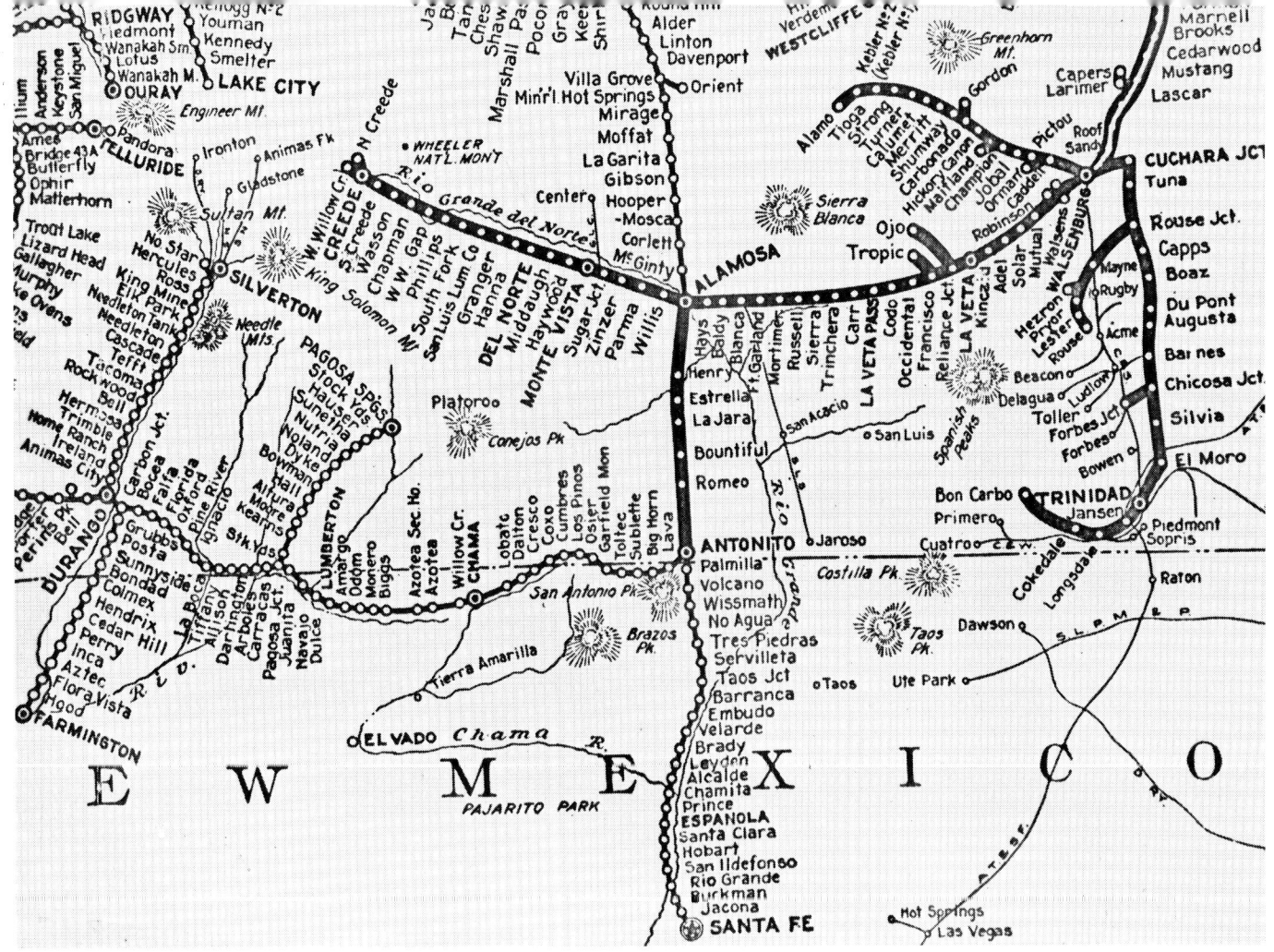

This map of about 1925, deleted La Madera and El Vado branches.

former sawmill operator, observed that the D&RG could have constructed and maintained a railway to the moon with all that "G.T." lumber.

By the government being so slow in resolving the timber pirating case, the timber and lumber interests had enjoyed relative freedom long enough to have accomplished the harvesting of the virginal timber. After the lifting of the injunctions and the closing of the case, lumbering regained most of its impetus but never returned to the wildly urgent stage that existed from the coming of the Narrow Gauge until about 1910.

During the peak 30 years, sawmill "towns" in the timber stands along the Narrow Gauge were built and occupied as long as there was timber to cut. It was then moved, with the mill, to a new location, and took a new name. Branches, spurs and side tracks—even three quasi-independent short railroads—and supporting facilities were built and abandoned as the timber harvest grew and then declined.

Few pictures exist to show us what most of these lumber towns looked like. We have to depend on descriptions and stories of old-timers to let us mentally picture what life was like in the heyday of the lumbering along the Narrow Gauge. The descriptions of these towns have a common sameness. The mill with its great sawdust piles, boilers and saws and piles of logs far enough from the town to prevent accidental fires. There was always one central road, or street, along which the homes and commissary were built; this street was wide enough to accommodate the great loads of logs being transported on high-wheeled wagons that were pulled by three or more spans of horses or oxen. And, that street was always dusty in dry weather so that the house interiors were always dust covered. In wet weather, there was mud inches, and feet, deep.

The houses (shacks) were constructed of the first boards cut (if material had not been moved from the last location). These boards were nailed to frail frames of scantlings that formed the walls and roofs. The sawed boards then had slabs nailed over the cracks. The roof was also boards and slabs. In summer the heat in these shacks was unbearable; in the winter the cold wind and snow came through the walls and ceiling to howl and freeze. The foundations were universally built of green logs with the tops flattened by work with a broad axe. Soon after the house was built, a second much smaller structure of coarse construction graced the backyard. Depending on the size of the family it was either a one-holer or a two-holer.

Farther away from the houses, down wind, were built the hay barns and stables and a large corral for work stock. In this vicinity was the blacksmith shop that, at large operations, worked day and night.

These short-lived towns were rough, and life in them hard and monotonous, but for the most part, they were law-abiding and not rowdy. The work was too hard and the pay too low to cause much celebrating—except the Fourth of July and Christmas. If the men's lives were hard, the women's were harder. There was the constant battle against dust and mud, cooking heavy meals (including much baking), washing clothes on a rubbing board, and changing diapers on their babies. If on the main line of the railroad, there was the excitement twice a day when the east-and west-bound passenger trains stopped.

At Pagosa Springs, the narrow gauge tracks came in just behind the dark line of trees over the river.

RAILROAD SPURS

Transitory as the mill camps were, the railroad spurs serving them were as impermanent. Nature soon removed all trace they had ever been there after abandonment and removal. Besides the numerous timber spurs, there were four of long enough life and length to be designated as branches. The ownership of them, due to the D&RG's early methods of financing and being quasi-partners in so many enterprises, is not always clear. They were built with D&RG material, used D&RG equipment and were operated by D&RG employees. If any question arose about ownership or operation damaging to the D&RG, any connection was vehemently disclaimed.

The first spur of any length built that shows of record was 3.16 miles long. Prior to its construction others had been built, used and abandoned. This one in 1888 left the main line just west of Chama at M.P. 345 and ran southwest to a sawmill owned and operated by J.D. Biggs and Son. The mill was called Law's Mill.

The following year, at M.P. 348, a siding to handle the loading of logs for Biggs was built. These logs were hauled to Biggs Jct. thence to Law's Mill. This siding was taken out in 1891 when Biggs began cutting at M.P. 350, one mile west of Willow Creek. A spur was built to the mill town, and it is possible the line was extended beyond into the timber. Records and remains of abandoned trackage cannot confirm this.

However, records of June, 1892, of the merger of the Chama Lumber Company and J.D. Biggs and Son, into one firm (the word "son" is sometimes written "sons") state that the new corporation had "two mills with a capacity of 75,000 feet each day and operate twenty-two miles of railroad with engines and rolling stock sufficient to do their business." We can surmise from this there must have been 10 miles or so of logging railroad into the timber being cut for the Willow Creek operation.

Or, possibly, the statement was anticipating the completion of track being laid as an extension from Law's Mill to a new stand of timber and mill town near Brazos, N. Mexico on the banks of a stream named Brazos. When this extension was completed, the Willow Creek mill and town was moved to Brazos. The railroad was organized and chartered as The Tierra Amarilla Southern Railroad. Not long after the road was in operation, it was delivering a trainload of lumber daily to the D&RG. A two-mile logging spur ran into timber from Brazos. In 1893, tracks were laid westward to the Chama River, crossed it and served a mill at a location called Sawmill Mesa. This was ten miles west of Brazos.

The Panic of 1893 caused a 50 per cent cutback in lumber production, but apparently conditions were better by 1895 for the TASRR built from Brazos to a small Mexican community named Ensenada and thence on to Tierra Amarilla, the present-day county seat of Rio Arriba County.

In 1902, the D&RG took over the Tierra Amarilla Southern and renamed the trackage the Chama Lumber Spur. Trains were run by the new owner until the end of the year when it was dismantled. This dismantling was caused by the depletion of timber and to obtain railroad material to build the Rio Grande & Southwestern from Lumberton, N. Mexico to a Biggs' mill and new timber at El Vado, N. Mexico. This branch was 33 miles long and crossed the Continental Divide via the old Horse Lake Indian trail.

SULLENBERGER SPURS

Another man, Alexander T. Sullenberger, loomed large in the lumbering west of Chama. He submitted a sketch to the D&RG for a spur to be built just west of Azotea to follow the Continental Divide southward from the D&RG to timber he was to cut. The spur was not built until early fall of 1888. The spur when completed was designated as "Sullenberger's No. 1."

A short time later another spur left the D&RG one mile

FIRST TRAIN TO DURANGO
Rio Grande No. 493 leads its freight across a level section in the Rocky Mountains enroute to Durango from Chama in 1965. It was the first consist in three weeks over the line after a washout halted train action. *Chris Burritt*

TRESTLE CROSSING ACTION
No. 484 passes over a road trestle at Highway 17 just west of Cumbres station with a freight train destined for Alamosa. No. 492 (not seen) is helping at the rear. *Chris Burritt*

COALING UP
No. 492 simmers at the coal tipple in Chama on a bright day in 1965. An unidentified locomotive sits behind it. *Chris Burritt*

WATER FOR A THIRSTY IRON HORSE
In the time-honored tradition, No. 493, a K-37 2-8-2 — and a sister locomotive — take on water at the Chama tank. *Chris Burritt*

ANOTHER ONE OVER THE HILL
No. 492, a helper engine, has just watered up, and now it and the caboose are ready to depart for Chama after helping another freight train over Cumbres. The train, headed by No. 484, is already on its way to Alamosa and is out of sight. *Chris Burritt*

MAN AND NATURE IN HARMONY
TOP. With Durango behind it in the background, No. 487 invades the quiet of the surrounding mountains with its clanking rods and rattle of things mechanical. Nature's brilliant yellow flowers adorn the right-of-way. *Chris Burritt*

THE *SAN JUAN*
NEXT PAGE. The *San Juan* was a special green and gold train: Porterhouse steaks, luxurious service and lavish fittings gave it an image of richness beyond what most expected of 3-foot trains. Clayton Tanner rode the *San Juan* on August 10, 1950 and recorded this view of the rear platform while the train was at Alamosa. *Clayton Tanner*

SILENT NIGHT AT DURANGO
A strange silence surrounds the roundhouse at Durango as two Rio Grande locomotives, one with a balloon stack, rest peacefully inside. No one appears to be around tonight to tend the engines. Chris Burritt took this night shot at 9 p.m. in the fall of 1965.

East end of Pagosa Springs. There was even a railroad named the Rio Grande & Pagosa Springs built north from Lumberton.

west of Sullenberger's No. 1. It ran north and was a logging line. Before being pulled up it reached a total of about three miles to the base of Chromo Peak. This was Sullenberger's No. 2.

Sullenberger's No. 3 was at MP 359. A mill and town were established here. To aid in logging, a light rail line was extended six miles to the summit of Spring Creek Divide. At the midpoint a spur ran west two miles to the head of Diamonte Canyon. Had this spur continued another three miles, it would have junctioned with the Narrow Gauge at Amargo, N. Mexico. Sullenberger operated at this location possibly until 1898. When the logging road miles were abandoned a 15-car capacity spur was left and named Bigg's Spur. (This was the second spur so-named, for earlier there had been a short spur that left the main line near the Monero water tank named Bigg's Spur.)

By 1900, most of the large tracts of virgin pine in the "Chama Pineries" had been harvested. Interest turned to the El Vado-Gallinas, Navajo River and Pagosa Springs stands. These tracts were too distant from the narrow gauge to be served by spurs. Because of this, three branch lines were built. Two junctioned with the main at Lumberton, N. Mexico and one at Pagosa Jct. (Gato). Much later, and not properly part of the story of the earlier harvesting, a fourth branch started from a large new mill built at Dulce, N. Mexico by the Pagosa Lumber Company. It went up a canyon in a southwest direction to some pine on the Jicarilla Apache Reservation. Construction began in 1916. Before fading away to abandonment in 1923, a total of 20 miles of track had been laid. These miles were not straight away miles and included spurs and sidings. The rail operation was a headache from the beginning, and never profitable.

Of the three lumber branches built contemporaneously with the early harvest, the Rio Grande & Pagosa Springs Railroad built north from Lumberton, N. Mexico to the Nava-

Conductor R.S. Murray sets a handbrake on a narrow gauge box car.

161

jo River at a new mill and town named Edith, Colorado. This was only six miles, but its presence raised a fever in Pagosa Springs whose inhabitants hoped for the line to extend to them. A survey was run and a segment was constructed. Building stopped at a place named Flaugh, almost in sight of Pagosa Springs. Track building for logging purposes was extended on up the Navajo River about five miles to Chromo, Colorado and later extended four miles to the holdings of an old settler named William Price.

Other spurs of this line went into Coyote Park, up several canyons to timber, up Webb Canyon, and one up the Little Navajo River. Local tradition says a spur left the main a mile up river from Chromo to the north side of Chromo Peak at Spring Creek Pass. Extensions of track were sporadic and coincided with new stands of timber being logged. Trackage diminished as the timber was cut off. The RG&PS RR quit running trains early in 1914 and was formally dissolved as a railroad October 24, 1917.

The approaching depletion of timber in the Brazos-Sawmill Mesa area expedited the acquisition of stands in the El Vado-Horse Lake-Gallinas (N. Mex) districts. All of these were relatively distant from the D&RG main line and would need a more ambitious rail system than earlier logging had required. The lumber people and railroad engineers made extensive surveys trying to find a way to serve the new timber by an extension of the existing Tierra Amarillo Southern Railroad. They were unable to find a feasible route due to terrain. The old Horse Lake Indian trail between the Chama and Navajo rivers was well known. Terrain and grade were favorable, so the decision was made to build the needed railroad starting from a junction with the D&RG at Lumberton, N. Mexico.

The cost of grading would be minimal and track materials from the TAS could be salvaged and used. In January, 1903, the D&RG and Biggs signed an agreement to jointly construct the new line, The Rio Grande & Southwestern. The route was 42 miles long from Lumberton to Gallinas, N. Mexico. D&RG was to furnish the 30-pound rail from the TAS and OTM (Other Track Material) excluding spikes. Jointly, 30 miles of track were to be completed by January, 1904 and the balance not later than January, 1906. The line was surveyed in the spring of 1903 and grading started at Lumberton in May. Track laying began a month later.

The summit of the Continental Divide was reached in August and a siding there was named Hillcrest. Progress beyond this point is not well recorded but there is knowledge that from a fork just beyond Hillcrest a line was started toward El Vado and reached there in the fall, probably early October.

BOULDER LAKE CUTTING

El Vado was 33.16 miles from Lumberton. From the RG&SW main, spurs were laid and operated as needed. One spur took off at a point named Lago and ran two miles to La Jara Lake. Just south of Lago a two-pronged spur served the Boulder Lake cutting. A few miles further south was Horse Lake Jct. Here a major spur ran north to Horse Lake and from this a secondary spur headed east toward the Willow Creek drainage and followed this valley to the southeast base of Sawmill Mesa, then as a perimeter line around the mesa. Two miles from El Vado a spur was built to harvest Thompson Mesa. Spurs were built and had hardly been put on a map before the timber served was cut and the spurs torn out to be used on others. Very few of the place names can be found on present-day maps. However, by their use the last remaining tall pines of northern New Mexico west of the Chama River were cut and went to market, except for the great stand in the Gallinas Mountains, and west of Stinking Lake.

The delays caused by the timber pirating case, some minor economic recessions and slackened demand made it unnecessary to continue track building to the Gallinas Mountains until 1917. Extensions did begin in 1917 and reached the New Mexican settlement of Gallinas in 1918 and a few miles beyond. From midpoint of the extension a spur took off generally northward to Stinking Lake and from this spur a dozen or so short, temporary spurs permitted cutting of individual stands.

This network of shortline railroad and spurs was used in the final harvesting of the virgin pine of northern New Mexico. As 1923 drew to a close, depletion was in sight. The year 1924 saw the mill at El Vado closed. It was dismantled and moved to the Dolores River Country on the Rio Grande Southern. All of the remaining Rio Grande & Southwestern had been abandoned and the rail pulled up by 1928 with the exception of the first three miles from Lumberton which remained to serve the Miller Coal Mine.

The fourth of the major lumber hauling branches to be built with a Narrow Gauge connection was the Pagosa Springs Branch. It was originally built by lumbering interests, then acquired by the D&RG. This branch had an operating life of 35 years. It was 30.85 miles long from Pagosa Jct. (Gato), Colo., to Pagosa Springs. Last operation was 1935 and rails were pulled up in 1936. Timber in the vicinity and along Cat (Gato) Creek, upper Stolsteimer Creek, and in and around Pagosa Springs was cut. Before the first-growth timber had been finally cut a large number of logging spurs had been built, used and abandoned in connection with the Pagosa Springs Branch.

The story of the Pagosa Springs Branch goes back to the Chama pineries and Alexander T. Sullenberger. He sold out to the Biggs group at Azotea, finished cutting the Spring Creek Pass-Diamonte stand, and moved to Pagosa Springs. Contrary to the then prevalent practice, Sullenberger found partners and they then incorporated as the Pagosa Lumber Company. His two most important partners were Whitney and Harry E. Newton of the Newton Lumber Company. In the same month the new lumber firm was incorporated, they incorporated and chartered the Rio Grande, Pagosa & Northern Railroad. The construction contract was let in August, 1899, and grading started at Pagosa Jct. the same month. By Christmas, 14.5 miles of track had been laid up Cat Creek and work stopped for the winter.

FIRST TRAIN

Work resumed in the spring of 1900 and just before dark, October 13, the first train of the RGP&N steamed into Pagosa Springs. True, it was only a work train, but it did have an engine, cars and a cracker box caboose. The inhabitants of Pagosa Springs were jubilant, even though regular train service was not inaugurated until nine days later.

Pagosa Springs was the first community in the D&RG sphere reached by any of the logging railroads that was not a lumber camp. The Pagosa Springs had for a long time been used by the Indians for their therapeutic properties and had become well known as a spa to the Americans. There was an important livestock industry, including haying, already active and some high altitude agriculture. The link-and-pin coupled cars, lettered either Pagosa Lumber Co. or P.L.Co. hauled the logs. D&RG power and other cars were used by the RGP&N. Four types of rail service were provided: passenger, freight, mail and express, and the log hauling. The RGP&N was classed as an interstate common carrier. (After 1904 Federal Law made it necessary for all equipment, including log cars, to be converted to semi-automatic couplers and automatic air brakes.)

Enthusiastically greeted by the residents of Pagosa Springs, within a year the RGP&N was being soundly cussed and criticized for its poor service (when available). Most of the complaints were justified, for Sullenberger was a logging and milling man and operated the RGP&N accordingly. The D&RG took over the RGP&N in 1906 but until the last train ran, complaints continued. Pagosa Lumber ceased all operations by April, 1917.

There was not much left for the Narrow Gauge to haul. Some small sawmills shipped a little lumber and there was some revenue from seasonal movements of cattle and sheep. There was a mail contract to contribute toward operating costs but there was never enough profit to allow providing the class of service Pagosa Springs wanted. Operations were continued essentially because Pagosa Springs was the county seat for Archuleta County and a strong political stronghold.

Finally, the 1929 Depression came. People did not have the money to go to the spa at Pagosa Springs. And, anyway they discovered they could throw a generous amount of Epsom salts in their hot bath water, and take a bit more internally to get the same results. Markets for lumber, cattle and sheep almost disappeared, and operation of the Pagosa Springs Branch became a losing game. The last operation was in 1935 and rails were removed in 1936 to end the most active and longest-lived of the Narrow Gauge lumber branches.

Too many old records have been destroyed; too many old-timers have passed on, as has too much time, to answer all the questions: Did the D&RG use the incorporators of the logging roads, or did those incorporators take advantage of the D&RG?; Was the D&RG the real owner of the four major logging branches, hiding behind the facade of the logging roads to evade operating as common carriers or did the loggers take the D&RG for the most expensive track material, the rails, to obtain rebates favorable to the lumbering enterprises?

It is anybody's answer and they have the privilege of changing their minds as desired. But the D&RG, later the D&RGW, did, in each case, end up publicly owning the Tierra Amarilla Southern Railroad; the Rio Grande & Southwestern Railroad and the Rio Grande, Pagosa & Northern. Formal declaration of ownership of the Rio Grande and Southwestern was held in abeyance until the very end by the D&RG operating it as a separate entity but strictly as a D&RG operation. The fourth, the railroad out of Dulce built by the Pagosa Lumber Company, was unquestionably not involved with the D&RG.

Whatever the answer, a lot of tall, virgin growth pines were felled, milled and transported. From logging road junctions with the Narrow Gauge, thousands of carloads of sweet, resinous smelling pine lumber moved to be hauled over Cumbres Pass to waiting markets.

It was a good time, a wild time and it swung to the music of the logger's cry—TIMBERRR!!!

Caboose No. 0578 was part of Nos. 0537-0580, all 17-foot long. The Rio Grande also had 30-foot cabooses. *Don Heimburger*

Chapter 13

Rio Grande steam

With the exception of some locomotives built by Grant and purchased in 1881 and 1882, the D&RG remained faithful to Baldwins on the Narrow Gauge. The first consolidateds came with the beginning of this century. It was also in 1900 that the first narrow gauge locomotive weighing over 72,000 pounds was used. The first *big* engines were the Class 125 (later K-27), Nos. 450 to 464, and they weighed 136,650 pounds.

It would require a book to list all the engines that worked on the Narrow Gauge—classification changes, number changes, dates purchased or retired, odd engines acquired second-hand and like information. In general, the Narrow Gauge fleet is best remembered as:

Class	Numbers	Tonnage on 4 per cent grade
C-16	268-278	79
C-19	340-345	92
C-18	315-319	106
C-21	360-361	113
K-27	450-464	183

In 1916, the D&RG bought three engines from the Crystal River Railroad—Nos. 430, 431, and 432. Engines 430 and 431 were renumbered as D&RGW Nos. 360 and 361; the 432 became D&RGW 375. The K-27 class was known on the Narrow Gauge as "Mudhens". They remained the biggest power used until the K-28 class, engines 470 to 479, were bought in 1923. For some reason, engine 375 could haul as much as the K-27 class engines, so she came to be called affectionately "The Little Mudhen."

Until the Rio Grande bought the 470's and 480's, plus producing the 490's in its own shops, there were no roadway restrictions that prevented any narrow gauge power from being worked on any district. Because of their greater hauling power, the K-27's were kept on assignments over the heavier grades. Repair and maintenance facilities, up to heavy shopping, were located at Chama and Durango. Alamosa could handle all types of work on engines. Power could be moved from district to district as demand required, although each chief dispatcher had a quasi-pool of engines assigned to him. He was given advance notice before an engine being used on his district was moved to another.

As a general rule, chief dispatchers operated patterns of power to the best advantage learned from experience. Engines working out of Alamosa usually turned at Chama; out of Durango, engines were turned at Chama or, if heavy work was needed, were traded for an east end engine at Chama and went through to Alamosa. The Chili Line, Silverton Branch and smaller branches came closer to having semi-permanent power assignments.

No. 471, a K-28 built in 1923 by Schenectady, swings on the turntable at Salida about 1940. Later in 1942, she and others saw service in Alaska during World War II on the White Pass & Yukon. All engines were later scrapped.

Engine No. 95 and her crew. No. 95 was built in 1880 as the *Embuda*. It was later sold to several companies, one being the Atlantic Coast Line RR. In later years it was converted to standard gauge.

LOCOMOTIVES—Narrow Gauge 1923

Numbers From–To	Class	Number Series	Number Total	Service	Size of Cylinders	Driver Diameter	Weight on Drivers	Weight on Trucks	Total Weight	Builder	Date Built	Interstate Commerce Classification
					in. in.	in.	lbs.	lbs.	lbs.			
166–168	47	3		Pass.	14x20	46	50,643	19,907	70,550	Baldwin	4—1883	OOOoo▷ C3
169–171	"	3		"	"	"	"	"	"	"	12—1883	" "
172–174	"	3		"	"	"	"	"	"	"	4—1884	" "
175–177	"	3	12	"	"	"	"	"	"	"	6—1884	" "
200–208	60	9		Freight	15x20	37	59,330	9,775	69,105	Grant	5—1881	OOOOo▷ B4
209–217	"	9		"	"	"	"	"	"	"	6—1881	" "
218–219	"	2		"	"	"	"	"	"	"	7—1881	" "
220–221	"	2		"	"	"	"	"	"	"	12—1881	" "
222	"	1		"	"	"	"	"	"	"	1—1882	" "
223	"	1		"	"	"	"	"	"	"	12—1881	" "
224–227	"	4		"	"	"	"	"	"	"	1—1882	" "
228	"	1		"	"	36¾	"	"	"	Baldwin	1877	" "
229	"	1		"	"	"	"	"	"	"	2—1880	" "
240–241	"	2		"	"	"	"	"	"	"	6—1881	" "
262–263	"	2		"	"	"	"	"	"	"	2—1882	" "
265–274	"	10		"	"	"	"	"	"	"	"	" "
276	"	1		"	"	"	"	"	"	"	3—1882	" "
278	"	1		"	"	"	"	"	"	"	"	" "
280–286	"	7	53	"	"	"	"	"	"	"	"	" "
400–401	70	2		"	16x20	"	64,000	10,260	74,260	"	5—1881	" "
403	"	1		"	"	"	"	"	"	"	"	" "
404–405	"	2		"	"	"	"	"	"	"	6—1881	" "
406–407	"	2		"	"	"	"	"	"	"	7—1881	" "
408	"	1		"	"	"	"	"	"	"	8—1881	" "
410–411	"	2		"	"	"	"	"	"	"	9—1881	" "
417–418	"	2		"	"	"	62,150	8,150	70,300	"	6—1887	" "
419	70	1		"	"	"	"	"	"	"	7—1887	" "
421–422	"	2	15	"	"	"	"	"	"	"	"	" "
424	72	1		"	"	38	64,000	8,000	72,000	"	1896	" "
425	"	1		"	"	"	"	"	"	"	7—1895	" "
426	"	1		"	"	"	"	"	"	"	2—1896	" "
427	"	1		"	"	"	"	"	"	"	10—1895	" "
428–429	"	2	6	"	"	"	"	"	"	"	3—1896	" "
430	93	1		"	17x20	"	85,650	10,000	95,650	"	6—1900	" "

LOCOMOTIVES—Narrow Gauge—Concluded

Numbers From	Numbers To	Class	Number Series	Number Total	Service	Size of Cylinders	Driver Diameter	Weight on Drivers	Weight on Trucks	Total Weight	Builder	Date Built	Interstate Commerce Classification
	431	93	1	2	Consol.	in. in. 17x20	in. 38	lbs. 85,650	lbs. 10,000	lbs. 95,650	Baldwin	5—1900	oOOOo▷ B4
	432	112	1	1	"	18x20	"	107,400	"	117,400	"	3—1903	" "
450–	464	125	15	15	Freight	17x22	40	105,425	E.T11,300 Tr. 19,925	136,650	"	4—1903	oOOOOo▷ E4
	554	71	1		Consol.	16x20	37	62,900	8,200	71,100	"	1884	OOOOo▷ B4
	555	"	1	2	"	"	"	"	"	"	"	7—1890	" "

RECAPITULATION

Class 47	12	Class 72	6
" 60	53	" 93	2
" 70	15	" 112	1
" 71	2	" 125	15
		Total	106

1923
ADDITIONAL LOCOMOTIVES (Six Months' Delivery)
Narrow Gauge

Numbers From To	Class	Number Series	Number Total	Service	Size of Cylinders	Driver Diameter	Weight on Drivers	Weight on Trucks	Total Weight	Builder	Date Built	Interstate Commerce Classification
470–479	140	10	10	Freight	in. in. 18x22	in. 44	lbs. 112,000	lbs. 28,000	lbs. 140,000	American	1923	oOOOOo E4

This K-37 was one of several K's converted from Class C-41 standard gauge engines. *John Krause/Dr. Richard Severance collection*

Narrow Gauge engine notes

(From an old faded, handwritten memo in D&RGW archives, unsigned and undated.)

The first engine ordered by the D&RG was built in England by Furness & Company. It never reached Denver. It was shipped from England on the same ship with the first consignment of rails. After the loco was unloaded at New Orleans, the newborn company had insufficient funds to prepay the freight on both shipments to Denver. The locomotive was sold at New Orleans to provide money to pay the freight on the rails.

Another English engine was the Mountaineer, No. 101. This was a double-ender having two boilers and one firebox with a side fire door. An English nobleman who visited Colorado in 1872 or 1873 was much taken by the new railroad and shipped the No. 101 to Palmer as a present. It was used mostly in work train service, expecially over La Veta Pass. Way it was built, whatever direction it was moving one of the two engines had to be in back motion.

Engines No. 1 and No. 4 were dismantled in 1888 and their boilers were taken to Salida and installed as the boilers for the heating plant of the D&RG hospital.

Engine 22 was renumbered as the 228 in 1894; engine 24 became the 41 the same year and a little later again renumbered to be the 229. Engine 25 became No. 42.

Engine 275, sold to the Rio Grande Western in 1886, was numbered RGW-1, and converted to standard gauge. When the RGW was consolidated with the D&RG it was renumbered as 553. In 1918, it was reconverted to narrow gauge and was renumbered 290.

Engines 287 and 288 were originally standard gauge San Pete Valley RR engines. Upon change of ownership, they were given the numbers 680 and 681. In 1918, after being converted to narrow gauge, they were given the numbers of 287 and 288 again. (The San Pete Valley RR was nicknamed and usually called the Polygamy Central.).

Engines 111 to 118 were obtained from the Utah & Pleasant Valley RR in Utah in 1883 and turned back to that line in 1884. When the RGW took over the U&PV these engines became RGW Nos. 2, 3, 4, 5, 6, 7, 8, and 9.

Engines 107, 108 and 109 were designed and built to burn anthracite coal which was mined near Crested Butte. They were not a success for they could not be kept hot.

Engines 166 to 177 were given wagon-top boilers in place of the original straight top boilers. They carried a steam pressure of 160 pounds with a tractive effort of 11,599. They were capable of speeds up to 60 mph.

Engines 430, 431 and 432 were purchased from the Crystal River RR Co. in 1916 (later known as Crystal River and San Juan RR). They were changed from standard gauge to narrow gauge at the Salida shops and renumbered. (Author's note—it is known that the 432 became the 375; the 431 became 361; and the 430 became 360.)

Engine 424 was bought from the Midland Terminal RR in 1920.

Engines 425 to 429, inclusive, were purchased from the Florence & Cripple Creek RR when that line was abandoned in 1917.

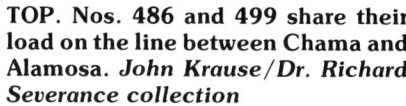

TOP. Nos. 486 and 499 share their load on the line between Chama and Alamosa. *John Krause/Dr. Richard Severance collection*

LEFT. No. 493, ex-1005, and No. 487, a K-36, are coupled together on the Rio Grande in August of 1965. *Chris Burritt*

NEXT TWO PAGES. Nos. 494 and 487 at Chama. *John Krause/Dr. Richard Severance collection*

TOP. No. 488 rests securely in the Alamosa roundhouse among tools and machines that can repair its workings. *Chris Burritt*

LEFT. Locomotives didn't always stay on the tracks. It's 8 a.m., March 27, 1952 and Engine No. 476 on the point of a train loaded with ore from Silverton hit ice and derailed into an outjutting rocky point. You can see the rails to the right of the locomotive in the snow.

Engine roster
January 1, 1940

LOCOMOTIVES

SERIES	SERVICE	ROAD CLASS	TYPE	M. P. CLASS	TOTAL EN-GINES	Diam. of Cyl.	Stroke	Steam Press.	Diam. of Drivers	Weight on Drivers	Total Weight Including Loaded Tender	Tractive Power	Coal Cap. (tons)	Tender Water Capacity (gal.)	Duplex D-1	Simplex B	Standard Modified Type B	Super-Heater	Power Reverse Gear	Elesco	Worth.	Elesco	Sellers	Syphon
01	S⊗		2-8-0		1	22	28	190 ♦	54	164,690	303,700	40,531	9	6,000										
50– 62	S	S-33	0-6-0	149	13	20	26	190	51	150,000	270,800	32,800 ‡	12	6,000					3.					
223–278	F	C-16	2-8-0	60 N.G.	4	15	20	160	36½	59,330	122,110	16,540	6	2,500										
315–319	F	C-18		72 N.G.	5	16	20	145⊗	38½	64,000	129,000	16,606	7	2 to 3,500										2.
340–346	F	C-19		70 N.G.	4	16	20	160	38½	64,000	127,260	19,947	6	2,500										1.
360–361	F	C-21		93 N.G.	2	17	20	160	38	85,650	160,950	20,686	5	2,900										
375	F	C-25		112 N.G.	1	18	20	170	38	107,400	181,400	24,641	6	3,000										1.
452–464	F	K-27	2-8-2	125 N.G.	10	17	22	200	40	105,425	219,950	27,000	8.5	4,100				9.						
470–479	P	K-28		148 N.G.	10	18	22	200	44	113,500	254,500	27,540	8	4,000				10.						
480–489	F	K-36		139 N.G.	10	20	24	195	44	143,850	286,600	36,200	9.5	4,000				10.						
490–499	F	K-37		– N.G.	10	20	24	200	44	143,280	307,250	37,100	9	4,000				10.						1.
605	S	C-26	2-8-0	120	1	20	24	160	50½	100,600	191,000	25,600	11	3,500										1.
633–688	S	C-28		113	6	20	24	160	50½	99,700	187,000	22,780x	9 to 10	3 to 4,500				2.						9.
760–781	P	T-31	4-6-0	184	2	21	26	200	63	145,000	331,400	30,940	15	5,000				15.						
782–789	P	T-29		184	15	21	26	200	67	145,000	332,600	29,093	15	5,000										
800–805	P	P-44	4-6-2	261	6	26	26	200	67	160,640	444,550	44,594	17	7,000				6.	6.			6.		6.
923	S	C-39	2-8-0	187	1	22	28	190	56	165,100	326,100	39,083	14	5,000										
930–934	S	C-40		199	5	21	30	200	57	177,200	310,000	39,500	14	5,000										3.
956	S	C-41		185	1	21	28	190	54	164,690	303,700	40,531	9	5,000					1.					
1000–1029		C-41		190	17	21	28	200	55	163,000	302,000	40,883	9	5,000				14.	6.	14.				3.
1131–1199	F & S	C-48		220	68	24	23	200	57	194,100	386,100	48,100	13	5,000				68.	10.	5⊗				21.
1200–1213	F & P	K-59	2-8-2	250	13	27	30	200	63	212,000	433,700	59,000	17	7½ to 8,600	10.	3.		13.	13.					1.
1400–1409		F-81	2-10-2	429	10	31	32	195	63	345,300	624,900	81,200	24	12,000	9.	1.		10.	10.	10.			9.	8.
1501–1510	F & P	M-67	4-8-2	377	10	28	30	210	63	257,500	654,600	65,640 †	25	13,000	10.			10.	10.			3.		10.
1511–1520	F & P	M-78		383 booster	10	28	30	210	63	266,700x	661,800	65,640 †	25	13,000	10.			10.	10.			2.		10.
1521–1530	F & P	M-67		378	10	28	30	210	63	266,700	656,200	65,640	25	13,000		10.		10.	10.			5.		10.
1600–1609	F	M-75		419 3 cyl.	10	25	23	210	67	290,530	710,310	74,970	25	13,000				10.	10.	6.	6.			
1700–1713	P	M-64	4-8-4		14	27	30	240	70	264,900	696,750	63,700	20	15,000		14.		14.	14.	14.				14.
1800–1804	P	M-68			5	26	30	235	73	279,172	873,360	67,200	26	12,000			5.	5.	5.	5⊗		9.		5.
3300–3307	F	L-62	2-6-6-2	340	8	20½x33	32	200	57	295,500	499,000	62,026	14	3,000				8.	8.					
3400–3415	F	L-95	2-8-8-2	458	16	26x40	32	200	57	394,000	639,000	95,000	20	9,000	10.	6.		16.	10.			11.		15. x
3500–3509	F	L-107		532	10	25x39	32	240	57	481,000	748,000	107,374	18	12,000	10.			10.	10.	10.				
3600–3609	F	L-131			10	26x26	32	240	63	559,500	992,500	131,800	30	25,000		10.		10.	10.	10.				10. x
3610–3619	F	L-132			10	26x26	32	240	63	572,000	1,008,500	131,800	30	25,000		10.		10.	10.	10.				10.
3700–3709	F	L-105	4-6-6-4		10	23	32	255	70	437,939	1,035,900	105,000	26	20,000			10.	10.	10.	9.	1.			10.
Totals					338										69.	54.	15.	290.	172.	63.	6.	23.	20.	137.

⊗ Shop Switch

⊗ = 315
♦ = 160
• = 60–62
• = 180

x or 25600
† with booster = 78907
‡ = 60–62 = 31200

x with booster = 330,500

x = 3606 = Circulator
x = 3405 = Circulator

⊗ = Coil Type.

173

TOP. A string of Rio Grande locomotives steam at Chama. BELOW. No. 495 and 498 at Chama. *Both photos, John Krause/Dr. Richard Severance collection*

1955
STEAM LOCOMOTIVES

SERIES	SERVICE	ROAD CLASS	TYPE	M.P. CLASS	TOTAL LOCO'S.	Diam. of Cyl.	Stroke	Steam Pres.	Diam. of Drivers	Weight on Drivers	Total Weight Including Loaded Tender	Tractive Effort	Coal Cap. (tons)	Tender Water Capacity (gal.)	STOKERS Duplex D-1	STOKERS Simplex B	STOKERS Standard Modified B or MB-1	Super- Heater	Elesco F.W. Heater	EXHAUST STEAM INJECTORS Elesco	EXHAUST STEAM INJECTORS Sellers	Syphon	Circu- lator	Year Built
268	F	C-16	2-8-0	60 N. G.	1	15	20	160	36¾	59,335	122,110	16,540	6	2,500										1882
463, 464	F	K-27		125 N. G.	2	17	22	200	40	108,300	223,550	27,000	8.5	4,100				2.						1903
473-478	P	K-28	2-8-2	148 N. G.	3	18	22	200	44	113,500	254,500	27,540	8	5,000				3.						1923
480-489	F	K-36		189 N. G.	9	20	24	195	44	143,850	286,600	36,200	9.5	5,000				9.						1925
490-499	F	K-37		– N. G.	9	20	24	200	44	148,280	307,250	37,100	9	6,000				9.				1.		1928-30
1034, 1035	F, P, & S	C-43	2-8-0		2	22	28	210	55	195,000	376,000	43,980	15	8,000			2.	2.				2.		1910
1134-1199	F & S	C-48		220	30	24	28	200	57	194,100	386,100	48,100	18	8,000			14	30.				14		1906 -8
1202-1209	F & P	K-59		280	3	27	30	200	63	212,000	444,700♦	59,000	17x	83 to 9,000x	3.			3.		1.	2.	1	1.	1913
1224	F & S	K-63	2-8-2		1	28	30	200	55	232,000	473,000	62,700	17	8,736	1.			1.		1.‡		1.		1915
1229	F	K-63			1	26	30	200	55	232,000	470,000	62,700	17	9,000			1♦	1.		1.‡		1.		1916
1400-1407	F	F-81	2-10-2	429	6	31	32	195	63	353,700	724,880	81,200	23	16,000	6.			6.	6.			5.	1.	1917
1509	F & P	M-67		377	1	28	30	210	63	257,500	654,600	66,640	25	14,000	1			1.	1			1.		1922
1519	F & P	M-67	4-8-2		1	28	30	210	63	266,700	661,800	66,640	25	14,000	1.			1.				1.		1923
1526-1529	F & P	M-67		378	3	28	30	210	63	266,700	656,200	66,640	25	14,000	3.			3.		2.		2.	1.	1923
1700-1713	P	M-64	4-8-4		4	27	30	240	70	264,900	696,750	63,700	20	14,000		4.		4.	4.			4		1929
3600-3609	F	L-131	2-8-8-2		10	26	32	240	63	559,500	992,500	131,800	30	18,000		10.		10.	10.			9.	1.	1930
3610-3619	F	L-132			10	26	32	240	63	572,000	1,008,500	131,800	30	18,000		10.		10.	10			10.		1930
3700, 3708	F	L-105	4-6-6-4		2	23	32	255	70	437,939	1,035,900	105,000	26	20,000			2.	2.	2.	3.		2.		1938
3710-3712	P	L-105			3	23	32	255	70	435,472	1,035,330	105,000	26	20,000								3		1941
					101										14	24.	22.	100	34.	7.	2.	57	4.	

♦=1202 =537,400 x=1202 =20 x=1202 =13,000 ♦=Type E ‡=Coffin. □ Coil type.

1968
STEAM LOCOMOTIVES
(NARROW GAUGE)

SERIES	TYPE	SERVICE	ROAD CLASS	MOTIVE POWER CLASS	TOTAL LOCO'S.	YEAR BUILT
473, 476, 478	2-8-2	Passenger	K-28	148	3	1923
480-489	2-8-2	Freight	K-36	189	6	1925
491-499	2-8-2	Freight	K-37		5	1928-30
					14	

SERIES	DIAMETER OF CYLINDER	STROKE	STEAM PRESSURE	SUPERHEATER	SYPHONS	TOTAL HEATING SURFACE SQ. FT.
473, 476, 478	18	22	200	3	0	1,600
480-489	20	24	195	6	0	2,118
491-499	20	24	200	5	1	2,159

SERIES	DIAMETER OF DRIVERS	WEIGHT ON DRIVERS	WEIGHT OF LOCO.	TRACTIVE EFFORT	WEIGHT OF TENDER (LOADED)	TOTAL WEIGHT INCLUDING LOADED TENDER	TENDER WATER CAPACITY (GALLONS)	COAL CAPACITY (TONS)
473, 476, 478	44	113,500	156,000	27,540	98,500	254,500	5,000	8
480-489	44	143,850	187,100	36,200	99,500	286,600	5,000	9.5
491-499	44	148,280	187,250	37,100	120,000	307,250	6,000	9

PRECEDING PAGE. Two K-37's and K-36 (No. 486) rest quietly at the roundhouse. **ABOVE.** A Schenectady-built K-28 is waiting to go against No. 115, the *San Juan* on July 4, 1941. *R.W. Richardson/Colorado RR Museum*

Engines 450 to 464 were built as Vauclain compounds by Baldwin and had fantail tanks. In operation during cold weather it was found signals could not be seen because of clouds of steam around the engines. They were converted to simple engines by the D&RG. (Engine 451 lost her original boiler in an explosion and received a new one.)

Engines 490 to 499 were built at D&RGW Burnham shops from standard gauge engines, class 190. These were Baldwin built in 1902. (See author's notes later.)

There were two engines numbered 71. The second 71 was obtained from the Santa Fe Southern. What became of the first 71 is not known. Neither is there much information about the second. (Author's note—the second 71 was obtained from the Texas, Santa Fe and Northern, or the Santa Fe Southern as the TS&N was later named in the course of some corporate changes. It was TS&N Engine 3, named the *General Meily*. The abbreviation of the Texas Santa Fe & Northern is found as TS&N and TSF&N. The first 71 was *Pacific Slope* sold to the D&RGW Ry. in 1886 and subsequently other lines, including the RGS.)

From the beginning to end a total of slightly more than 300 locomotives saw service on the narrow gauge lines.

AUTHOR'S NOTES

Engine 168 was presented to Colorado Springs when retired.

Engine 169 was sent as an exhibit to the New York World's Fair, 1940 and 1941, upon return was presented to Alamosa.

Engine 223 was presented to Salt Lake City.

Engine 268 was donated to Gunnison and 278 to Montrose.

Upon retirement, 485 was presented to Salida and 486 to Canon City.

Engine No. 6 was sold to the Denver Circle Ry. and in turn sold to the short-lived Colorado Eastern. Engine No. 6 was finally dismantled in the Union Pacific shops at Denver. Date unknown.

Engine 268 was a movie queen and went to the Chicago World's Fair in the summer of 1949. While there she powered a passenger train that earned the highest per-train-mile revenue in the history of railroading. A total of 606,901

Nos. 490, 492 and 488 waiting for orders in May of 1955.
John Krause/Dr. Richard Severance collection

In August, 1965, Chris Burritt shot 487 in the Alamosa roundhouse, with snowplow attached, ready for the winter white stuff.

No. 486, a K-36, was retired in 1962.

No. 492 bides her time in front of the coal tipple at Chama, New Mexico before being called to work. *Chris Burritt*

passengers paid a dime each to ride the half-mile long railroad that was a replica of the approach to and of the Moffat Tunnel.

Engine 432, obtained from the Crystal River, was without doubt, at the beginning, the poorest steamer ever on the D&RGW. She simply killed firemen trying to make her steam. Then, one time on a trip going up Marshall Pass, fireman Gilbert Lathrop, all tuckered out, just dumped a few scoops of coal barely through the fire-door. A few minutes later the 432 rammed her needle over against the peg and started popping off. And that was the secret—she did not want coal heaved in each corner and one in the middle like other engines but just a supply in front of the door. The 432 was later given the number of 375 and became a favorite of all firemen and was called "The Little Mudhen" because she would haul as much as one of the 450's, the Mudhens.

Another story told of the 375 which cannot be authenticated from the records is that, either as the 432 or 375, she was loaned or leased to Mears and used on his Silverton lines. According to the story, during that period she was given a superheater modification by Mears' master mechanic, a man named John C. Woods, who later worked for the D&RG at Chama as a machinist. The 375 was dismantled in 1949.

There has been considerable confusion about the K-37 class engines, Nos. 490 to 499, inclusive. The Rio Grande records have contributed some to this as they show the K-37s rebuilt by D&RGW from C-41 class engines Nos. 1003-1005, 1009, 1014, 1020, 1021, 1023, 1025, and 1026. D&RGW obtained from Baldwin in 1913 engines 1001 to 1006, inclusive. Then engines 1050 to 1057 had been received from American in 1909 and Nos. 1060 to 1075 from Baldwin in 1913. The engines used in the conversion listed as 1009 to 1026 must have been some of the Class 190, Nos. 1101 to 1130, obtained from Baldwin in 1902 and renumbered. (Engines 490 to 495 rebuilt in 1928; engines 496 to 499 in 1930.)

Engine 1130 was renumbered as the 1000 and assigned to the San Luis Valley where she hauled so much produce, livestock, ore and lumber during her years of service she was called the "Billion Dollar Engine." Engine 1000 was always a reliable engine and would steam all day on a few scoops of coal.

Another engine donated upon retirement to a city was the 315 which was given to Durango.

Check *Locomotives of the Rio Grande* by the Colorado RR Museum for more details of steam locomotives.

(All of above listings of numbers from and to, are inclusive.)

Nos. 493 and 487 are both 2-8-2's, the 487 a K-36, the 493 a K-37. *Chris Burritt*

This Baldwin 2-8-0 started life as *Grand River* No. 401 and later was renumbered to #803, then #405, then #345. *Clayton Tanner*

Engine #268 was built by Baldwin in 1882. Its original Class was 60, but was later changed to C-16. After serving branchlines because of its light weight, No. 268 was sent to the Chicago World's Fair where it pulled passenger trains under the orange and silver with black striping livery. When it was returned, it retained its lively paint scheme.

No. 268 was the last of its class in active D&RGW service. The locomotive hauled the last revenue train west of Gunnison. *Photo by H. Bender from C.T. Felstead collection*

PREVIOUS PAGE. No. 4700N works the Silverton branch without a freight consist on this day. *John Krause/Dr. Richard Severance collection.*

ABOVE. No. 50 had the Durango yard assignment; it was acquired to save maintenance expenses. It was built by the Davenport Locomotive Works. *A.M. Payne*

Engine No. 318 was built by Baldwin and put in service in 1896. It was re-built in 1917. Class C-18. *Photo by J. Ehrenberger, taken in 1956, from C.T. Felstead collection*

186

Engine No. 340 was built by Baldwin and placed in service in July, 1881. Class C-19. Photo by R.M. Hanft taken in 1950 from C.T. Felstead collection

Engine No. 343 was in service July, 1881, Baldwin-built. Class C-19. Photo by R. Collins, taken August, 1939 from C.T. Felstead collection

Engine No. 346, the *Cumbres* was sold to the Montezuma Lumber Co., then Robert Richardson, then the Colorado Railroad Museum where it now rests.

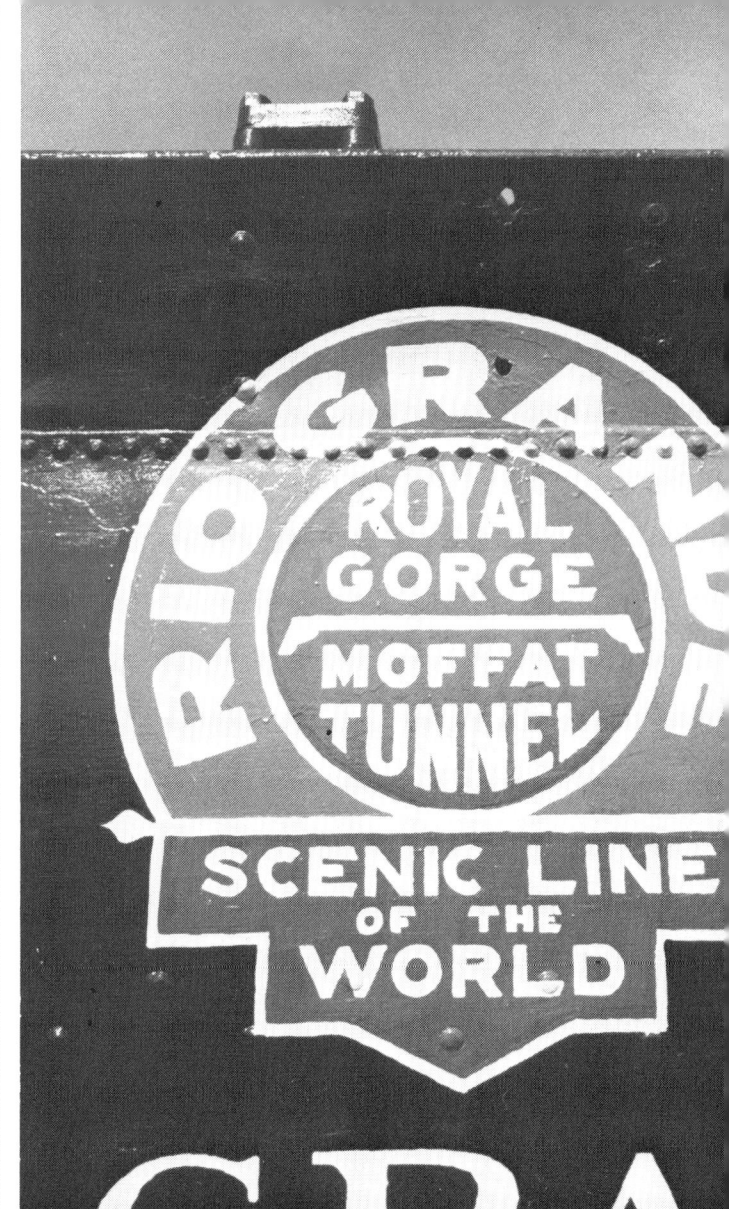

No. 346 preserved

All photos by Don Heimburger

Engine 346 started life in 1881 as No. 406. It was one of a dozen Class 70 consolidations which the railroad used on its main line over the Continental Divide and Marshall Pass. In 1903 the locomotive was assigned to Durango as a switcher and then went to helper service on Cumbres Pass. Later, the engine replaced one on the Montezuma Lumber Co. line, the last lumber railroad in Colorado. The #346 now rests at the Colorado Railroad Museum where it is occasionally fired up.

Engine No. 453, a Baldwin, was part of the "Mudhen" fleet of engines Nos. 450 to 464. They were originally built as Vauclain compounds, but were converted to simple engines by the Rio Grande because of difficulty of seeing signals in cold weather due to steam vapor. *Photo by C. Ulrich from C.T. Felstead collection*

Engine No. 461, in service in 1903, built by Baldwin. The Class K-27's, 2-8-2's, were another of the Mudhens. *Photo by R. Trepton, taken in August, 1940, from C.T. Felstead collection*

Engine No. 471, a 2-8-2 of the Class K-28 (sport models). This locomotive went to Alaska during World War II to serve the narrow gauge lines there. *Photo by A. Hale, taken August, 1939, from C.T. Felstead collection*

Engine No. 476, an American Locomotive product, was built and placed in service in October of 1923. It's a 2-8-2 of the Class K-28 and part of a 10-engine order; seven went to Alaska for service with the Army during WWII; three engines—Nos. 473, 476 and 478—stayed at home on the D&RGW. Affectionately known as sport models. *Photo by R.H. Kennedy taken July 13, 1947 from C.T. Felstead collection*.

Engine No. 481, Baldwin, in service in September, 1925. Class K-36. Sometimes these were mistakenly called sport models but on the Rio Grande only the K-28's were given this designation. This was really a beautiful locomotive and most efficient — it could pull plenty of freight tonnage or very capably handle passenger trains. They were the fireboy's pets. *Photo by H. Bender from C.T. Felstead collection*

Engine No. 482, Baldwin, Class K-36. This locomotive was retired in 1962 and was delivered to the Cumbres and Toltec Scenic RR in 1970. *Photo by C.T. Felstead*

Engine No. 491 was rebuilt by the Rio Grande to narrow gauge proportions from standard gauge Class C-41 engines Nos. 1003-1005, 1009, 1014, 1020, 1021, 1023, 1025 and 1026. Engines 490-495 were placed in service in 1928. Engines 496-499 were in service in 1930. Tractive effort was 37,1000 compared with K-36's tractive effort of 36,200. The K-37's were never the success hoped for. *Photo by H. Bender from C.T. Felstead collection*

Engine No. 493, Class K-37, rebuilt from standard gauge C-41's. *Photo by H. Bender from C.T. Felstead collection*

Engine No. 496, Class K-37, 2-8-2. *Photo by R. Trepton, taken August 1940, from C.T. Felstead collection*

Chapter 14

The *San Juan*

Occasionally some writer or story teller gets carried away about the last of the scheduled narrow gauge passenger trains and mentions the "San Juan Express". There never was such a train.

But the *San Juan,* a proud pair of trains, did exist. They did not require the pseudo glamor attached to an "Express". They had all they needed without being gilded. Right up to discontinuance of passenger service between Alamosa and Durango, February 1, 1951, they held onto their style, elan and exclusiveness. They were the only luxury pair of narrow gauge passenger trains. They quit running, not as anachronisms, but as still glamorous, paint and brass bright and still serving the best T-bone steak with all the fixings.

The *San Juan* belonged. Their forebears were born to and grew with the Narrow Gauge. The last of the line, they were more than worthy of all that had gone into the making. In a country even at a late date still essentially primitive and for many miles otherwise inaccessible, they blended and fit in.

In 1947, when the *San Juans* were then 10 years old, *Holiday Magazine* published "Narrow Gauge Holiday" written by Lucius Beebe. He correctly used the name *San Juan* and stated "...on the next track stood one of the most beautiful trains you had ever seen and, on second glance, one of the smallest."

The old maestro is off to a good start on his favorite subject, railroads and trains, so we may as well let him have his say about the *San Juan:*

> "Right out of the '70's, too, is the equipment of the *San Juan,* gleaming, immaculate and wonderfully maintained, from the pilot beam of its diminutive but powerful locomotive to the brass rail of the observation platform. It is one

The *San Juan* on July 2, 1941, powered by Engine No. 477 with four cars at 15 miles an hour is at the highway crossing just west of Cresco and the Colorado-New Mexico line. *Richard Kindig*

Here the *San Juan* is eastbound (Train No. 116) with Engine No. 476 and a standard operating consist. The date is September 16, 1948 and the place is the Carracas-Arboles area which is about midway between Chama and Durango. *R.W. Richardson/Colorado RR Museum*

of the most beautiful trains in the world. Usually its 'consist', as trainmen call it, includes a railway-post-office car, a mail and baggage car, two day coaches and a combination parlor-observation-lounge and dining car at the rear.

"The cars are dark green and gold, and the chair car is a minuscule version of all train luxury in a single unit, its walls paneled with white birch, its lighting fixtures plated with silver from Colorado's own mines. Only its tiny kitchen where the venerable steward-chef prepares your meals is the last work in metal modernity, with electric stove and ice boxes as spotless as those of the *Super Chief*."

Aye...the sister *San Juans* were all that and more. In them the wonders and richness of the Narrow Gauge came to fruition, all that the General had ever dreamed of for "his little railroad."

Behind the *San Juan* sister trains was a long line of ancestors that carried people and their gear into a new and developing frontier. Trains of "varnish", always for the times, the best to be had, carrying rich and poor, the serious and the frivolous, the illiterate and the pedant, trains that gave no thought to segregation of race, color or creed. The only separation being whether you rode chair car or parlor car. Money was the determining factor—if you had just sold a gold mine or herd, you could ride the parlor car without first getting rid of your mining clothes or the smell of sheep.

SILVER PALACES

From the beginning, when the schedules were night time ones, narrow gauge passenger trains carried sleeping cars leaving Alamosa, Silverton and Durango. Legend would have it that Pullman's Silver Palaces originated to accommodate the newly-rich silver kings commuting between Silverton and Denver. The ornateness and lavish fittings did develop here, but the sleeping car, as such, did not.

This shows the front cover of a 1913 compilation of passenger schedules used by the Denver & Rio Grande passenger traffic department. *Colorado State Historical Society*

The eastbound *San Juan* (Train No. 116) and Engine No. 478 with its regular consist of cars. The head coach was given the "Rio Grande Gold" paint treatment in this October 21, 1950 photo. *R.W. Richardson/Colorado RR Museum*

The Cumbres Horseshoe shows a passenger train — perhaps a special — with three cabooses in the consist. *John Krause/Dr. Richard Severance collection*

Train No. 115, the westbound *San Juan*, approaches the east switch at Coxo, a distance of 80.49 miles from Alamosa and just the other side of Cumbres. *R.W. Richardson/Colorado RR Museum*

Lt. John Gregory Bourke, a soldier-ethnologist, described a trip from Santa Fe to Antonito, thence to Durango in 1881 (the Narrow Gauge had only recently reached Durango). He wrote: "The train from Denver was at least an hour late. It had attached to it, a Pullman in which I secured a seat, much to my delight. Leaving Antonito, our course was upgrade, cutting first through a basalt formation and then through one of drift, winding up a wonderful series of curves through and around ranges of great height, but of gently sloping contour."

He mentions that he saw the lights come on in Chama as the train approached, and arrived Durango at 1:30 a.m. in the morning of October 4, 1881. There was no bugler to blow reveille so he stayed sleeping in his Pullman berth until 7:00 a.m. One comment he made on this 1881 trip was to be repeated many times in future years: "Many of the 'bits' of landscape on this road would make the fame and fortune of the artist who could reproduce them."

Of course, passenger cars were not always first class or properly maintained. There was the story of the well-known traveling man, enroute Denver to Santa Fe, who heard it was raining steadily on the Chili Line. He wired ahead to the Alamosa ticket agent: "Please have an umbrella waiting for me at Antonito. I want to stay dry from there to Santa Fe."

Prior to 1910 there may have been some named Narrow Gauge passenger trains but the first one most likely showed in 1910 when a pair of trains appear on the public timetable as *San Juan* and *New Mexico Express*. Later, in 1917, the designation was changed to *Colorado-New Mexico Express*.

This pair of trains remained on the public timetable without a name change through the Great Depression. But toward the end of this period the equipment, hardly changed from the days of Lieutenant Bourke, was deteriorating. Management started a refurbishing program that cost $79,526 before it was completed.

The project was finished in 1937 and the *San Juan* sister trains were unveiled for service between Alamosa and Durango (another train named the *Shavano* was put on the Salida-Gunnison run. When discontinued the equipment was used as *San Juan* standby.)

There should have been bells ringing, salutes firing and champagne popping to commemorate the occasion. But the Rio Grande put them in service without fanfare except for schedule renumbering. From Denver to Pueblo the train was No. 15; Pueblo to Alamosa, No. 115, and Alamosa to Durango, No. 215. Eastward the numbers were No. 216, No. 116 and No. 16. At the top of the schedule column between Alamosa and Durango, appearing with the train number in bold black type was *The San Juan*. And a low key announcement was in the new public timetable:

RIO GRANDE NARROW GAGE LINES
Longest Narrow Gage System in U.S.
And narrow gage trains are modern trains. The *Shavano* on the Salida-Gunnison run, and the *San Juan*, operating between Alamosa and Durango, are modern vestibuled trains, steam heated and equipped with 110-volt current. Smartly appointed are the coaches and lounges.

Engine No. 463 leads a mixed freight between Durango and Silverton in this John Krause photo. *Dr. Richard Severance collection*

Baker's Park (Silverton) is a beautiful spot for the end point of a steam train ride. Note the *Silver Vista* at the rear of this train. *John Krause/Dr. Richard Severance collection*

A mixed train on the Silverton Line with a combination of box cars, a caboose, dark green and also gold and silver passenger cars is led by Engine No. 478, a 2-8-2, Class K-28. *John Krause/Dr. Richard Severance collection*

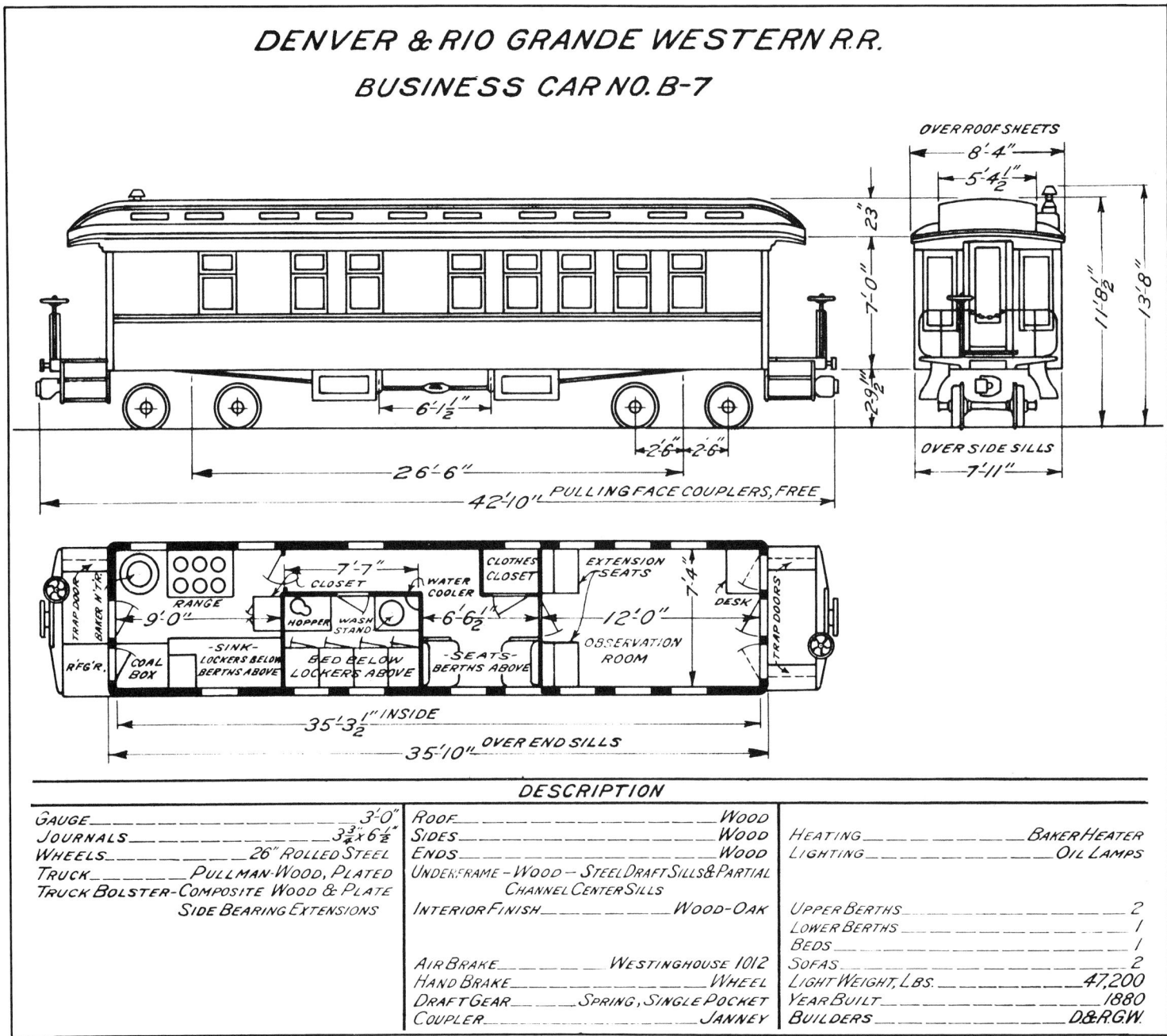

In fact, no globe-trotter can claim he has been everywhere until he has traveled over the Rio Grande's narrow gage system.

The schedules between Alamosa and Durango were such as to permit passengers to have daylight through the most scenic part of the 200-mile trip. The schedule time of nine hours was not bad considering grades and curvatures.

Although most people liked it, one doctor in Alamosa did not approve of the arrival time from Denver and the whistle blowing of the arriving engine. His gripe was that his sleeping pattern had been disrupted because too many of his patients, awakened by the early arriving train, could not go back to sleep. With time on their hands they did what came naturally and, the doctor swore, all the babies he delivered came into the world as No. 115 whistled for Alamosa.

No. 216 was due to stop at the Alamosa station at 8:30 p.m. It whistled for the State Street crossing at 8:29 p.m. Residents depended on this whistle to check their watches before retiring. They would admit their watches or clocks might be wrong, but only an act of God could keep the *San Juan* from whistling for State Street at 8:29 p.m.

Who rode these little gems with their bright new wood and metal works, and modern comforts? If you are conversant with railroad passenger train history you have already guessed the answer.

The clientele did not change. The same passengers who had patronized the old *Colorado-New Mexico Express* rode the *San Juan,* and unfortunately their numbers did not increase. Granted the Rio Grande did an extremely poor job of advertising the new trains; still you cannot deny plain economic and historical facts.

The country had just emerged from a great depression and few people had money to spend on the luxury of traveling for pleasure, especially in the Narrow Gauge world where the major portion of the population did not even own an automobile. People rode the *San Juan* because they wanted to travel from one place to another, and it was the only logical means. The highway system along or approaching the

At Gunnison we see #0524 caboose, #280 coach and #126 baggage-REA car. *R.W. Richardson/Colorado RR Museum*

DENVER & RIO GRANDE WESTERN RAILROAD
NARROW GAUGE - MAIN LINE
THE SAN JUAN

Courtesy Rocky Mountain RR Club

	WESTBOUND		STATIONS		EASTBOUND	
Photo stops	PASSENGER SCHEDULE	Mile Posts		Elev.	PASSENGER SCHEDULE	Photo stops
	Lv. 8:00 AM	252	ALAMOSA	7546	Ar. 5:45 PM	
	8:30	266	LA JARA	7609	5:15	
*	9:10	280	ANTONITO	7888	4:45	
#	9:55	291	LAVA	8468	4:20	
	10:30	300	BIG HORN WYE	9022	4:00	#
*	11:25	316	TOLTEC GORGE	9595	3:00	
#	11:45 AM	320	CASCADE TRESTLE	9637	2:45	
#	12:30 PM	330	CUMBRES	10015	2:15	#2
	12:35	332	COXO	9753	2:10	
	12:50	340	LOBATO	8303	1:20	
*	Ar. 1:00	344	CHAMA	7863	Lv. 1:00	*
	Lv. 1:20	344	CHAMA	7863	Ar. 12:45	
	1:40	354.5	CONTINENTAL DIVIDE	7733	12:15 PM	
	2:00	363	MONERO	7252	11:50 AM	
	2:20	370	LUMBERTON	6856	11:30	
	3:20	390	GATO (PAGOSA JCT.)	6271	10:15	
#	4:20	404	ARBOLES	6013	9:30	#
	5:00	419	LA BOCA	6177	8:40	
	5:20	426	IGNACIO	6437	8:20	
	5:35	433	OXFORD	6611	8:00	
	5:50	437	FLORIDA	6717	7:45	
	6:20	449	CARBON JCT. (Farmington Branch)	6425	7:10	
	Ar. 6:30 PM	452	DURANGO	6520	Lv. 7:00 AM	
			(Overnight stop)			
	Lv. 8:00 AM	452	DURANGO	6520	Ar. 6:00 PM	
	8:45	463	HERMOSA	6645	5:00	
#1	9:30	469	ROCKWOOD	7367	4:30	
#	9:50	470	ANIMAS GORGE	7350	4:25	
	10:05	472	TACOMA	7350	4:15	
	10:25	475	CASCADE TANK	7600	4:00	#
*	11:05	484	NEEDLETON TANK	8293	3:30	
#	11:45 AM	491	ELK PARK	8883	3:00	
	Ar. 12:30 PM	497	SILVERTON	9300	Lv. 2:30 PM	

The train will be double-headed between Durango and Silverton (except over trestles), and between Chama and Cumbres.

SYMBOLS: * indicates standing photo stop. # indicates train will back up and return for photos.

#1---On curve beyond the Animas Gorge "Shelf Line."
#2---Below "Windy Point", near the summit of Cumbres Pass.

PHOTO STOP RULES

You are asked to conform to the following rules at photo stops:

1. Use care to avoid walking in front of persons about to photograph the locomotive or train.

2. At moving photo stops, a line of photographers is to be formed at the location most beneficial to all. PLEASE do not take a position in front of this line.

3. Passengers not taking photos, who disembark from the train at photo stops, are asked to remain behind the line of photographers.

4. To avoid unnecessary delay, kindly board the train immediately upon the completion of each photo stop.

A Rocky Mountain Railroad Club special slips around the upper loop of Tanglefoot Curve just east of Cumbres on May 29, 1965. No. 483 is almost to the east switch of Cumbres. *Richard Kindig*

railroad consisted of dirt roads; at best gravel-surfaced. In the spring, mud made them impassable. In the winter they were blocked by snow, and during the balance of the year they were rough, hot and dusty.

Thus, the clientele of the *San Juan* continued to be mainly the natives such as New Mexicans, Indians, some Anglos, miners, sawmill workers and sheepherders. During the summer, fishermen rode No. 215 from Alamosa to fishing waters on Cumbres and returned in the afternoon on No. 216.

On the lounge-dinette car, the patron mix was a little different. The patrons were traveling salesmen, cattle and sheep owners, sawmill operators, mine owners, railroad officials, school teachers on a junket and those travelers with a little spare cash used to the better things of life. Passenger revenue did not support the train and it was only the existence of a favorable mail contract that the *San Juan* lasted as it did.

The facts behind the demise of the *San Juan* sisters are sometimes a bit more obscure. The answer lies in the accumulative facts of economic and historical circumstances. When WWII was over many people had money and a yen to travel and relax. As quickly as it became available they spent their money on an automobile. Having this conveyance, they wanted to see a lot of places fast—speed, speed, and more speed—and a nine hour journey to travel only 200 miles did not answer their wants.

Passenger Train Memories

Veteran conductor Alva Lyons helps unload passengers from the *San Juan* sometime in the late 1940's.

Among memories of riding on the Narrow Gauge varnish was one that was missing on the *San Juan*. It was a novelty that should not have been taken away. That was the newsbutch. Those who earlier had patronized the *Colorado-New Mexico Express* missed him. The spit-and-polish, well-served meals of the *San Juan's* diner-lounge, and the availability of iced drinks could not take the place of the sandwiches, fruit, cookies and candies displayed for sale on the two forward seats of the coach where the newsbutch set up his business.

You were awfully close to heaven when you climbed on the *Colorado-New Mexico Express* at a way station with a few dimes and quarters in your pocket to spend on a big, bright yellow banana, an orange twice as big as your fist, and a boiled-ham sandwich with almost enough meat in it to see.

Years later you would remember that the banana was often overripe and that sometimes concealed in it was a cinder that played hob with your bad tooth when you bit down. When peeled, the great, beautiful orange was no bigger than those bought in any store for two bits a dozen.

And you recalled the envy in your heart when you watched and listened to the whispered sales pitch of the newsbutch peddling a set of those naughty French postcards. Or the feeling of being part of a conspiracy as he gave a Mexican dandy or reservation Indian a story, sotto voce, of the "hot" five-carat diamond mounted in solid gold he was trying to dispose of for a pal of his who had sticky fingers. Believe it or not, he sold enough each trip to require visiting Woolworth's regularly to replenish his supply. He bought these choice diamond and gold rings for fifty cents each.

Yes, management made a mistake when it did not keep the newsbutch on the *San Juan*. With him went a little bit of tradition that, even though the new trains were an effort to improve and became part of the Narrow Gauge, left a void.

With the new schedule, the *San Juan* left Alamosa at 7 a.m., and an hour and five minutes later was leaving the San Luis Valley at Antonito to start its climb to Cumbres, 50.3

Later, another group would appear which promised a turn for the better for the *San Juans*—steam railroad buffs. But, in modernizing, the Rio Grande had gone too far. The vestibules and sealed windows eliminated the cinders and smell of coal smoke that were part of riding a steam train. The insulated walls and rugs on the floor muffled the sound of the steam whistle and the clickety-clack of wheels passing over rail joints. Found only on a steam train, these "inconveniences" were, to rail buffs, sensuous pleasures.

211

A doubleheaded special, with passenger cars and cabooses, makes its way between Chama and Alamosa. *John Krause/Dr. Richard Severance collection*

miles west. It departed Chama at 11:15 a.m., and the sister *San Juan* left Durango at the same time. They met at Carracas. No. 215 arrived Durango at 4:05 p.m.; No. 216 reached Alamosa at 8:30.

The westbound trip was considered the scenic part of the round trip and the "oh's" and "ah's" began about 8:30 a.m. as the west switch and water tank at Lava were passed. The track layout at Lava was in a large loop that served as a "balloon" track on which trains or engines could be turned if for any reason they were not to continue westward. Leaving Lava, for the next 10 minutes the train moved through a series of cuts to maintain grade and climb to the next level of the escarpment. During the original building of the line, blocks of this lava material were used to build the depot at Antonito. In the winter, snow drifted them full and the cuts were tough to get through—they sometimes stalled even a rotary snowplow.

For those choosing to do their scenic viewing of the mountains the easy way, fall was the preferred season and riding the *San Juan* the preferred mode. From the moment the train started around the Lava Loop, the travelers were awestricken by what they saw. For across the San Luis Valley stood Mount Blanca crested with an early snowfall and the Sangre de Cristo Range flowing south from the high peak. Sometimes this range was also tipped with the early snow. And the immense dead sea bottom of the Valley stretched away, mile after mile.

At the south end of the Valley was the moonscape of lava flows and the rounded cones of the extinct volcanoes from which the lava came. The major ones were San Antone Peak, Ute and Kettle Mountains. When the upper escarp-

The kerosene lamps in the Rio Grande's passenger cars were silver plated.

The interior of a Rio Grande passenger coach, taken August 12, 1950. *Clayton Tanner*

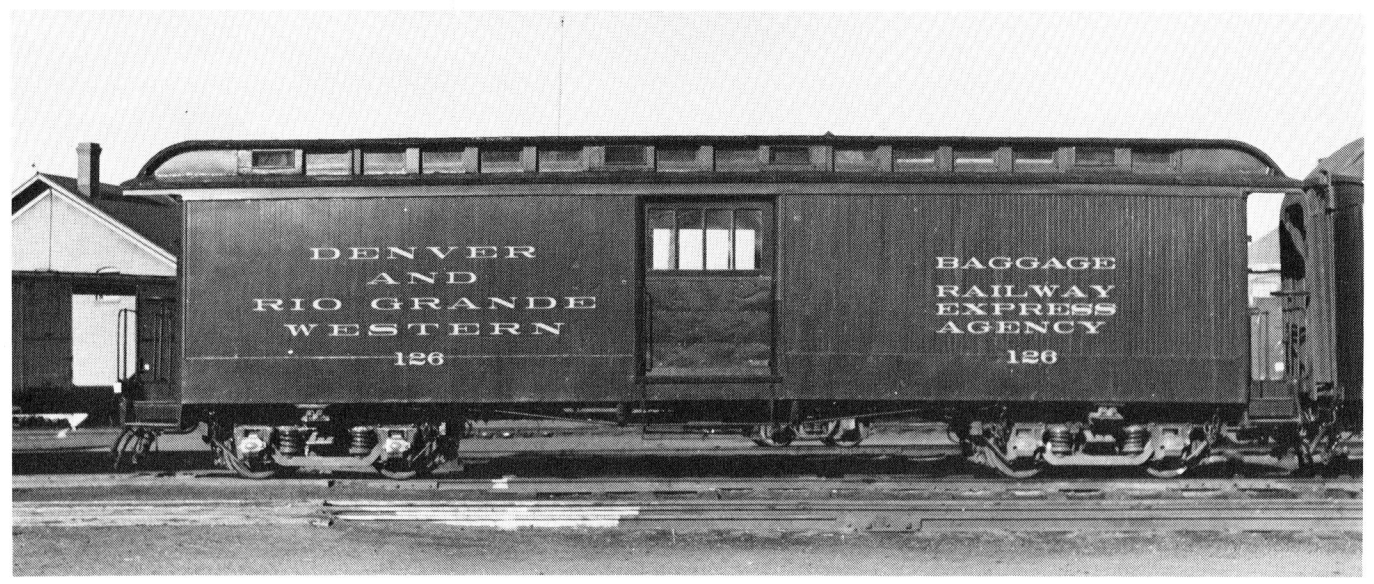

Here's a close-up view of #126 baggage-REA car. ***R.W. Richardson/Colorado RR Museum***

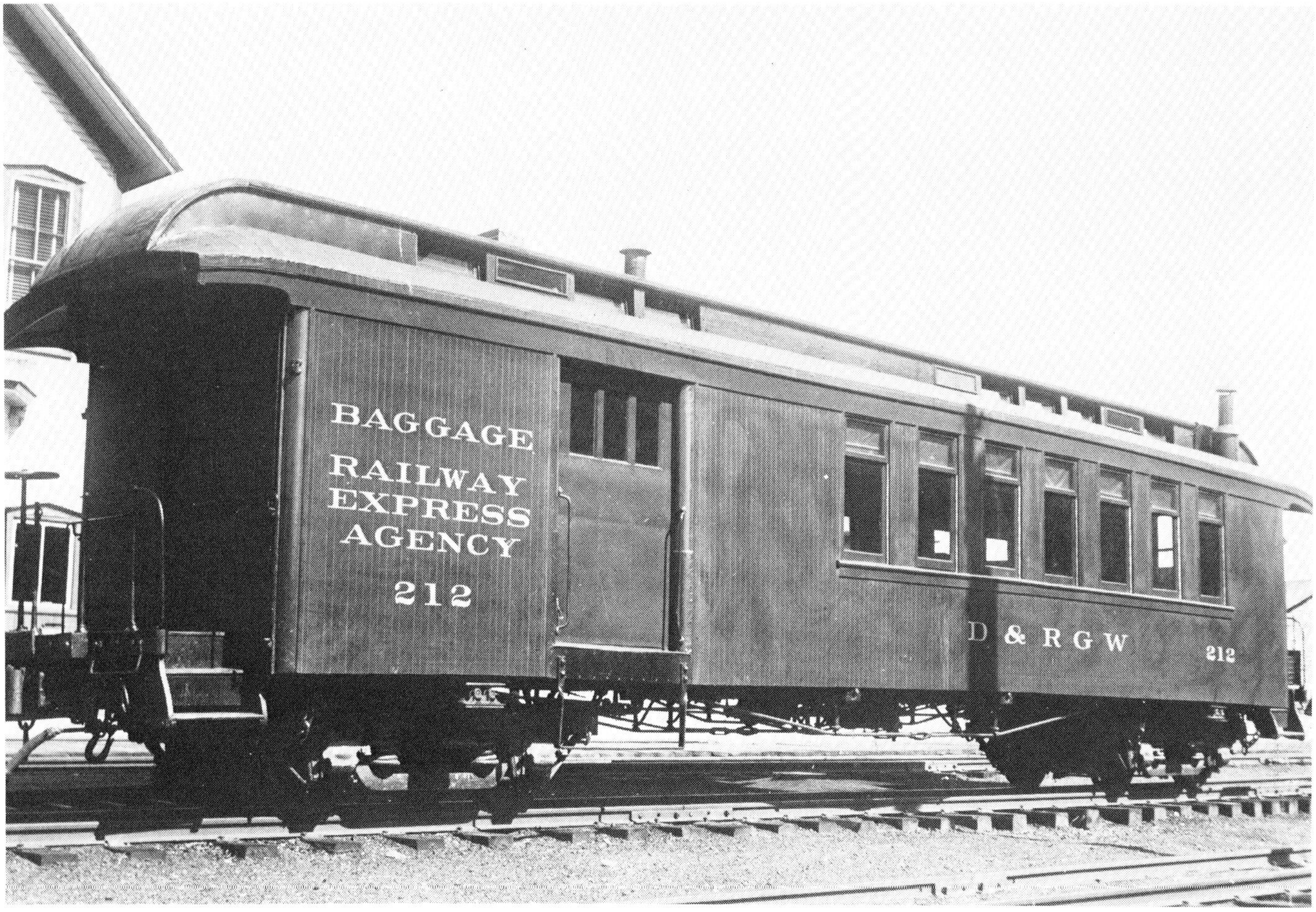

Combination car #212 at Durango. ***Don Grace-John Charles/Colorado RR Museum***

Rio Grande

THE DENVER AND RIO GRANDE WESTERN RAILROAD COMPANY

Coach #296 at Durango now in use on the Silverton Train.

ment was reached at Big Horn, the triple cones of Los Mogotes could be seen.

The way from Big Horn Loop westward was on top of the hogback that divided the Los Pinos and Conejos drainages through tall pines and, approaching Sublette, a deep, curving excavation through an ancient glacial moraine. Emerging from this, the track was built on the rim of a gorge whose steep slopes were studded with pine trees and spires of eroded basalt.

So began the scenery that made the Cumbres route such an attraction. From here to Chama one vista closely followed another. Though the train's speed was only about 20 miles per hour, you still did not have time to absorb all the sights.

A cluster of hewed log buildings stood at the Sublette section headquarters. To the left, while the engine took water, there was time to fully appreciate the grand and breathtaking depths of the valley of the Los Pinos River. Far below on the valley's floor the trees and foliage were still green, while at track elevation were all the shades of orange and red that autumn painted aspens can assume. Down the middle of the valley flowed the blue, blue river broken by occasional whitewater rapids and cascades. Nestled on the floor of green were a few tawny adobe houses with a haze of wood smoke above them. Horses, cows and sheep grazed contentedly on the rich grass.

On westward as the train proceeded, the eyes moved from wild distant panoramas of mountains ablaze with the fall colors, to those closer at hand. There were Calico Cut, Phantom Curve and Brigham's Monument, and the broken grandeur of the granite uplift of the lower portion of Toltec Gorge. The Los Pinos erupted at the base of the great cleft and the east portal of Toltec Tunnel appeared as a small black spot high up toward the upper righthand side of the view.

If for nothing else, General Palmer and his engineers should be remembered for the way the line is laid out from M.P. 307 to Toltec Tunnel. For four miles all the beauty, inspiration and natural greatness of the world can be seen in some form. Because of the chosen line of construction, each site could be viewed precisely at the most scenic angle. Everything couldn't be seen in one trip so fans developed a fever in the blood to keep coming back again and again.

At the west portal of Toltec Tunnel a stop was made to view and pay homage at a monument to an assassinated President, James Abram Garfield. However, few spent much time at the monument. Instead they walked out on the man-built wall that bridged the crevice at the west portal. There they leaned over the protecting balustrade to look down into the depths of Toltec Gorge at the tumbling, roaring river at the bottom, tearing and grinding savagely between and over the smoothly-polished granite boulders. Across the gorge a wide, deep vee ran from the crest of the granite, narrowing as it led downward. In this rough fissure ran a microcosm of the parent river below. A dense grove of wind and snow-dwarfed aspen fought for survival. As if to atone for these gnarled and crooked trunks and branches a picture was created each year at leaf-turning time that has never been equaled.

Leaving Toltec Gorge the roadway paralleled the Los Pinos on a high shelf to Osier. The river began to flow more gently as it approached the high alpine valley that began at Osier. The aspen growth become sparser and was replaced by willows along the stream and acres of grass surrounding copses of spruce and balsam. Beyond Osier, after crossing several brawling tributaries of the Los Pinos and moving around a sheer cliff on a narrow shelf roadbed, a spindly trestle built on a curve bridged a larger stream of water.

Beyond this, the summit of Cumbres Pass came into view, but there were several miles of treeless, grass-blanketed alpine meadow and gently contoured slopes to be traversed before Tanglefoot Curve and the depot at Cumbres was reached. By this time, passengers were surfeited with scenery and were ready to eat. But they interrupted their meal at Windy Point, reached immediately after beginning the descent.

The parlor buffet cars, *Chama* and *Durango*, were built in 1880 and rebuilt in 1937. Interior finish was walnut—and there was carpeting. There was room for four at the dining table, 10 in the plush chairs. *R.W. Richardson/Colorado RR Museum*

Rounding this black, massive outcrop of breccia, the whole world was laid out before you—at least that portion that lay beyond the Colorado-New Mexico state line only a few miles farther on and extending 100 miles into northern New Mexico. Then there was the immense canvas painted by Jack Frost; miles of mountain slopes that formed the Wolf Creek drainage to its junction with the Chama River Gorge and on to the flats where the Chama lay.

If you thought that by now you had viewed the most vivid and spectacular scenes to be found anywhere, you had one more view in store that would dwarf all that had gone before. After crossing Wolf Creek a mile beyond Dalton Spur on a steel spider web of a trestle, you rounded a curve and came to Lobato. Looking to the right across the Chama River, May Day Canyon, you simply quit breathing. The aspens on the mountain side there were a solid mass of the colors of a raging forest fire.

It would be an insult to try to find words that were appropriate. Lieutenant Bourke said it best: "Many of the 'bits' of landscape on this road would make the fame and fortune of the artist who could reproduce them."

Then it was out of Chama and over the Continental Divide at Azotea through scenes of grasslands and decaying pine stumps still standing after the pickings of the Chama pineries, and through the sedimentaries of Monero Creek to the sage-covered park that lay from Amargo to Dulce. There were the blanketed Apaches at Dulce with their colorful, tightly woven baskets for sale and into Navajo Canyon.

The Navajo River ran between walls of vari-colored sandstone that nourished tall yellow pine trees on the slopes and nearer the river, along where the rails ran, were thickets of mountain maple, mountain mahogany and chokecherry. Bordering the water were gnarled cottonwoods. At places, entirely covering the rocks, were tapestries and mats of woodbine highlighted, where springs seeped from the base of rocks, with ferns and beds of flowers. Occasionally, where an area near the river was large enough, there was a cluster of adobe or cedar pole buildings of a ranchito. And in these small enclaves grazed a few sheep, goats, cattle and horses or burros tended by a barelegged Nuevo Mejico boy or girl.

With few variations, this was the scene until the San Juan River (earlier joined by the Navajo) was left. There were none of the brilliant red of aspens, but there were all the shades of yellow, from pale lemon to tangerine. The mountain maple and mahogany, with their small leaves, produced a shade of red all their own, and the woodbine turned a color rivalling the clearest claret wine.

Many people were concerned when the Narrow Gauge no longer had passenger trains to ride on—for many reasons. But none were as disappointed and heartbroken as those who made an annual tour to view the mountains painted by autumn.

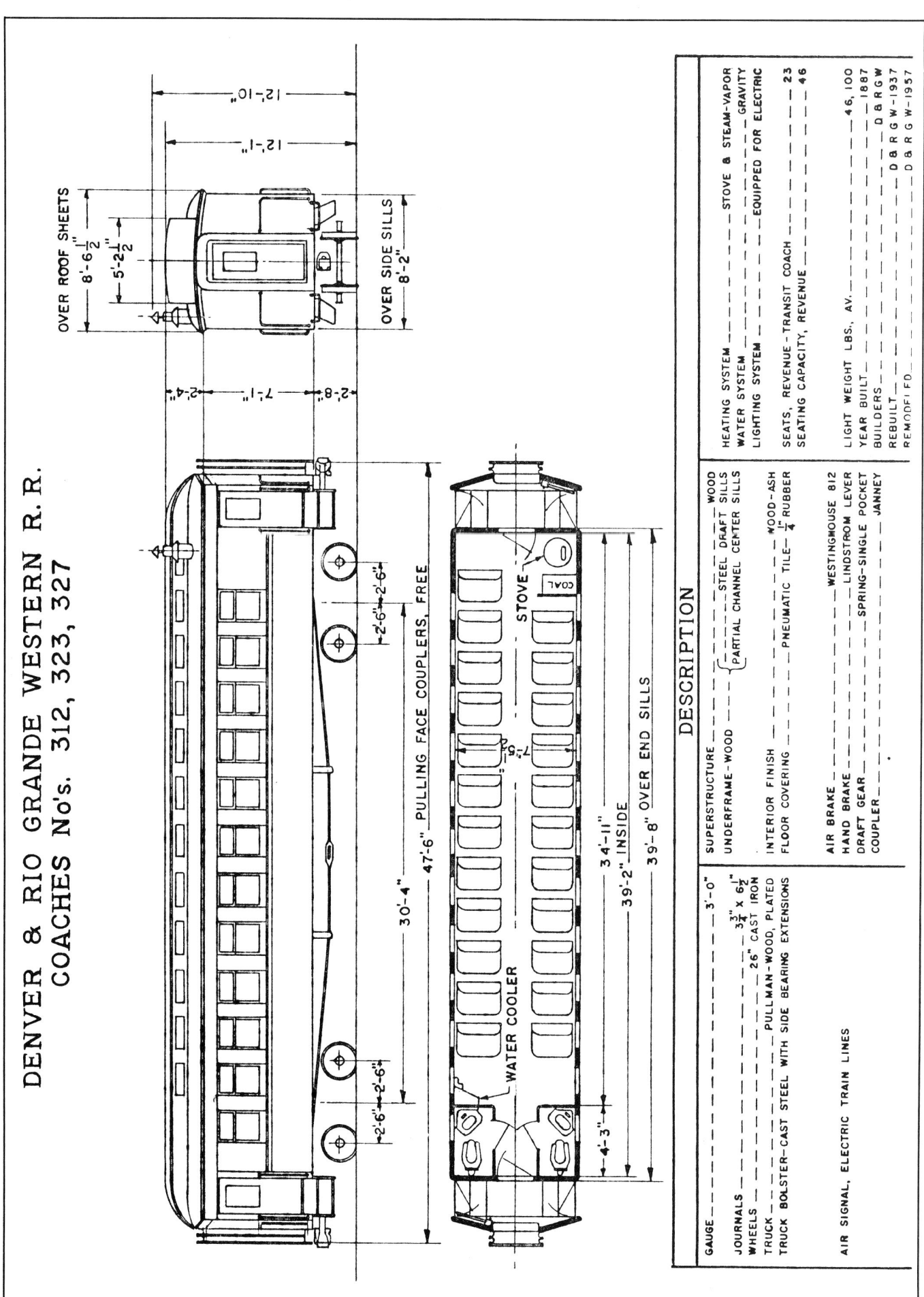

Engine No. 499 derailed at east switch Coxo, just west of Cumbres.

Chapter 15

Derailments

The word "wreck" was never used on the Narrow Gauge — telegraphers and train dispatchers were forbidden to send the Morse abbreviation, "wrk". They could abbreviate and send "TA", for train accident, but *never* "wrk". It was taboo and a firing offense.

If you read all the records of the 3-foot gauge line, you would reach the conclusion there was never one of those catastrophies that occurred on other railroad lines called wrecks. On the Narrow Gauge, regardless of other circumstances, if the wheels of engines or cars were still on the rail, the situation was normal. If any wheels were off the rail, then you had a "derailment", never a "wreck". On the Narrow Gauge it did not matter how far the engine or cars had come to rest from the roadbed, or how much equipment was totaled, it was still a "derailment" and not a "wreck."

Considering the millions of train miles run on the Narrow Gauge, there were very few bad "derailments" or "wrecks." The reasons were simple. The ball of rail was not very far above the ties; loads were light compared to standard gauge, and the center of gravity was low, while train speeds came a long ways from that necessary to break the sound barrier. In most cases the term "derailment" was the apropos one.

LEFT AND RIGHT. The K-36 engines sometimes had more tractive effort than was needed especially going downhill. Some K-2 triple valves failed to release out of the east portal of Mud Tunnel on Cumbres.

219

Picking up the pieces where the *San Juan* went into Toltec Gorge after it was hit by a snowslide.

However, if you were a cynic, and present at the picking up of the pieces, it is only with difficulty that you could refrain from using the word "wreck".

The taboo started a long time back, in 1881, in fact, when headlines screamed: "Terrible Railroad Accidents on Conejos Range - Criminal Liability of the D. & R. G. Railway Company - The Miner Warned the Public of the Unsafe Condition of the Road Weeks Ago - Eight Persons Killed and Six Seriously Injured."

The train consisted of a coach, a caboose and an engine. The accident, late in 1881, reportedly was caused by a washout that allowed the rails to spread. There were sixteen passengers in the coach and six railroad men in the caboose. From contemporary reports it was a gory "derailment."

Sixty-seven years later, February 11, 1948, train No. 216, with Conductor Ed Morgan and Engineman Dan Holly aboard, eastbound, was struck within a few hundred feet of the same location by a snowslide. Part of the *San Juan's* equipment tobogganed into Toltec Gorge. On this occasion there were no deaths and only minor injuries.

There was a "derailment" on the Silverton Branch just east of Rockwood caused by snow and ice that involved a passenger special. This was the so-called "Million Dollar Special Wreck" that occurred in January, 1918. The special received its name because of the many important people aboard making an inspection trip of properties in the San Juan area. No one was killed or injured, but two business cars designated as the "B" and "N" were destroyed by fire which

A derailment at Pinkerton on the Silverton Branch. A falling rock broke a rail that grounded this engine.

TOP. A sun kink on the curve at Needleton threw No. 473 off the rails and into the drink. The load of 900 tons of silver concentrates remained on the rails.

RIGHT. The same derailment at Needleton from another perspective.

was caused by a can of kerosene (coal oil) rupturing close to the hot kitchen stove. The engine involved was the 169, now in the park at Alamosa, Colorado. The train was made up of three cars—the "P", an observation-business car with sleeping compartments; "B", the dining car and "N" the kitchen car.

Another passenger train wreck on the Silverton Branch happened just east of Tacoma and west of the high Animas River bridge. On December 21, 1921, a train with engine 270 on the point followed by engine 263, then a flanger, struck some rocks. The two engines and flanger went into the Animas River. Fireman John Connor was killed and engineman Jim Connor spent six months in a hospital because of an injured leg. Enginemen Louis Johnson and Ben Hindelang were not injured.

However, Louis Johnson was living on borrowed time. He was engineman of engine 375, pulling a string of varnish, on March 11, 1927. It struck a sunkink in the track and the engine turned over into the Animas. Fireman Jack Dieckman joined the bird-gang and lived. Engineman Louis Johnson was caught and crushed.

One of the dangerous snowslides on the Silverton Branch

This derailment was called the last big pile-up on the Narrow Gauge. It occurred between Los Pinos and Cumbres.

was named "The Red Young Slide" because engineman William S. (Red) Young was killed when his engine struck this slide, just freshly run.

On the Santa Fe Branch (the Chili Line) one of the wrecks of a passenger train occurred at the foot of Barranca Hill. This happened to a mixed train enroute from Antonito, Colorado, to Santa Fe. The date was July 17, 1929, and the train was being pulled by engine 474, with engineman Johnny Reddington and fireman John (Jack) Fish. Both were killed and 11 passengers were injured. The cause was excessive speed resulting from a failure to set the required number of retainers at the top of Barranca Hill.

In the 70 years of passenger operation over Cumbres Pass, and elsewhere on the Narrow Gauge, with well over a million passengers carried, those killed or injured were mighty few. Crew members who suffered injury or death were also few in number.

That is not to say, traveling or working conditions, at times, were not hazardous or that there were only a few accidents. The work was demanding; passenger travel did offer the chance of accidents, but on the whole the accidents were few. There were accidents and "derailments"—some were freaks; some an act of God; some due to man failure and a lot simply were not explainable. But, there were no "wrecks."

During July, 1951, a movie company was engaged in filming the picture Rio Grande in the Animas Canyon. The Rio Grande made a special effort to have its ore hauling done out of Silverton before it was time to shoot a crucial scene. This was to be a realistically simulated head-on collision between two obsolete scrapper engines.

No. 462, engine 473, in charge of engineman John Dieckman, with fireman M. Rhodes manning the shovel, and skippered by W.L. Bruce, drifted by the east switch at Needleton with 900 tons of ore and concentrates. At the rocky point and curve immediately east of the switch, the sun had caused a sunkink in the track. Fireman Rhodes, a practicing lay-preacher, was caught in a squeeze between the apron and a corner of the cab. Just as Rhodes thought he was going to be crushed to death, the Man Above remembered all the good Rhodes had done and halted the squeezing movement long enough for Rhodes to escape.

All the cars remained upright and on the rail, but the 473 jackknifed between locomotive and tender, and when all movement stopped, the pilot was being washed by Las Animas River water.

There were other mishaps, but the Narrow Gauge men had more to do than remember derailments. If you know where to look and have a lot of time, you can root around in the rocks and undergrowth below grade, usually on a curve, and find bits of rusting metal that are relics of some of the older mishaps.

For the first time in motion picture history, two trains were crashed head-on for the 1952 Nat Holt motion picture *Rio Grande*. Paramount Pictures Corporation

Engine No. 491 is finally released from its snow-covered grave in January, 1952.

Chapter 16

Snowstorms on Cumbres

Cumbres Pass was a meteorological conundrum in the way snow came to it, or did not come to it. In cycles of five or six years snowfall was extraordinary, not infrequently being as much as 500 inches total fall. Other years snowfall was such the railroad was kept open without extreme difficulty. Occasionally there were winters when snowfighting equipment spent most of the season stored on backtracks, unused.

But when she was bad, she was very, very bad. (Cumbres was always referred to by those working on or over it as "she".) To the men who worked the track, and to those who operated the trains, snow was a white devil that beat, tortured

This 1952 winter scene is about halfway between Osier and Los Pinos. The flanges were getting so bad that Rotary OY backed out to allow section men to hand-pick them.

There are three engines in front and one at the rear. *John Krause/Dr. Richard Severance collection*

and scrouged them. To management, snow was a nemesis that threatened constantly. Clearance of one snow blockade could wipe out any profit made during the balance of the year. The empirical rule was that a season of light snowfall on Cumbres Pass meant at least $100,000 more profit than in a season beset by storms.

The management team at the beginning of each winter became extra attentive to the Almighty and said prayers with sincerity and devotion—"And, God, please give us a year with no snow."

Fremont, in writing of his ill-fated fourth expedition crossing the San Luis Valley: "Even along the river bottoms the snow was already breast deep for the mules, and falling frequently in the valleys and almost constantly on the mountains. The cold was extraordinary. At the warmest hours of the day the thermometer stood, in the shade of a tree trunk, at zero; and that was a favorable day, the sun shining and a moderate breeze. Judge of the nights and the storm!"

That was down in the Valley. Of the mountains that ringed it, Fremont said: "Along these naked heights it storms all winter, and the raging winds sweep across them with remorseless fury."

Fremont's words describes the winter of 1848 in the Colorado San Juan mountains. They could as well have been written to describe conditions later over Cumbres Pass in the same range when the Narrow Gauge was operating.

Rio Grande railroaders, when telling stories of snowstorms on Cumbres, dated and measured them against the winter of 1883-1884. (Winters were designated by using the fall year plus the spring year.) This was known as the year of the Big Snow, and until the granddaddy of all snows in 1951-1952, could rightfully be used as a gauge for comparison years. The Big Snow was not the sole property of Cumbres Pass—it affected all the Rocky Mountain and Plains areas. It hit all the new mining and logging camps along the D&RG, causing privations and sometimes near starvation in many of them. Sporadically a few relief trains were dispatched with food over Cumbres to the people at Chama and west by digging out the railroad.

DIGGING OUT

"Digging out" is the only way to describe the way the line was cleared of snow that year, for rotaries and other mechanical aids were not yet available. Trains of outfit cars with gangs of up to 100 men, supplied to stay at the working face of snow clearance, moved out of Alamosa enroute to Cumbres or the Chili Line as each storm abated for a while. Clearing was accomplished by literally digging out a snow trench down to the rails, foot by foot.

Engines Nos. 495 and 498 are a dozen cars apart, but together in spirit in this overview. *John Krause/Dr. Richard Severance collection*

Breakthrough at the Twin Slides on the Silverton Branch.

It was cold work shoveling snow to open the rail line. Digging a trench in drifted snow sometimes 30 to 40 feet deep is not child's play, at least not when the mercury in a thermometer retreats to the bulb at the bottom of the column and stays there, and gale force winds keep blowing the snow back into the trench. Or, when you are bundled in so many clothes you can hardly move, and the driven snow sifts down your collar and up your pant legs to melt and lay clammy on the skin and your nose is dripping and an icicle starts near your nostrils until eventually your moustache becomes icebound and keeps you from opening your lips.

That winter, Durango was without train service a total of 94 days; Silverton even longer. Smaller settlements and isolated families survived as well as they could on available resources.

If crews tried to handle more snow than the equipment could handle, a little shovel work was needed to open the fan chutes.

How many teetered on the brink between life and death—or did not survive—is not known, for the country was still too raw to have a widespread news coverage or historical recordings.

One incident involving Cumbres Pass and a number of people came close to becoming a Narrow Gauge Donner Party. There are records of this.

The westbound passenger train of January 6, 1884, stalled in snow near the summit of Cumbres Pass in the east loop of Tanglefoot Curve, about one mile from Cumbres station. In later years, this location was to be the scene of more marooned trains.

It was not a large train, for passengers to carry were not yet plentiful. There were eight men, eight women and the crew. The train did not carry means for feeding passengers, but there was a sleeping car.

The wind continued to blow and the snow to drift after the train stalled. Periodically the locomotive whistle was used to sound the signal of distress, but the engine whistles of that era more closely resembled the ones on a peanut vendor's cart and the whistle sound was blown away by the screaming wind. Station and section forces at Cumbres heard nothing and the telegraph line was down somewhere and the telegraph operator had no knowledge the train was enroute.

When the storm ceased, on the third day, the crew using axes from emergency kits, started cutting dead timber near the tracks to fire the sleeping car and express car stoves. Coal, including that on the engine, was saved to be used to bank fires at night. One crew member fought his way to Cumbres station. By the time the storm lulled, the cars and locomotive were buried by snow. It was necessary to erect walls of snow blocks around the stovepipes in order to keep a draft and tunnels from doors to the top of the snow to provide exits and admit air.

Later on the third day, section men from Cumbres, led by the crew member who had struggled to the station, returned through the snow dragging a sled load of food, including a quarter of beef.

SERIOUS SITUATION

Conductor Tweed and Engineer Willis Swoop took charge and informed the passengers how serious the situation was and that it might be days, even weeks, before the train was rescued. Faced with the hard facts of reality, the passengers accepted without wasting time complaining and pitched in to organize for making out in the ordeal they faced.

Life on the train was reduced to primitive simplicity. During periods of calm the crew and male passengers cut more wood and transported coal from the engine to the cars, kept tunnels clear and melted snow for water. The women cooked what scanty food supplies there were and kept the cars swept out. Without any argument, everyone on the train accepted the need for rationing and played fair, with one exception. Anyone who had a bottle of whisky in their luggage kept this knowledge quiet and secretly took a nip occasionally.

A trail was kept as open as possible between the train and Cumbres station. The people there pooled their food supplies and, going on rations themselves, divided equally with those on the train. Offers were made for any passenger desiring to do so to come to the houses at Cumbres; but no one accepted the offer. By this time, the marooned train seemed almost like home. The women even heated water and laundered everyone's underclothes.

The old records fail to say how many days the train (and those at Cumbres) were marooned, but they do say it continued to snow.

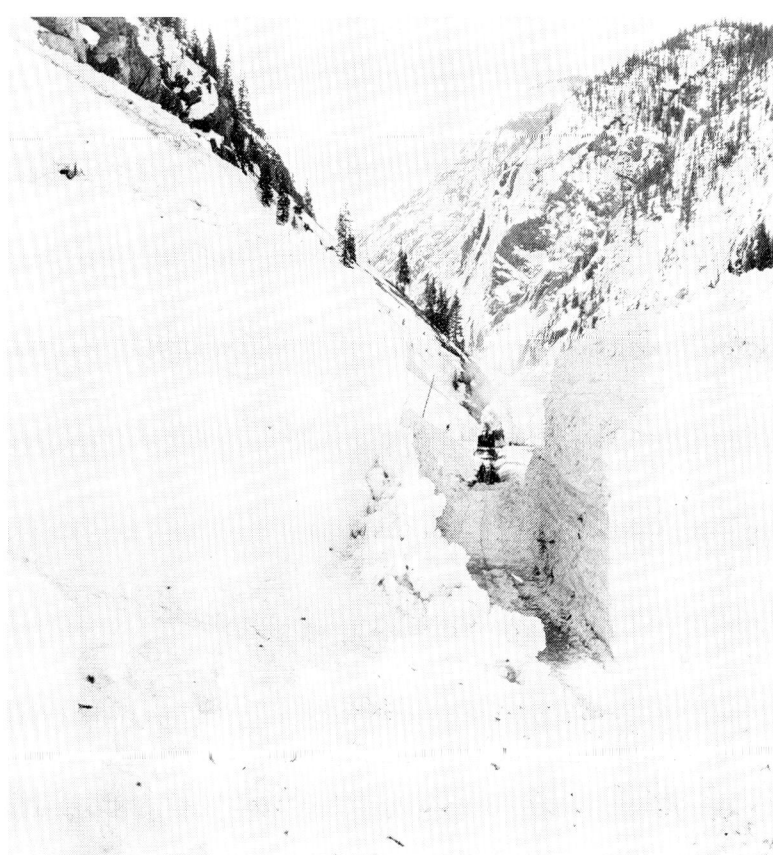

It's March 20, 1952, at MP 492.50 showing cut wall on the river side after breakthrough!

March 19, 1952 west of Whitehead water chute, MP 491. Work train was derailed by snowslide.

Rotary OM waits for the next winter season. *Chris Burritt*

Rotary outfit heading for home at Big Horn.

The records also recount an incredible trip through the snow that became a Narrow Gauge legend. When Conductor Tweed left Alamosa with the marooned train his wife was in the hospital critically ill. He worried about her, always with the feeling she was worsening and would not live. He wanted to be at her bedside.

After several days of agonizing, he could take no more, so leaving the train in charge of Engineer Swoop he departed on foot for Alamosa.

He arrived 10 days later and only God knows how or what kept him going, for Tweed would never talk about the trip. It is known he progressed from section headquarter to section headquarter to obtain some shelter, rest and food, but how he survived in the intervals between we know nothing. He fought it out from the train to Antonito, then rode a local train to Alamosa.

His determined struggle was in vain; all the frostbite, tortured muscles and suffering did not get him home in time. His wife was dead.

AWAIT BETTER WEATHER

Tweed's report did confirm that rescue of the marooned passengers must await a better break in the weather. As bad as the situation was at Cumbres and on the train, a rescue attempt might endanger even more people and create a much worse blockade.

However, Division Superintendent Cole Lyden did not think it proper to leave the crew and passengers without some word or outside presence to boost their morale. Neither would he ask another to attempt making the trip to Cumbres. Equipping himself and bidding his wife goodbye, he rode a

Just around the curve from Osier comes the rotary and two locomotives—the outfit cars are about a half mile behind.

train to Antonito, then strapped on his snowshoes (skis) and made Tweed's journey in reverse and much faster.

Snow continued to fall, but eventually linemen working out of Chama on skis (not to be confused with today's sophisticated equipment) found the break and re-established telegraphic communication. Trains of snow shovelers started working east from Chama and west from Antonito. Men from Chama using skis and sleds got through to the people on top of the Pass with food and other supplies.

After the trail was broken from Chama to the train, a second trip was made to bring more skis and sleds to the site.

The passengers and crew members who could use skis did so and others rode man-pulled sleds to a meeting with the snow train working out of Chama. They then rode this to the town at the foot of the mountain.

The snowbound passenger equipment was not dug out until April 12, 1884. Part of the crew and Superintendent Lyden stayed with the equipment until it was free and dragged into Chama.

With the line open again and trains running, Superintendent Lyden caught the first eastbound train for Alamosa. At last he was in a hurry to get home to get acquainted with his

Rotary, two engines and outfit cars leave Osier westbound for day's work.

Everything is back on the rails after a derailment at Osier in January, 1952.

new daughter, born shortly after he had left Antonito on skis. She was almost three months old before he first saw her.

After the spring thaw, in the vicinity of the stalled train, could be seen a large area containing stumps of trees that had provided wood for the train's stoves. Depth of the snowdrifts were reflected in the height of the stumps that measured from as short as 15 feet to a high of 40 feet.

LATER REMEMBERED SNOWSTORMS

Until the car-type snow flanger became available in 1885 and the rotary snowplow in 1891, the task of snow removal involved tough men, shovels and guts. Wedge plows mounted on the front of an engine with up to a half dozen pusher engines behind it could knock a hole in drifts up to 12 feet deep. If a narrow trench was dug through the drift at the center of the track, the wedge could knock out a bit more. But the basic pattern was an army of shovelers heaving snow.

Depending upon the depth of the snow to be removed, the shovelers would start a cut on the surface of the necessary width to reach track level with clearance and sufficient slope angle to be free-standing. As the cut deepened, terraces or benches were left. Men at lower levels passed snow to the one above and the process continued until the snow had been relayed to the top and disposed of away from the track. It was slow, cold, backbreaking work.

The first "Big Snow" of 1884 set two patterns. First, every succeeding "Big Snow" was named for the year that ended the season. Second, every man who was part of the team that fought the snow of a bad year just naturally thereafter referred to his year as the "Big Snow." For that reason, trying to form a chronology of "Big Snows" on the Narrow Gauge is a lesson in futility. Regardless of the year, each man who was stalled or starved, froze and ached in one of the bad storms, was convinced his was the "Big Snow."

The snows bad enough to be remembered, on Cumbres Pass and the Silverton Branch, did not occur every year. The belief, not always true, was that there would be a bad snow about each five or six years. This idea of cyclic occurances was just near enough to being true to lull everyone to sleep.

Following 1884's "Big Snow," there were no snow troubles worth mentioning until 1888, which was bad, but never rated as a "Big Snow." The next one of note came in 1891 and tied up the Chili Line while Cumbres remained relatively open.

The 1891 storm initiated the new rotary plow, just put in service, by using it to bore a hole from Antonito to Volcano on the Santa Fe Branch. An eastbound passenger train, fortunately with no passengers, and a snowplow with a wedgeplow engine on the nose, sent to rescue the passenger train, both stalled in deeply drifted cuts. The new rotary performed and released the stalled trains after they had been stuck three weeks. By this time, crews working in snow territory were getting smart and those on these two stalled trains did not suffer for food. This snow did rate a "Big Snow" so far as Chili Line men were concerned.

Then the Narrow Gauge went almost seven unbelievable years with only light snowfall. But the storms of 1897 did break finally and the snowfighting of that year rated it a "Big Snow." The years 1905 and 1906 did not quite rate this designation, but 1907 was a real stem-winder. The year 1909 was bad enough to be remembered. The next really bad year, area wide, was 1911.

The year of 1911 is remembered as a "Big Snow" but also as the year when miles of track were washed out and lost on the segment of railroad along the Navajo and San Juan rivers. The year 1911 is also one of the years that is dated by the actual year of occurence because it came during the latter part of October and early November. The snow had hardly stopped falling in November when warm rains started. This combination caused heavy flooding of the Navajo and San Juan rivers with consequent washing away and destroying miles of roadbed that was built on their banks. This was the greatest water-connected track damage ever to be suffered by the Narrow Gauge.

FINANCIAL CATASTROPHE

The year 1912, while hardly half as bad as 1911, was almost a financial catastrophe to the Narrow Gauge coming so close behind the costly debacle of 1911. But, almost as to make amends, nature relented until 1916-1917. Great snowfall was not the problem as much as the unceasing gale-force winds that kept the snow moving into deep, hard-packed drifts. Many track and train workers who, as young men, were in the action of 1884 and, later, the 1916-1917, rated the latter as the most hazardous working conditions.

Following in succession were 1920, 1923, 1927, 1932, 1936, 1942, 1947, 1952, 1957 and 1964. Or, you can talk to old-timers and they will give you an entirely different list. Some won't bother to list individual years. Ask them which were the worst years and they will reply, "Son, what you talking about? They was all bad."

Old-timers are often asked how people on the stalled trains

The rotary has stopped to have its discharge chutes cleaned.

conducted themselves and passed the time waiting for rescue. Actually, by 1900, conditions and possibilities connected with travel over Cumbres Pass in the winter were familiar to all.

The number of trains, especially passenger trains, that were marooned on Cumbres Pass was small in proportion that did stall. A lot of sleeping was done; everything available was read; some card games were played and a few women knitted or embroidered. The two favorite pastimes or time-killers were eating, if food was plentiful or available, and blowing the big breeze; that is, trying to out-lie each other.

On the Silverton Branch, snow conditions were different than on Cumbres. Snow slides were the bugaboo, and a train coming up against one of these simply stopped and retreated to Durango or Silverton. Consequently, there were no incidents of marooned passenger trains, or freights.

During the years that the Rio Grande attempted to maintain service during the winter between Durango and Silverton, the greatest feeling of futility in later years came to those working in the depths of Animas Canyon clearing slides when they looked up on the mountain side and saw modern, high-speed, state-owned snow-bucking equipment opening the new, paved Million Dollar Highway so trucks and buses could operate.

The sight made them recall that less than three-quarters of a century before teamsters were probably up on the mountain side looking down into the canyon at the smoke-belching, cinder-throwing engines—with the same forlorn thoughts the railroaders now had of the trucks and buses.

Don Heimburger

Chapter 17

Forewarnings of abandonment

From the turntable at Alamosa in 1965, Engine No. 490 appears to be cannibalized for spare parts. In the rear sits standard gauge No. 101 diesel switcher. *Chris Burritt*

The ultimate abandonment of the Narrow Gauge came in the late 1960's, and many factors were involved to bring it about.

Fundamentally, abandonment became necessary because the reasonings of Palmer's concept of building a mountain railroad to the three foot gauge had weaknesses that developed over the changing years. To this were added some inescapable economic and historic occurrences.

The Narrow Gauge was built to harvest frontier resources—timber, coal, ore, and livestock grazed on abundant free range. It was built in a period when government restrictions and taxes were still far in the future. Labor and materials were cheap, and equipment cost relatively little. Labor, besides being plentiful, had yet to begin its demands for better working conditions and high wages.

Too, very few rules restricted financing or the accounting for the use of money or returns to the investor.

When all of these factors changed and became governing aspects after World War I, the handwriting on the wall predicting the decline of the Narrow Gauge appeared.

The many travails of the Rio Grande's main operation on the standard gauge contributed to later abandonment. There was the bankruptcy brought about because of the Western Pacific being built using the Rio Grande as collateral by the Missouri Pacific. Then there was the closing of the Ogden gateway by the Southern Pacific. And the Rio Grande, following heavy use during WWI, was in poor physical condition requiring repairs.

At the beginning of 1918 the Rio Grande went into receivership and was able to start rehabilitation, and under this situation, was able to improve its plant. However, most of the improvement was on the standard gauge.

On September 17, 1917, the Missouri Pacific published a report entitled "Report on the Denver & Rio Grande Railroad Company and the Western Pacific Railroad Company." This report dealt rather heavily on the position and needs of the Narrow Gauge. Much written in the report was prophetic of latter events. Unfortunately, the report estimated it would require the amount of $31 million to upgrade the Rio Grande, and $5 million for the Western Pacific. The report, carefully documented and replete with many practical recommendations, was shelved.

It is the planning and insight where the Narrow Gauge is covered that is the most intriguing and leads to speculation as to what would have happened to the Narrow Gauge and the areas it served had all or part of the study been implemented.

Two proposals were made, either of which would have resulted in standard-gauging the line west of Alamosa to the San Juan and beyond.

One proposed the digging of a tunnel from South Fork, on the Creede Branch, to Pagosa Springs, thence back to the Narrow Gauge at Juanita. The other proposed standard gauge from Antonito to an elevation below the heavy snowline at Cumbres where a tunnel would be started that would emerge on the Chama side at a favorable point to escape the snow hazard and eliminate the 4 per cent grades.

As late as 1920 the Cumbres Pass tunnel was still under consideration. At a meeting held in Denver on March 21 a tri-tunnel project to be funded by a state bond issue of $18.5 million was offered to the public. The three tunnels were to be: the Moffat Tunnel, a tunnel under Monarch Pass and one under Cumbres Pass. Eventually, only the Moffat Tunnel was built.

The report prefaced operating statistics for a five-year period with this statement: "The operation of the Company's narrow gauge lines is unduly expensive." The highest narrow gauge revenue for the period was only $1,970,305 for the entire mileage of narrow gauge trackage. The most damaging statistics were the operating ratios that went as high as 117.08.

By 1948 the narrow gauge operating ratio had climbed to 171.77. One year later it was even higher and still climbing. It cost six times as much in wages, and three times as much in fuel, to move one thousand gross tons one mile on the narrow gauge as it did on the standard gauge, again demonstrating a fallacy of the narrow gauge concept. Tonnage could not be moved in heavily-curved mountainous territory over steep grades with equipment and at a speed that would permit a resulting favorable unit cost.

Rio Grande management was faced with a conclusion reached in the 1917 report: "It is necessary that the railroad reach an early decision as to whether operation of the narrow gauge lines shall be perpetuated, or whether such of these lines as have further traffic development possibilities shall be relocated and reconstructed to provide economical standard gauge operations." The oil-gas boom at Farmington delayed the decision a few years.

TIMES WORSEN

In the aftermath of WWI there was a feeling that better times would come. On the Narrow Gauge, people began to dream of prosperous years ahead.

There were dreamers in the mining and lumber industries, and livestock growers saw great herds of cattle and flocks of sheep fattening and streaming to market. All of them overlooked the basic isolation of the Narrow Gauge territory and that the frontier resources had been used and were not renewable.

Rio Grande management rushed down the primrose path along with others. New, heavier power was bought for the Narrow Gauge, as well as new cars of greater capacity. There was an active program of upgrading rails, ties and roadbed.

In the Rio Grande Valley and the San Juan Basin, grandiose irrigation projects totaling over a million acres were projected. The terrain was not favorable for these, nor was there enough water to fill proposed canals. The farms and small ranches continued to be hardly more than subsistence ones and the orchards failed to develop.

Some ore, not in great volume, continued to come from the mines, and coal was a major source of revenue until gas lines began to bring gas to the industries and homes in the Denver-Front Range area in the Thirties. Lumber was still important, but not to the extent it had been prior to 1915. And livestock, as always, was a seasonal unprofitable commodity. The isolated, depleted land west and south of Antonito could not compete with more productive parts of the country.

So, in the wild, hectic climate of a nation gone speculation and credit crazy, the clouds over the Narrow Gauge grew darker and more threatening. Dreams for a bright future, a productive and active one, became less frequent.

Then the bottom fell out of things and the Great Depression hit. The Rio Grande was again in receivership and there was but little business to haul. Surprisingly the Narrow Gauge was not as hard hit as the standard gauge, for another of the concepts of Palmer's had been that narrow gauge roadway, facilities and equipment could be maintained more cheaply than standard. Tonnage to move, already low before 1929, did not fall off in proportion to that on other portions of the Rio Grande. The Narrow Gauge did not wax fat, but neither did it loose weight.

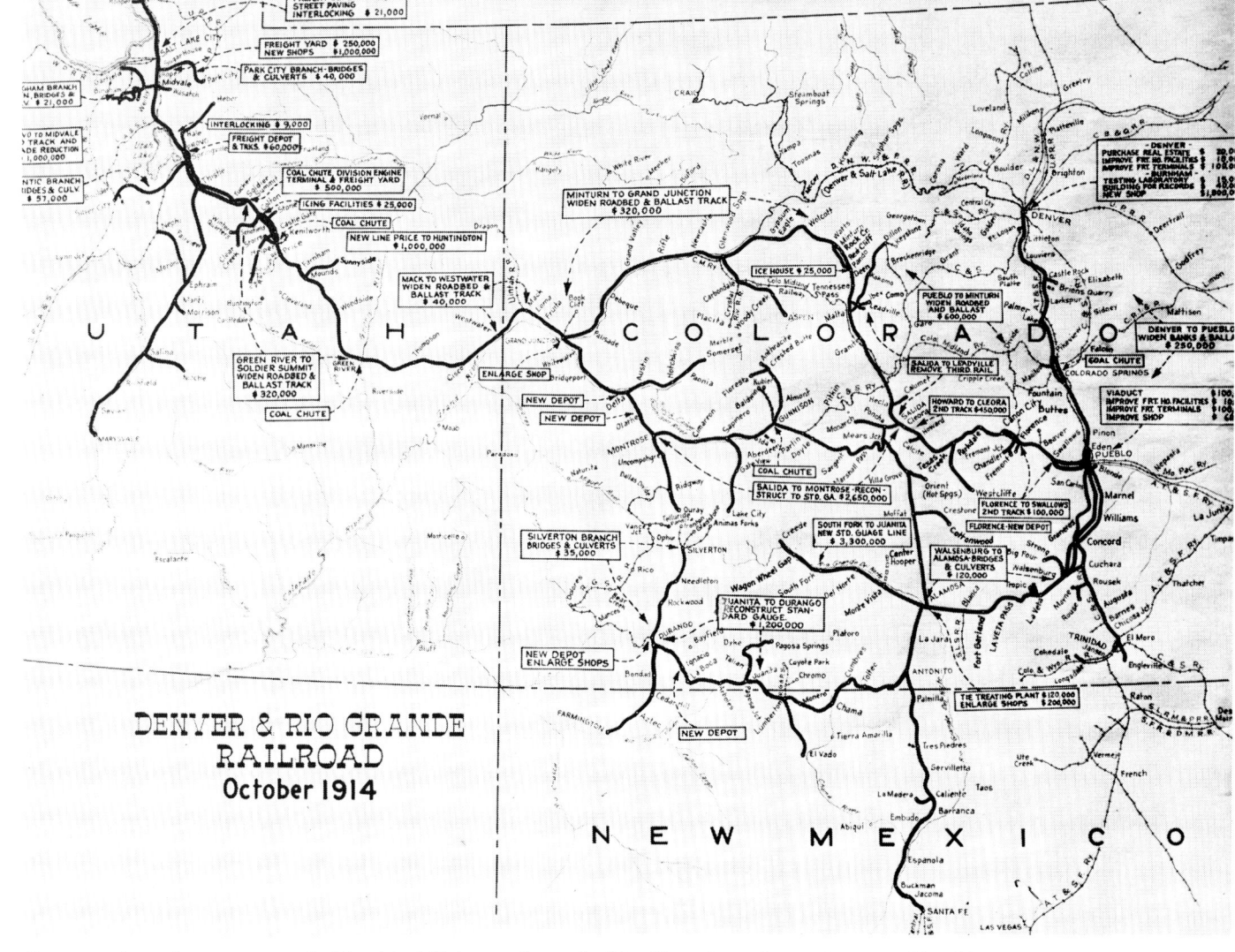

Construction plans are revealed in this 1914 map from the Rio Grande archives. *Renewed by Clarence Froid*

Contrary to common belief, the Rio Grande made most of the early abandonments resulting from the Depression on the standard gauge. On the Narrow Gauge, as a whole, abandonments did not start until 1932. The first to go were those where practically all sources of revenue had dried up. They were:

La Madera Branch - 1932
Parlin to Quartz (Salida-Montrose line) - 1934
Lake City Branch
  (also Salida-Montrose line) - 1936
Pagosa Springs Branch - 1936

Then followed the Orient Branch (on Mears Junction - Alamosa line) in 1942, and the entire Santa Fe line (The Chili Line), also in 1942. The latter was the first abandonment to be contested by the public.

An uncontrollable earth slide on the Gunnison-Montrose segment caused abandoning Gunnison to Cedar Creek in 1949.

In 1951 the tracks between Mears Junction (on the Gunnison line) were abandoned to Hooper. The remainder of this trackage, Hooper to Alamosa, was not abandoned until 1959.

The Gunnison line, Salida to Gunnison, was not abandoned until 1955. As part of this abandonment and in the same year, the Crested Butte and Baldwin coal hauling branches were abandoned.

Two other small abandonments came in 1953. They were the remainder of the Gunnison-Montrose line, Cedar Creek to Montrose, and Ridgway to Ouray.

After these abandonments, all that was left of the General's narrow gauge empire, was the Cumbres Pass line to the San Juan Basin and the Silverton Branch. These remaining miles of rails laid three feet apart came to be known to a developing army of steam railroad fans as *The Narrow Gauge*.

Adding to the uncertain future of the Narrow Gauge was the loss of business, not then large but important, coming to Durango from the Rio Grande Southern. This railroad, Otto Mear's contribution to the Rocky Mountain narrow gauge system, ceased operations in 1951.

By this time the movement of oil-gas well casing, line pipe and other supplies for the Farmington gasfield was tapering off. Highways were being improved into and along the Narrow Gauge and trucking operations were breaking out all over—along with highway passenger buses.

There were many who continued to dream of saving the Narrow Gauge, including many in the Rio Grande management team, but their dreams were not realistic, and the clouds grew darker.

THE END APPROACHES

In a magazine article in 1965, Stanley J. Wotjas, wrote about two narrow gauge railroads, the Black Hills Central and the Rio Grande Silverton Branch. Referring to the latter, he wrote: "In southwestern Colorado, a ghost has captured the spotlight, the ghost of the Silverton train which runs between

On February 20, 1953, Engine No. 484 and a caboose seem to pose for a parting shot from the Narrow Gauge. *Richard Kindig*

Durango and Silverton. For all practical reasons the narrow gauge line should have ceased to exist many years ago." At the time this was in the process of being accomplished. There is always one point in the history of any existing situation when hope comes to a head-on collision with reality. At that point, the stage is set irrevocably for a final decision.

That point for the Narrow Gauge was reached a few days before Christmas, 1964 when one of the cyclical big snowstorms struck Cumbres Pass. A westbound freight train encountered extreme snow conditions near Osier. Personnel on the train were dubious about being able to move further without becoming stalled, so wisely started retreating eastward. By having taken this early, sensible action, it was able to return to Antonito without mishap and without the usual attendant misery of having to rescue a marooned train.

After the storm was over, employees of the Rio Grande and the Colorado Highway Department undertook a joint snow condition inspection using over-the-snow vehicles. The results of this inspection caused cessation of train operations until May 12 with the consent of the Colorado Public Utilities Commission.

The *Denver Post* of January 24, 1965 carried a statement from Rio Grande president, G.B. Aydelott: "We have just made an inspection of the conditions and find snow 25 to 30 feet in depth and under prevailing wind conditions we do not feel we can risk men and equipment on the (Cumbres) pass at this time. I am also advised that shippers have been contacted and have indicated their willingness to cooperate with us by receiving their freight by truck during this emergency."

The point in history of the Narrow Gauge had been reached from which the chain of events would lead to final abandonment. For five months, no trains operated over Cumbres Pass and during this period the people west of Chama learned their freight transportation needs could be handled as expeditiously and as cheaply by trucks.

When the snow season of 1965-1966 started, the Rio Grande, again with the permission of the Colorado PUC again quit operating trains over the pass, and shippers and

Eleven Gramps Oil Company crude oil tank cars head eastbound up Cumbres a mile east of the high trestle over Wolf Creek, between Lobato and old Dalton spur. Engine No. 495 on the point, No. 498 ahead of caboose. February 26, 1954. *Richard Kindig*

receivers of freight continued to be served by trucks without complaining.

In September, 1967, the Rio Grande applied to the Interstate Commerce Commission and to the utility commissions of Colorado and New Mexico for authority to abandon the last vestigial remains of the 86-year-old narrow gauge railroad. The application did not include a request to also abandon the Silverton Branch.

Not until this occurred did the people along the Narrow Gauge and the nation's steam railroad fans awaken to what was in the wind. Local newspapers reported developing events.

On October 20, 1967 there appeared in the *Farmington (N.M.) Daily Times:* "RAILWAY SERVICE APATHY INDICATED. ...Patten, (Farmington Chamber of Commerce manager) said he had talked to 90 firms which have tonnage shipments, only to find apathy. Patten, noticeably upset by the turnout of only 15 county residents from more than 60, said he was not in favor of 'sending good money after bad,' in reference to hiring a lawyer to combat abandonment of the narrow gauge railroad."

Durango citizens felt a bit more strongly. The *Durango Herald* of November 14 carried an article: "The Denver and Rio Grande Western Railroad's application to abandon about 238 miles of narrow gauge line from Alamosa to Durango and Farmington has stirred up a big protest in the San Juan Basin."

The *Daily Sentinel*, Grand Junction, on the same date, ran an article that quoted a letter from a Fred W. Schmidt of Durango. He alleged, according to the news report, that the D&RGW was guilty of: "1. Lack of maintenance of equipment; 2. Excessive maintenance of track during the last two years to enlarge its deficit; 3. Lack of any form of solicitation of business; 4. Deliberate destruction of facilities to discourage business, such as destruction of tank cars and stock pens."

A week later an editorial in the *Durango Herald* said, "The D&RGW has been building its case for abandonment for decades, by foot dragging, by deliberately downgrading their freight service, and by discouraging the movement of any freight."

The following week the *Durango Herald* informed its readers that there was $7,000 in hand for a "D&RGW Fight" and that attorneys Frank McKelvey of Durango and Herb Boyle of Denver had been hired to represent La Plata and Archuleta counties.

Almost a month later, November 29, the *Pueblo Chieftan* carried a headline, "RAILROAD BUFFS CONCERNED OVER D&RGW PROPOSAL." The accompanying article says in part that "Brad Dobbins of Roanoke, Va., who is a railroad buff, wrote to the ICC at the same time, stating, 'I sincerely feel that this line should be preserved as a memorial to the railroaders of America.' "

After these first flurries, the matter ceased to be newsworthy and not much was written.

A more-or-less related matter received occasional notice. On March 16, 1967 the *Alamosa Valley Courier* announced that a newly-organized corporation with Thomas T. Hinman as president had filed an application with the ICC to issue $300,000 in securities. He had previously filed for a certificate of convenience to operate a narrow gauge excursion train out of Alamosa.

This application, dated January 17, 1967 was for "a permit to operate a narrow gauge excursion train between Alamosa and Chama, N.M." The application went on to state that "the RG&SJ railway company has acquired 23 steel narrow gauge cars in Mexico at a cost of $2,375 each." It further stated that the refurbishing cost of the cars would be $21,000. The cars, when finished, were to closely resemble the stock used by the famous "San Juan Express" (sic) in the early days of the narrow gauge.

The May 1, 1967 issue of the *Durango Herald* carried an AP release from Alamosa headlined: "HINMAN WITHDRAWS HIS ICC REQUEST FOR TRAIN."

In the spring of 1968 the proposed abandonment was revived as news but mostly only short notices that read similar to the one appearing in the *Valley Courier* (Alamosa) dated April 1: "The Interstate Commerce Commission (ICC) has scheduled hearings for three cities on narrow gauge freight track between Durango and Alamosa. The ICC will hold hearings April 29 in Farmington, N.M., May 1 in Durango, and May 3 in Alamosa, all of which are served by the line."

The same day, the *Durango Herald* ran an editorial: "They're getting ready to pronounce the death sentence on one of the most colorful working railroads left in the continental United States. We don't like to be pessimistic, but it looks as though the last train of any kind—freight, passenger or

Engine No. 492 at Chama in the morning. *Chris Burritt*

Class K-37 No. 498 lined up for action.

mixed—has run on the Denver & Rio Grande's narrow gauge branch from the San Luis Valley to Durango and Farmington."

Ten days before the hearings were to get under way at Farmington, the *Silverton Standard* had this to say: "RAILROAD PROTESTS GET LOW ON STEAM... With the hearings less than two weeks away, the fight against the abandonment of the Denver and Rio Grande Western Railroad's narrow gauge connections between Alamosa, Durango and Farmington has yet to take on any of the fervor of the fight several years ago to save the Silverton Branch."

The story in the *Silverton Standard* went on to say: "The committee formed a year ago to combat abandonment attempts—The Colorado-New Mexico Better Transportation Association—has not functioned anything like its founder intended, and it is virtually inactive as the hearings approach.

"Alamosa involvement in the abandonment fight has been negligible since early in the game, and the Alamosa Chamber of Commerce is formally on record as saying it will not oppose the abandonment.

"Farmington was an early source of enthusiasm, but many observers feel the award of D&RGW land there to a vitally needed hospital expansion program after abandonment cooled the community feeling against loss of the railroad."

So the stage was set and the curtain was ready to raise on the hearings to determine the fate of the Narrow Gauge.

HEARINGS BEFORE THE ICC

The hearing of ICC Finance Docket No. 24745 was opened at Farmington, New Mexico, on April 29, 1968 and continued into April 30. The hearings at Durango were held May 1 and 2. The final hearing, at Alamosa, lasted one day, May 3. An ICC docket, No. 34843, which covered an application made by the Colorado-New Mexico Better Transportation Association for improved transportation for the area was heard at the same location and dates.

Docket 24745 designated the petition entered by the

The #485 has finished putting its train together along with cars from two Chama-Cumbres Turns operated earlier and is strung around Tanglefoot Curve (Cumbres Loop). It's waiting for the rear trainman to complete walking the train and then it'll get the highball and head out for Alamosa. *R.W. Richardson/Colorado RR Museum*

A doubleheader is coming into Chama on this August, 1965, morning with No. 492 on the point. *Chris Burritt*

Denver and Rio Grande Western Railroad Company seeking a certificate of public necessity permitting the abandonment of the remaining narrow gauge lines of the company, excluding the Durango-Silverton line.

Nearly 30 years had intervened between the bloody battle to abandon the Chili Line (Santa Fe Branch) and the present petition. However, memories of the bitter strife of 30 years previous were not forgotten, and the Rio Grande went to the hearings of Docket 24745 fully prepared for what they expected to be an epic attempt by the public to squash the Rio Grande's bid for abandonment.

The ICC hearing examiner was Robert N. Burchmore. Ernest Porter and John S. Walker represented the Rio Grande.

New Mexico State Corporation Commission had four representatives, James D. Childress, Floyd Cross, Howard L. Frisbie and Ralph B. Harlan.

Robert Lee Kessler, Ralph H. Knull and John L. McNeill appeared for the Public Utilities Commission of Colorado. Other attorneys were present to represent railway labor organizations or other protestants. They were: Herbert M. Boyle, James I. Davidson, M. Carl Feather, Edward Hamilton, Phillip F. Icke, LaVerne McKelvey, R. Franklin McKelvey and Linville I. Prell.

Including the Examiner, his recording reporter and the attorneys listed, there were 19 persons actively involved. In addition, a scant two score other persons were present in the hearing room. More than half were witnesses for either the Rio Grande or some protestant. The remaining bodies were spectators. In the large room that had been arranged to care for a huge crowd, the Examiner faced dozens of vacant seats and before opening the case requested those present as witnesses and spectators to congregate in a more compact group.

So much for the public's and the petitioner's belief there would be intense interest in the case. The second morning at Farmington there were even fewer present. A total of only 15 witnesses appeared for the protestants. None was on the stand more than five or ten minutes. Many scheduled to appear simply did not show up.

One such witness whose testimony would have been important, the San Juan Lumber Company, submitted a letter on the first morning to the Examiner withdrawing its opposition to the petition. Protestants had counted heavily on the lumber company testimony and the Rio Grande attorneys were much concerned.

Telling testimony opposing abandonment was also expected to be given by the executive director of the newly-

Superintendent's Bulletin No. 44 announcing abandonment of the last of the Narrow Gauge, excluding the Silverton Branch.

organized Four Corners Regional Commission. This commission consisted of parties interested in the four states that have a common corner in the area known as the Four Corners, New Mexico, Utah, Colorado and Arizona. It had federal financing behind it.

The testimony this witness gave was telling, but negative, and brought smiles of incredulity to many, including the face of the Examiner. The executive director was not a native and had been on the job only 30 days. It became clear under cross-examination that he was unfamiliar about where the railroad operated, how it operated or of its past history. He was not even vaguely familiar with which communities were directly or indirectly served. He did develop the Commission's object as being to develop transportation in the area, but quickly and without doubt made it clear that, in the Commission's view, this would consist of an improved network of highways and airline capabilities.

The hearing at Durango came closer to promising a reinactment of the Santa Fe Branch hearing. Almost 100 people were on hand. The witnesses represented lumber, mining, livestock and other interests. For a while it looked like there was to be some worthwhile testimony given by the protestants.

A matchsplint plant operator and a plywood manufacturer assessed their future and need for rail transportation. Stockmen appeared. One sheepman testified that he did not use the railroad because in his opinion, the narrow gauge stock cars had got so bad "sheep fall out of the cars enroute."

A Silverton mining man testified there were expectations that a 1,000 ton mill would be built at Silverton to process ore reserves. On cross-examination he admitted the project was speculative in nature and at best was two years in the future before construction would start.

A coal mine operator developed that there was a small market for coal in Denver but that due to poor service, known losses enroute and a freight rate that was high due to the necessity of transferring to standard gauge cars at Alamosa, he was not able to compete for the market.

Another item of a speculative nature involved the possibility that a paper pulp mill might be built on nearby Indian lands. Testimony established this idea had not yet come to the stage of serious study or investigation.

A railroad attorney asked a Durango witness what his constituents thought of Thomas T. Hinman's Rio Grande and San Juan R.R. The witness quickly glossed over the importance of this and even more quickly dropped the subject. People of the San Juan Basin and those of the San Luis Valley were very reluctant to discuss anything connected with the RG&SJ RR.

The Durango Pepsi-Cola distributor had a tale of woe to tell about having built this plant to unload directly from cars, only to learn he could not do so. Asked why, he said he learned the track he proposed to use would be unavailable to him because a large trucking terminal was being constructed over the track. Unfortunately, he had not considered this in building his plant.

The hearing adjourned at Durango and moved to Alamosa for the final hearing to be held there May 3. The attendance

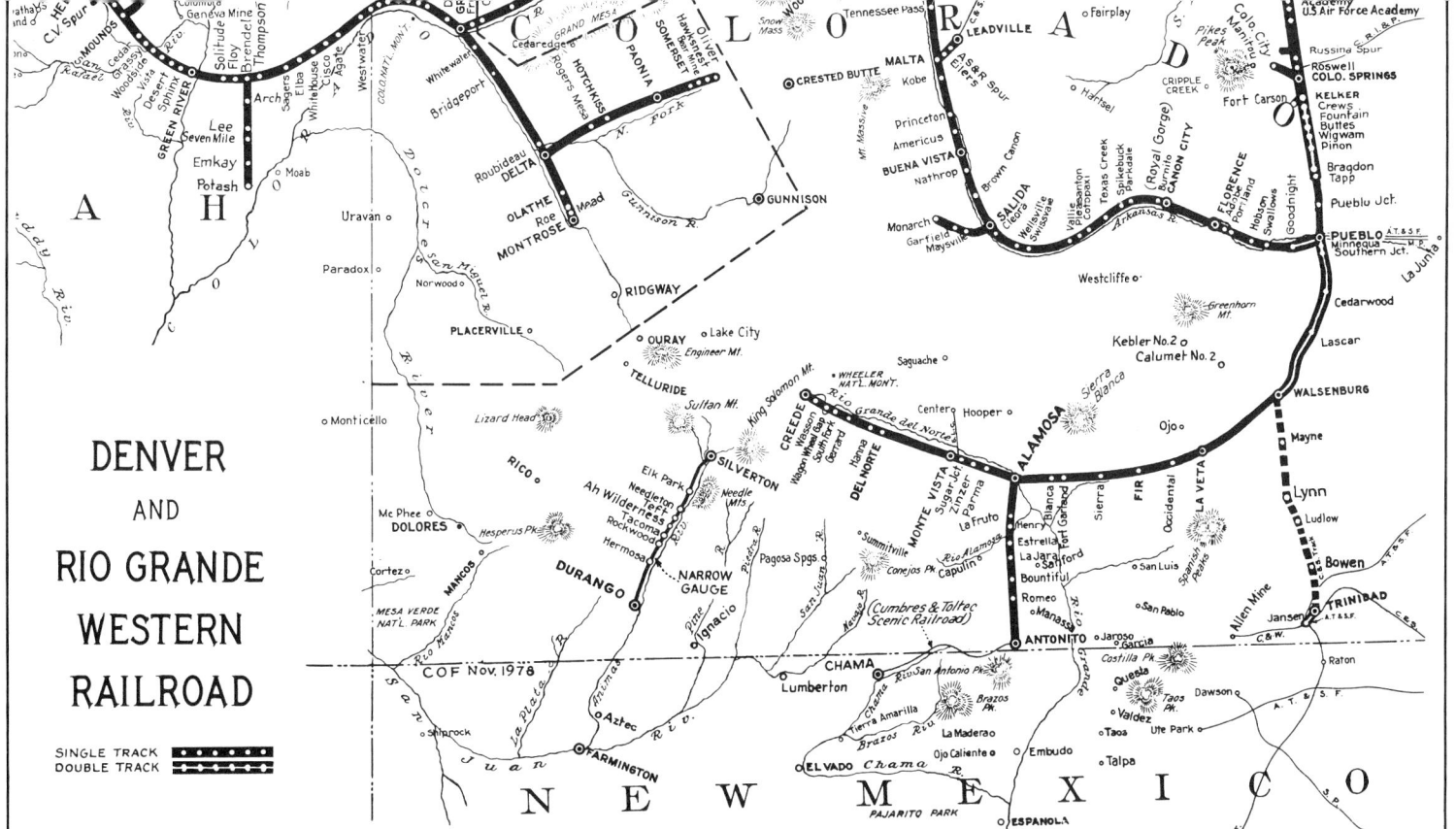

was meager to the extreme—almost to zero for spectators.

Upon opening at Alamosa, the Examiner asked if there were any witnesses to appear for the protestants—only silence answered him. At the morning session not a single public witness appeared. Considering how deeply involved San Luis Valley people had been in the Santa Fe Branch about 30 years before, the present situation was noticeably unique.

In the afternoon, the Examiner accepted in evidence a rather voluminous Economic Feasability Study from a representative of the Transportation Management Division, General Services Administration. The Examiner then questioned the applicant's attorneys to clarify a few points of testimony he wished more information about.

Then at about 2 p.m. he again asked if there were further witnesses to appear. An ex-president of the Alamosa Chamber of Commerce responded and entered a brief statement which was read into the record and accepted without any questions.

The hearing closed at 2:50 p.m. and the Examiner announced that June 17 was the final date for submitting briefs.

The Rio Grande people had great feeling for what the pending abandonment of the last remaining miles of narrow gauge railroad meant. The feeling was deep, sincere, and emotional—the pathos and nostalgic involvement held sadness for most Rio Grande people.

The State Corporation Commission of New Mexico filed a brief entitled "Abandonment-Downgrading-D&RGW Co. Narrow Gauge." It was inflammatory, attempted to enter new unsupported testimony, and above all grossly abusive. It went far beyond the limits of accepted conduct and in the end defeated its own purpose.

The Rio Grande, in answering it, took exception on the basis it was "garish," "gaudy," "relied unfairly on erroneous transcriptions of the reporter's notes," "unprofessional" and "inflammatory." They moved that the brief be overruled.

A two-page document entitled as "Further Supplemental Particulars" was offered by a James D. Childress to serve as a "Brief and Argument of Protestants and Complaintants," but was not accepted as it missed the June 17 deadline.

These were the only briefs offered for, after seeing the New Mexico presentation, other attorneys of protestants either chose not to join such an acrimonious attack or could perceive the futility of a brief after such a poor public appearance of protest.

The New Mexico brief, although a masterpiece of hyperbole, accomplished nothing and later apologies for its bias and thoughtless contents, with retractions, robbed it of its sting. It never became necessary for the Rio Grande to challenge the New Mexico attorneys to a High Noon shootout.

On July 30, 1968 the Secretary of the ICC published the recommendations of Robert N. Burchmore, hearing examiner. The document was not served to interested parties until August 16.

When received it read:

"Decided

---

1. Present and future public convenience and necessity found to permit abandonment by the Denver and Rio Grande Western Railroad Company of that portion of its narrow gauge line of railroad between Farmington, N. Mex. and Alamosa and Antonito, Colo. Conditions and certificates issued in F.D. 24745.

2. The Denver and Rio Grande Western Railroad Company found not shown to have failed to provide transportation or reasonable facilities therefor.

Complaint in F.D. 34843 dismissed."

The handwriting that had been appearing on the wall since about 1910 and World War I, predicting the demise of the last of the Narrow Gauge which people had been too busy to read or heed, had come to pass.

The General's dream of a 3-foot gauge railroad had come to an end, but memories of it, especially on *The Narrow Gauge*, would live on and on.

One of the Grande's wooden flat cars. Alamosa, January, 1953. *R.W. Richardson/Colorado RR Museum*

D&RGW dump bottom coal car 884. In earlier times, when the coke ovens were operating in Durango, some dump cars had high racks on the sides and ends so a profitable load of coke could be carried to Alamosa for transfer to the Pueblo steel mills. When equipped, they were called "longhorns." *A.M. Payne*

A low-sided 800-series dump car. *Don Heimburger*

D&RGW gondola No. 1554 as built with wooden side and end sills. *A.M. Payne*

LEFT. D&RGW No. 1423 high-side gondola. *Don Heimburger*

BELOW. Box car No. 3426 in Farmington, 1965. *Chris Burritt*

Stock car No. 5717 was one of the series 5500-5849 of 28-foot length. *Don Heimburger*

RIGHT. Another 28-foot-long stock car. *Don Heimburger*

BELOW. No. 159 refrigerator car is from the series Nos. 150-169. *Don Heimburger*

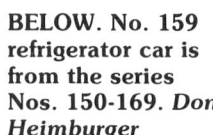

Carbody flanger at the Colorado RR Museum.

LEFT. D&RGW flanger OC. *Don Heimburger*

BELOW. Caboose #0587 was built prior to 1920. *John Parker collection/Colorado RR Museum*

Chapter 18
Local color on the Narrow Gauge

Don Heimburger

"Auz" — telegrapher, philosopher, piddler

C.D. Poage was a traveling cartoonist and a telegrapher who was liable to show up anywhere there was a seasonal need for a lightning slinger. Judging from the dates shown with his name and written on the planked interior of the baggage room of the Rio Grande depot at Pagosa Junction in the marking ink of early days, lampblack and kerosene, he was employed at Pagosa Junction several times for short periods. He left, in addition to his name and dates, a number of drawings that were true Poage on the same walls.

In 1930 he put together all his recollections of old-time depots and drew a cartoon entitled *At the Old Depot*. This was published widely in various railroad publications and later issued and sold in framing quality and size as a railfan collector's item.

Poage shows that the station agent was named J. Pluto Bolivar, and the holder of other titles, including justice of the peace, mayor, et cetera.

J. Pluto Bolivar was still alive in 1930, but his true name was H. Austin "Auz" Rogers. He was retired from the Rio Grande but living across the tracks from "The Old Depot" and, with his wife, Helen, running a small trackside eating house and providing a few overnight room accommodations.

Most of the signs and some of the other relics, Helen had collected when Auz retired and put on display in the restaurant dining room.

Helen had a copy of Poage's cartoon and she said there was not much missing in the way Auz' office always looked.

Auz learned to telegraph on the old Kansas & Pacific, but left the K&P to come to Colorado. He went to work first on the D&RG as a mail and express messenger, but finding this too strenuous, returned to telegraphing. One of his assignments was as station agent at Fort Garland where he met his future wife, Helen. She was a schoolteacher, an excellent cook and possessed of a nature that allowed her, after marriage to Auz, to live with his many eccentricities.

NEW BID AT GATO

Auz was past forty when he bid in the new agency at Gato, later renamed Pagosa Junction. He went there as a bachelor but with intentions of changing this by taking Helen as wife.

Very shortly after arrival at Gato, he decided that it was where he wanted to spend the rest of his life. He bought a piece of land across the tracks from the depot and on the banks of the San Juan River, built a house, furnished it and planted some cottonwood saplings to grow into shade for the lawn he planned.

With all this done, he called the agent at Fort Garland on the Morse wire and asked him to take a message to Helen telling her to come on down to Gato to marry him. He had been so busy building, he had given no thought to keeping Helen advised of his intentions or progress. But Helen, in her own way, was a match for Auz and a sensible young lady.

While Auz had been busy preparing a home, Helen had been just as busy filling a couple of hope chests with linens, bedding and other household necessities. When the command came to come to Gato to marry Auz, she caught the next westbound passenger. At forty years of age, Auz was set in his ways, and Helen, fifteen years younger, was not about to try to change those ways.

The train arrived at Gato and Auz finished loading and unloading the mail and express and only then walked back where his bride-to-be was waiting on the platform. He picked up her valise with one hand and patted Helen on the shoulder with the other—no tender bussing for him—and they walked into the telegraph office. Auz "OS'd" the train and asked for permission to be absent a short while.

Ten minutes later they were in the parlor of the local justice of the peace and Auz is telling him, "Like I told you this morning, we want to get married. Make it short and fast as you can, just so it's legal. Helen and I will take care of the binding part."

The JP called his wife and an aunt in as witnesses and asked Auz if he had a ring. He did not, so the aunt slipped a silver ring off her finger and handed it to him. Forty years later it was worn very thin, but Helen still wore it.

The JP told them to take each other by the right hand. They did, and he said, "Do you, Austin Rogers, take this

No. 493 engulfs itself in a cloud of steam in a shot by Chris Burritt.

D&RGW refrigerator car No. 159 close-up. *Don Heimburger*

woman, Helen, as your wife?"

Auz answered, "I do," and the JP said, "Do you, Helen, take this man, Austin Rogers, for your husband?"

She replied, "I do." The JP pronounced them man and wife. Auz gave him some silver dollars and they walked out. Still no loving embraces but the short ceremony was a binding one. As Auz approached 85 years of age he still worshipped the ground Helen walked on and she thought Auz was the only man in the world.

DUTIES NOT BURDENSOME

Duties as station agent at Gato were not burdensome. Over the years, Auz waded through most of the ancient philosophers' works and a lot of modern literature. When he was not reading, he was "piddling," making drawings and models of his "inventions." Periodically Helen had to go to his workroom and throw out enough junk to make room for newer piddlings. Auz was prone to drop projects midway and forget them, especially if the local Catholic priest came around to talk. That poor padre spent many hours trying to bring Auz to God, but he died an atheist and agnostic.

Auz eventually became Justice of the Peace at Gato and performed numerous marriage ceremonies for Ute and Mexican couples. Helen used to say they were much different than hers had been, for Auz made them long and impressive. The time spent on the ceremony depended on whether he read a poem from Kipling, Keats or Tennyson. If the couple understood English, Auz would read them a few verses from the Book of Ruth and pronounce them man and wife.

Often Helen chided him for his actions in performing the wedding ceremony, but he would just tax her to give him a single example of his marriage ceremonies not being effective. She could not do so, for the people Auz married stayed married.

Over the years Auz read, piddled and got in Helen's way as she worked. She straightened up after him and put up with him. Auz had no money sense whatever, but Helen did, and she was thrifty. He did not always know how some of the things that happened to him came to pass, such as being elected to a directorship in the bank at Pagosa Springs and finding himself the owner of a number of buildings and businesses. Helen did, but she just let him think he alone was responsible.

"And he died in a good old age, full of days, riches and honour."

House by the side of the road

No. 487 enroute between Chama and Alamosa in May of 1953. *John Krause/Dr. Richard Severance collection*

When Poet Sam Walter Foss wrote *The House by the Side of the Road* he surely was not describing hewed pine logs or rough-sawed pine boards hastily thrown together and painted brownish yellow. But a lot of such houses were beside the road on the Narrow Gauge. Some were on mountain tops; some in canyons or desert land; and some were built among the leafy cottonwoods of the river bottoms. In them lived section men and their families, pumpers, telegraphers, car inspectors and others who were needed to keep the tracks in passable condition, water in the tanks and train orders in the hoops for trains.

Without these men who lived in the houses beside the road—and their wives who had the courage and love to make homes at isolated locations and under conditions often adverse, and often lonely—the Narrow Gauge could not have operated. They were the humble, lonely and often forgotten. But these employees kept the ties tamped, the rail joints tight and curves lined, and kept the gauge on the water tanks at the full mark. They sat at a telegraph key, fighting sleep and cold in order to be ready when the train dispatcher pounded out call letters in Morse and the sounders spelled out, *"9 - cy 4 west."* The lightning slinger slipped the zinc plate below four sheets of the flimsy train order tissue and in beautiful flowing script copied the train order for delivery to a westward train.

These men, and women, were the backbone, the mainstay, of operations over the mountains, through canyons and along the rivers. They put in a full day's work every day and when the waters ran high or the snow fell and drifted, or the trains were in trouble, they let the clock run down and did not wind it again until conditions returned to normal. Lack of food, sleep and rest never prevented them from giving their all. They sometimes fell asleep with a shovel of snow or mud in midswing, or collapsed in their tracks from fatigue—but when the next emergency arose, they responded to the call.

If the men were strong, the women were stronger. The time of night meant nothing if their man was called out. He left the house after eating a hot meal, carrying a lard pail lunch bucket full of food and a whiskey bottle full of coffee. When he was gone she comforted the awakened children and returned to bed.

OS JOBS

Until the advent of the motorized section car, the usual spacing of section headquarters was about six miles apart. Wayside telegraph offices were spaced depending upon the density of train movements, weather conditions and the need for communications or prompt reporting of train location. Centralized Traffic Control was unheard of and a train dispatcher had to have frequent train reports in order to properly dispatch train movements. The old telegraph code abbreviation to announce to the dispatcher a train report of a passing train was the two letters *OS*, followed by the station call letters and the train identification and time. So operators who worked the small, isolated train order offices came to be called *OS Operators* and the small stations were known as *OS jobs*.

All of the section headquarters were replicas of one another. If the pumper, coal-heaver or telegrapher was also stationed at a section headquarters, their homes did not differ from those of the section men. The foreman's home was slightly bigger than the laborers' as a status symbol. Architecture, material and paint job did not vary. The effect of giving a foreman a bit larger house was lost when the paint gang finished its work since the dull, yellow paint made every building assume the same uniform drabness.

There was a day-in, day-out sameness in general in the homes by the side of the road. By the light of coal oil lamps the wives and older daughters sewed and mended, knitted or embroidered. The man of the house smoked, read an old newspaper or just rested. Daytimes there was cooking, washing of clothes and housekeeping.

What did the children do? In good weather they played outside until the last light was gone—a thousand games of make-believe. In bad weather they stayed indoors, but without clamor or complaint. Story-telling was learned at an early age for there were no elaborate toys, games or amusements.

What did any of these people do to amuse themselves, gauged to leisure time today? No radio, no television, no sports, no diversions of any kind as we know them. But they must have possessed a secret that gave them happiness and contentment in measures that satisfied them.

WHAT HAPPINESS WAS

Happiness was the man's arm resting for a moment on his wife's shoulder, a plentiful meal and security from the snow and rain raging outside.

Happiness to the children was to hear a train whistle, then race to be in position to pick up the roll of newspapers, maybe some gum or candy, their friends, the train and engine crews, often threw off to them. Adventure was the excitement of unrolling the packet to see what was hidden inside—peppermint lozenges, barberpole stick candy, marshmallow bananas or peanuts; best of all, maybe chewing gum. Contentment came as they sat and divided the treats into equal shares and looked at the funnies. Happiness to those on the trains came from the wide smiles and waves of thanks. Some of the donors were not too long from having been one of the kids at the side of the road.

Then there was wonder when the train came by in the late dusk with its windows all lit up and the polished men and women sitting at the tables eating and the light glowing on the tall bottles of wine in the hands of the white-dressed waiters. And the dreams of being "growed up" and rich and pretty and getting on that train and eating, drinking and looking out the windows.

For the people in the brownish-yellow houses at the side of the road and the people who lived in them, the unknown poet said it all:

"Courage and toil and service, old, yet forever new...
"Yes, we reckon we're a failure,
When it comes to being rich...
But there's a desert that's now bloomin'
'Cause we helped to dig a ditch.
Yes, we reckon we're a failure,
In regard to winnin' fame...
But there's a desert that's now gentle
'Cause we helped to make it tame."

D&RGW No. 499 with a short train between Chama and Alamosa. *John Krause/Dr. Richard Severance collection*

Appendix

Don Heimburger

OFFICIAL ROSTER

of

THE DENVER AND RIO GRANDE WESTERN RAILROAD SYSTEM

JOSEPH H. YOUNG, Receiver

The Denver and Rio Grande Western Railroad System
The Rio Grande Southern Railroad Company

No. 11

APRIL 1, 1923

Compiled in the Office of the
General Auditor

General Offices
DENVER, COLORADO

MAP OF
THE DENVER AND RIO GRANDE WESTERN RAILROAD
AND CONNECTIONS

January 1, 1966

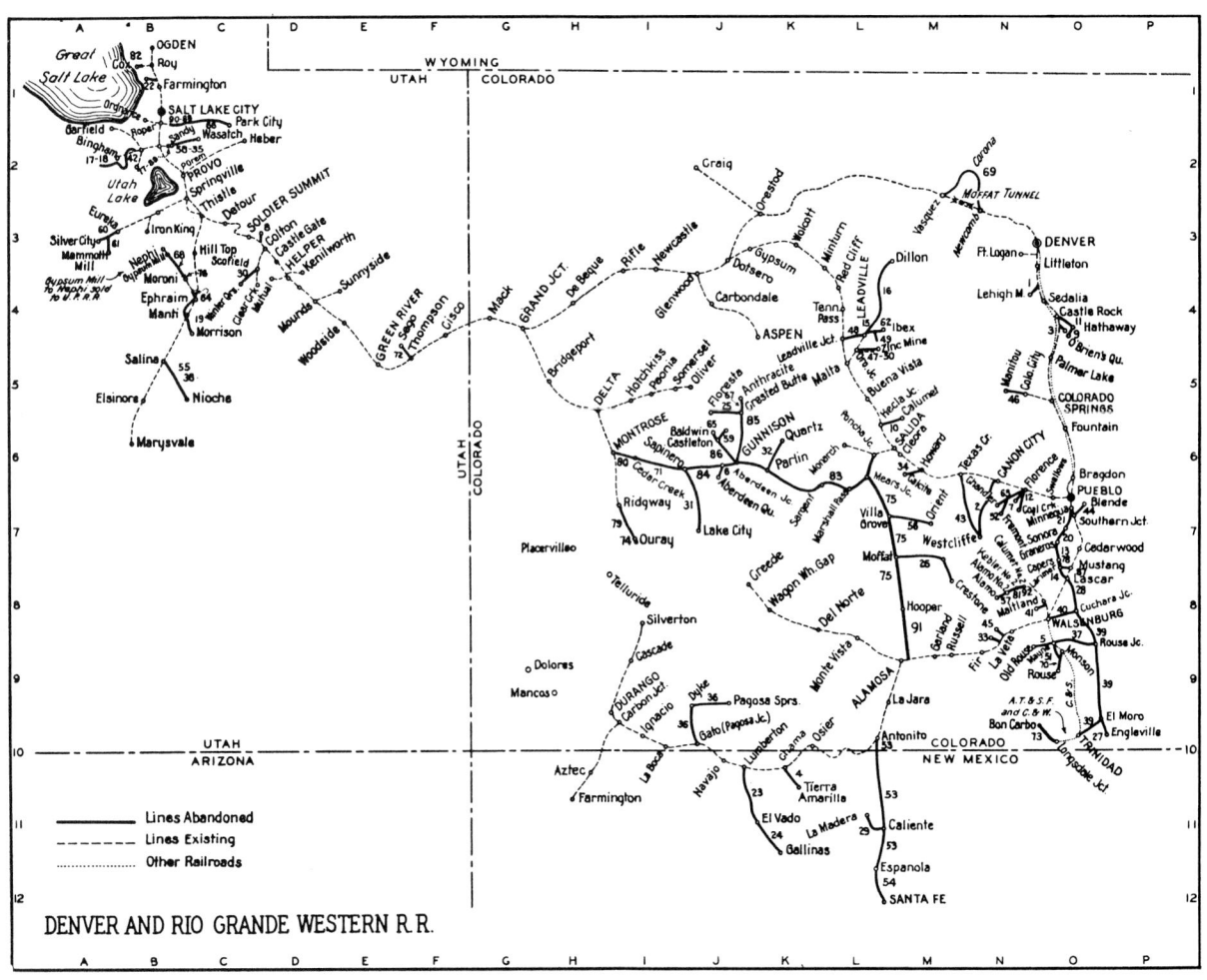

LINES ABANDONED   3-1-1961

No. on Map	Name of Line	Index
1	Lehi Branch	N-4
2	Grape Creek Branch	N-7
3	Douglas Quarry Spur	O-4
4	Chama Lumber Spur	K-10
5	Old Rouse Branch	O-8
6	Aberdeen Branch	J-6
7	Oak Creek Branch	N-7
8	Jennings & Potter Quarry Br'h	D-3
9	O'Brien's Quarry Spur	O-4
10	Calumet Branch	L-6
11	Castle Rock Branch	O-4
12	Coal Creek Branch	N-7
13	Graneros Br'h. Capers to Graneros	O-7
14	" " Lascar to Larimer	O-8
15	Blue River Br'h. in Leadville	L-4
16	" " " Leadville-Dillon	L-4
17	Copper Belt Branch	A-2
18	Copper Belt - Carr Fork Br'h.	A-2
19	Morrison Branch	C-4
20	Part of Old Main Line Sonora to Graneros	O-7
21	Sonora Branch	O-7
22	Lake Park Branch	B-1
23	Rio Grande Southwest'n. R.R.	K-11
24	" " " "	K-11
25	Ruby-Anthracite Branch	J-5
26	Crestone Branch	M-7
27	Engleville Branch	O-10
28	Part of Old Main Line Lascar to Cuchara Jct.	O-8
29	La Madera Branch	L-11
30	Winter Quarters Spur	C-3
31	Lake City Branch	J-7
32	Pitkin Branch (C.&S.)	K-6
33	Tropic Spur	N-8
34	Howard Branch	M-6
35	Little Cottonwood Br'h. (Part)	C-2
36	Pagosa Springs Branch	J-9
37	Rouse Branch	O-8
38	Castle Valley Br'h. Crystal to Niocha	B-5
39	Part of Old Main Ln. Cuchara Jct. to Trinidad	O-9
40	" " " " Cuchara Jct. to Walsenburg	O-8
41	New Pacific Mine Spur	N-8
42	Bingham Br'h. Extension	B-2
43	Westcliffe Branch	M-7
44	Zinc Smelter Spur	O-7
45	Reliance Branch	N-8
46	Manitou Branch (Part)	N-5
47	California Gulch Br'h (Part)	L-5
48	Ryan Cut-off	L-4
49	Graham Park Branch	L-4
50	California Gulch Branch (Part)	L-5
51	Rouse Branch (Part)	O-8
52	Fremont Branch	N-7
53	Santa Fe Br'h. Antonito to Espanola	L-10
54	" " " Espanola to Santa Fe	L-11
55	Castle Valley Br'h. Salina to Crystal	B-5
56	Orient Branch	M-7
57	Loma Branch (Part)	N-8
58	Little Cottonwood Br'h. (Part)	C-2
59	Kubler Branch	J-6
60	Tintic Branch (Part)	A-3
61	Mammoth Spur	A-3
62	Ibex Branch	L-4
63	Chandler Creek Branch	N-6
64	San Pete Valley Branch (Part)	C-4
65	Baldwin Branch (Part)	J-6
66	Park City Branch (Part)	C-1
67	Crested Butte Branch (Part)	J-5
68	San Pete Valley Br'h. (Part)	B-3
69	Corona Line (Former D.&S.L.)	N-2
70	Rouse Branch	O-9
71	Sapinero to Cedar Creek	I-6
72	Ballard & Thompson R.R.	F-5
73	Reilly Canon Branch	O-10
74	Ouray Branch (Part)	I-6
75	Mears Jct. to Alamosa (Part)	L-7
76	Moroni Spur (Part)	B-4
77	Little Cottonwood Br'h. (Part)	B-2
78	Capers Branch (Part)	O-8
79	Ouray Branch (Part)	I-7
80	Cedar Creek Branch	I-7
81	Loma Branch (Part)	N-8
82	Hooper Branch, Utah (Part)	B-1
83	Poncha Jct. to Gunnison	K-7
84	Sapinero Branch	J-7
85	Crested Butte Branch	J-7
86	Baldwin Branch	J-7
87	Capers Branch	O-8
88	Sugar House Spur (Part)	B-1
89	Little Cottonwood Br'h. (Part)	B-2
90	Sugar House Spur (Part)	B-1
91	Hooper Spur	L-8
92	Loma Branch (Part)	N-8

DENVER AND RIO GRANDE WESTERN R.R.   SYSTEM 31   1-1-1966

LINES ABANDONED

	LINE	STATE	FROM	TO	MILES OF MAIN TRACK	YEAR BUILT	DATE OF LAST OPERATION	TRACKS REMOVED	REMARKS
1	LEHIGH BRANCH	COLORADO	LEHIGH JCT.	LEHIGH COAL MINE	4.50	1883	ABOUT 1890	1890	Off Main Line near Louviers.
2	GRAPE CREEK BRANCH	"	GRAPE CREEK JCT.	WESTCLIFFE	31.20	1881		1890	" " " Canon City. Washed out 1889
3	DOUGLAS QUARRY SPUR	"	DOUGLAS	MADGE QUARRY	2.55	1881		1902	
4	CHAMA LUMBER SPUR	NEW MEXICO	CHAMA (BIGGS JCT.)	TIERRA AMARILLA	14.72	1888 & 1896		1902	3.16 Miles Const'd in 1888, 11.56 Miles in 1896.
5	OLD ROUSE BRANCH	COLORADO	OLD ROUSE JCT.	OLD ROUSE MINES	1.17	1888		1904	
6	ABERDEEN BRANCH	"	ABERDEEN JCT.	ABERDEEN QUARRY	4.47	1889	ABOUT 1903	1904	Near Gunnison. Granite for State Capitol Bldg.
7	OAK CREEK BRANCH	"	OAK CREEK JCT.	OAK CREEK	2.63	1881		1905	Near Florence.
8	JENNINGS & POTTER'S QUARRY BRANCH	UTAH	JENNINGS JCT.	QUARRIES	4.97		1907	1917	Near Kyune.
9	O'BRIEN'S QUARRY SPUR	COLORADO	HATHAWAY	O'BRIEN'S QUARRY	1.39	1880	1905	1917	Near Castle Rock.
10	CALUMET BRANCH	"	HECLA JCT.	CALUMET	7.13	1881	1908	1923	Near Brown Canon.
11	CASTLE ROCK BRANCH	"	CASTLE ROCK	HATHAWAY	2.87	1880	1913	1924	Part of former Main Line.
12	COAL CREEK BRANCH	"	FLORENCE	COAL CREEK MINE NO. 2	3.19	1872	1913	1924	" " " " "
13	GRANEROS BRANCH	"	CAPERS (M.P. 143.85)	GRANEROS (M.P. 151.75)	2.80	1876	1924	1924	" " " " "
14	"	"	LASCAR	LARIMER	4.18	1876	1924	1924	
15	BLUE RIVER BRANCH	"	LEADVILLE (M.L. JCT)	LEADVILLE (N. End of Yard)	0.80	1881	ABOUT 1924	1924	
16	"	"	LEADVILLE	DILLON	35.68	1881-1882	1909	1924	
17	COPPER BELT BRANCH	UTAH	BINGHAM (Copper Belt Jc.)	MONTANA-BINGHAM	1.91	1901-1902		1924	
18	COPPER BELT-CARR FORK BRANCH	"	YAMPA MINE CONN.	YAMPA MINE	1.11	1903	ABOUT 1916	1924	
19	MORRISON BRANCH	"	EPHRAIM	MORRISON	13.74	—	1914	1925	
20	PART OF OLD MAIN LINE	COLORADO	SONORA	GRANEROS (Near)	17.91	1876	1924	1925	Purchased in 1907.
21	SONORA BRANCH	"	MINNEQUA (Sonora Jct)	SONORA (End of Old Main Line)	4.71	1876		1925	
22	LAKE PARK BRANCH	UTAH	LAKE PARK JCT.	LAKE PARK	2.70	1903	1907	1925	Near Farmington, Utah.
23	RIO GRANDE & SOUTHWESTERN R.R.	NEW MEXICO	LUMBERTON	EL VADO	33.18	1918		1928	
24	"	"	EL VADO	GALLINAS	7.18	1893		1928	
25	RUBY-ANTHRACITE BRANCH	COLORADO	CRESTED BUTTE	FLORESTA	10.71		1929	1929	
26	CRESTONE BRANCH	"	MOFFAT (M.P. 262.26)	COTTONWOOD (M.P. 273.70)	11.44	1901	1913	1929	
27	ENGLEVILLE BRANCH	"	ENGLEVILLE JCT.	ENGLEVILLE	6.40	1877	1913	1930	
28	PART OF OLD MAIN LINE	"	LASCAR	CUCHARA	13.30	1876		1932	
29	LA MADERA BRANCH	NEW MEXICO	TAOS JCT.	LA MADERA	16.43	1914	1932	1932	Hallack & Howard Lumber Company.
30	WINTER QUARTERS SPUR	UTAH	SCOFIELD	WINTER QUARTERS	2.20	1890		1933	
31	LAKE CITY BRANCH	COLORADO	SAPINERO	LAKE CITY	35.81	1889	1932	ABOUT 1936	Built by predecessor of C.&S. and retired by C.&S. Part of old Main Track to Gunnison. Operated by D.&R.G.W. from 1911 to 1934.
32	PITKIN BRANCH (C.&S. Ry.)	"	PARLIN	QUARTZ	17.90	1882	1931	1934	
33	TROPIC SPUR	"	TROPIC JCT.	TROPIC	1.95	1908	1935	1935	Near La Veta.
34	HOWARD BRANCH	"	HOWARD'S QUARRY JCT.	CALCITE	5.83	1903	1936	1936	
35	LITTLE COTTONWOOD BRANCH (Part)	UTAH	SAND PIT	WASATCH	6.79	—	ABOUT 1934	1934	Purchased in 1881.
36	PAGOSA SPRINGS BRANCH	COLORADO	PAGOSA JCT.	PAGOSA SPRINGS	30.85	1900	1935	1936	Near Present "Gato".

Continued on Page 32

DENVER AND RIO GRANDE WESTERN R.R.   SYSTEM 32   1-1-1966

LINES ABANDONED

Continued from Page 31

	LINE	STATE	FROM	TO	MILES OF MAIN TRACK	YEAR BUILT	DATE OF LAST OPERATION	TRACKS REMOVED	REMARKS
37	ROUSE BRANCH	COLORADO	ROUSE JCT.	MAYNE	4.17	1888	1936	1936	Near Salina
38	CASTLE VALLEY BRANCH (Part)	UTAH	CRYSTAL	NIOCHE	2.33	1903	1907	"	
39	OLD MAIN LINE (Part)	COLORADO	CUCHARA JCT.	TRINIDAD	39.93	1876 & 1887	—	—	Const'd Cuchara to Engleville in '76 and to Trinidad in 87
40	"	"	"	WALSENBURG JCT.	5.59	1876	1936	1937	
41	NEW PACIFIC MINE SPUR	"	NEW PACIFIC JCT.	NEW PACIFIC MINE	2.69	1927	—	—	Near Picbou
42	BINGHAM BRANCH EXTENSION	UTAH	LOLINE JCT.	CUPRUM	11.93	1906	1923	1925 to 1928	Track reconstructed and operation resumed (Upper Jc. to Midas in 1929 and removed in 1931.
43	WESTCLIFFE BRANCH	COLORADO	TEXAS CREEK (Jct.)	WESTCLIFFE	25.49	1900	1936	1938	
44	ZINC SMELTER SPUR	"	ZINC JCT.	BLENDE	3.36	1902	1937	1939	Near Minnequa
45	RELIANCE BRANCH	"	RELIANCE JCT.	OJO	5.41	1912	1939	1939	Near La Veta, Along former Veta Pass N.G. Main Line.
46	MANITOU BRANCH (Part)	"	COLORADO CITY	MANITOU	2.60	1880	1939		
47	CALIFORNIA GULCH BRANCH (Part)	"			0.34	1880	—	1940	Leadville Mining District
48	RYAN CUT-OFF	"	LEADVILLE	LEADVILLE	3.06	1887	1940	1941	Also called Leadville Cut-Off
49	GRAHAM PARK BRANCH	"	GRAHAM PARK JCT.	TUCSON	1.61	1900	1941	"	Leadville Mining District
50	CALIFORNIA GULCH BRANCH (Part)	"			0.76	1880	1939 & 1940	"	"
51	ROUSE BRANCH (Part)	"	MAYNE	MONSON	2.25	1888			
52	FREMONT BRANCH	"	FREMONT JCT.	FREMONT MINE	1.74	1893	1942	1942	
53	SANTA FE BRANCH	COLO.-N. MEX.	ANTONITO	ESPANOLA	{20.04	1880	1941	"	
54	"	NEW MEXICO	ESPANOLA	SANTA FE		1882 — 1886			
55	CASTLE VALLEY BRANCH (Part)	UTAH	SALINA	CRYSTAL	17.67	1903	1942	"	
56	ORIENT BRANCH	COLORADO	VILLA GROVE	ORIENT	8.20	1881	1940	"	
57	LOMA BRANCH (Part)	"	ALAMO NO. 2	ALAMO	0.88	1923	1942	"	
58	LITTLE COTTONWOOD BRANCH	UTAH	SANDY	SAND PIT	1.36	—	1943	1943	Purchased in 1881
59	KUBLER BRANCH	COLORADO	CASTLETON	KUBLER	1.56	1883	"	"	Built by predecessor of C.&S. Acquired by D&R.G.W. in '37
60	TINTIC BRANCH (Part)	UTAH	EUREKA	SILVER CITY	3.49	1891 & 1892	1943	"	
61	MAMMOTH SPUR	"	MAMMOTH JCT.	MAMMOTH MILL	0.47	See Note Page 4		▪1944	D&R.G.W. owned ½ interest {D&R.G.W ½ interest sold to U.P.R.R}
62	IBEX BRANCH	COLORADO	LEADVILLE	IBEX	7.19	1898	1944	"	Leadville Mining District
63	CHANDLER CREEK BRANCH	"	CHANDLER JCT.	CHANDLER MINE	4.61	1890	"	"	Purchased in 1907.
64	SAN PETE VALLEY BRANCH (Part)	UTAH	IN EPHRAIM		0.53	—	1945	1945	Built by predecessor of C.&S., Acquired by D&R.G.W. in '37
65	BALDWIN BRANCH	COLORADO	CASTLETON	BALDWIN	2.09	1883	1946	1946	
66	PARK CITY BRANCH	UTAH	CEMENT QUARRY	PARK CITY	24.10	1889	1946	1946	
67	CRESTED BUTTE BRANCH (Part)	COLORADO	CRESTED BUTTE	ANTHRACITE	4.06	1882		1947	
68	SAN PETE VALLEY BRANCH (Part)	UTAH	MORONI	NEPHI	23.02			1948	Purchased in 1908. Gypsum Mill to Nephi (2.34 Mi) sold to U.P.R.R Co. in 1948.
69	CORONA LINE (Former D&S.L.)	COLORADO	NEWCOMB	VASQUEZ	31.76	1904	1928	1937	{Abandoned by D&S.L. when Tunnel operation was started.
70	ROUSE BRANCH	"	MONSON	ROUSE	2.53	1888	1949	1949	
71	GUNNISON TO MONTROSE	"	SAPINERO	CEDAR CREEK	26.63	1882	1950	1950	
72	BALLARD & THOMPSON R.R.	UTAH	THOMPSON	SEGO	4.95	1914	"	"	
73	REILLY CANON BRANCH	COLORADO	LONGSDALE JCT.	BON CARBO	8.91	See Note Page 4			

Continued on Page 33

258

DENVER AND RIO GRANDE WESTERN R.R.
SYSTEM 33
1-1-1966

LINES ABANDONED

Continued from Page 32

	LINE	STATE	FROM	TO	MILES OF MAIN TRACK	YEAR BUILT	DATE OF LAST OPERATION	TRACKS REMOVED	REMARKS
74	OURAY BRANCH (Part)	COLORADO	M.P. 387.64 AT OURAY	M.P. 387.81 AT OURAY	0.17	1887		1950	
75	MEARS JCT. TO ALAMOSA (Part)	"	MEARS JUNCTION	HOOPER	53.21	1881 and 1890		1951	Formerly San Pete Valley Branch - Purchased 1908
76	MORONI SPUR (Part)	UTAH	M.P. 23.02 AT MORONI	M.P. 23.27 AT MORONI	0.25			1951	Purchased 1881
77	LITTLE COTTONWOOD BRANCH (Part)	"	M.P. 1.94 AT SANDY	M.P. 2.08 AT SANDY	0.14			1951	
78	CAPERS BRANCH (Part)	COLORADO	M.P. 151.46 AT CAPERS	M.P. 151.75 AT CAPERS	0.29	1876 and 1924		1952	
79	OURAY BRANCH (Part)	"	M.P. 377.56 AT RIDGWAY	M.P. 387.64 AT OURAY	10.08	1887	1952	1953	Remaining Portion of Ouray Branch S.G. in 1953
80	CEDAR CREEK BRANCH	"	M.P. 350.86 AT MONTROSE	M.P. 340.81 AT CEDAR CR.	10.05	1882	"	"	
81	LOMA BRANCH (Part)	"	M.P. 192.09 NEAR ALAMO NO.2	M.P. 193.27 AT ALAMO NO. 2	1.18	1923	"	"	
82	HOOPER BRANCH	UTAH	M.P. 3.74 " HOOPER	M.P. 5.06 AT COX	1.32	1905 to 1917		1952	
83	PONCHA JCT. TO GUNNISON	COLORADO	M.P. 220.66 PONCHA JCT.	M.P. 288.41 AT GUNNISON	67.75	1881	12-18-1953	1955	
84	SAPINERO BRANCH	"	M.P. 288.41 AT GUNNISON	M.P. 314.18 AT SAPINERO	25.77	1882	"	"	
85	CRESTED BUTTE BRANCH	"	M.P. 288.55 " "	M.P. 316.79 AT CRESTED BUTTE	28.24	1881	"	"	
86	BALDWIN BRANCH	"	M.P. 288.72 "	M.P. 304.55 AT CASTLETON	15.83	1883	May 1948	"	
87	CAPERS BRANCH	"	M.P. 148.85 AT MUSTANG	M.P. 151.46 AT CAPERS	2.61	1876 and 1924		1956	
88	SUGAR HOUSE SPUR (Part)	UTAH	M.P. 5.67 AT ALEXANDER	M.P. 8.18 AT CEMENT QUARRY	2.51	1889		"	
89	LITTLE COTTONWOOD BRANCH (Part)	"	M.P. 1.64 AT SANDY	M.P. 1.94 AT SANDY	0.30			"	
90	SUGAR HOUSE SPUR (Part)	"	M.P. 3.15 AT SUGAR HOUSE	M.P. 5.67 AT ALEXANDER	2.55	1889	1957	1957	Built Standard Gauge in 1930.
91	HOOPER SPUR	COLORADO	M.P. 279.49 AT HOOPER	M.P. 299.72 AT ALAMOSA	20.23	1890	1959	1959	
92	LOMA BRANCH (Part)	"	M.P. 185.09 End of Track	M.P. 192.09 AT KEBLER #2	7.02	1904 to 1907	1959	1959	
93	OREM BRANCH (Part)	UTAH	M.P. 6.36 End of Track	M.P. 6.43 End of Track	0.07		1961	1961	Purchased from SL&URR in 1946.
94	LOMA BRANCH (Part)	COLORADO	M.P. 185.09	M.P. 184.70 AT CALUMET #2	0.39	1907	1962	1962	
95	CALIFORNIA GULCH BRANCH	"	M.P. 274.30 ORO JCT.	M.P. 276.45 AT ROWE MILL	2.15	1880	1957	1963	Leadville Mining District.
96	FORT LOGAN BRANCH (Part)	"	M.P. 9.47 Federal Blvd.	M.P. 10.62 AT FORT LOGAN	1.15	1889	1962	1963	
97	BINGHAM BRANCH (Part)	UTAH	M.P. 11.81	M.P. 14.26 AT BINGHAM	2.45	1873	1964	1964	Sold 2,000 ft. to Kennecott Copper Co.
98	LITTLE COTTONWOOD BRANCH	UTAH	M.P. 0.00 AT MIDVALE	M.P. 1.64 End of Track	1.64		1964	1965	Purchased 1883.

CONDENSED PROFILE
OF THE
D. & R.G.W.R.R.
SYSTEM

OFFICE OF CHIEF ENGINEER

DENVER, COLORADO

CORRECTED TO JAN. 1, 1966

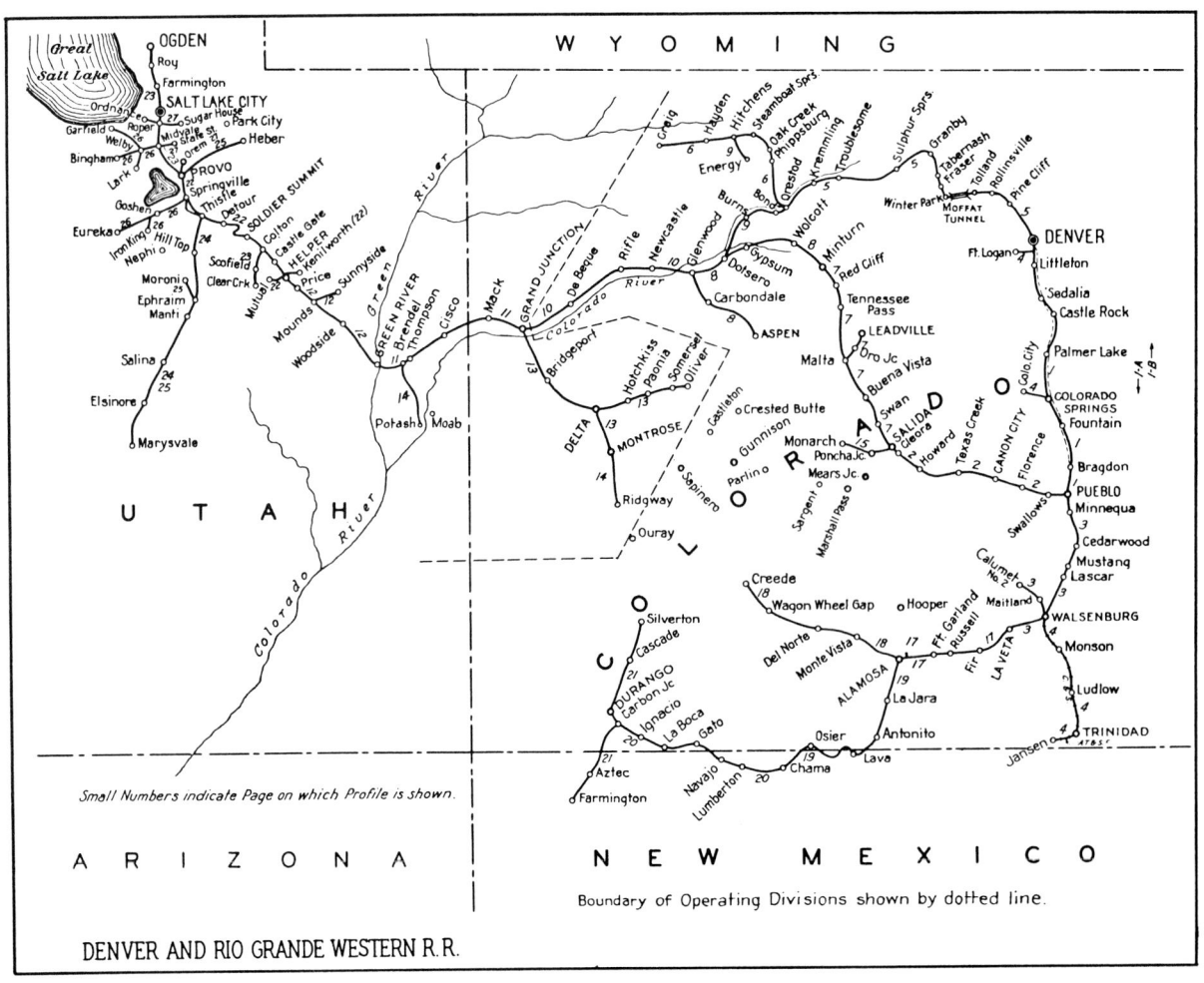

DENVER AND RIO GRANDE WESTERN R.R.

Small Numbers indicate Page on which Profile is shown.

Boundary of Operating Divisions shown by dotted line.

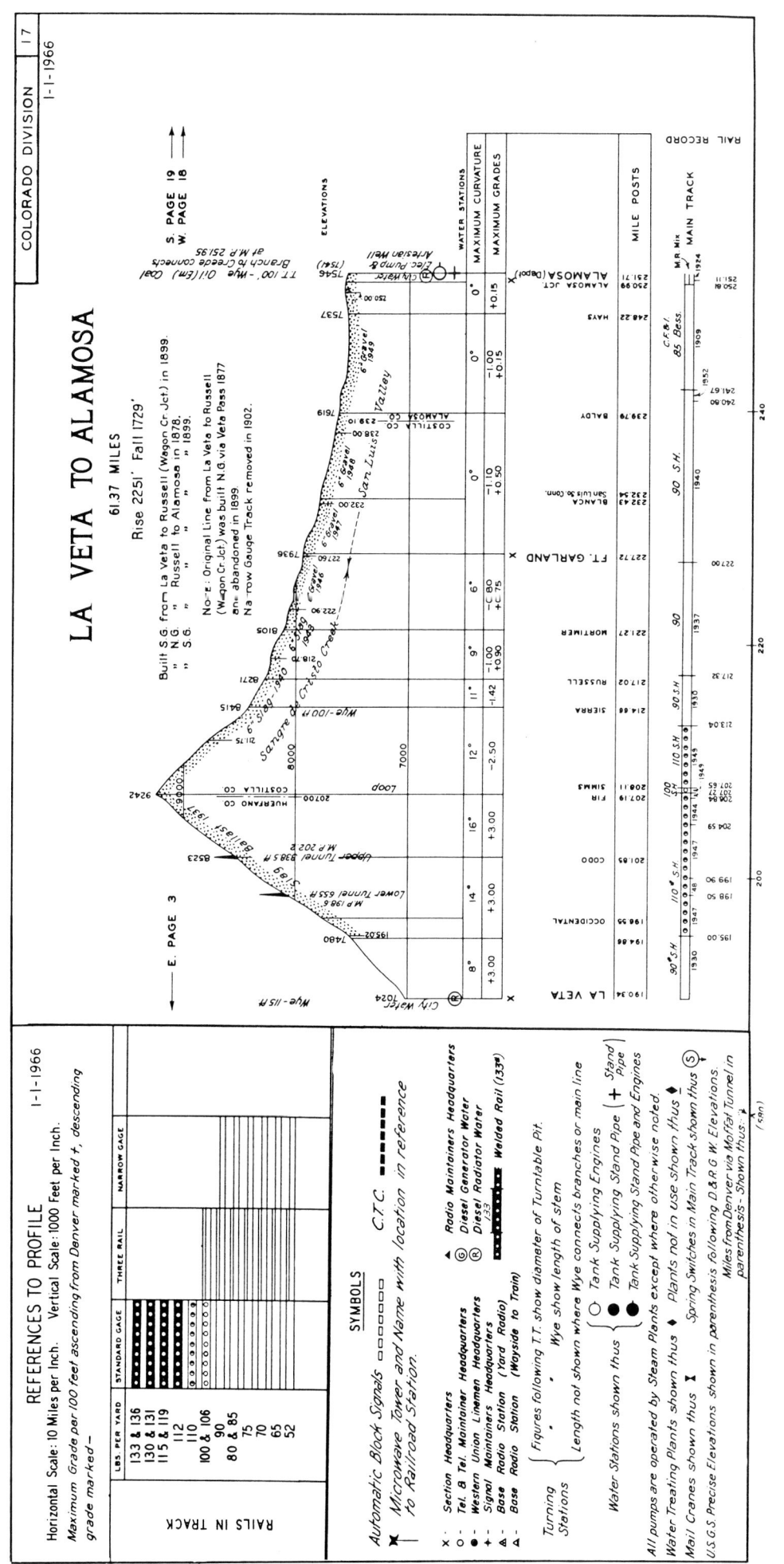

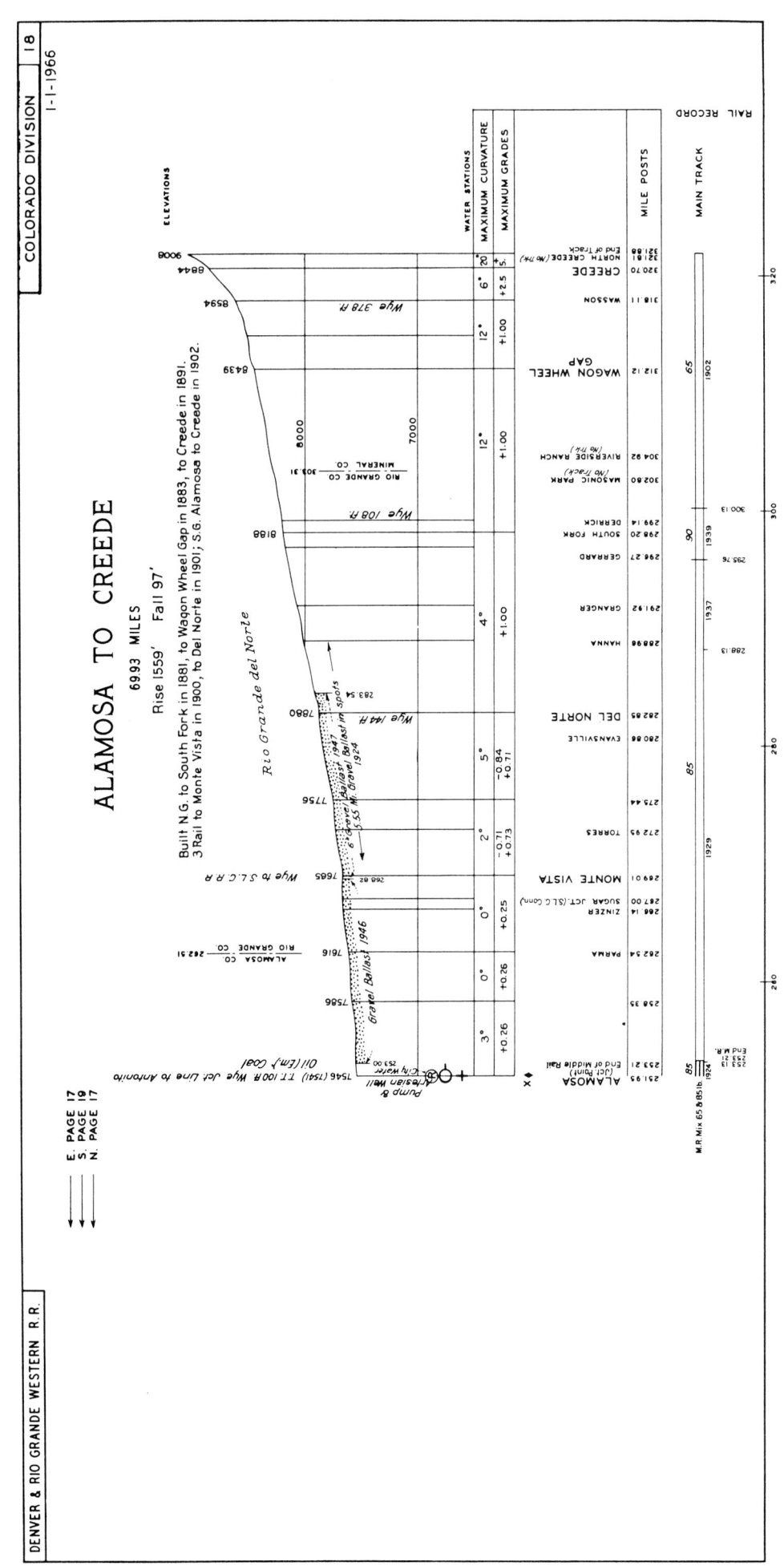

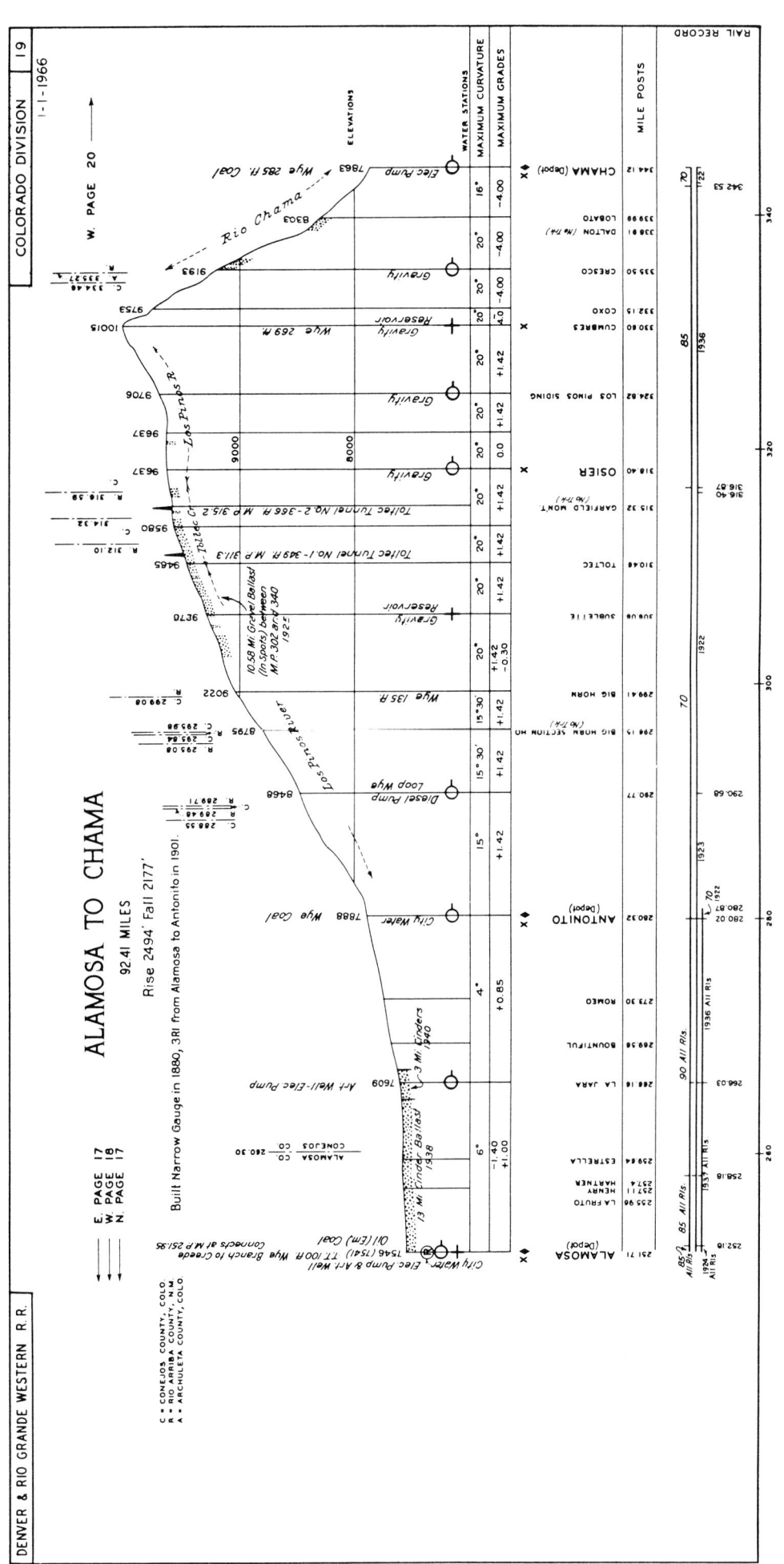

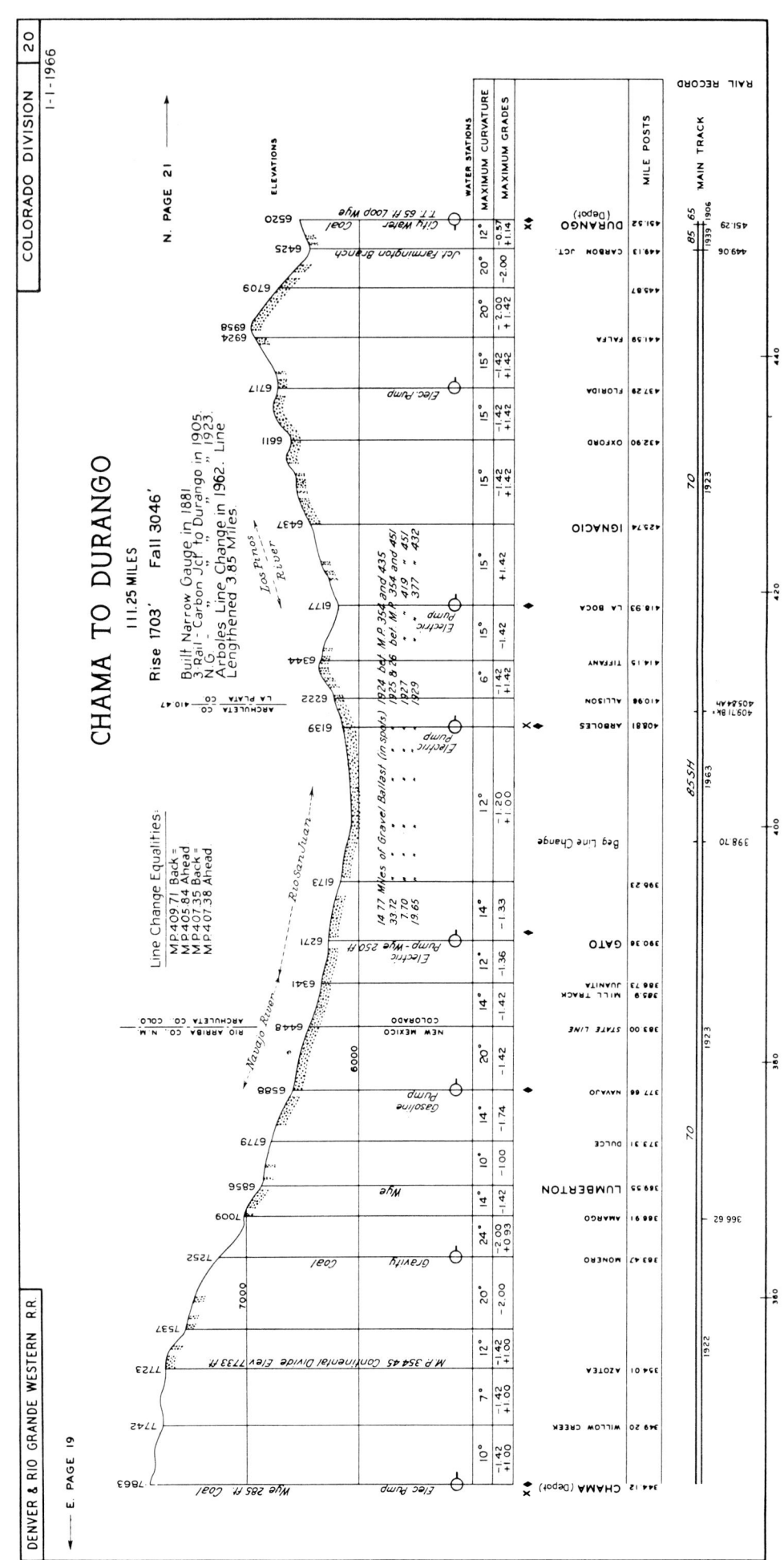

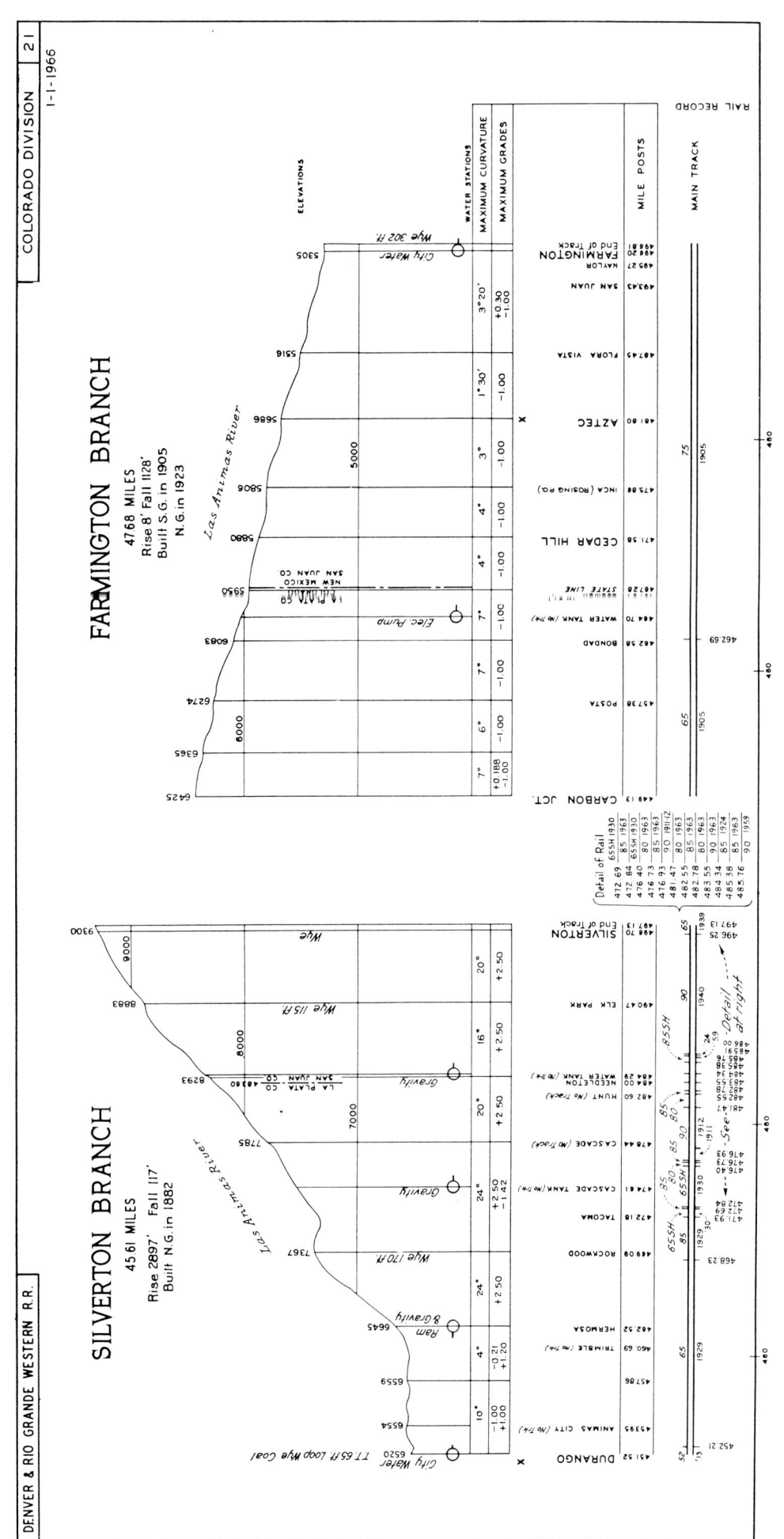

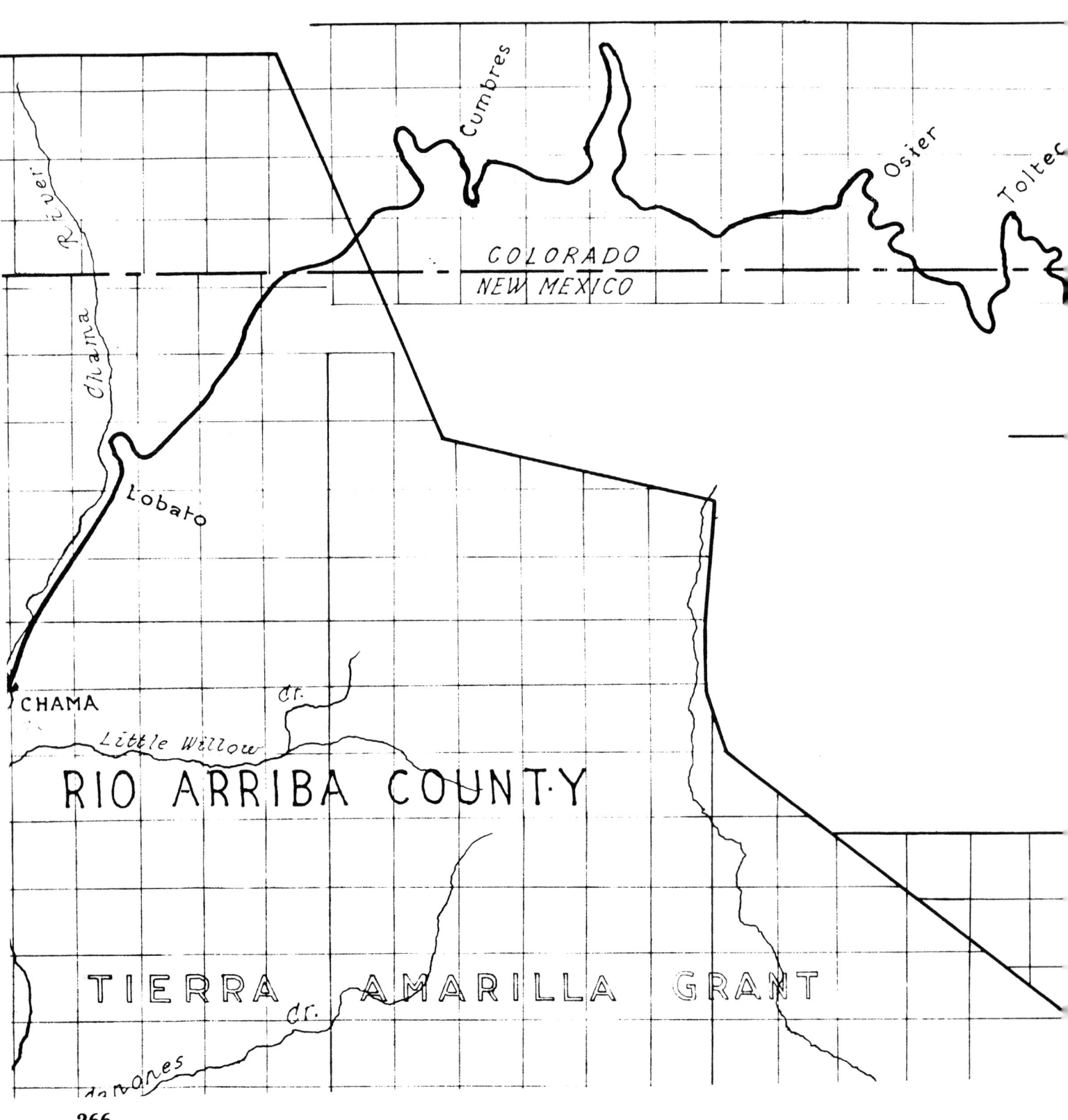

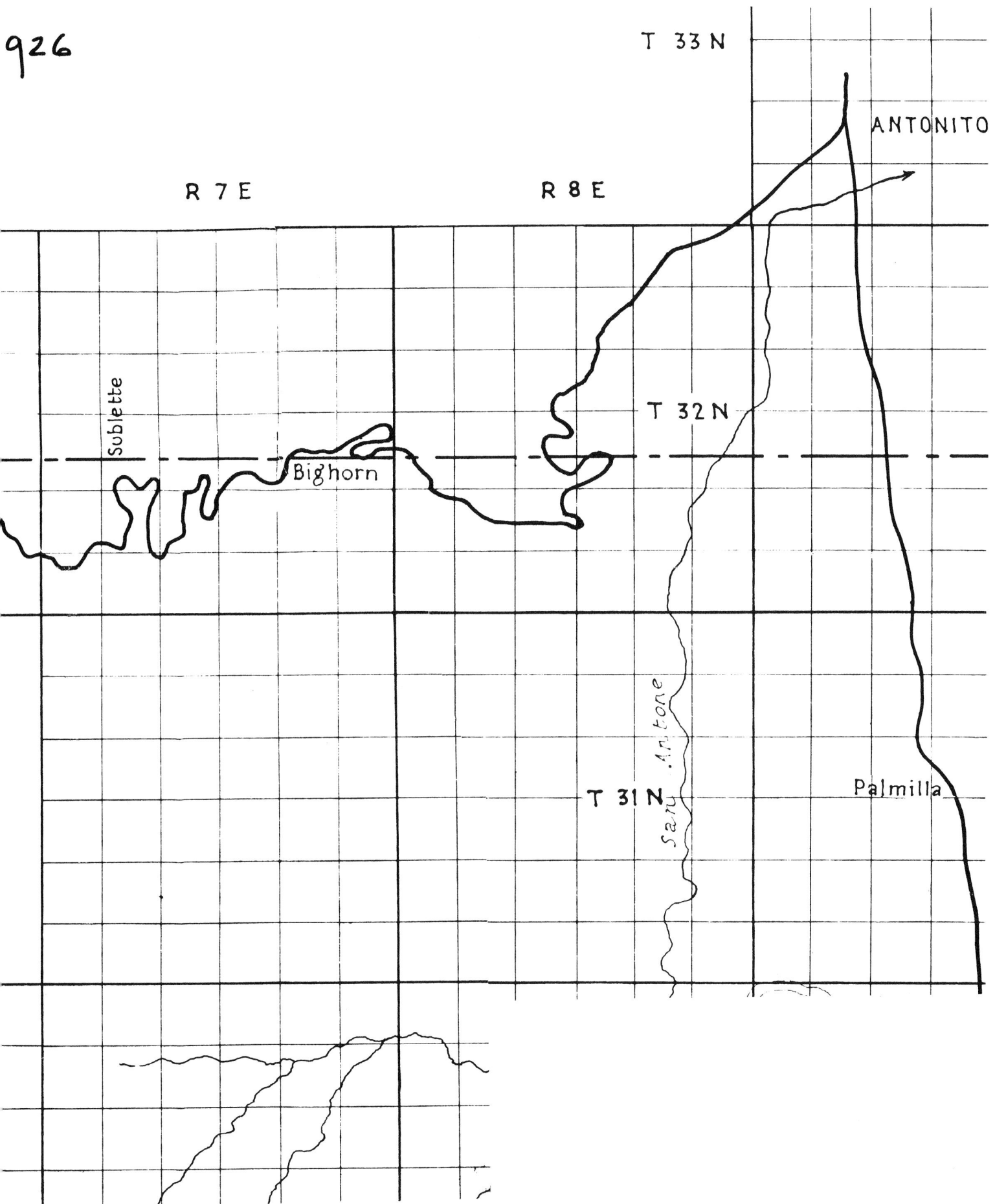

NAMES OF OTHER LINES AND POINTS OF CONNECTION WITH D. & R. G. W. R. R.

ATCHISON, TOPEKA & SANTA FE RY.
    Denver, Palmer Lake, Colorado Springs (via Colo. Mid.), Pueblo, El Moro, Trinidad, Portland, Chandler Jct. (via A. T. & S. F. Transfer), Canon City, Santa Fe (Transfer only).

BALLARD & THOMPSON R. R.
    Thompson, Utah.

BAMBERGER ELECTRIC RAILROAD.
    North Salt Lake Jct.
    Ogden (via Utah Idaho Central Railroad).

BINGHAM & GARFIELD RAILWAY.
    Magna.

CARBON COUNTY RAILROAD.
    Mile Post 13.1, Sunnyside Branch.

CHICAGO, BURLINGTON & QUINCY RAILROAD.
    Denver.

CHICAGO, ROCK ISLAND & PACIFIC RY.
    Denver (via U. P. R. R.), Roswell, Colorado Springs.

COLORADO & SOUTHEASTERN R. R.
    Barnes.

COLORADO & SOUTHERN RY.
    Denver, Colorado Springs (via Colo. Mid.), Pueblo, Southern Jct. Lascar, Walsenburg Junction, Mayne Junction, Forbes Junction, Trinidad.—Narrow Gage: Buena Vista, Leadville, Dillon.

COLORADO & WYOMING RY.
    Hezron Jct. and Jansen.

CRYSTAL RIVER & SAN JUAN R. R.
    Carbondale.

DENVER & INTER-MOUNTAIN R. R. (Electric).
    Denver.

DENVER & SALT LAKE RAILROAD.
    Denver (via C. B. & Q. R. R).

GRAND RIVER VALLEY RAILWAY (Electric).
    Grand Junction.

LOS ANGELES AND SALT LAKE RAILROAD.
    Eureka, M. P. 39.7, Tintic Branch.
    Mammoth Jct., M. P. 42.0, Tintic Branch.
    Tintic Mill, M. P. 43.1, Tintic Branch.
    Provo.
    Utah Sugar Works.
    Salt Lake City (via O. S. L.).
    Garfield (via A. S. & R. Co.).
    Nephi, San Pete Valley Branch.

MIDLAND TERMINAL RAILWAY.
    Colo. Springs, and Hulbert, Transfer.

MISSOURI PACIFIC R. R.
    Pueblo.

NEW MEXICO CENTRAL RY.
    Santa Fe.

OREGON SHORT LINE RAILROAD.
    Smelter Passing Track.
    Fireclay.
    Salt Lake City.
    North Salt Lake.
    Ogden Sugar Works Jct.
    Evona.
    Ogden.
    Midvale, Utah Steel Corporation.

RIO GRANDE SOUTHERN R. R. (Narrow Gage).
    Ridgway, Durango.

RIO GRANDE & SOUTHWESTERN R. R. (Narrow Gage).
    Lumberton.

SALT LAKE, GARFIELD & WESTERN RAILWAY (Electric).
    Salt Lake City.

SALT LAKE & UTAH R. R. (OREM LINES) (Electric).
  Provo, Spanish Fork Sugar Factory, West Jordan Sugar Factory, Lehi, Utah Sugar Works.
SAN LUIS CENTRAL R. R.
  Monte Vista.
SAN LUIS SOUTHERN RAILWAY.
  Blanca.
SILVERTON RY. AND SILVERTON NORTHERN R. R. (Narrow Gage).
  Silverton.
SOUTHERN PACIFIC COMPANY.
  Ogden.
UINTAH RAILWAY.
  Mack (Narrow gage) (Transfer only).
UNION PACIFIC R. R.
  Denver.
  Park City, M. P. 31.6, Park City Branch.
  Ogden.
UTAH-IDAHO CENTRAL RAILROAD (Electric).
  Ogden.
UTAH RAILWAY.
  Utah Ry. Jct., Thistle, Springville, and Provo.
WESTERN PACIFIC RAILROAD.
  Salt Lake City.

SILVERTON NORTHERN RAILROAD
LIST OF OFFICERS

OTTO MEARS, PRESIDENT
J. R. PITCHER, JR...........Vice-President, Treasurer and General Manager
J. H. SLATTERY............................Assistant to Vice-President
J. B. FRANK..............................Secretary and General Agent
J. E. DRESBACK..................................General Auditor
F. L. ROSS......................................General Counsel
W. E. BOOKER................................General Superintendent

Station No.	Miles from Silverton	Local Mileage	Telephone Calls	STATIONS	AGENTS	Elevation above sea level, ft.
0	0	0		Silverton	F, T & E	9,300
1	1	1		Power		
2	2	1		Waldheim		
3	3			Robin		
4	3.2	1		Collins		
5	4.7	1		Howardsville		
6	6.1	1.25		Howardsville		
	6.3	1.30		Old Hundred		
				Green Mountain		
7	6.2	1		Hamlet		
9	7.4	1		Minnie Gulch		
10	8.5	2		Eureka		10,000
11				Astor		
12				Lion Tunnel		
13	12.5			Animas Forks		11,200
0				Silverton		9,300
Y.M.1	3.2	3.2		Yukon Mills		
P.G.2	5	1.8		Porcupine Gulch		
F.M.3	7	2		Fisher's Mill		
G.4	7.5	.5		Gladstone		10,600

SILVERTON RAILWAY
LIST OF OFFICERS

OTTO MEARS...President
J. R. PITCHER, JR...........Vice-President, Treasurer and General Manager
J. B. FRANK..Secretary
J. E. DRESBACK..General Auditor
F. L. ROSS..General Counsel
W. E. BOOKER..General Superintendent

Station No.	Miles from Silverton	Local Mileage	Telephone Calls	STATIONS	AGENTS	Elevation above sea level, ft.
0	0.00	0.0		Silverton	F, T & E	9,300
5	5.30	6.4		Burro Bridge		10,236
7	7.23	2.5		Chattanooga		10,400
10	10.64	4.0		Summit		11,235
A12	11.97	1.6		Red Mountain		11,025
B12	12.66	0.4		Vanderbilt		
C12	12.85	0.2		Yankee Girl		
13	13.26	0.4		Robinson		
D13	13.46	0.1		Guston		
E13	13.93	1.3		Paymaster Coal Track		
14	14.38	0.6		Corkscrew Gulch		
F15	14.81	0.5		Paymaster Ore Track		
G15	15.03	0.1		Silver Belle		
16	16.06	2.5		Joker		

THE CRYSTAL RIVER & SAN JUAN RAILROAD CO.

General Offices, Marble, Colo.

LIST OF OFFICERS

JAMES H. BLOOD, President	Denver, Colo.
A. J. MITCHELL, Vice-President and General Manager	Denver, Colo.
H. E. BUCHENAU, Treasurer	Denver, Colo.
W. W. BLOOD, Secretary	Denver, Colo.
F. V. MUELLER, General Superintendent	Marble, Colo.
V. T. BROWN, Freight Claim Agent	Marble, Colo.

MAIN LINE

(Standard Gauge)

Connection with Crystal River R. R. at Redstone, Colo.

Miles from Redstone	Local Mileage	STATIONS	AGENTS
0.00	0.00	Redstone	
1.40	1.40	Crystal Ranch	
3.50	2.10	Placita	
4.30	.80	McClures	
6.50	2.20	Chair Creek	
7.50	1.00	Prospect	
9.30	1.80	Holland's	
9.80	.50	Fortsch's	
10.90	1.10	Marble	

THE RIO GRANDE & SOUTHWESTERN R. R. CO.

(Narrow Gauge)
LIST OF OFFICERS

W. P. McPHEE, President	Denver, Colo.
R. G. LINDSTROM, Vice-President	Denver, Colo.
H. E. WOODARD, Secretary-Treasurer	Denver, Colo.
H. F. McCARTHY, Auditor	Denver, Colo.

Miles from Lumberton	Telegraph Calls	STATIONS	AGENTS	Elevations
0.00		Lumberton		6,856
7.36		Mundo		7,469
12.00		Hillcrest		7,714
19.00		Lago		7,292
27.22		Horse Lake Junction		6,994
32.21		Gallina Junction		6,838
33.16		El Vado		6,792
40.02		Gallinas Mountain		6,882

THE SAN LUIS SOUTHERN RAILWAY COMPANY

LIST OF OFFICERS

H. S. THOMPSON	President	Boston, Mass.
CHAS. A. ROBINSON	Treasurer and General Manager	San Acacio, Colo.
G. W. BIERBAUER	Secretary	Colorado Springs, Colo.
ROBERT B. RAMSEY	Auditor and Superintendent	San Acacio, Colo.
HOWARD T. WELLS	Master Mechanic	Blanca, Colo.

Station Number	Miles From Blanca	Stations	Agents	Elevation
1	0.00	Blanca	F, T & E	7,750
7	7.41	Ojito		7,724
16	15.81	San Acacio	F T & E	7,737
24	24.44	Mesita		7,671
32	32.00	Jaroso	F, T & E	7,579

Stock yards at San Acacio, Mesita and Jaroso.

THE SAN LUIS CENTRAL RAILROAD COMPANY

LIST OF OFFICERS

GEO. McLEAN	President	Denver, Colo.
A. T. YOUNG	Vice-Pres., Gen. Manager & Treasurer	Denver, Colo.
F. C. KRAUSER	Secretary and Auditor	Denver, Colo.
A. W. CORNELL	Superintendent and General Agent	Monte Vista, Colo.

No Express. Operated by Telephone.
Use D. & R. G. W. track, Monte Vista to Sugar Factory............ 3 miles
Main Line, Sugar Factory to Center................................ 12 "
      Total mileage operated.. 15 "
Mileage owned by Counties—Rio Grande, 11.71; Saguache, 0.50; all in Colorado.

Miles From Monte Vista	Stations	Agent	Elevation
0	Monte Vista (Joint)	F & P	7,665
3	*Sugar Factory		
5	*North Farm		
9	*Dunul		
11	*Ansel		
15	Center	F & P	7,675

*No Agent.

THIRD DIVISION—3RD DISTRICT

Station No.	Miles from Denver	Local Mileage	Telegraph Calls	STATIONS	Kind of Agency	Elevation above sea level, feet
215	215.11	0.00	S	SALIDA..................W T	FC	7,050
P226	226.02	10.91		Mears Junction...............W T	N	8,431
	227.96			County line, Chaffee and Saguache.		
R230	229.57	14.46	PB	Poncha Pass............(Tel. Box)	N	9,059
R233	232.86	17.75		Round Hill....................W	N	8,687
R235	235.10	19.99		Alder.......	N	
R239	238.99	23.88		Linton.....	N	
R240	239.67	24.56		Davenport....	N	8,179
R245	245.34	30.23	VG	VILLA GROVE...............W	FC	7,972
	245.43	30.32		Orient Junction........	N	7,973
	250.80	5.37		Decorate....	N	
Q254	253.56	8.13		Orient.....	N	9,024
R251	250.93	35.82		Mineral Hot Springs......	FT	7,767
	253.69	38.58		Watonga..........No Track	N	
R257	257.01	41.90		Mirage......	N	7,628
R262	262.26	47.15		Crestone Junction....	N	
R263	262.69	47.58	MF	Moffat....................W	FC	7,579
R269	268.90	53.79		La Garita...	N	7,561
R274	274.30	59.19		Gibson.....	N	7,559
	280.04			County line, Saguache and Alamosa.		
R280	280.27	65.16	GR	Hooper....	FC	7,576
R287	286.84	71.73	MK	Mosca.....	FT	7,572
R291	291.13	76.02		Corlett....	N	
R294	294.11	79.00		McGinty...	N	7,563
	299.50	84.39		End of Third Division......		
	299.72	84.61		Garland Junction...........	N	
R300	300.44	85.33	AS	ALAMOSA.................W T	FC	7,546

THIRD DIVISION—CRESTONE BRANCH

Station No.	Miles from Denver	Local Mileage	Telegraph Calls	STATIONS	Kind of Agency	Elevation above sea level, feet
R262	262.26	0.00		Crestone Junction..............W	N	7,582
AG266	265.74	3.48		Travis......	N	7,589
AG274	273.70	11.44		Crestone (End of Operated Track)....	N	7,881
AG278	278.30	16.04		Mill.........................W	N	8,371
AG279	279.12	16.86		Cottonwood....	N	8,407
	279.22	16.96		End of Track........		

FOURTH DIVISION—1ST DISTRICT

Station No.	Mile Post	Miles from Denver via C. & S. Joint D. T.	Local Mileage	Telegraph Calls	STATIONS	Kind of Agency	Elevation above sea level, feet
B186	190.34	185.54	0.00	X	LA VETA.............W T	FC	7,024
B187	191.75	186.95	1.41		Reliance Junction........	N	
B192	196.97	192.17	5.22		Ojo (Reliance Mine)......	N	
					" (Reliable Mine)........	N	
B190	194.54	189.74	4.20		Oakdale Junction........T	N	7,433
B191	195.96	191.16	1.42		Alliance....	N	
B191½	196.34	191.54	1.80		Tropic (Oakdale M.) (Oakview P.O.)	N	7,603
B190¼	194.86	190.06	4.52		Francisco....	N	7,480
B192½	197.14	192.34	6.80		Occidental..............T	N	7,820
B197	201.89	197.09	11.55		Codo...................W T	N	8,523
	207.00	202.20			County line, Huerfano & Costilla		
B202	207.19	202.39	16.85	VA	La Veta Pass.............T	FT	9,242
B203	208.26	203.46	17.92		Carr........	N	
B204	208.80	204.00	18.46		Trinchera.....	N	
B210	214.56	209.76	24.22		Sierra.................W T	N	8,415
B212	216.87	212.07	26.53		Russell................T	N	8,271
B216	221.07	216.27	30.73		Mortimer...............T	N	8,104
B223	227.72	222.92	37.38	FT	Ft. Garland.............W	FT	7,936
B228	232.43	227.63	42.09	NK	Blanca.....	FC	
	232.54	227.74	42.20		San Luis Southern Connection.		
	239.10	234.30			County line, Costilla & Alamosa.		
B235	239.79	234.99	49.45		Baldy..................T	N	7,619
B244	248.47	243.67	58.13		Hays.......	N	7,537
	250.99	246.19	60.65		Garland Junction..........	N	
B247	251.71	246.91	61.37	AS	ALAMOSA.............W T	FC	7,546

FOURTH DIVISION—CREEDE BRANCH

Station No.	Mile Post	Miles from Denver via C. & S. Joint D. T.	Local Mileage	Telegraph Calls	STATIONS	Kind of Agency	Elevation above sea level, feet
B247	251.71	246.91	0.00	AS	ALAMOSA.............W T	FC	7,546
	252.91	248.11	1.20		Tie Treating Plant........	N	
B254	258.35	253.55	6.64		Willis......	N	7,586
	262.51	257.71			County line, Alamosa and Rio Grande.		
B258	262.54	257.74	10.83		Parma.....	N	7,616

W Water.   T Telegraphone.

FOURTH DIVISION—CREEDE BRANCH—Concluded

Station No.	Mile Post	Miles from Denver via C. & S. Joint D. T.	Local Mileage	Telegraph Calls	STATIONS	Kind of Agency	Elevation above sea level, feet
B261	266.14	261.34	14.43		Zinzer....................	N	
	267.00	262.20	15.29		Sugar Junction............	N	
B263	267.70	262.90	0.70		Sugar Works..............	N	
B263½	268.32	263.52	16.61		Continental Oil Co.........	N	
B264	269.01	264.21	17.30	MV	MONTE VISTA........W	FC	7,665
B268	272.95	268.15	21.24		Torres...................	N	7,756
B271	275.44	270.64	23.73		Haywood.................	N	
B272	276.42	271.62	24.71		Freeman.................	N	
B274	279.02	274.22	27.31		Middaugh................	N	
B278	282.85	278.05	31.14	DE	Del Norte................	FC	7,880
B284	288.89	284.09	37.18		Hanna...................	N	
B287	291.95	287.15	40.24		Granger..................	N	
	296.88	292.08	45.17		Hutchison................	N	
B292	297.08	292.28	45.37		San Luis Lumber Co.......	N	
B293	298.20	293.40	46.49		South Fork...........W	N	8,188
B294	299.14	294.34	47.43		Derrick..................	N	
B297	301.67	296.87	49.96		Phillips..................	N	
	302.36	297.56	50.65		Masonic Park....No Track	N	
	303.31	298.51			County line, Rio Grande and Mineral.		
	304.92	300.12	53.21		Riverside Ranch...No Track	N	
	310.29	305.49	58.58		Cunningham......No Track	N	
B307	312.12	307.32	60.41	W	Wagon Wheel Gap.......W	N	8,449
	315.04	310.24	63.33		Chapman.........No Track	N	
B313	318.09	313.29	66.38		Wasson..................	N	8,603
B315	320.12	315.32	68.41		South Creede.............	N	8,784
B316	320.70	315.90	68.99	JI	CREEDE...............W	FC	8,852
	321.51	316.71	69.80		West Willow Creek Junction..	N	
B316½	321.62	316.82	0.11		Humphrey's Mill...........	N	
B316¾	321.72	316.92	0.21		Commodore Ore Bins.......	N	
B317	321.81	317.01	70.10		North Creede.............	N	9,016

FOURTH DIVISION—2ND DISTRICT

Station No.	Mile Post	Miles from Denver via C. & S. Joint D. T.	Local Mileage	Telegraph Calls	STATIONS	Kind of Agency	Elevation above sea level, feet
B247	251.71	246.91	0.00	AS	ALAMOSA...........W T	FC	7,546
Y252	257.04	252.24	5.33		Henry...................	N	7,558
Y255	259.64	254.84	7.93		Estrella...............T	N	
	260.30	255.50			County line, Alamosa and Conejos.		
Y261	266.16	261.36	14.45	JR	La Jara...............W	FC	7,609
Y265	269.71	264.91	18.00		Bountiful................	N	
Y268	273.27	268.47	21.56	OM	Romeo...................	FT	7,736
Y276	280.32	275.52	28.61	NA	Antonito.............W T	FC	7,888
	288.55	283.75			Conejos Co., Colo., & Rio Arriba	Co.,	N. M.
	289.48	284.68			Rio Arriba Co., N.M., & Conejos	Co.,	Colo.
	289.71	284.91			Conejos Co., Colo., & Rio Arriba	Co.,	N. M.
Y286	290.77	285.97	39.06		Lava.................W T	N	8,468
	295.08	290.28			Rio Arriba Co. N.M., & Conejos	Co.,	Colo.
	295.84	291.04			Conejos Co., Colo., & Rio Arriba	Co.,	N. M.
	295.98	291.18			Rio Arriba Co., N.M., & Conejos	Co.,	Colo.
	296.15	291.35	44.44		Big Horn Sec. House, No Track	N	8,795
	299.09	294.29			Conejos Co., Colo., & Rio Arriba	Co.,	N. M.
Y295	299.41	294.61	47.70		Big Horn..............T	N	9,022
Y301	306.06	301.26	54.35	SU	Sublette.....(Tel. Box) W T	N	9,276
Y306	310.46	305.66	58.75		Toltec...................	N	9,465
	312.10	307.30			Rio Arriba Co., N.M., & Conejos	Co.,	Colo.
	313.44	308.64	61.73		Toltec Sec. House, No Track W	N	9,580
	314.32	309.52			Conejos Co., Colo., & Rio Arriba	Co.,	N. M.
	315.32	310.52	63.61		Garfield Monument, No Track	N	
	316.59	311.79			Rio Arriba Co., N.M., & Conejos	Co.,	Colo.
Y314	318.40	313.60	66.69	BO	Osier.................W T	N	9,637
Y317	322.12	317.32	70.41		Los Pinos................	N	9,637
	325.50	320.70	73.79		Los Pinos Sec. Ho. No Tr'k W	N	9,706
	330.49	325.69			County line, Conejos and Archuleta.		
Y326	330.60	325.80	78.89	BR	Cumbres..............W T	FT	10,015
Y327	332.20	327.40	80.49		Coxo....................	N	9,753
	335.27	330.47			Archuleta Co., Colo., & Rio Arriba	Co.,	N. M.
Y331	335.50	330.70	83.79		Cresco................W T	N	9,193
Y334	338.91	334.11	87.20		Dalton...................	N	
Y335	339.99	335.19	88.28		Lobato..................	N	8,303
Y338	343.00	338.20	91.29		Broad...................	N	
Y339	344.12	339.32	92.41	CH	CHAMA..............W T	FC	7,863

FOURTH DIVISION—SANTA FE BRANCH

Station No.	Mile Post	Miles from Denver via C. & S. Joint D. T.	Local Mileage	Telegraph Calls	STATIONS	Kind of Agency	Elevation above sea level, feet
Y276	280.32	275.52	0.00	NA	Antonito.............W T	FC	7,888
	285.86	281.06			Conejos Co., Colo., & Rio Arriba	Co.,	N. M.
Z287	291.75	286.95	11.43		Palmilla.................	N	8,258
Z294	298.68	293.88	18.36		Volcano...............T	N	8,487
Z295	299.96	295.16	19.64		Wissmath................	N	

W Water.   T Telegraphone.

Station No.	Mile Post	Miles from Denver via C. & S. Joint D. T.	Local Mileage	Telegraph Calls	STATIONS	Kind of Agency	Elevation above sea level, feet
Z297	301.48	296.68	21.16		Lawton....................	N	
	302.35	297.55			County line, Rio Arriba and Taos.		
Z303	307.87	303.07	27.55		No Agua................W	N	8,205
Z310	315.05	310.25	34.73	PF	Tres Piedras............W	FT	8,088
	322.17	317.37	41.85		Connell Tank............W	N	
Z320	324.68	319.88	44.36		Servilleta.................T	N	7,727
Z332	336.52	331.72	56.20	CJ	Taos Junction............T	FC	7,324
	338.75	333.95	58.43		Carson..........No Track	N	
Z340	345.13	340.33	64.81		Barranca................T	N	6,949
	350.19	345.39			County line, Taos and Rio Arriba.		
Z348	352.58	347.78	72.26	MD	Embudo................W	FT	5,821
Z351	355.60	350.80	75.28		Velarde...................	N	
Z352	357.17	352.37	76.85		Brady....................	N	
	358.50	353.70	78.18		Leyden..........No Track	N	
Z356	360.56	355.76	80.24		Alcalde...................	N	5,709
Z362	366.76	361.96	86.44		Chamita..................	N	5,641
Z365	369.67	364.87	89.35		Prince....................	N	
Z367	371.62	366.82	91.30	NO	ESPAÑOLA.............T	FC	5,590
	372.61				County line, Rio Arriba and Santa Fe.		
	374.60	369.80	94.28		Santa Clara......No Track	N	5,659
	376.30	371.50	95.98		Hobart..........No Track	N	5,595
	377.49	372.69	97.17		Pajarita Ranch....No Track	N	
Z374	378.55	373.75	98.23		San Ildefonso.............	N	5,571
	380.55	375.75	100.23		Otowi....................T		
Z376	380.93	376.13	100.61	WT	Rio Grande.............W	N	5,516
Z379	384.14	379.34	103.82	WC	Buckman.................	N	5,545
	388.01	383.21	107.69		Jacona Sec. House..No Track	N	
Z389	393.82	389.02	113.50	JA	Jacona..........(Tel. Box)	N	6,282
Z400	405.35	400.55	125.03		SANTA FE, Old Depot Closed	N	6,968
	405.90	401.10	125.58	Z	" Union Depot..W	FC	
Z401	406.05	401.25	125.73		" Transfer Platform		

FOURTH DIVISION—La Madera Branch

Station No.	Mile Post	Miles from Denver	Local Mileage	Telegraph Calls	STATIONS	Kind of Agency	Elevation
Z332	336.52	331.72	0.00	CJ	Taos Junction.............	FC	7,324
ZA339	343.70	338.90	7.18		Solo.....................	N	
ZA344	348.83	344.03	12.31		Ojo Caliente..............	N	
	350.09	345.29			Co. Line, Taos and Rio Arriba.		
	353.14	348.34	16.62		End of D. & R. G. W. Track..		
ZA348	353.22	348.42	16.70		La Madera (Mill)........W	FC	

FOURTH DIVISION—3rd District

Station No.	Mile Post	Miles from Denver	Local Mileage	Telegraph Calls	STATIONS	Kind of Agency	Elevation
Y339	344.12	339.32	0.00	CH	CHAMA..............W T	FC	7,863
Y344	349.20	344.40	5.08		Willow Creek.....(Tel. Box)	N	7,742
Y349	354.01	349.21	9.89		Azotea..........(Tel. Box)	N	7,723
	357.53	352.73	13.41		Azotea Sec. House..No Track	N	7,537
Y355	359.56	354.76	15.44		Biggs....................	N	
Y359	363.47	358.67	19.35	M N	Monero...............W T	FT	7,252
Y360	364.74	359.94	20.62		Odom....................	N	
Y362	366.89	362.09	22.77		Amargo..................	N	7,009
Y365	369.55	364.75	25.43	FC	Lumberton................	FC	6,856
	369.76	364.96	25.64		R. G. & So. W. Junction.....	N	6,852
Y369	373.33	368.53	29.21	DY	Dulce....................	FT	6,779
Y373	377.66	372.86	33.54	JO	Navajo.........(Tel. Box) W	N	6,588
	383.00	378.20			Co. line, Rio Arriba Co., N.M., & Archuleta.		
Y382	386.73	381.93	42.61		Juanita...................	N	6,341
Y386	390.36	385.56	46.24	PG	Pagosa Junction........W T	FC	6,271
Y390	395.23	390.43	51.11		Carracas..................	N	6,173
Y399	403.63	398.83	59.51		Arboles...............W T	N	6,013
Y401	406.30	401.50	62.18		Darlington................	N	
	410.47	405.67			County line, Archuleta and La Plata		
Y406	410.81	406.01	66.69	A	Allison...................	FT	6,222
Y410	414.34	409.54	70.22		Tiffany..........(Tel. Box)	N	6,344
Y414	418.86	414.06	74.74		La Boca................W	N	6,177
Y421	425.74	420.94	81.62	IG	Ignacio...................	FC	6,437
Y424	429.02	424.22	84.90		Pine River................	N	
Y428	432.90	428.10	88.78		Oxford...................	N	6,611
Y432	437.29	432.49	93.17		Florida.................W	N	6,717
Y437	441.59	436.79	97.47		Falfa (Griffith P. O.).......	N	6,924
Y441	445.87	441.07	101.75		Bocea....................	N	6,709
Y444	448.79	443.99	104.67		West.....................	N	
	448.91	444.11	104.79		Carbon Sec. House.No Track	N	6,424
	449.13	444.33	105.01		Carbon Junction...........	N	6,425
Y446	450.86	446.06	106.74		Standard Smelter Junction....	N	
Y446½	451.33	446.53	107.21		San Juan Smelter Junction....	N	
	451.52	446.72	0.19		R. G. S. Junction..........	N	
Y447½	452.26	447.46	0.93		A. S. & R. Co. Smelter......	N	
Y447	451.52	446.72	107.40	DG	DURANGO............W T	FC	6,520

W Water. T Telegraphone.

FOURTH DIVISION—Pagosa Springs Branch

Station No.	Mile Post	Miles from Denver via C. & S. Joint D. T.	Local Mileage	Telegraph Calls	STATIONS	Kind of Agency	Elevation above sea level, feet
Y386.	390.36	385.56	0.00	PG	Pagosa Junction........W T	FC	6,271
	391.48	386.68	1.12		Stock Yards...............	N	
	398.13	393.33	7.77		Kearns....................	N	
AY396	400.38	395.58	10.02		Moore.....................	N	
AY398	402.84	398.04	12.48		Altura....................	N	7,173
AY401	405.58	400.78	15.22		Hall......................	N	6,901
AY402	407.00	402.20	16.64		Bowman...................	N	
AY403	407.47	402.67	17.11		Dyke (Platform)...No Track	N	6,816
	408.18	403.38	17.82		Tank..........No Track W	N	
AY404	408.42	403.62	18.06		Noland....................	N	
	408.56	403.76	18.20		Kline.....................	N	
AY407	411.34	406.54	20.98		Nutria....................	N	7,054
AY408	413.15	408.35			Smith.....................	N	
AY409	413.28	408.48	22.92		McAlpen...................	N	
AY410	414.91	410.11			Lake......................	N	
AY411	416.31	411.51	25.95		Sunetha...................	N	7,514
AY412	416.42	411.62	26.06		Hauser....................	N	
AY414	419.27	414.47	28.91		Shields...................	N	
AY415½	420.68	415.88	30.32		Stock Yards...............	N	
AY416	421.13	416.33	30.77	BA	PAGOSA SPRINGS......W	FC	7,108

FOURTH DIVISION—Farmington Branch

Station No.	Mile Post	Miles from Denver	Local Mileage	Telegraph Calls	STATIONS	Kind of Agency	Elevation
Y447	451.52	446.72	0.00	DG	DURANGO..........W T	FC	6,520
	449.13	444.33	2.39		Carbon Junction...No Track	N	6,425
	450.14	445.34	3.40		Grubbs....................	N	
AX448	453.00	448.20	6.26		Lodo..............No Track	N	
AX453	457.38	452.58	10.64		Posta.....................	N	6,274
	459.06	454.26	12.32		Sunnyside.........No Track	N	
AX458	462.58	457.78	15.84		Bondad....................	N	6,083
	464.70	459.90	17.96		Bondad Tank............W	N	
AX462	467.04	462.24	20.30		Colmex....................	N	
	467.28	462.48			*La Plata Co., Colo., and San Juan*	Co.,	N. M.
AX464	468.70	463.90	21.96		Riverside.................	N	
	468.93	464.13	22.19		Hendrix...................	N	
AX465	470.00	465.20	23.26		Ralston...................	N	
AX467	471.66	466.86	24.92		Cedar Hill................	N	5,880
	473.75	468.95	27.01		Perry.............No Track	N	
AX471	475.86	471.06	29.12		Inca (Rosing P. O.)........	N	
AX477	481.80	477.00	35.06	AZ	AZTEC....................	FC	5,686
AX483	487.48	482.68	40.74		Flora Vista...............	N	5,516
AX487	491.39	486.59	44.65		Hood......................	N	
AX491	496.20	491.40	49.46	FX	FARMINGTON..........W	FC	5,305

FOURTH DIVISION—Silverton Branch

Station No.	Mile Post	Miles from Denver	Local Mileage	Telegraph Calls	STATIONS	Kind of Agency	Elevation
Y447	451.52	446.72	0.00		DURANGO..........W T	FC	6,520
Y449	453.95	449.15	2.43		Animas City, No Siding or Spur	N	6,554
Y450	454.32	449.52	2.80		Ireland...................	N	
Y453	457.86	453.06	6.34		Home Ranch................	N	6,559
Y456	460.69	455.89	9.17		Trimble...................	N	6,578
Y458	462.52	457.72	11.00		Hermosa..............W	N	6,645
Y463	468.15	463.35	16.63		Bell......................	N	
Y464	469.09	464.29	17.57	R W	Rockwood........(Tel. Box)	N	7,367
Y467	472.28	467.48	20.76		Tacoma....................	N	
Y470	474.61	469.81	23.09		Cascade Tank............W	N	
Y473	478.02	473.22	26.50		Tefft.....................	N	
Y474	478.44	473.64	26.92		Cascade...................	N	7,785
Y478	482.31	477.51	30.79		Needleton.................	N	8,141
	483.60	478.80			*County line, La Plata and San Juan.*		
	484.40	479.60	32.88		Needleton Tank...........W	N	
Y486	490.47	485.67	38.95		Elk Park................T	N	8,883
Y489	494.16	489.36	42.64		Silverton Tank, No Track W	N	
Y490	494.79	489.99	43.27		King Mine.................	N	
	495.36	490.56	43.84		Ross......................	N	
Y491	496.00	491.20	44.48		Hercules..................	N	
	496.31	491.51	44.79		Silverton Smelter Junction....	N	
	496.86	492.06	0.55		Silverton Ry. Junction....	N	
	497.26	492.46	0.95		North Star Mill....No Track	N	
Y492	496.70	491.90	45.18	SV	SILVERTON............T	FC	9,300
	496.93	492.13	45.41		Silverton Northern R. R. Jct...	N	
	497.13	492.33	45.61		End of Track.............	N	

W Water.   T Telegraphone.

PASSENGER CARS—Narrow Gauge

KIND	Car Nos.	No. in Series	Length Over Sills ft. in.	Width Over Sills ft. in.	Height Over All ft. in.	Trucks	Weight lbs.	Seating Cap.	Heat	Light
Mail & Baggage	53		38 6	8 0½	12 1½	4-Wheel	34,800		Stoves	Lamps
"	54		45 10¾	7 11¾	12 5	"	54,900		B. H. & Stove	"
"	60		45 10¾	7 11¾	12 5	"	53,580		" "	"
"	61		38 6	8 0½	12 1½	"	34,900		Stoves	"
"	62		38 6	8 0½	13 4½	"	36,800		"	"
"	63		38 6	8 0½	13 1½	"	37,700		"	"
"	64		45 11½	8 0	12 5	"	40,700		"	"
"	65		45 11½	8 0	12 0	"	55,300		"	"
"	66		45 11½	8 0	12 5	"	38,000		"	"
"	118		36 0	8 1	12 8	"	31,500		"	"
"	119		45 11½	8 0	12 5	"	42,300		"	"
"	120		45 10¾	7 11¾	12 5	"	34,400		B. H. & Stove	"
"	121		36 0	8 1	12 8	"	33,300		Stoves	"
"	122		45 10¾	7 11¾	12 5	"	55,800		B. H. & Stove	"
"	123	15	36 0	8 1	12 8	"	32,400		Stoves	"
Baggage	111		38 6	8 1	12 1½	"	33,200		"	"
"	125		36 0	8 1	12 1½	"	30,600		"	"
"	126		36 0	8 1	12 2½	"	31,400		"	"
"	127		38 6	8 1	12 7	"	31,480		"	"
"	128		36 0	8 1	12 2½	"	32,900		"	"
"	129		36 0	8 1	12 2½	"	33,400		"	"
"	151		36 0	8 1	12 2½	"	30,800		"	"
"	152		36 0	8 1	12 7	"	34,400		"	"
"	154		36 0	8 1	12 2½	"	31,400		"	"
"	155		36 0	8 1	12 2½	"	34,600		"	"
"	156		36 0	8 1	12 2½	"	29,500		"	"
"	158		36 0	8 1	11 2½	"	35,460		"	"
"	159		36 0	8 1	12 7	"	28,660		"	"
"	163		38 6	8 1	12 7	"	37,700		"	"
"	164		38 6	8 1	12 7	"	34,100		"	"
"	165		38 6	8 1	12 7	"	33,300		"	"
"	167		38 6	8 1	12 1½	"	36,140		"	"
"	168		38 6	8 1	12 1½	"	36,800		"	"
"	169	19	38 6	8 1	12 1½	"	33,900		"	"
Coach and Baggage	202		35 11	7 11½	12 6	4-Wheel	30,900	26	Stoves	Lamps
"	204		35 11	7 11½	12 1½	"	33,300	27	"	"
"	209		35 11	7 11½	12 6	"	33,400	28	"	"
"	210		35 11	7 11½	12 1½	"	31,200	28	"	"
"	211		38 4	7 11½	12 6	"	32,400	24	"	"
"	212		34 10	7 11½	12 6	"	34,100	28	"	"
"	214		34 10	7 11½	12 6	"	34,200	26	"	"
"	215	8	38 4	7 11½	12 6	"	30,500	28	"	"
Coach and Mail	240		35 11	8 0½	12 2	"	35,400	20	"	"
"	241		35 11	8 0½	12 7	"	33,400	20	"	"
"	242	3	35 11	8 0½	12 7	"	33,360	18	"	"
Coach	256		38 4	7 11½	12 1½	"	34,800	44	"	"
"	270		38 4	7 11½	12 1	"	32,700	44	"	"
"	271		38 4	7 11½	12 6	"	32,700	44	"	"
"	272		39 8	8 2	13 1½	"	35,100	46	"	"
"	274		38 4	7 11½	12 6	"	30,800	46	"	"
"	280		38 4	7 11½	12 1½	"	33,700	44	"	"
"	281		38 4	7 11½	12 6	"	31,700	44	"	"
"	282		38 4	7 11½	12 6	"	32,980	44	"	"
"	283		38 4	7 11½	12 6	"	35,000	44	"	"
"	284		38 4	7 11½	12 6	"	36,200	44	"	"
"	285		38 4	7 11½	12 2	"	34,400	44	"	"
"	287		38 4	7 11½	11 1½	"	34,500	44	"	"
"	289		38 4	7 11½	12 1	"	35,140	44	"	"
"	290		38 4	7 11½	12 1	"	34,100	44	"	"
"	291		38 4	7 11½	12 6	"	31,100	44	"	"
"	292		38 4	7 11½	12 6	"	32,900	44	"	"
"	296		38 4	7 11½	12 6	"	31,400	46	"	"
"	297		38 4	7 11½	12 6	"	32,800	44	"	"
"	300		38 4	7 11½	12 1½	"	35,200	44	"	"
"	301		38 4	7 11½	12 6	"	33,900	44	"	"
"	302		38 4	7 11½	12 1½	"	35,100	44	"	"
"	304		38 4	7 11½	12 6	"	33,400	44	"	"
"	305		38 4	7 11½	12 2	"	36,400	44	"	"
"	306		38 4	7 11½	12 2	"	33,000	44	"	"
"	307		38 4	7 11½	12 6	"	30,300	44	"	"
"	309		38 4	7 11½	12 1½	"	34,100	44	"	"
Coach	310		39 8	8 2	12 9	4-Wheel	36,400	46	Stoves	Lamps
"	311		38 4	7 11½	11 10½	"	36,000	44	"	"
"	312		39 8	8 2	12 9	"	34,400	46	"	"
"	313		38 4	7 11½	11 10½	"	31,000	44	"	"
"	316		38 4	7 11½	12 6	"	33,500	44	"	"
"	317		38 4	7 11½	12 6	"	33,200	44	"	"
"	318		38 4	7 11½	12 6	"	34,600	44	"	"
"	319		38 4	7 11½	12 2	"	34,340	44	"	"
"	320		38 4	8 0	12 3½	"	34,760	44	"	"
"	321		38 4	7 11½	12 1	"	34,040	44	"	"
"	323		39 8	8 2	13 1½	"	35,580	46	"	"
"	324		39 8	8 2	13 1½	"	35,800	46	"	"
"	325		39 8	8 2	12 9	"	37,800	46	"	"
"	326		39 8	8 2	12 9	"	34,400	46	"	"
"	327	41	39 8	8 2	13 1½	"	35,480	46	"	"
Chair Car	401		40 8½	8 0	12 2	"	34,960	27	B. Heater	"
"	403	2	42 0	8 1	12 6	"	37,100	29	"	"
Observation	Royal Gorge 500	1	35 11	8 0⅝	5 11½	"	34,300	48		
"	Black Canon 501	1	38 6	8 0⅝	6 0	"	31,800	52		
"	Argus 502	1	38 0	8 2	6 9½	"	34,600	52		
Parlor	Camp Bird		41 11	8 1	11 11	"	41,800	46	B. Heater	Lamps
"	Ouray		48 0	8 2	12 6½	"	41,500	48	"	"
"	Pagosa		41 11	8 1	11 3	"	41,200	46	"	"
"	Durango		42 0	8 1	12 5½	"	47,400	24	"	Lamps, Gas
"	Silverton	5	42 0	8 1	12 5½	"	47,100	24	"	"
Total		96								

DENVER & RIO GRANDE WESTERN

ADDITIONAL WORK EQUIPMENT (Six Months' Delivery)
Narrow Gauge

KIND	Car Nos.	No. of Cars		Capacity	Average Weight	Inside Dimensions					
		Series	Total			Length		Width		Height	
						ft.	in.	ft.	in.	ft.	in.
Steam Derrick	OZ	1	1	lbs. 148,000	lbs. 200,000	28	2	9	6	14	10¾
Rotary Snow Plow	OY	1	1		140,500						

NOTE

Business Car B-8 has Standard and Narrow Gauge Trucks.
Pile Driver OB has Standard and Narrow Gauge Trucks.
Construction Derrick OP has Standard and Narrow Gauge Trucks.
Cook and Dining Outfit 0450 has Standard Gauge Trucks.
Box Outfit Cars 04910 and 04980 used as supply cars by Store Department.
Coal " " 09744 used as cinder car.
Flat " " 06010, 06047, 06052, 06054 used as water cars.
" " " 06063, 06051 and Box Outfit Car 04549 used with Derrick OP.
Coal " " 01283, 01524, 01672 used on RGS with Ditcher.
Flat " " 06008 used with Pile Driver OB.
Coal Cars 7048, 8803, 8818, 8860, 8932, 8980, 9029, 9062, 9085, 9088, 9120, 9143, 9158, 9193, 9738 used as flat cars, having had coal sides removed.
Box Cars 4402, 4425, 4433, 4435, 4437, 4451, 4456, 4457, 4478, 4487, 4490 fitted up as automobile cars.

WRECKING OUTFIT CARS

Box Outfit Cars 04252, 04511, 04909.
Flat " " 06084, 06405, 06410.
Coal " " 01513, 01616, 09160.
Tool and Material Outfit Car 0278.
Cook and Dining Outfit Car 0460.

SUMMARY OF EQUIPMENT
PASSENGER CARS

Standard Gauge	301
Narrow Gauge	96
Total	397

FREIGHT CARS

Standard Gauge	13,348
Narrow Gauge	3,211
Total	16,559

WORK AND ROADWAY EQUIPMENT

Standard Gauge	899
Narrow Gauge	189
Total	1,088

Don Heimburger

FREIGHT CARS—Narrow Gauge

KIND	Car Nos.	No. of Cars: Series	No. of Cars: Total	Capacity	Average Weight	Inside Dimensions: Length ft.	Length in.	Width ft.	Width in.	Height ft.	Height in.
				lbs.	lbs.	ft.	in.	ft.	in.	ft.	in.
Refrigerator	32 to 81	50		40,000	24,400	23	10⅛	6	9⅞	6	3 11/16
"	84, 85, 89 and 95	4		40,000	24,500	28		6	7	5	7
"	100 and 133	2		40,000	24,500	19		6	10	5	7
"	107 to 114, 117 to 119	11		40,000	24,000	28		6	7	6	3
"	124, 126, 127, 135, 138 to 141, 144 to 147, 149	13	80	40,000	24,300	28		6	7	5	7
Box	2611, 2647 and 2823	3		40,000	19,100	23	6	6	10	5	9
"	3000 to 3749	724		50,000	21,800	29	5	7		6	1¾
"	3752	1		40,000	19,000	23	6	6	10	5	9
"	4000 to 4099	24		40,000	19,000	27		6	10	5	11
"	4100 to 4999	207	959	40,000	19,800	29	6	6	10	5	11
Stock	5500 to 5849	348	348	50,000	21,700	29	4	7	3	6	1¾
Coal	1000 to 1499	452		50,000	20,700	31		6	10	3	4
"	1500 to 1899	396		50,000	19,400	31	1	6	11	3	4
"	1900 to 1925	26		50,000	19,300	31	1	6	11	4	2
"	8168 to 8760	24		30,000	15,400	25	10	6	10	3	
"	8800 to 9199	242		40,000	16,900	28	1	6	10	2	6
"	9200 to 9574	328		50,000	19,000	31		6	10	3	4
"	9719, 9729, 9738, 9756, 9767, 9791, 9793, 9795 and 9939	9	1477	40,000	16,800	28	1	6	10	2	6
Coal, National Dump	700 to 899	200	200	50,000	21,700	31		7	9	3	4
" Ingolsby Dump	901 to 941	41	41	50,000	24,700	29		6	10	4	4
Flat	6000 to 6098	48		40,000	14,700	30		7	5½		
"	6200 to 6209	10		50,000	15,400	34		7	6		
"	6210 to 6219	10		40,000	16,200	34		7	6		
"	6401, 6403, 6407, 6409, 6413	5		30,000	13,600	26	9	7	5½		
"	6746, 6798, 6875, 6950, 7447	5	78	20,000	13,600	26	9	7	5½		
Caboose	0500, 0501, 0503, 0504, 0517, 0518, 0524, 0526, 0528, 0540, 0548, 0556, 0573 to 0580, 0584 to 0589	26			11,800	15	4½	*8	3	*12	7½
" Box	04982 and 04990	2	28			29	6	6	10		
Total			3211								

ADDITIONAL FREIGHT CARS (Six Months' Delivery)

Narrow Gauge

KIND	Car Nos.	No. of Cars: Series	No. of Cars: Total	Capacity	Average Weight	Inside Dimensions: Length ft.	Length in.	Width ft.	Width in.	Height ft.	Height in.
				lbs.	lbs.	ft.	in.	ft.	in.	ft.	in.
Stock	5900 to 5999	100	100	50,000	36,000	33	4	7	3¾	6	1¾

WORK AND ROADWAY EQUIPMENT—Narrow Gauge

KIND	Car Nos.	No. of Cars: Series	No. of Cars: Total	Capacity	Average Weight	Inside Dimensions: Length ft.	Length in.	Width ft.	Width in.	Height ft.	Height in.
Business	B-1	1			53,500	38	6	*7	11	*12	¾
"	B-2	1			54,400	40	10	*8	2	*11	10
"	B-3	1			51,300	40	7	*8	1¼	*12	3
"	B-7	1			48,500	35	10	*7	11	*12	1½
"	B-8	1	5		43,100	35	10½	*8	2	*12	4
" Pay Car	0275	1	1		32,500	38	4	*7	11½	*12	6
Cook and Dining Outfit	051	1			20,000	*30		*7	11½	*14	
"	0450	1			29,900	*38	6	*8		*13	2
"	0460	1	3		32,000	*40	6	*8	1	*12	7
Cook Outfit	0452	1	1		35,200	*40	8	8	1	*12	8
Dining Outfit	0457	1	1		35,200	40	8	8	1	*12	8
Bunk Outfit	0566	1	1		21,000	*36		*8		*12	8
Tool and Material Outfit	0278	1	1		18,400	26	9	7	4		
Box Outfit	02701 and 03679	2		40,000	18,400	23	6	6	10	5	9
"	04013, 04022 04036, 04041	4		40,000	18,500	27		6	10	5	11
"	04100 to 04999	117	123	40,000	19,800	29	6	6	10	5	11
Flat Outfit	06006, 06008, 06010, 06020, 06026, 06029, 06038, 06047, 06050 to 06052, 06054, 06063, 96067, 06084, 06092	16		40,000	14,700	30		7	5½		
"	06400, 06402, 06405, 06410 to 06412	6	22	30,000	13,600	26	9	7	5½		
Coal Outfit	01259 and 01269	2		50,000	20,700	31		6	10	3	4
"	08916, 09104, 09160, 09163, 09744	5	7	40,000	16,900	28	1	6	10	2	6
Water Outfit	0458	1	1	20,000							
Wrecking Outfit	04909	1	1	40,000	19,300	29	6	6	10	5	11
" Derrick	OA	1	1	20,000		26	9	7	5½		
Pile Driver	OB	1	1	40,000	63,500	30		7	5		
Flanger	OC to OL	10			27,500						
"	OT	1	11								
Rotary Snow Plow	OM and ON	2			101,500	*38	8	*9	10	*14	4½
"	OO	1	3	80,000		*30	4	*9	5½	*12	2
Derrick	OP	1	1	50,000	37,700	31		6	11	*14	4
Excavator	OQ	1	1								
Air Dump	OR and OS	2	2	30,000		*21	3	*8	2	*5	11
Ditcher	OW	1	1	76,000		*18	6	*6	2½	*11	7
"	OX	1	1	"		*19	11	*7		*11	8
Total			189								

*Length, Width and Height to clear.

TELEGRAPH OFFICES AND CALLS
FIRST DIVISION—1st District

OFFICES	Calls	Day or Night	Phone	Block	R. R. WIRES					W. U. WIRES																
					1	3	5	7	11	P	102	104	106	108	110	122	123	124	128	132	134	136	202	206	208	214	215	216	217	218
Denver, W. U.	V	N	†		†	*	†	*	†		*	*	*	*	*	*	*	*	*	*	*	*	*	*	*	*	*	*	*	*
Denver Gen. Office	Dc	N			*	*	*	*	*																					
Denver Supt. Teleg.	Tg	D			†	†	†	†																						
Denver C.R.I.& P. Tkt	Kn	D								*		*																		
Denver CB&Q Loc Frt	Fh	N			*																									
Denver Union Station	Dn	N	*		*	*	*	*	*			*																		
Denver M.T. Gen. Of.	Go																				*	*	*							
Denver Yard Office				*																										
Burnham	Fs			*																										
South Denver Tower				*																										
Overland Park	Ov			*																										
Military Junction	Jc			*																										
Ft. Logan Depot	Fn	D					*					†																		
Ft. Logan	Fg	D										*																		
Littleton	F	N	*	*	*	*	†	*	†	†		†	†	*	†	†	†	†	†	†	†	†	†	†	†	†	†	†	†	†
Wolhurst	Wh			*	*																										
Acequia	Aq			*																										
Magazine Spur				*																										
Louviers	Au	D		*	*		*					*																		
Sedalia	Z	N		*	*	*		*	†			*	†					†	†											
Plateau	Pa			*																										
Castle Rock	Ck	N		*	*	*		*	†			*	†		†		†	†	†											
Douglas	Dl			*																										
Glade	Gl			*																										
Larkspur	Rk	D		*	*	*		*				*																		
Greenland	G	D		*	*	*		*																						
Palmer Lake	Di	N		*	*	*	†	*	†			†	†	*	†	†	†	†	†	†	†	†	†	†	†	†	†	†	†	†
Monument	Mu	N		*	*	*		*																						
Borst				*																										
Husted	Hu	D		*	*	*		*				*																		
Edgerton				*																										
Pikeview	Vi	D		*	*	*																								
Roswell C. R. I. & P.	Rj	N		*	*	*				*		*																		
Colorado Spgs, W. U.	Cg	N										*	†	†	*		†	†	†					†	†	†	†	†	†	†
Colorado Spgs., Depot	Cs	N	*	*	*	*	†	*	†	†		*	*	†				†	†											
C. Spgs. C.R.I.&P.Tkt	Ri	D								*		*																		
Colorado City	Ot	D			*			*				*																		
Manitou, W. U.	Mc	D										*																		
Manitou, Depot	Ma	D			*		*					†																		
Kelker	K	D		*	*																									
Widefield				*																										
Fountain	Fo	N		*	*	*		*				*																		
Buttes	Bu	N		*	*	*		*				*																		
Wigwam	Wg	D		*	*	*		*				*																		
Pinon	Po			*	*																									
Cuba	Cb			*	*																									
Bragdon				*	*																									
Eden	Un			*																										
Fuego				*																										
Pueblo, W. U.	P	N			†	†	†	†	†		*	*	*	*	*	*	*	*	*	*	*	*	*	*	*	*	*	*	*	*
Pueblo, C.R.I.P. Tkt	Kt	D								*		*																		
Pueblo, Dispatchers	Rg	N		*	*	*	*											†	†	†											
Pueblo, Chief Dispr	Ny	N		*	†	†			†			†						†	†											
Pueblo, Union Depot	Sb	N		*				†	*	*		†																		

Duplex loops from "V" office, Denver, on Nos. 3 and 7 to "Dc," "Dn" and "Tg."
C. B. & Q. Pony wire is in "V," "Dn," "Fh" and "N" offices, Denver.
No. 1 loops from "Dn" to "Fh" C. B. & Q. local freight office, Denver.
Nos. 5 and 108 loop from Military Junction to Fort Logan.
Santa Fe Nos. 1, 3, 5, 9, 102, 104, 106, 107, 108, 123, 125, 144, 201, 203, 204 and 215 in switchboard at Littleton.
Manitou Branch Nos. 1 and 5 loop from "Cs" Colorado Springs.
Manitou Branch No. 108 loops from "Cg" Colorado Springs.
C. R. I. & P. Ry. Nos. 6-7 and 31 wire are in "Cs" office Colorado Springs.
No. 106 north connects with C. R. I. & P. No. 31 east at "Cg" Colorado Springs.
No. 106 south connects with C. R. I. & P. No. 17 east at Colorado Springs.
Denver, W. U. Wire Chief, call "DV."
Pueblo, W. U. Wire Chief, call "QP."

FOURTH DIVISION—1st, 2nd and 3rd Districts, Silverton and Farmington Branches

OFFICES	Calls	Day or Night	R. R. WIRES								W. U. WIRES		REMARKS
			1	3	01	5	S1	So 102	2		108	109	
La Veta	X	N		*	*						*	†	
La Veta Pass	Va	N		*	*						*	†	
Garland	Ft.			*	*						*	†	
Blanca	Nk	D	*	*	*						*	†	
Alamosa, Dispatchers	Rm	N	*	*	*	*	*				†		No. 01 to Santa Fe.
Alamosa, Supt.	As	D	*	*	*	*	*						
Alamosa, W. U.	Ax	D	†	†	†						*	*	No. 5 ends at Alamosa.
La Jara	Jr	D	*	*	*						*	†	
Estrella													
Romeo	Om	D	*	*	*						†	†	
Antonito	Na	D	*	*	*						*	†	
Lava					†								
Big Horn					†								
Sublette	Su				†								
Osier	Bc	D		*									
Cumbres	Br	N	*	*							*	†	
Cresco					†								
Chama	Ch	N	*	*							*	†	
Monero	Mn	D	*	*							*	†	
Lumberton	Fc	D	*	*							*	†	
Dulce	Dy	D	*	*							*	†	
Pagosa Junction	Pg	D	*	*							*	†	
Pagosa Springs	Ba	D											Pagosa Spgs. Branch loops from Pagosa Jct., can connect with any wire.
Arboles					†								
Allison	A	D	*	*							*	†	
Ignacio	Ig	D	*	*							*	†	
Florida	Fa				†								
Bocea	Bs				†								

Offices	Calls	Day or Night									Remarks
Durango, W. U.	Du	D	†	†			*		*	*	
Durango, Depot, Pass.	Dg	N	*	*			*	†	*	†	No. 3 ends at "Dg" Durango.
Rockwood	Rw			†							
Cascade	Ca			†							
Needleton	N			†							Silverton Branch.
Elk Park	Kp			†							
Mile Post 492.60	Bo			†							
Silverton, Depot	Sv	D	*					*			
Aztec	Az	D	*				*				
Farmington	Fx	D	*				*				Farmington Branch repeaters at Durango.
Farmington, W. U.	Fa	D	*				*				

FOURTH DIVISION—Creede Branch

OFFICES	Calls	Day or Night	R. R. WIRES							W. U. WIRES			REMARKS
			1							118			
Alamosa Dispatchers	Rm	N	*							†			
Alamosa	As	D	*							*			
Alamosa, W. U.	Ax	D	†							*			
Monte Vista	Mv	D	*							*			
Monte Vista, W. U.	Mn	D	*							*			
Del Norte	De	D	*							*			
Wagon Wheel Gap	W	□	†							*			
Creede, Depot	Ji	D	*							*			

FOURTH DIVISION—Santa Fe Branch

OFFICES	Calls	Day or Night	Joint W. U. and R. R. Wire							REMARKS
			01							
Antonito	Na	D	*							
Tres Piedras	Pf	D	*							
Taos Jct.	Cj	D	*							
Embudo	Md	D	*							
Espanola	No	D	*							
Water Tank	Wt	□	†							
Buckman	Wc	□	†							
Jacona	Ja	□	†							
Santa Fe	Z	D	*							
" W. U.	Sz	D	*							

TELEGRAPH OFFICES AND CALLS—Concluded

GENERAL NOTES

Instruments on wires marked * must always be cut in during office hours and properly adjusted.
† indicates wires in Switchboard only.

Explanation of Characters: D, Day Offices; N, Day and Night Offices; NO, Night Office Only; DN, Part Day and Part Night; P, Pony Wire; R.I., C. R. I. & P. Wire; C. S., Colo. & Southern Wire; S., R. G., Sou Wire; J., R. G., Jct. Wire.

The following signals will take precedence in the order in which they are assigned and must be obeyed without question or exception. The individual signals must not be used unless authorized by those to whom they belong or for answers to messages sent under signals. Signals on messages and answers thereto must be sent and copied at the beginning of such message by sending and receiving operators:

First—"Time." Must not be interrupted.

Second—"Wire." Used only by those authorized to test wires and for that purpose only.

Third—"9." Train orders; may also be used by all to prevent or report accident.

Fourth—"91." Receiver, Chief Operating Officer, Asst. Chief Operating Officer, General Superintendents and Supt. of Transportation.

"Dc" and "Dn" Denver will relay business between offices not reached direct. Glenwood will relay Aspen Branch. Gunnison will relay for points on Third Division except Montrose and Delta, and between Mears Jct. and Alamosa. Alamosa will relay Creede and Espanola Branches. Durango will relay Silverton Branch. Ridgway and Durango will relay Rio Grande Southern business.

"Wk." Call for wrecks, washouts, or any case of temporary cutting-in on wires where no regular assigned call is given.

Signal and Telephone Maintainers located at Burnham, Colorado Springs, Pueblo, Glenwood, Grand Junction and Provo.

Western Union Linemen are located as follows: Denver, Colorado Springs, Pueblo, Salida, Buena Vista, Glenwood, Grand Junction, Gunnison, Alamosa, Durango, Helper, Provo and Salt Lake City.

Telegraph Wrecking Boxes located as follows:

First Division—Special cars A1, A2, A3, A4, A5, B1, B2, B3, B4, also at "Sb" Pueblo, Cuchara Jct and La Veta; also Conductor J. W. Donley.

Second Division—Special cars B8 and B5.

Third Division—At Salida and Gunnison in N. G. wreckers; also at following telegraph offices: Marshall Pass, Gunnison, Montrose.

Fourth Division—Alamosa, Superintendent's Office, two boxes and special car B7, La Veta Pass Chama wrecker, Durango telegraph offices.

Operators' call bells located as follows:

First Division—Barnes, Rouse Junction, Cuchara Junction, La Veta.

Fourth Division—Antonito, Cumbres, Durango, La Veta and Chama.

MAXIMUM LIMIT OF LOAD MEASUREMENT

Number	COLORADO LINES	1 foot Wide		2 feet Wide		3 feet Wide		4 feet Wide		5 feet Wide		6 feet Wide		7 feet Wide		7 ft. 6 in. Wide		8 feet Wide		8 ft. 6 in. Wide		9 feet Wide		9 ft. 6 in. Wide		10 feet Wide		10 ft. 6 in. Wide		11 feet Wide		11 ft. 6 in. Wide		Maximum Height		Maximum Width	
		Ft.	In.	Ft.	In.	Ft.	In.	Ft.	In.	Ft.	In.	Ft.	In.	Ft.	In.	Ft.	In.	Ft.	In.	Ft.	In.	Ft.	In.	Ft.	In.	Ft.	In.	Ft.	In.	Ft.	In.	Ft.	In.	Ft.	In.
	STANDARD GAUGE																																			
1	Denver to Pueblo	17	9	17	9	17	9	17	9	17	9	17	9	17	9	17	9	17	9	17	9	17	9	17	9	17	9	17	9	17	9	17	9	17	9	11	6
2	Pueblo to Leadville and Minturn	17	..	17	..	17	..	17	..	17	..	16	1	15	11	15	9	15	6	15	4	15	2	15	..	14	10	14	7	14	..	17	..	11	6
3	Pueblo to Cuchara Jct.	19	1	19	1	19	1	19	1	19	1	19	1	19	1	19	1	19	1	19	1	19	1	19	1	19	1	19	1	19	1	19	1	11	6
4	Cuchara Jct. to Trinidad																																			
5	Cuchara Jct. to Antonito	20	..	20	..	20	..	19	6	19	4	19	..	18	9	18	6	18	6	18	6	18	6	18	3	18	..	18	..	17	9	20	..	11	6
6	Alamosa to Creede	19	6	19	6	19	6	19	6	19	6	19	6	19	6	19	6	19	6	19	6	19	6	19	6	19	6	19	6	19	6	19	6	11	6
7	Minturn to Grand Jct.	17	..	17	3	17	3	17	3	17	..	17	..	16	10	16	5	16	3	17	..	16	9	16	..	15	9	15	8	15	4	15	..	14	9	17	..	11	6
8	Montrose to Grand Jct.	18	8	18	8	18	8	18	8	16	8	18	2	17	6	17	3	17	..	16	9	16	6	16	4	16	..	15	..	13	..	12	..	18	8	11	6
9	Manitou Branch																																			
10	Westcliffe Branch																																			
11	Aspen Branch	16	7	16	7	16	7	16	7	16	7	16	7	16	7	16	7	16	7	16	7	16	7	16	7	16	7	16	7	16	7	16	7	11	6
12	Farmington Branch	22	..	22	..	22	..	22	..	22	..	22	..	22	..	22	..	22	..	22	..	22	..	22	..	22	..	22	..	22	..	22	..	11	6
13	North Fork Branch	18	6	18	6	18	6	18	6	18	6	18	6	18	6	18	6	18	6	18	6	18	6	18	6	18	6	18	6	18	6	18	6	11	6
	NARROW GAUGE																																			
14	Leadville to Dillon	18	4	18	4	18	4	18	4	18	4	18	4	18	4	18	4	18	4	18	4	18	4	18	4	18	4	18	4	18	4	18	4	11	6
15	Salida to Gunnison	15	4	15	4	15	4	15	4	15	3	14	6	14	..	13	5	13	1	12	10	12	7	12	3	11	11	11	7	11	4	10	9	15	4	11	6
16	Mears to Alamosa																																			
17	Gunnison to Montrose	16	..	16	..	16	..	16	..	16	..	16	..	16	..	15	..	14	4	14	..	13	9	13	6	13	..	13	..	13	..	13	..	16	..	11	6
18	Antonito to Durango	15	4	15	4	15	4	15	4	15	3	14	6	14	..	13	5	13	1	12	10	12	7	12	3	11	11	11	7	11	4	10	9	15	4	11	6
19	Antonito to Santa Fe	19	6	19	6	19	6	19	6	19	6	19	6	19	6	19	6	19	6	19	6	19	6	19	6	19	6	19	6	19	6	19	6	11	6
20	Durango to Silverton	14	6	14	6	14	5	14	4	14	3	14	2	14	1	14	..	13	11	13	10	13	8	13	3	13	1	13	..	14	6	11	6
21	Crested Butte Branch	19	..	19	..	19	..	19	..	19	..	19	..	19	..	19	..	19	..	19	..	19	..	19	..	19	..	19	..	19	..	19	..	11	6
22	Lake City Branch	16	..	16	..	16	..	16	..	16	..	16	..	16	..	16	..	16	..	16	..	16	..	16	..	16	..	16	..	16	..	16	..	11	6
23	Ouray Branch	21	3	21	3	21	3	21	3	21	3	21	3	21	3	21	3	21	3	21	3	21	3	21	3	21	3	21	3	21	3	21	3	11	6

STRUCTURES CONTROLLING THE ABOVE CLEARANCES

- No. 1. Colorado Midland Crossing, Colorado Springs.
- No. 2. Red Hill Tunnel. A., T. & S. F. Crossing near M. P. 153 and at Swallows.
- No. 3. Northern Ave. Viaduct, Pueblo.
- No. 4. No overhead structures.
- No. 5. Tunnel M. P. 206+1,809 ft. near La Veta Pass (Upper Tunnel).
- No. 6. Bridge 306A.
- No. 7. Tunnels at Shoshone and Glenwood. Tunnel at "Tunnel" Station, R. G. J. Ry.
- No. 8. Bridgeport Tunnel and Bridge 378A.
- No. 9. No overhead structures.
- No. 10. No overhead structures.
- No. 11. Colorado Midland Crossing at M. P. 371 (Overhead structures at Aspen, ample clearance).
- No. 12. Bridge 465A.
- No. 13. Bridge 380A.
- No. 14. Colorado & Southern Crossing near Kokomo.
- No. 15. Snowshed 237B.
- No. 16. No overhead structures.
- No. 17. Bridge 289B, 289C, 291B and Snow Shed 335A.
- No. 18. Mud Tunnel near Toltec, Snowsheds 326C, 329B and 332A, B, C, D and E.
- No. 19. Bridge 367C.
- No. 20. Snowshed 492A.
- No. 21. Bridge 299A.
- No. 22. Overhead Flume near M. P. 343.
- No. 23. Bridge 376B.

MILEAGE BY STATES

DIVISION	OWNED LINES						LEASED LINES							Total All Tracks
	First Track				Add'l Track			First Track				Add'l Track		Total	
	Main		Sidings		Main	Sid'gs	Total	Main		Sidings		Main	Sid'gs		
	S.G.	N.G.	S.G.	N.G.	S.G.	S.G.		S.G.	N.G.	S.G.	N.G.	S.G.	S.G.		
FIRST—Operated	446.81		230.80		56.84		734.45	9.71		4.88		151.20	36.34	202.13	936.58
Not Operated															
Total	446.81		230.80		56.84		734.45	9.71		4.88		151.20	36.34	202.13	936.58
SECOND—Operated	238.92		131.78	4.24	20.67		395.61	62.08		13.92				76.00	471.61
Not Operated		42.81		4.55			47.36								47.36
Total	238.92	42.81	131.78	8.79	20.67		442.97	62.08		13.92				76.00	518.97
THIRD—Operated	117.54	357.73	25.58	41.20			542.05		37.26			4.72		41.98	584.03
Not Operated		5.52					5.52						0.73	0.73	6.25
Total	117.54	363.25	25.58	41.20			547.57		37.26			5.45		42.71	590.28
FOURTH in Colorado—Operated	188.92	180.30	36.03	22.63			427.88								427.88
GREEN RIVER in Colorado—Operated	34.04		7.29				41.33								41.33
SUMMARY—Colorado—Operated	1,026.23	538.03	431.48	68.07	77.51		2,141.32	71.79	37.26	18.80		4.72 151.20	36.34	320.11	2,461.43
Not Operated		48.33		4.55			52.88					0.73		0.73	53.61
Total in Colorado	1,026.23	586.36	431.48	72.62	77.51		2,194.20	71.79	37.26	18.80		5.45 151.20	36.34	320.84	2,515.04
FOURTH in New Mexico—Operated	29.51	206.08	1.61	14.22			251.42								251.42
GREEN RIVER in Utah—Operated	217.04		95.26		26.68		338.98	3.68		2.60				6.28	345.26
SALT LAKE—Operated	467.61		175.18		41.15		683.94	6.78		5.82		20.62	3.32	36.54	720.48
Not Operated	27.18		4.33				31.51								31.51
Total	494.79		179.51		41.15		715.45	6.78		5.82		20.62	3.32	36.54	751.99
SUMMARY—Utah—Operated	684.65		270.44		67.83		1,022.92	10.46		8.42		20.62	3.32	42.82	1,065.74
Not Operated	27.18		4.33				31.51								31.51
Total in Utah	711.83		274.77		67.83		1,054.43	10.46		8.42		20.62	3.32	42.82	1,097.25
SUMMARY—All States—Operated	1,740.39	744.11	703.53	82.29	145.34		3,415.66	82.25	37.26	27.22		4.72 171.82	39.66	362.93	3,778.59
Not Operated	27.18	48.33	4.33	4.55			84.39					0.73		0.73	85.12
Total All States	1,767.57	792.44	707.86	86.84	145.34		3,500.05	82.25	37.26	27.22		5.45 171.82	39.66	363.66	3,863.71

STOCKYARDS

LOCALITY	FACILITIES	Car Capacity Stock		Car Capacity Sheep	
		S. G.	N. G.	S. G.	N. G.
Acequia		2		1	
Alamosa	S. F. W.	50	75	70	100
Amargo			10		5
American Fork	S. F. W.	5		3	
Antonito	W.	32	40	16	20
Arboles			8		10
Aspen		2		1	
Augusta		14			
Austin		8		4	
Avon (Private)		13		7	
Aztec			20		10
Blanca		2		1	
Bonita		10			
Buckman			10		5
Buena Vista		4		2	
Buttes (Private)		4			
Canon		3			
Carbondale		9		4	
Carlile		1			
Cascade			16		8
Castle Rock		3			
Chama	S. W. F.		14		27
Cimarron			15		7
Cisco	F. W.	5		3	
Cleora	S. F. W.	107	134	52	67
Colona			5		2
Colorado City	Chute only				
Colorado Springs	F. W.	14			
Colton	S. F. W.	20		16	
Cotopaxi		6			
Crested Butte			4		2
Crookton			7		3
Cuchara		8			
De Beque		25		12	
Del Norte	W.	20		10	
Delta	F. W.	11		7	
Denver (C. R. I. & P.)		1			
Denver (Union Yards)	S. F. W.				
Dotsero		18		9	
Dulce					20
Durango	F. W.		40		20
Durham	S. F. W.	100		90	
Eagle		12		6	
El Moro		3			
Elsinore		16		8	
Emma		8		4	
Ephraim		7		4	
Espanola			3		14
Estrella		4		2	
Farmington	S.	5		10	
Florence		4			
Florida			2		1
Fountain		12			
Fountain Green		7		4	
Fruita		3		2	
Garland		20		10	
Glenwood	F. W.	11		6	
Glenwood, Red Canon		3		2	
Grand Junction		12		6	
Grand Valley		2		1	
Granger		2		1	
Granite	Chute only				
Greenland		2			
Green River	F. W.	14		8	
Gunnison, Colo.			9		4
Gunnison, Utah		14		7	
Gypsum		17		8	
Heber	W.	22		11	
Hillside, Colo.		2			
Hillside, Utah		6		25	
Hooper			9		4
Hotchkiss	W.	6		3	
Howard		4			
Huerfano		1			
Ignacio			1		1
Indianola		5		3	
Iola			7		3
Jack's Cabin			5		2
Kebler Pass	Chute only				
Kelker		2			
Kimball		5		3	
La Jara		14		7	
Larkspur		1			
La Veta	W.	14		7	
La Veta Pass		1		1	
Layton		2		1	
Leadville		6	8	3	4
Leland		5		3	
Littleton		1			
Loma		4		2	
Mack		25		20	
Malta	Chute only	7		4	
Manti		6		4	
Mapleton		9		5	
Marysvale		25		13	
Mill Fork		15		8	
Minturn	F. W.	42		21	
Moffat			22		11
Monte Vista	W.	30		15	
Montrose	S. F. W.	20	26	10	13
Monument		9			
Moroni		3		2	
Mosca			11		5
Mounds		32		24	
Mt. Pleasant		4		2	
Murray		3		2	
Nathrop		6	7	3	4
Newcastle		12		6	

Location					
Olathe			4		2
Oro Junction		5	6	2	3
Osier	Chute only				
Overland Park		1			
Oxford			1		
Pagosa Junction	S. F.				20
Pagosa Springs			20		
Pando		33		17	
Parkdale		1			
Parlin			7		3
Payson		10		7	
Pines		2		1	
Price	W.	30		20	
Provo	F. W.	4		2	
Pueblo, Union Yards	S. F. W.				
Richfield		30		16	
Rifle	F. W.	40		20	
Riverton		3		2	
Romeo		3		2	
Roper	F. W.	6		4	
Rose Spur		3		2	
Roswell (C. R. I. & P.)		80		50	
Roubideau		10		5	
Rouse		2			
Russell		2			
Salida	F. W.	25	31	12	15
Salina		25		13	
Salt Lake Union Yards	S. F. W.				
San Carlos		10			
Santa Fe	F. W.		50		25
Sapinero			17		8
Sargent			3		1
Sedalia		4			
Servilleta	S.		10		30
Sigurd		2		1	
Silt	F.	20		10	
Silverton			2		1
South Fork		8		4	
Springville		2		1	
Sunetha	S.				35
Tennessee Pass		40		20	
Texas Creek		5			
Thompson	F W.	17		30	
Tiffany			20		10
Tres Piedras		2			1
Trinidad		2			
Vaca		7		5	
Villa Grove			13		6
Wagon Wheel Gap		2		1	
Walsenburg		8			
Wasson		7		16	
Westcliffe		10			
Westwater		8		28	
Whitewater		19		10	
Whittaker		2		1	
Wolcott	S.	55		27	
Wolhurst		2			
Woodside		20		11	
Woody Creek		3		2	

Sheep dipping vats: Antonito, Chama and Thompson.
NOTE: F—Feed; S—Scales; W—Water.

ENGINE HOUSES

LOCATION	Stalls S. G.	Stalls N. G.	LOCATION	Stalls S. G.	Stalls N. G.
Alamosa	6	9	Leadville	9	2
Antonito		2	Minturn	15	
Aspen (not in use)	24		Montrose	2	4
Burnham	24		Manti	2	
Burnham (used for erecting shop)	13		Marysvale	2	
Canon City	6		Midvale (not used)		
Chama		7	Ogden	6	
Chama (used for shop)		2	Ouray		2
Crested Butte		2	Park City	1	
Cuprum	4		Pueblo	34	
Colton (not used)			Pueblo (used as shop)	15	
Durango	2	8	Salida	20	12
El Moro	6		Salida (used as shop)		10
Glenwood	8		Salt Lake	19	
Grand Junction	24		Salt Lake (used as shop)	9	
Green River	6		Sargent		6
Gunnison		10	Silverton		2
Husted (not used)			Spring Canon (not in use)		
Helper	16		Soldier Summit	24	
Helper (used as shop)	3		Thistle	12	
Lake City		2	Westcliffe	1	
La Veta	8		Welby	6	

ASH PITS

LOCATION	Type	Material	Lgth. Feet	LOCATION	Type	Material	Lgth. Feet
Alamosa	Double	Concrete	64	Minturn	Double	Concrete	90
Burnham	Single	Concrete	120	Montrose	Single	Concrete	30
Canon City	Single	Stone	34	Pueblo	Single	Concrete	120
Chama	Single	Concrete	30	Pueblo	Single	Concrete	120
Durango	Single	Concrete	64	Pueblo	Single	Concrete	34
El Moro	Single	Concrete	34	Salt Lake	Double	Concrete	125
Glenwood	Single	Concrete	60	Salida	Double	Concrete	90
Grand Junction	Double	Concrete	90	Santa Fe	Single	Wood	34
Green River	Single	Concrete	90	Santa Fe	Single	Wood	34
Gunnison	Single	Stone	40	Soldier Summit	Double	Concrete	15
Helper	Double	Concrete	90	Thistle	Single	Concrete	60
La Veta	Single	Concrete	30	Walsenburg	Single	Concrete	60
Leadville	Single	Stone	14	Welby	Double	Concrete	90
Midvale	Single	Concrete	90				

TRACK SCALES

LOCATION	Gauge	Capacity Tons	Length Feet	REMARKS
Alamosa	3-Rail	100	50	
Antonito	3-Rail	80	50	
Aspen	S. G.	60	44	
Burnham	S. G.	115	50	
Canon City	S. G.	115	50	
Cameo	S. G.	100	50	
Colorado Springs	S. G.	115	50	
Colton	S. G.	70	42	Not used
Crested Butte	N. G.	100	50	
Chama	N. G.	50	34	
Denver	S. G.	125	50	
Durango	3-Rail	80	42	
Eureka	S. G.	80	42	
Gunnison	S. G.	60	42	Colo. & Southern R. R.
Grand Junction	S. G.	115	50	
Lake City	N. G.	40	32	
Leadville	S. G.	100	50	
Mack	S. G.	100	50	Owned by Uintah R. R.
Montrose	3-Rail	60	44	
Manti	S. G.	60	34	Not used
Oro Junction	S. G.	115	50	
Ogden	S. G.	70	42	Not used
Pueblo Walker Yard	S. G.	125	50	
Pueblo West Yard	S. G.	115	50	
Roswell	S. G.	60	34	C. R. I. & P. R. R.
Ridgway	N. G.	40	32	
Roper	S. G.	115	50	
Salida	S. G.	100	50	
Salida	N. G.	60	44	
Salt Lake	S. G.	115	50	
Santa Fe	3-Rail	63	38	N. M. C. R. R. Joint
Silverton	N. G.	40	29	Silverton R. R. Joint
Springville	S. G.	115	50	
Trinidad	S. G.	115	50	
Walsenburg	S. G.	115	50	
Westcliffe	S. G.	60	44	

ICE HOUSES

LOCATION	Capacity Tons	Refrigerator Car Icing Platform Feet	Elevators	LOCATION	Capacity Tons	Refrigerator Car Icing Platform Feet	Elevators
Alamosa	2,000	176	1	Moroni	50		
Burnham	2,500			Manti	50		
Canon City	100			Ogden	200		
Cimarron	100			Pueblo	10,000	220	1
Colorado Sp'gs	400			Provo	5,000	120	
Colton	6,000			Pando	3,000		
Delta	6,500	500	1	Salida	2,000		
Denver	9,000	540	2	Salt Lake	2,500		
Durango	1,000	80		Santa Fe	70		
Glenwood	700			Sargent	20		
Green River	500			Soldier Summit	800		
Grand Junction	30,000	1,500	8	Thistle	350		
Gunnison	100			Welby	500		
Helper	800			Woodside	200		
Leadville	100						
Minturn	5,000	375	1	Total	89,940		
Montrose	400						

TUNNELS
Colorado Lines

NAME	Location	Length
Red Hill	M. P. 206.3	508 feet
Tennessee Pass	M. P. 281.2	2577 "
Pando	M. P. 286.6	242 "
East Belden	M. P. 296.0	275 "
West Belden	M. P. 296.1	66 "
Rock Creek	M. P. 296.8	408 "
Shoshone No. 1	M. P. 349.9	276 "
Shoshone No. 2	M. P. 350.9	134 "
Glenwood	M. P. 359.0	1327 "
Beaver Tail Tunnel	M. P. 428.5	763 "
Bridgeport	M. P. 400.0	2252 "
La Veta Line—Lower Tunnel	M. P. 198.6	655 "
La Veta Line—Middle Tunnel	M. P. 202.2	338 "
La Veta Line—Upper Tunnel	M. P. 206.3	234 "
Toltec Tunnel—No. 1	M. P. 311.3	349 "
Toltec Tunnel—No. 2	M. P. 315.2	366 "

TURNTABLES

LOCATION	Type	Length Feet	Heaviest Engine Advisable
Alamosa	3-Rail	65	190
Anthracite (not used)	N. G.	50	70
Aspen (not used)	S. G.	62	190
Bingham	S. G.	60	180
Burnham, Tank Shop	S. G.	50	
Burnham	S. G.	100	439
Canon City	S. G.	65	190
Chama	S. G.	50	70

Crestone (not used)	S. G.	50	70
Cuprum	S. G.	86	340
Durango	3-Rail	50	106
El Moro	S. G.	62	190
Embudo	N. G.	50	70
Floresta	N. G.	50	70
Glenwood	S. G.	80	220
Grand Junction	S. G.	80	280
Gunnison	N. G.	60	125
Helper	S. G.	80	280
Ibex	S. G.	80	280
La Veta	S. G.	65	100
Leadville	3-Rail	62	190
Marshall Pass	N. G.	62	125
Minturn	S. G.	100	340
Monarch (not used)	N. G.	50	000
Ogden	S. G.	67	220
Orient (not used)	N. G.	50	000
Osier	N. G.	50	70
Ouray	N. G.	50	70
Palmer Lake	S. G.	65	220
Pueblo	S. G.	100	439
Ridgway	N. G.	50	70
Salida	3-Rail	62	190
Salida	S. G.	100	439
Salt Lake (Through)	S. G.	80	280
Sargent	N. G.	62	125
Somerset (Cast iron)	S. G.	60	113
Thistle	S. G.	67	220
Walsenburg	S. G.	80	220
Welby	S. G.	90	340
Westcliffe	S. G.	56	113

COALING STATIONS

LOCATION	TYPE	No. of Chutes	Capacity Tons
Alamosa	Locomotive Incline, Dump Bottom Cars	8	240
Antonito	Locomotive Incline, Shovel into pockets	6	30
Burnham	Balanced Bucket	5	400
Canon City	Locomotive Incline, Dump Bottom Cars	8	240
Castle Gate	Mine Tipple	1	
Chama	Incline Hoist, Dump Bottom Cars	12	60
Chester	Bin		15
Cimarron	Bin		100
Colorado Springs	Locomotive Incline, Shovel into Pockets	32	150
Colorado Springs	Locomotive Incline, Dump Bottom Cars	2	60
Cuchara	Locomotive Incline, Shovel into Pockets	4	32
Cuprum	Locomotive Incline, Shovel into Pockets	6	30
Delta	Locomotive Incline, Dump Bottom Cars	4	120
Durango	Shovel from Cars		
Embudo	Locomotive Incline, Shovel into Pockets	3	30
Glenwood	Locomotive Incline, Dump Bottom Cars	8	240
Grand Junction	Balanced Bucket	4	300
Grand Valley	Incline Hoist, Dump Bottom Cars	6	180
Grays	Bin		10
Green River	Balanced Bucket	3	200
Gunnison	Locomotive Incline, Shovel into Pockets	24	60
Helper	Balanced Bucket	4	300
Heber	Bin		25
Lake City	Bin		35
Leadville	Bin		30
La Veta	Balanced Bucket	2	150
Manti	Bin		17
Marysvale	Bin		50
Malta	Locomotive Incline, Dump Bottom Cars	6	180
Marshall Pass	Bin		35
Mears Junction	Bin		20
Minturn	Balanced Bucket	4	300
Monero	Mine Supply	6	30
Mounds	Bin		15
Ogden	Bin		40
Pagosa Junction	Derrick and Buckets		8
Park City	Bin		25
Pryor	Mine Tipple	1	
Pueblo	Balanced Bucket	5	600
Salida	Balanced Bucket	4	300
Salina	Bin		20
Salt Lake	Balanced Bucket	4	300
Sargent	Locomotive Incline, Dump Bottom Cars	4	100
Sommerset	Mine Tipple	1	
Springville	Bin		40
Soldier Summit	Locomotive Incline, Dump Bottom Cars	10	300
Texas Creek	Bin		15
Thistle	Balanced Bucket	4	300
Villa Grove	Bin		20
Walsenburg	Locomotive Incline, Dump Bottom Cars	6	180
Westcliffe	Bin		40
Welby	Locomotive Incline, Dump Bottom Cars	6	180
Winter Quarters	Mine Tipple	1	

WYES

STATION	Degree of Curve	Gauge	Length of Stem	Remarks
Alamosa	18° 30'	3-Rail	To Creed	
Antonito	14°	3-Rail	To Santa Fe	
Artwell	16°	S. G.	Main Tracks	Disconnected
Aspen		S. G.		Colo. Midland Ry.
Barnes	12°	S. G.	Main Tracks	Colo. S. E. Ry.
Barranca	24°	N. G.	332 ft.	
Big Horn	20°	N. G.	135 ft.	
Burnham	16°	S. G.	575 ft.	
Carbondale	15° 42'	S. G.	To Marble	Joint with C. R. R. R.
Castle Gate	11° 30'	S. G.	303 ft.	
Castleton	24°	N. G.	To Kubler	
Castle Rock	24°	S. G.	To Hathaway	
Cedar Creek	21° 42'	N. G.	112 ft.	
Cerro Summit	24°	N. G.	122 ft.	
Chama	12° 30'	N. G.	285 ft.	

Station	Degree	Gauge	Notes	Other
Chicosa Junction	15°	S. G.	To Forbes Jct.	
Cimarron	11° 48'	N. G.	1,398 ft.	
Cisco	10°	S. G.	666 ft.	
Colorado Springs	16°	S. G.	To Manitou	
Colton	15°	S. G.	261 ft.	
Crested Butte	10° 16'	N. G.	3,260 ft.	
Cuchara Junction	12°	S. G.	Main Tracks	
Cumbres	20°	N. G.	269 ft.	
Delta	10° 15'	S. G.	N. Fork Branch	
Dillon	16°	N. G.	350 ft.	
Divide	20°	S. G.	120 ft.	
Elk Park	23°	N. G.	115 ft.	
Ephraim	14° 18'	S. G.	Main Tracks Marysvale & San Pete Valley Branches	
Farmington	12°	S. G.	302 ft.	
Flora	15° 06'	S. G.	Iron King Branch & Goshen Valley R. R. Maintenance	
Florence	18°	S. G.	Coal Creek Branch	
Funston	20°	S. G.	242 ft.	
Gogorza	20°	S. G.	828 ft.	
Goshen	12°	S. G.	285 ft.	
Grand Junction	10° 12'	S. G.	Main Tracks	
Green River	12° 30'	S. G.	208 ft.	
Gunnison	16° 40'	N. G.	To Crested Butte	
Heber	12° 30'	S. G.	382 ft.	
Helper	16°	S. G.	261 ft.	
Hotchkiss	20°	S. G.	232 ft.	
Kenilworth	18°	S. G.	450 ft.	
Kenilworth Jct.	15°	S. G.	To Kenilworth	
Kokomo	24°	N. G.	450 ft.	
Kyune	16°	S. G.	129 ft.	
Lake City		N. G.	Loop	
La Madera	24°	N. G.	150 ft.	H. & H. Lumber Co.
Larsen	14° 30'	S. G.	Sugar Works Spur	
Lascar	12°	S. G.	To Graneros	
La Veta	16°	S. G.	115 ft.	
La Veta Pass	11° 05'	S. G.	Loop	
Littleton	15°	S. G.	740 ft.	
Lumberton	11° 48'	N. G.	To Edith	New Mexico Lumber Co.
Malta	16°	S. G.	To Leadville	
Manitou	20°	S. G.	262 ft.	
Manti	12°	S. G.	357 ft.	
Marysvale	14°	S. G.	1,075 ft.	
Mears Junction	20° 30'	N. G.	To Alamosa	
Midvale	19° 30'	S. G.	Bingham Branch	
Military Junction	12°	S. G.	To Ft. Logan	
Moffat	8° 26'	N. G.	Crestone Branch	
Monte Vista	15°	S. G.	To Center	San Luis Cent. R. R.
Montrose	9° 40'	3-Rail	Ouray Branch	
Mounds	13° 14'	S. G.	896 ft.	
Nephi	15° 30'	S. G.	Main Tracks	Joint with L. A. & S. L. R. R.
Nibley	13° 10'	S. G.	Sugar Wks. Spur	
Nioche	16°	S. G.	170 ft.	
Oak Creek	16° 24'	S. G.	207 ft.	
Ogden	13°	S. G.	Union Dep. Tracks	
Pagosa Junction	24°	N. G.	Loop	
Pagosa Springs	24°	N. G.	Loop	
Pando	16°	S. G.	1,681 ft.	
Park City	16°	S. G.	246 ft.	
Pearl Jct.	12°	S. G.	Goshen Valley R. R.	
Pitkin	24°	N. G.		
Poncha Junction	23°	N. G.	Monarch Branch	
Poncha Pass	24°	N. G.	120 ft.	
Price	16°	S. G.	502 ft.	Joint with S. U. R. R.
Provo	15°	S. G.	284 ft.	
Pueblo	17°	S. G.	Main Tracks	
Richfield	12°	S. G.	373 ft.	
Ridgway	9° 34'	N. G.	Main Tracks	R. G. S. R. R.
Rifle	16°	S. G.	360 ft.	
Riter	12° 30'	S. G.	182 ft.	
Rockwood	19°	N. G.	170 ft.	
Round Hill	24°	N. G.	93 ft.	
Rouse Junction	9° 30'	S. G.	To Rouse	
Salida	8° 26'	S. G.	325 ft.	
Salina	13°	S. G.	Castle Valley Brch.	
Salt Lake City	15° 45'	S. G.	Main Tracks	
Santa Fe	24°	N. G.	220 ft.	
Sapinero	21°	N. G.	205 ft.	
Sargent	21°	N. G.	572 ft.	
Scofield	20° 40'	S. G.	146 ft.	
Sevier	15°	S. G.	911 ft.	
Sierra	14°	S. G.	100 ft.	
Silver City	17° 10'	S. G.	263 ft.	
Silverton	17° 30'	N. G.	Main Track	Silverton R. R.
Soldier Summit	12°	S. G.	323 ft.	
Spring Canon Jct.	12°	S. G.	Spring Canon Brch.	
Springville	15°	S. G.	503 ft.	
Sunnyside (new)	16°	S. G.	Coke Oven Tracks	
Sunnyside (old)	16°	S. G.	1,094 ft.	
Taos Junction	20°	N. G.	To La Madera	
Tennessee Pass	8° 26'	S. G.	247 ft.	
Texas Creek	12°	S. G.	260 ft.	
Thistle	14°	S. G.	Marysvale Branch	
Thompson	14°	S. G.	To Sego	Joint with B. & T. R. R.
Tres Piedras	29°	N. G.	245 ft.	
Trinidad	19° 20'	S. G.	Main Tracks	C. & S. Ry.
Villa Grove	19° 30'	N. G.	To Orient	
Wagon Wheel Gap	17°	S. G.	420 ft.	
Walsenburg	12° 06'	S. G.	300 ft.	
Wasson	17°	S. G.	378 ft.	
Welby	10°	S. G.	Main Tracks	Bingham & Garfield Branches
West Salida	26° 15'	N. G.	288 ft.	
Wild Horse	16°	S. G.	Main Tracks	Joint with Colo. Mid. Ry.
Woodside	15° 30'	S. G.	175 ft.	

Safety  Service

J. F. Selby
Trainmaster
Alamosa

J. R. Murray
Trainmaster—Roadmaster
Gunnison

T. J. Cummins
Ass't. to Superintendent and
Road Foreman of Equipment
Alamosa

J. B. Norwood, Jr.
Chief Dispatcher
Alamosa

The
Denver and Rio Grande Western Railroad
Company

ALAMOSA DIVISION

TIME-TABLE
No. 125

Takes Effect Wednesday, June 1, 1949

at 12:01 A. M.
Mountain Time

Superseding Time-Table No. 124
and Supplements Thereto

NOTE IMPORTANT CHANGES IN
TIME-TABLE RULES

For the exclusive guidance of Employes; not for
the information of the Public

The Management reserves the right to vary
from it at pleasure

A. E. PERLMAN
General Manager

L. F. WILSON
Assistant General Manager

L. H. HALE
Superintendent
Transportation

E. B. HERDMAN
Superintendent

ALWAYS BE CAREFUL

WESTWARD		MAIN LINE			EASTWARD
FIRST CLASS 115 Passenger	Mile Posts	Sub-Division 10 STATIONS TIME-TABLE No. 125 JUNE 1, 1949	Miles from Alamosa	Capacity of Siding	FIRST CLASS 116 Passenger
Leave Daily					Arrive Daily
1 45 AM	190.3	x **LA VETA** KSBWFYDN	61.4	Yard	12 10 AM
		4.6			
f 2 01	194.9	FRANCISCO P	56.8	19	f 12 01 AM
		1.7			
f 2 07	196.6	OCCIDENTAL P	55.1	65	f 11 56
		5.3			
f 2 27	201.9	CODO PW	49.8	39	f 11 37
		5.3			
s 2 45	207.2	va **FIR** YN	44.5	89	s 11 19
		7.4			
f 3 07	214.6	SIERRA PWY	37.1	70	f 10 52
		2.3			
f 3 12	216.9	RUSSELL P	34.8	25	f 10 46
		4.4			
f 3 23	221.3	MORTIMER P	30.4	64	f 10 35
		6.4			
s 3 40	227.7	rt **FORT GARLAND** WD	24.0	81	s 10 23
		4.7			
s 3 55	232.4	Nk **BLANCA** D	19.3	73	s 10 13
		7.4			
f 4 12	239.8	BALDY	11.9	21	f 10 00
		8.4			
f 4 32	248.2	HAYS	3.5	43	f 9 47
		1.4			
f 4 35	249.6	EAST YARD	2.1	127	9 45
		1.4			
4 39	251.0	ALAMOSA JCT. J	0.7		9 42
		0.7			
4 45 AM	251.7	AS **ALAMOSA** KBOWFYDN		Yard	9 40 PM
Arrive Daily		(61.4)			Leave Daily
3.00 20.5		Schedule Time Average Speed per Hour			2.30 24.5

WESTWARD		MAIN LINE			EASTWARD
FIRST CLASS 215 Passenger	Mile Posts	Sub-Division 11 STATIONS TIME-TABLE No. 125 JUNE 1, 1949	Miles from Chama	Capacity of Siding	FIRST CLASS 216 Passenger
Leave Daily					Arrive Daily
7 00 AM	251.7	AS **ALAMOSA** PBSOJKTWFYDN	92.4	Yard	8 30 PM
		5.3			
f 7 10	257.0	HENRY	87.1	128G 14NG	f 8 19
		2.6			
f 7 15	259.6	ESTRELLA P	84.5	44SG 58NG	f 8 14
		6.6			
s 7 30	266.2	Jr **LA JARA** PWD	77.9	148SG 191NG	s 7 59
		3.5			
f 7 37	269.7	BOUNTIFUL	74.4	228G 29NG	f 7 49
		3.6			
s 7 45	273.3	om **ROMEO** PD	70.8	38SG 54NG	s 7 42
		7.0			
s 8 05	280.3	Na **ANTONITO** PWFYD	63.8	Yard	s 7 25
		10.5			
f 8 31	290.8	LAVA YPW	53.3	25	f 6 55
		8.6			
f 8 52	299.4	BIG HORN PY	44.7	28	f 6 35
		6.7			
f 9 09	306.1	SUBLETTE PW	38.0	25	f 6 15
		4.4			
f 9 22	310.5	TOLTEC P	33.6	75	f 6 01
		7.9			
f 9 45	318.4	bc **OSIER** PFW	25.7	43	f 5 35
		6.4			
f 10 03	324.8	LOS PINOS W	19.3	46	f 5 18
		5.8			
s 10 20	330.6	br **CUMBRES** PWFYD	13.5	105	s 5 02
		1.6			
f 10 26	332.2	COXO	11.9	18	f 4 53
		3.3			
f 10 39	335.5	CRESCO PW	8.6	43	f 4 39
		4.5			
f 10 56	340.0	LOBATO	4.1	28	f 4 19
		4.1			
11 10 AM	344.1	ch **CHAMA** SPOKBWFYDN		Yard	4 05 PM
Arrive Daily		(92.4)			Leave Daily
4.10 22.1		Schedule Time Average Speed per Hour			4.25 20.9

Telephones also located in booths at M. P. 311.3, M. P. 315.2, M. P. 323.0, M. P. 328.0 and M. P. 333.0

TABLE OF SPEEDS

MILES PER HOUR	ONE MILE IN	
	Minutes	Seconds
5	12	0
8	7	30
10	6	0
12	5	0
15	4	0
18	3	20
20	3	0
25	2	24
30	2	0
35	1	43
40	1	30
45	1	20

WESTWARD	CREEDE BRANCH			EASTWARD
	Mile Posts	Sub-Division 10-A STATIONS TIME-TABLE No. 125 JUNE 1, 1949	Miles from North Creede	Capacity of Siding
	251.7	AS **ALAMOSA** PBKOJBWFYDN	70.1	Yard
		10.8		
	262.5	PARMA	59.3	20
		3.6		
	266.1	ZINZER	55.7	81
		2.9		
	269.0	MV **MONTE VISTA** YWD	52.8	130
		3.9		
	272.9	TORRES	48.9	47
		9.9		
	282.8	De **DEL NORTE** YD	39.0	50
		6.1		
	288.9	HANNA	32.9	23
		3.0		
	291.9	GRANGER	29.9	18
		6.3		
	298.2	SOUTH FORK W	23.6	27
		0.9		
	299.1	DERRICK Y	22.7	Wye
		3.7		
	302.8	MASONIC PARK	19.0	
		9.3		
	312.1	WAGON WHEEL GAP	9.7	18
		6.0		
	318.1	WASSON Y	3.7	28
		2.6		
	320.7	ji **CREEDE** WD	1.1	27
		1.1		
	321.8	NORTH CREEDE		
		(70.1)		

D. & R. G. W.—Alamosa

ALWAYS BE CAREFUL

MAIN LINE

Sub-Division 12 — STATIONS — TIME-TABLE No. 125 — JUNE 1, 1949

WESTWARD FIRST CLASS 215 Passenger Leave Daily	Mile Posts		STATIONS		Miles from Durango	Capacity of Siding	EASTWARD FIRST CLASS 216 Passenger Arrive Daily
11 15 AM	344.1	ch	CHAMA	POSKBWFTDN	107.4	Yard	4 00 PM
			5.1				
f 11 26	349.2		WILLOW CREEK		102.3	17	f 3 44
			4.8				
f 11 37	354.0		AZOTEA	P	97.5	32	f 3 30
			5.6				
f 11 50	359.6		BIGGS SPUR		91.9	19	f 3 14
			3.9				
f 11 59	363.5		MONERO	FTW	88.0	63	f 3 04
			3.4				
f 12 10 PM	366.9		AMARGO	P	84.6	30	f 2 53
			2.6				
s 12 18	369.5		LUMBERTON	PT	82.0	63	s 2 47
			3.8				
s 12 27	373.3	Dy	DULCE	PD	78.2	67	s 2 36
			4.4				
f 12 40	377.7		NAVAJO	FW	73.8	23	f 2 23
			9.0				
f 1 03	386.7		JUANITA	P	64.8	23	f 1 59
			3.7				
s 1 21	390.4	pg	GATO	FWYD	61.1	75	s 1 49
			4.8				
f 1 35 216	395.2		CARRACAS	P	56.3	39	f 1 35 215
			8.4				
s 1 56	403.6		ARBOLES	FW	47.9	45	s 1 13
			7.4				
f 2 15	411.0		ALLISON	P	40.5	16	f 12 56
			3.3				
f 2 24	414.3		TIFFANY	P	37.2	33	f 12 48
			4.6				
f 2 35	418.9		LA BOCA	FW	32.6	28	f 12 37
			6.8				
2 53	425.7	Ig	IGNACIO	PD	25.8	62	s 12 22
			7.2				
f 3 11	432.9		OXFORD		18.6	10	f 12 03 PM
			4.4				
f 3 23	437.3		FLORIDA	FW	14.2	30	f 11 53
			4.3				
f 3 34	441.6		FALFA		9.9	11	f 11 43
			7.5				
s 3 57	449.1		CARBON JCT.	PJ	2.4	27	s 11 22
			2.4				
4 05 PM	451.5	Dg	DURANGO	YOKBSJPWFTD		Yard	11 15 AM
Arrive Daily			(107.4)				Leave Daily
4.50 22.2			Schedule Time Average Speed per Hour				4.45 22.6

SILVERTON BRANCH

Sub-Division 12-B — STATIONS — TIME-TABLE No. 125 — JUNE 1, 1949

WESTWARD SECOND CLASS 461 Mixed Leave Tues., Thurs. & Sat.	Mile Posts		STATIONS		Miles from Silverton	Capacity of Siding	EASTWARD SECOND CLASS 462 Mixed Arrive Tues., Thurs. & Sat.
9 15 AM	451.5	Dg	DURANGO	YKOSBJPWFTD	45.2	Yard	5 00 PM
			9.2				
f 9 50	460.7		TRIMBLE		36.0		f 4 26
			1.8				
s 9 57	462.5		HERMOSA	W	34.2	13	s 4 19
			6.6				
s 10 26	469.1		ROCKWOOD	Y	27.6	24	s 3 53
			3.2				
s 10 50	472.3		TACOMA		24.4	18	s 3 30
			10.3				
f 11 35	482.6		HUNT		14.1		f 2 40
			1.4				
f 11 40	484.0		NEEDLETON	W	12.7	13	f 2 35
			6.5				
f 12 14 PM	490.5		ELK PARK	YP	6.2	14	f 2 05
			6.2				
12 40 PM	496.7	sv	SILVERTON	YD		Yard	1 40 PM
Arrive Tues., Thurs. & Sat.			(45.2)				Leave Tues., Thurs. & Sat.
3.25 13.2			Schedule Time Average Speed per Hour				3.20 13.6

No. 461 is superior to No. 462.

FARMINGTON BRANCH

Sub-Division 12-A — STATIONS — TIME-TABLE No. 125 — JUNE 1, 1949

WESTWARD	Mile Posts		STATIONS		Miles from Farmington	Capacity of Siding	EASTWARD
	449.1		CARBON JCT.	JP	47.1	27	
			8.3				
	457.4		POSTA		38.8	13	
			5.2				
	462.6		BONDAD		33.6	15	
			9.1				
	471.7		CEDAR HILL		24.5	19	
			4.2				
	475.9		INCA		20.3	10	
			5.9				
	481.8	As	AZTEC	D	14.4	23	
			5.7				
	487.5		FLORA VISTA		8.7	16	
			8.7				
	496.2	Fx	FARMINGTON	WTD		Yard	
			(47.1)				

D. & R. G. W—Alamosa

ALWAYS BE CAREFUL

WESTWARD MAIN LINE EASTWARD

Miles from Denver		Sub-Division 13 STATIONS TIME-TABLE No. 125 JUNE 1, 1949		Miles from Gunnison	Capacity of Siding
215.1	s	**SALIDA**	PJKBSDNWFTTO	73.3	Yard
		5.0			
220.1	PN	PONCHA JCT.	JPY	68.3	52
		3.8			
223.9		OTTO		64.5	27
		2.1			
226.0		MEARS JCT.	JPWY	62.4	30
		2.3			
228.3		SHIRLEY		60.1	35
		3.6			
231.9		KEENE		56.5	18
		2.1			
234.0		GRAY'S	P	54.4	60
		3.6			
237.6		POCONO		50.8	18
		3.1			
240.7	MP	**MARSHALL PASS**	SNWTP	47.7	120
		4.1			
244.8		SHAWANO	PW	43.6	36
		3.7			
248.5		CHESTER	P	39.9	28
		2.3			
250.8		TANK 7	W	37.6	
		2.0			
252.8		BUXTON	P	35.6	43
		4.4			
257.2	Sj	SARGENT	KBSDWFTP	31.2	100
		4.8			
262.0		ELKO	P	26.4	45
		3.5			
265.5		CROOKTON	P	22.9	22
		4.0			
269.5		DOYLE	P	18.9	18
		0.9			
270.4		BONITA		18.0	44
		6.4			
276.8		PARLIN	PW	11.6	29
		5.4			
282.2		STEELE		6.2	41
		6.2			
288.4	Gu	**GUNNISON**	PJKBDWFTTO		Yard
		(73.3)			

Westward CRESTED BUTTE BRANCH Eastward

Miles from Denver		Sub-Division 13-B STATIONS TIME-TABLE No. 125 JUNE 1, 1949		Miles from Crested Butte	Capacity of Siding
288.4	Gu	**GUNNISON**	PSJKBDWFTTO	27.9	Yard
		10.7			
299.1		ALMONT		17.2	43
		5.6			
304.7		JACK'S CABIN	W	11.6	24
		11.6			
316.3	Bc	CRESTED BUTTE	DWTP		Yard
		(27.9)			

WESTWARD BALDWIN BRANCH EASTWARD

Miles from Denver		Sub-Division 13-C STATIONS TIME-TABLE No. 125 JUNE 1, 1949		Miles from Castleton	Capacity of Siding
288.4	Gu	**GUNNISON**	BSKJDTWFYOP	15.6	Yard
		6.7			
295.1		WYLIE		8.9	6
		2.4			
297.5		TEACHOUT		6.5	5
		3.5			
301.0		DOLLARD		3.0	5
		3.0			
304.0		CASTLETON	WY		26
		(15.6)			

WESTWARD MONARCH BRANCH EASTWARD

Miles from Denver		Sub-Division 13-A STATIONS TIME-TABLE No. 125 JUNE 1, 1949		Miles from Monarch	Capacity of Siding
220.1	PN	PONCHA JCT.	JPY	16.2	52
		6.9			
227.0		MAYSVILLE	Y	9.3	60
		6.4			
233.4		GARFIELD		2.9	14
		2.9			
236.3		MONARCH	Y		126
		(16.2)			

D. & R. G. W.—Alamosa

ALWAYS BE CAREFUL

SAPINERO BRANCH

		WESTWARD		EASTWARD	
Miles from Denver		Sub-Division 14 STATIONS TIME-TABLE No. 125 JUNE 1, 1949		Miles from Sapinero	Capacity of Siding
288.4	gu	**GUNNISON** PJKBSDWFYTO		25.6	Yard
		10.8			
299.2		IOLA		14.8	12
		0.9			
300.1		KEZAR		13.9	28
		7.1			
307.2		CEBOLLA	P	6.8	45
		6.8			
314.0		SAPINERO	PT		57
		(25.6)			

TRACKS NOT SHOWN AS STATIONS IN TIME-TABLE

LOCATION		NAMES	CAR CAPACITY		SWITCH CONNEC-TIONS
Sub-Division	MP		S G	N G	
10	197.1	Nixon	11		East End
10	208.1	Simm's Spur	8		East End
10-A	258.4	Willis	7		East End
"	267.0	S. L. C. Jct.	7		
"	268.3	Continental Oil	3		West End
"	276.4	Freeman	21		East End
"	280.8	Evansville	25		Both Ends
"	296.3	Gerrard	24		Both Ends
11	256.0	La Fruto	8		Both Ends
"	257.4	Hartner	6		Both Ends
13-B	298.9	Spring Creek		9	East End

Telegraph line between Antonito and Chama does not follow main track at the following points:

MP 289 to MP 291   MP 300½ to MP 306¾
MP 294 to MP 294½   MP 312 to MP 314
MP 296 to MP 298   MP 322 to MP 327½

WESTWARD MAIN LINE EASTWARD

Miles from Denver		Sub-Division 15 STATIONS TIME-TABLE No. 125 JUNE 1, 1949		Miles from Alamosa	Capacity of Siding
226.0		MEARS JCT.	PJWY	74.4	30
		3.6			
229.6		PONCHA PASS	PY	70.8	33
		3.3			
232.9		ROUND HILL	W	67.5	46
		12.4			
245.3		VILLA GROVE	PWY	55.1	45
		5.6			
250.9		MINERAL HOT SPRINGS		49.5	16
		11.8			
262.7	Mf	MOFFAT	PW	37.7	42
		17.6			
280.3	Hg	HOOPER	PD	20.1	45
		6.5			
286.8		MOSCA	P	13.6	45
		12.9			
299.7		ALAMOSA JCT.	P	0.7	
		0.7			
300.4	As	**ALAMOSA** PSJKBDNWFYTO			Yard
		(74.4)			

D. & R. G. W—Alamosa

Special Time-Table Rules
Superseding General Rules and Regulations which are Inconsistent Therewith

1. EASTWARD TRAINS ARE SUPERIOR TO WESTWARD TRAINS OF THE SAME CLASS.

1-A. No. 461 is superior to No. 462.

2. Trains will leave Creede, Silverton, Fir and Cumbres without clearance card when there is no operator on duty.

Trains on Sub-Division 12-A will leave Carbon Junction without clearance card.

Trains on Sub-Division 13-A will leave Poncha Junction and Monarch, and on Sub-Division 15 will leave Mears Junction without clearance card when there is no operator on duty.

2-A. There is no train order signal at Farmington or Marshall Pass. No trains will leave these stations without clearance card, except all trains will leave Farmington and Marshall Pass without clearance card when there is no operator on duty.

3. TRAIN REGISTER BOOKS are located at:

La Veta	Durango
Alamosa	Farmington
Creede	Silverton
Cumbres	Salida
Chama	Marshall Pass
Carbon Jct. (for trains 215 and 216 only)	Gunnison

Register stations are shown in body of the Time-Table in FULL FACED TYPE.

3-A. When necessary to move Salida Branch train to Farm Track, Alamosa, for purpose of tieing up, yardmaster on duty will give crew register check on overdue first class trains on Sub-Division 11.

4. YARD LIMIT STATIONS:

La Veta	Wasson	Carbon Jct.
Occidental	Creede	Durango
Fir	LaFruto-Henry-Hartner	Silverton
Sierra	Estrella	Aztec
Ft. Garland	La Jara	Farmington
Blanca	Romeo	Poncha Jct.
Alamosa-Hays	Antonito	Mears Jct.
Willis	Big Horn	Marshall Pass
Parma	Cumbres	Buxton
Zinzer	Chama	Sargent
Monte Vista-SLC Jct.	Monero	Parlin
Torres	Lumberton	Gunnison
Hanna	Dulce	Poncha Pass
Del Norte	Juanita	Round Hill
Granger	Gato	Villa Grove
Gerrard	Carracas	Moffat
South Fork	Arboles	Hooper
Freeman	Ignacio	Mosca

4-A. Yard limits, Sub-Division 13-A extend between Poncha Jct. and Monarch.

Yard limits, Sub-Division 13-B extend between Gunnison and Crested Butte.

Yard Limits, Sub-Division 13-C extend between Gunnison and Castleton.

Yard Limits, Sub-Division 14 extend between Gunnison and Sapinero.

4-B. Trains have no time-table superiority between Alamosa Junction, MP 251.0 and junction with Creede Branch, Alamosa Yard, MP 251.9. Trains must run at restricted speed expecting to find tracks occupied by other trains.

4-C. Spur track at Zinzer with east end connection, capacity four cars, serving Colorado Potato Growers' Association warehouse. Crews using this spur will be governed as follows:

Before crossing main highway, trains or engines serving this warehouse will stop to clear the highway. A member of crew with proper flagging equipment will proceed to center of the highway to protect the further movement of train against highway traffic. Movement over the highway will be made only on his signal.

In case of poor visibility during daylight hours, red fusees will be used to flag highway traffic. The move across the highway should be a continuous one and the highway will not be blocked by standing equipment if it can be avoided.

No cars are to be left on this spur between the main track and highway or between the highway and potato warehouse.

5. When retainers are in use trainmen and enginemen must keep close watch while train is in motion for indications of excessively heated wheels, and when observed, the retainer on such car or cars must be placed in normal release position (turned down) until wheels have had sufficient time to cool.

5-A. On westward trains at Cumbres, and before leaving Fir, Marshall Pass, Poncha Pass, Monarch, Garfield and Silverton, members of the train crew must assist in looking over the air brakes, as well as the general condition of the train.

Particular attention must be devoted to all rods and brake connections, brake shoes and levers, key bolts and split keys, and to all draft gear.

5-B. After brakes have been released, retainers must be turned up before trains leave any station on a descending grade where use of retainers is required.

5-C. Between Fir and Sierra; Fir and La Veta:

On trains consisting of empty cars, retainers will be used on every other car in 10-lb. position, alternated at inspection point. When cars are equipped with 4-position release control retaining valve, these retainers will be used in slow direct exhaust position instead of 10-lb. position on empty cars.

On trains consisting of loaded cars or mixed loads and empties, retaining valves will be used in 20-lb. position on all cars having gross weight of 50 tons or more, in 10-lb. position on other loaded cars, and in 10-lb. position or slow direct exhaust position on empty cars.

5-D. The following will govern the use of retainers in handling trains on descending grade movements on Poncha Pass, Marshall Pass and Monarch Branch:

On trains consisting of heavily loaded cars, all retainers will be used in 20-lb. position. On trains consisting of light loaded cars, all retainers will be used in 10-lb. position. On trains consisting of mixed, loaded and empty cars, retainers will be used in 20-lb. position, on heavily loaded cars, in 10-lb. position on other loaded cars, and in 10-lb. position or slow direct exhaust position on 50% of empty cars. On trains consisting entirely of empty cars, 50% of retainers will be used in 10-lb. position or slow direct exhaust position. Where the use of all retaining valves is not required, retainers will be used on forward portion of train.

5-E. In handling trains on descending grade movements Cumbres to Chama, retainers will be used as follows:

On trains consisting of heavily loaded cars, all retainers will be used in 20-lb. position. On trains consisting of light loaded cars, mixed loaded and empty cars, or entirely of empty cars, all retaining valves will be used in 10-lb. position. If it is found that the retaining power is excessive a few retaining valves on the rear of train may be turned to release position to avoid slack action or stalling on the grade, 4-position (release control) retainers will be used in slow direct exhaust position instead of 10-lb. position on **EMPTY** cars.

5-F. In handling trains on descending grade movement, Silverton to Durango, all retaining valves will be used in 10-lb. position. If it is found that retaining power is excessive, a few retaining valves on rear of train may be turned to release position to avoid slack action or stalling on the grade.

5-G. In handling of freight trains down Cumbres, Poncha Pass, Monarch Branch and Marshall Pass, not more than one (1) car having non-air or inoperative brakes will be permitted to descend in solid coal, ore or steel trains, not more than two (2) cars having non-air or inoperative air brakes in other freight or mixed trains.

At all times the number of operative air brakes in a train must not be less than 85% of the total number of cars in the train.

5-H. Eastward freight trains will stop at Occidental to cool wheels and inspect train.

Eastward freight trains will stop 5 minutes at Big Horn and Mears Junction to cool wheels and inspect train.

Westward freight trains will stop at Buxton to turn down retaining valves.

5-I. Freight trains consisting of heavily loaded cars, brake pipe pressure will be increased to 90-lbs. before departing eastward from Monarch and Poncha Pass, westward from Cumbres and before departing in either direction from Marshall Pass.

5-J. Following are maximum length and tonnage of trains on descending grades:

Fir-LaVeta:

Engines equipped with 1 or 2—8½" CC compressors—85 cars or 4250 tons.

Engines equipped with 2—11" compressors—70 cars or 3500 tons.

D. & R. G. W.—Alamosa

Fir-Sierra:—100 cars or 4500 tons.
Cumbres to Antonito—70 cars.
Monarch to Maysville—8½" CC compressors—25 loaded cars.
Maysville to Poncha Jct.—8½" CC compressors—45 loaded cars.
Crested Butte to Gunnison—8½" CC compressors—70 loaded cars.
Narrow Gauge Territory—On 4% descending grades:

Engines Equipped With	Coal or Other Heavy Loading	Stock or Other Light Loads	Empties or Mixed Loads and Empties
1—9½" Compressor	15 cars	30 cars	40 cars
2—9½" Compressors	20 cars	40 cars	50 cars
1—11" Compressor	18 cars	35 cars	45 cars
2—11" Compressors	25 cars	45 cars	60 cars
1—8½" CC Compressor	40 cars	45 cars	60 cars

On 4% descending grades in narrow gauge territory, gross weight of train must not exceed an average of 38 actual tons per operative car brake.

5-K. Not more than 100 cars will be handled in any narrow gauge freight or mixed train.

6. Where locomotives are equipped with water brakes enginemen must know that they are in proper working condition and use them where required.

6-A. Drawhead knuckles must be properly coupled when pushing engines or cars on sharp curves and on heavy grades, to avoid possibility of couplers passing and resultant damage therefrom.

7. Persons accompanying live stock or other freight will be carried on any freight train handling such live stock or freight when holding proper transportation, and when permission to accompany same is covered by contract. Passengers on freight trains should be informed that cabooses will not be pulled up to platform to receive or deliver passengers or baggage. Employes holding passes will be carried on any freight train to and from points at which trains stop when passes are stamped: "Good on Freight Trains."

To comply with Rule 91, Conductors on freight trains will wire dispatcher from first telegraph station where they pick up passengers for movement on their trains, including caretakers of livestock, banana messengers, etc., also sectionmen, bridgemen and other employes riding as passengers.

7-A. Passengers may be carried on freight trains between Chama and Durango and between Salida and Sargent.

7-B. Cars must not be "dropped" over main highways.

8. All employes are hereby notified of close clearance of structures, etc., located on the main track and on sidings, as follows:

Sub-Division	Mile	Description		Side or Overhead
		MAIN TRACK		
10	190.5	Water column	Main Track	Side
10	198.6	West Occidental	Tunnel	Side and Overhead
10	202.2	West Codo	Tunnel	Side and Overhead
10-A	287.1	East Hanna	Wire Crossing	Overhead
10-A	306.4	East Wagon Wheel Gap	Bridge 306.39	Side and Overhead
		SIDINGS		
10	216.9	Russell	Stock Chute	Side
10	227.7	Ft. Garland	Stock Chute	Side
10	232.4	Blanca	Freight Platform	Side
10-A	298.2	South Fork	Sheds, Stk. Chute	Side
10-A	318.1	Wasson	Stock Chute	Side
		MAIN TRACK		
11	306.0	Sublette	Water Column	Side
11	311.3	West Toltec	Mud Tunnel	Side and Overhead
11	315.2	West Toltec	Rock Tunnel	Side and Overhead
'1	330.6	Cumbres	Water Column	Side
.1	343.6	East Chama	Bridge 343.61	Side and Overhead
12	377.4	East Navajo	Bridge 377.39	Side
12	377.5	East Navajo	Bridge 377.52	Side and Overhead
12	380.2	West Navajo	Bridge 380.23	Side
12	386.1	East Juanita	Bridge 386.07	Side and Overhead
12	387.7	West Juanita	Bridge 387.67	Side and Overhead

Sub-Division	Mile	Description		Side or Overhead
		MAIN TRACK		
12	390.4	Gato	Bridge 390.45	Side and Overhead
12	404.1	West Arboles	Bridge 404.07	Side and Overhead
12	418.6	East La Boca	Bridge 418.62	Side and Overhead
12	437.0	East Florida	Bridge 437.01	Side and Overhead
		SIDINGS		
12	367.0	Amargo	Stock Chute	Side
12	373.3	Dulce	Stock Chute	Side
12	403.6	Arboles	Stock Chute	Side
12	414.0	Tiffany	Stock Chute	Side
12	419.0	La Boca	Stock Chute	Side
12	425.7	Ignacio	Stock Chute	Side
12	437.3	Florida	Stock Chute	Side
		SIDINGS		
12-A	481.8	Aztec	Stock Chute	Side
12-A	496.2	Farmington	Stock Chute	Side
12-A	496.2	Farmington	Oil Loading Trestle	Side and Overhead
		MAIN TRACK		
12-B	452.4	West Durango	Bridge 452.42	Side and Overhead
12-B	462.42	East Hermosa	Bridge 462.42	Side
12-B	474.5	West Tacoma	Rock Cuts	Side
12-B	477.81	West Tacoma	Bridge 477.81	Side and Overhead
		MAIN TRACK		
13	215.1	Salida	Bridge 215.14	Side and Overhead
13	220.7	West Poncha Jct.	Bridge 220.75	Side
13	226.5	Mears Junction	Bridge 226.48	Overhead
13	240.5	Marshall Pass	Snow Sheds	Side and Overhead
13	257.2	Sargent	Coal Chute	Side
13	312.2	East of Cr. Butte	Water Column	Side
13-B	320.6	Crested Butte	Stock Chute	Side
13-C	295.1	Wylie	Stock Chute	Side
		SIDINGS		
13	257.2	Sargent	Stock Chute	Side
13	265.5	Crookton	Stock Chute	Side
13	276.8	Parlin	Stock Chute	Side
13	288.6	Gunnison	Stock Chute	Side
13-B	304.7	Jack's Cabin	Stock Chute	Side
13-B	316.3	Crested Butte	Upper Tramway	Side and Overhead
13-B	316.3	Crested Butte	Lower Tramway	Side and Overhead
13-C	301.0	Dollard	Stock Chute	Side
		MAIN TRACK		
14	300.7	West Kezar	Bridge 300.68	Side
		SIDINGS		
14	299.2	Iola	Stock Chute	Side
14	314.0	Sapinero	Stock Chute	Side
		SIDINGS		
15	245.3	Villa Grove	Stock Chute	Side
15	262.7	Moffat	Stock Chute	Side
15	280.3	Hooper	Stock Chute	Side
15	286.8	Mosca	Stock Chute	Side

All employes are also hereby notified that there are coal chutes, buildings, platforms and other structures located on tracks, other than the main track and sidings, that WILL NOT CLEAR a man riding on the side of a car or engine or on the top of the car; and all employes must protect themselves from injury in passing such structures.

9. The speed of trains should be so restricted that absolute safety will be assured, and the maximum speed will ordinarily be that necessary to make the schedule.

9-A. Trains must not exceed the maximum speeds prescribed below:

Speed restrictions governing freight trains govern the speed of mixed trains and govern the speed of light engines unless otherwise provided.

	Passenger Trains MPH		Freight Trains MPH	
	NG	SG	NG	SG
Sub-Division 10				
La Veta-Francisco		35		20
Francisco-Fir		20		15
Fir-Sierra		20		18
Sierra-Alamosa		45		35
Westward trains or engines over Spring Switch MP 249.9 East Yard, Alamosa		25		20
Sub-Division 10-A				
Alamosa-Del Norte	45		40	
Del Norte-Hanna	45		30	
Hanna-Creede	35		25	
Sharp Curves	20		18	
Sub-Division 11				
Alamosa-Antonito	40	45	30	35
Antonito-Lava	40		25	
Cumbres-M.P. 342.8 descending	18		12	
Cumbres-Lava	30		18	
Sharp Curves	20		15	
Cumbres-Antonito, Snow Plow Trains	25		25	
Sharp Curves, Snow Plow Trains	18		18	
Over Bridges 319.95 and 339.78	10		10	
Sub-Division 12	35		25	
Sharp Curves	20		15	
Sub-Division 12-A	30		25	
Sharp Curves	20		15	
Sub-Division 12-B	25		20	
Sharp Curves	20		15	
Between Rockwood and Animas River Bridge 471.23	8		8	
Over Bridge 471.23	5		5	
Over Bridges 489.88, 495.64 and 496.12	10		10	
Sub-Division 13	35		25	
Sharp Curves	20		15	
Marshall Pass-Poncha Jct.—descending	18		12	
Marshall Pass-Buxton—descending	18		12	
Sub-Division 13-A	25		20	
Monarch-Maysville—descending	10		10	
Maysville-Poncha Jct.—descending	20		18	
Sub-Division 13-B	30		25	
Sharp Curves	20		15	
Sub-Division 13-C	15		15	
Over Gunnison River bridge and Ohio Creek bridge between Gunnison and Wylie	6		6	
Around sharp curves in shu-fly MP 301 plus 2000 ft., and MP 301 plus 4500 ft. between Dollard and Castleton	6		6	
Sub-Division 14	35		25	
Sharp Curves	20		15	
Sub-Division 15	30		25	
Sharp Curves	20		15	
Poncha Pass-Mears Jct.—descending	18		12	
Poncha Pass-Round Hill—descending	20		15	
Durango yard, between Continental Oil Spur and depot, westward	12		10	
Marshall Pass (first switch) East and West ends of shed	5		5	
Gunnison, over Tomichi and Virginia Ave's.	5		5	
Alamosa yard, trains and engines main track and track No. 2 between Hunt Avenue and Ross Avenue	6	6	6	6

All Sub-Divisions, except where specific restrictions in certain territories require lower speed:

	Miles Per Hour
In or out of turnouts	15

Maximum speeds permissible in any service by various classes of power and equipment as follows:

	Miles Per Hour
K-36 and K-37 class engines	35
C-48 L-95 and L-107	40
L-131-132	45
Engines backing up	15
Trains handling dead engines with side rods up	25
Dead engines with side rods all down	15
Dead engines with one pair wheels swinging	10
Steam Derricks, Shovels, Clam Shells, Short Scale Test cars except 010897, Ditchers and Pile Drivers moving on own wheels, also K & J and Western Air Dumps and loaded system coke racks	25

Restrictions on sharp curves refer to those of 8 or more degrees.

9-C. City Ordinance speed limits as follows:

	Miles Per Hour
Between MP 279.7 and 280.6 at Antonito	12

9-D. K-36 and K-37 engines must not be double-headed over bridges 319.95 and 339.78, Sub-Division 11.

9-E. C-25 class engines must not be double-headed with K-27 or K-28 class engines, nor must K-27 or K-28 class engines be double-headed over bridges on Sub-Division 12-B. Engines of the classes listed must not be operated over bridge 471.23, near Rockwood, unless separated by at least one hundred feet and this separation should consist of lightly loaded equipment. It is not permissible to operate two of these engines over this bridge with only a flanger between them.

9-F. When second engine is used on trains of over 35 cars on Sub-Division 11 between Antonito and Cumbres, second engine must be cut into train.

When second engine is used on Sub-Division 12, place it on head end.

9 G. No engine larger than C-21 class must be used in service between Gunnison and Sapinero, Sub-Division 14.

9-H. No engine larger than C-16 Class must be operated between Gunnison and Castleton, Sub-Division 13-C.

9-I. Double-heading between Salida and Marshall Pass is prohibited. Place one engine on head end, cut one engine into train about twenty-five cars from head engine and place one engine on the rear end, ahead of caboose. In operating three engine trains out of Sargent and Chama eastbound use two engines on head end of train and one engine on rear end, the rear engine either just ahead of caboose, or drover's car when latter is used. Engines will not be double-headed over bridges between Gunnison and Sapinero—must be at least five cars between engines on these bridges. On two engine trains out of Gunnison and Villa Grove, eastbound, place them on head end of train.

9-J. Between La Veta and Fir, two engine trains may be double-headed. When handling three engine trains, two engines may be used on head end and one engine just ahead of caboose, except that Class M engine must not be placed ahead of caboose. When Class M engines are used, they will be placed on head end of train.

Between Sierra and Fir, two engine trains may be doubleheaded. When handling three engine trains, the two helpers will be cut in train approximately 30 cars behind train engine.

9-K. L-131, L-132 class engines must not be doubleheaded with other mallet engines when handling trains.

9-L. Passenger trains must not exceed schedule running time between Osier and Big Horn.

9-M. Do not exceed a speed of fifteen (15) miles per hour over bridge 299.01 near Almont, Sub-Division 13-B, with K-36 or K-37 class engines.

10. Company Surgeons are located as follows:

DR. E. A. HINDS, Chief Surgeon, Denver
DR. C. R. FULLER, Assistant Chief Surgeon, Salida

SIDNEY ANDERSON......Alamosa	A. L. BURNETT..............Durango
J. R. HURLEY...............Alamosa	M. D. MORAN............Farmington
J. D. DAVIES—Oculist....Alamosa	R. A. HOOVER...................Salida
R. D. TAYLOR..........Monte Vista	LEO J. LEONARDI..........Salida
A. B. GJELLUM..........Del Norte	A. J. BENDER....................Salid
GEORGE R. DAVIS........Antonito	H. D. SMITH......................Salid.
J. I. DUNHAM..................Chama	L. E. THOMPSON, Eye.....Salida
J. R. C. CARTER..................Dulce	J. P. McDONOUGH......Gunnison
O. B. RENSCH..............Durango	J. W. HUDSON........Crested Butte

10-A. Hospitals are located as follows: Durango, "Mercy," Salida, "D. & R. G. W.," Alamosa "Community."

10-B. PROMPT TELEGRAPHIC REPORT (Form 3884) MUST BE MADE OF ALL ACCIDENTS. In the event Form 3884 cannot be furnished without unduly delaying the train a message must be filed at first open telegraph office giving principal facts concerning the accident and Form 3884 filed as quickly as possible thereafter. When a personal injury occurs on a train an additional message must be sent immediately to the Superintendent and Claim Department and if the injured person is not an employe on duty the following information must be given: Kind of transportation injured person holds, giving number of ticket or pass, description of injured party, whether coach or pullman passenger, with number or name of car and, if injured party stopping over enroute, state where stopover will be made and address at point of stopover.

In addition to the telegraphic reports (Form 3884) and messages above described, mail reports of all accidents and casualties must be promptly made and forwarded, using the following forms according to the instructions thereon and in the Book of Rules:

Form 3922—All personal injuries and all crossing accidents.
Form 4009—When accident occurs on train to be filled out by passengers.
Form 4012—Inspection of Equipment (Mechanical Dept.)
Form 4119—Fire Report (Section Foreman)
Form 3511—Stock Struck Report (Enginemen)
Form 4117—Stock Report (Section Foreman)

10-C. SURGICAL ATTENTION. (Passengers and employes.) Whenever passengers or employes are injured, everything must be done to care for them properly, either calling the Company's nearest Surgeon to treat them (and if seriously injured, calling the nearest competent Surgeon to be had, until the Company's Surgeon can get to the place of accident), or if they are able to be moved, taking them to the nearest place at which the Company has a Surgeon and turning them over to him for care and treatment. If other than a Company Surgeon is called, he is to be advised that he is called for first attention only, beyond which the Company assumes no responsibility for his bill.

(Others). When persons not employes or passengers (for example, persons injured at crossings, trespassers, outsiders at work around depot or other industries, etc.) are injured, if they are unable to care for themselves, and if no friends or others are at hand to care for them, the nearest Company Surgeon should be called, or if he cannot be reached, the nearest other competent Surgeon, which Surgeon must be advised that he is called for emergency attention only and that the Company does not assume responsibility for his bill. If trespassers are not taken charge of by friends or others, they should be turned over to the public authorities as soon as possible, and no expense incurred in behalf of the Company except the emergency attention above noted.

10-D. Parties calling Surgeons should explain fully as possible the nature of the injuries so that the Surgeon may know what equipment to bring with him.

10-E. When any accident, collision of trains, or any collision of trains with vehicles or pedestrians, resulting in loss of life or injury to persons in Colorado or New Mexico, the superior officer, agent or employe on ground at time of such accident shall immediately notify the Public Utilities Commission of Colorado, Capitol Building, Denver, Colo., or the State Corporation Commission, Santa Fe, New Mexico, by telegram, the details of such accident stating the immediate location and nature of accident and number of persons killed or injured.

Information concerning such accidents must be sent by Western Union Telegraph Company's wires and all agents will accept and so transmit, making notation that same shall be charged against CAK 33.

11. Westward trains arriving Marshall Pass will use west siding, in shed, instead of main track, and eastward trains will use the main track. Normal position of main track switch at east end of Marshall Pass Shed is for west siding and switch at west end of Marshall Pass is for main track. These switches must always be left lined to normal position, when not in use.

11-A. Siding inside of shed, Marshall Pass, will be known as WEST SIDING. Siding east of the shed will be known as EAST SIDING.

12. SPRING SWITCHES:

Miles from Denver	Location Spring Switch	Normal Position
249.9	East Yard (Alamosa)	Main Track

12-A. 2-position color light signal located fifty feet east of spring switch MP 249.9 indicates position of spring switch, East Yard. Signal will indicate "GREEN" when spring switch points are in running position for main track; and will indicate "RED" if spring switch points are open one-quarter inch or more. When signal indicates "RED" spring switch points must be inspected on ground before passing over same.

13. Water Tanks or Cranes between Stations.
Sub-Division 12-A, located M.P. 464.7
Sub-Division 12-B, located at M.P.'s 474.60 and 484.10.
Sub-Division 13, located M.P. 239.4
Sub-Division 13-A, located M.P. 229.6
Sub-Division 13-A, located M.P. 234.1
Sub-Division 14, located M.P. 305.1

14. The following are auxiliary lines (Rules 14-T, 14-U):
Carbon Jct., Sub-Division 12-A.
Poncha Jct., Sub-Division 13-A.
Mears Jct., Sub-Division 15.

15. Trains 215 and 216, only, on Sub-Division 12 will register at Carbon Junction. It will not be necessary for trains on Sub-Division 12 to check register at Carbon Junction.

16. When handling cars on coal chute inclines air must be coupled through and operative on the entire string of cars.

17. Open or stock cars loaded with creosoted ties should be trained at least ten cars from engine to avoid fire hazard.

18. Headlight of diesel locomotives must be kept burning during daylight hours when in road service except when necessary to comply with Operating Rules 17(b) and 17(c).

19. On Cumbres turns, when helper engine returns light from Cumbres, train crew and their engine will return from Cumbres to Chama ahead of helper engine except when there is switching to be done at Cumbres or on the return trip westbound between Cumbres and Chama, in which event helper engines will precede train.

20. In making doubles Sargent to Marshall Pass place the cars on spurs at Marshall Pass when there is room to do so. In case it becomes necessary to leave cars on main track notify Dispatcher and train order will be issued to cover.

21. On arrival Monarch, stop clear of tipple track and trainmen line tipple track switch to south passing track before proceeding into yard. Enginemen sound two (2) long and two (2) short blasts of whistle on approaching and passing tipple. When ready to depart from Monarch, trainmen line tipple track switch to south passing track before giving enginemen proceed signal. Clear south passing track before departing on each trip.

22. When cars are stored or left standing on Monarch Branch the west wye switch at Poncha Jct. on this Branch must be lined for the wye instead of main track to prevent cars running away.

23. When engines equipped with Priest or Ray flanger are working under snow conditions, flanger must be used on the ascending as well as the descending grade.

24. Engines handling steam heated passenger equipment must not be detached from train to buck snow, nor shall they be detached for other purposes unless an emergency exists. In winter weather, before detaching engine, steam line must be thoroughly blown out to prevent freezing and subsequent damage of steam appliances.

25. Discontinue whistling at 7th to 13th streets, inclusive, Durango yard, but engine bell must be rung. At Sixth Street, which is State Highway, Rule 14 (l) is modified as follows: "Two short blasts, space, two short blasts" will be used approaching this crossing. Keep whistle tone to as moderate a pitch as possible.

26. Following instructions govern movements in yards listed as follows:

ALAMOSA: Air hose must be coupled and air operative through cuts of cars handled between all of the various yards at this point, which are Old Yard, New Yard and Farm tracks.

GUNNISON: Air must be cut through and air brakes in operation on all trains, or cuts of cars handled between main yard and points on Crested Butte and Baldwin Branches in both directions.

9

D. & R. G. W—Alamosa

DURANGO: Air must be cut through and air brakes in operation on all trains, or cuts of cars handled between Durango yard and yard at Smelter.

27. Conductors will provide themselves with supply of forms to be used in giving tie-up instructions to Trainmen and Enginemen when necessary to tie up at intermediate points where trains are out of communication with Train Dispatcher. When trains are enroute over sub-division and on account of delays caused by obstructions, or for any reason whatever crews will be overtaken by Federal Rest Law, and cannot reach terminal within the allowed sixteen hours of service, and cannot get in touch with Train Dispatcher, conductor will, after fourteen hours on duty, and not to exceed sixteen hours on duty, tie up all members of train and engine crews, filling out the regular tie-up form, a copy to be given each member of all crews involved, including himself, and mail one copy to Superintendent and one copy to Chief Dispatcher. Tie up should be made, in all cases, at a point where eating and sleeping accommodations are available, if possible, unless in work train or snow service and accompanied by properly equipped outfit and cook cars, but must not, in any case, be tied up at a point where outfit will be endangered by snow slides or other hazards, or is likely to become badly snowed in. Three hours, or more release from duty are necessary to break continuity of service.

28. Trains Nos. 215 and 216 will stop daily at meeting point to permit express messenger on No. 215 to transfer express remittance picked up at La Jara and Romeo, to No. 216. In making stop, spot baggage cars opposite each other to expedite exchange.

Conductor on No. 215 ascertain from train messenger at Chama whether or not necessary to make stop as quite often there will be no transfer to make.

29. Any passenger who by reason of intoxication, or otherwise is guilty of such disorderly conduct as to annoy, threaten or insult other persons on the train, and who refuses to desist therefrom when requested to do so by the Conductor, may be ejected, with his baggage, at the next station where Agent is on duty. The Conductor shall use only such force as may be necessary to accomplish such removal, and he may command other railroad employes to assist in such removal, and when necessary wire ahead for assistance. Before ejecting a passenger the Conductor shall tender to such passenger the unused portion of any fare which has been paid.

Whenever a passenger is ejected the name and address of such passenger and the names and addresses of all witnesses, and their statements in writing if possible, should be obtained. All facts connected with such ejectment should be at once reported to the Division Superintendent.

LOCAL TIME INSPECTORS ARE LOCATED AS FOLLOWS:

VELHAGEN BROS. .... Alamosa

J. C. LINDHOLM .... Durango

MRS. MARTHA B. McCRUMB .... Salida

L. D. PATTERSON .... Gunnison

OPEN HOURS OF OFFICE OF COMMUNICATION

STATIONS	WEEK DAY HOURS	SUNDAY AND HOLIDAY HOURS
La Veta	8:00 AM to 4:00 PM 11:00 PM to 7:00 AM	8:00 AM to 4:00 PM 11:00 PM to 7:00 AM
Fir	10:00 PM to 7:00 AM	Closed
Ft. Garland	7:30 AM to 4:30 PM	Closed
Blanca	9:00 AM to 6:00 PM	Closed
Salida	Continuous	Continuous
Alamosa	8:00 AM to 4:00 PM 8:00 PM to 4:00 AM	8:00 AM to 4:00 PM 8:00 PM to 4:00 AM
Monte Vista	8:00 AM to 5:00 PM	Closed
Del Norte	9:00 AM to 6:00 PM	Closed
Creede	8:00 AM to 5:00 PM	Closed
La Jara	7:00 PM to 4:00 AM	7:00 AM to 9:00 AM
Romeo	7:15 AM to 4:15 PM	Closed
Antonito	7:30 AM to 4:30 PM	7:30 AM to 9:30 AM
Cumbres	8:00 AM to 5:00 PM	Closed
Chama	8:30 AM to 4:30 PM 11:00 PM to 7:00 AM	8:30 AM to 4:30 PM
Dulce	8:00 AM to 5:00 PM	Closed
Gato	9:00 AM to 6:00 PM	Closed
Ignacio	8:30 AM to 5:30 PM	10:30 AM to 12:30 PM
Durango	7:45 AM to 4:45 PM	9:45 AM to 11:45 AM
Silverton	9:00 AM to 6:00 PM	Closed
Aztec	8:00 AM to 5:00 PM	Closed
Farmington	7:30 AM to 4:30 PM	Closed
Hooper	8:00 AM to 5:00 PM	Closed
Sargent	8:00 AM to 5:00 PM	Closed
Gunnison	7:30 AM to 6:00 PM	Closed
Crested Butte	8:00 AM to 5:00 PM	Closed

FOLLOWING ARE LEGAL HOLIDAYS:

New Years Day; Washington's Birthday; Decoration Day; Fourth of July; Labor Day; Thanksgiving Day and Christmas (provided when any of the above Holidays fall on Sunday the day observed by the State, Nation or by proclamation shall be considered the holiday).

D. & R. G. W.—Alamosa

ADJUSTED TONNAGE RATINGS

FROM	TO	Class 6000 HP Diesels 555-564	Class 6000 HP Diesels 552-554	Class 5400 HP Diesels 540-547 549-551	Class 5400 HP Diesels 548	Class L-131 L-132 Engines 3600-3619	Class L-95 Engines 3400-3415 xx	Class M-78 Engines 1511-1519 Except 1515	Class M-64, M-67 Engines 1501-1510 1520-1530 1515 1700-1713	Class K-59 Engines 1200-1213	Class C-48 Engines 1131-1199	Adjustment Factor
		Tons	Tons	Tons	Tons	Tons	Tons	Tons	Tons	Tons	Tons	Tons
La Veta	Fir	2050	1550	1450	1400	1350	985	750	675	580	470	2
Alamosa	Russell	7200	6000	5800	5300	4600	3135	2900	2625	2060	1860	5
Russell	Sierra	4800	3600	3650	3500	3000	2375	1750	1600	1420	1120	4
Sierra	Fir	2800	2200	2050	1850	1750	1275	975	875	760	655	3
Alamosa	Monte Vista										5000	5
Monte Vista	South Fork										2900	8
South Fork	Wasson										2000	5
Wasson	Creede										1100	2
Alamosa	Antonito										3000	7

FROM	TO	Class of Engine K-37 No. of Engines 490-499	Class of Engine K-36 No. of Engines 480-489	Class of Engine K-28 No. of Engines 473-478	Class of Engine K-27 No. of Engines 452-464	Class of Engine C-21 No. of Engines 360-361	Class of Engine C-18 No. of Engines 315-319	Class of Engine C-19 No. of Engines 340-345	Class of Engine C-16 No. of Engines 268-278	Adjustment Factor
		Tons	Tons	Tons	Tons	Tons	Tons	Tons	Tons	Tons
Alamosa	Antonito	1635	1615	1240	1190	780	680	630	560	5
Antonito	Cumbres	840	825	630	600	390	350	320	280	4
Chama	Cumbres	252	232	187	183	113	106	92	79	1
Chama	Azotea	1715	1700	1375	1325	740	540	540	510	6
Arboles	Durango	940	925	720	680	410	360	340	290	4
Carbon Jct.	Falfa	660	650	490	460	290	250	230	210	3
Falfa	Gato	1160	1150	875	800	410	360	340	290	4
Gato	Dulce	1060	1050	825	785	560	510	440	390	4
Dulce	Lumberton	1320	1300	980	920	600	500	460	420	3
Lumberton	Monero	660	650	490	460	300	250	230	210	3
Monero	Azotea	710	700	535	485	375	285	275	265	3
Azotea	Chama	1020	1000	735	685	475	385	375	365	3
Durango	Hermosa			735	735	380	340	300	270	5
Hermosa	Silverton			315	315	150	140	120	105	2
Silverton	Durango			800	800	500	360	360	290	4
Farmington	Carbon Jct.	1070	1050	810	780	430	390	350	300	5
Carbon Jct.	Durango	1100	1070	835	820	490	460	420	380	5
Poncha Junction	Marshall Pass	252	232	187	183	124	106	92	79	1
Buxton	Marshall Pass	252	232	187	183	124	106	92	79	1
Poncha Junction	Maysville	373	353	301	301	127	120	105	89	2
Maysville	Monarch	203	195	159	159	95	88	75	65	1
Mears Junction	Poncha Pass	252	232	187	183	124	106	92	79	1
Alamosa	Mineral Hot Spgs.	2975	2950	2220	2030	1560	1190	1190	1120	5
Mineral Hot Spgs.	Villa Grove	1490	1475	1190	1105	600	480	480	420	5
Villa Grove	Round Hill	770	755	570	520	380	300	300	270	3
Round Hill	Poncha Pass	390	378	298	293	175	160	140	120	2
Gunnison	Sargent	1475	1430	1000	950	625	555	505	450	5
Gunnison	Crested Butte	830	820	660	630	410	360	340	290	4
Gunnison	Castleton						380	380	235	4
Sapinero	Gunnison			855	615	570	520	465		5

xx Tractive effort engines 3400, 3401, 3402, 3403, 3409 and 3414 have been increased to 99,000 pounds and are rated 4.2% more than other 3400 series engines.

These ratings are the usual tonnage ratings for dead Freight trains. Chief dispatchers are authorized to increase or decrease these ratings in their discretion in accordance with standing instructions, to adjust for slack grades, conditions of power, necessity for maintaining stock schedules, or for any other reasons which justify.

In computing tonnage, the adjustment factor represents the number of tons which shall be added to the total weight of each car, loaded or empty. The caboose shall count as a car. Tonnage hauled may exceed the rating by a fraction of a car.

D. & R. G. W—Alamosa

A LESSON IN "MONOPOLIES"

Train and Engine Crews and Yard Employes

THE ALAMOSA DIVISION of the Rio Grande is unique in that it comprises the only railroad, other than short lines, within the territory it serves.

That does not mean, by any stretch of the imagination, that the Rio Grande has a "monopoly" on the traffic that originates within the productive borders of the territory, or that moves into the territory from outside for local consumption.

Not by a long shot!

Shippers are looking for just one thing—**prompt** and **dependable** service. If they can count on getting it from the Rio Grande, that appears to be the logical way for them to move their products. But if the Rio Grande service is **NOT** prompt and dependable, there are still "other forms of transportation" they can utilize.

Here are a few typical figures to paste up in your cab or caboose or in the switch shanty as examples of what we mean: In 1935, 10 per cent of all livestock moving into the Denver market came in by truck. By 1945, this figure has grown to **25 percent!** In the year 1946, approximately **1,000 car loads** of San Luis Valley potatoes moved out of the valley by truck, and that's a lot of potatoes.

We supply just one product—transportation service. That product, properly supplied, means that we are playing our part in helping to develop the rich resources of the territory we serve. It also means that we will be getting our fair share of the traffic from the territory.

We all know the Rio Grande has a superior plant and an organization of ability, capable and energetic, which can supply transportation equal to or better than any other system under tough competitive conditions.

But mishandling of a train or even a single car usually means delay or damage to shipments, and may—and usually does—result in loss of future business.

On-time performance and smooth handling, combined with courteous treatment of all with whom we do business, is what it takes to make a transportation service of quality, and that means a busy railroad.

General Traffic Manager.

DENVER & RIO GRANDE WESTERN R.R.
TYPE-2-8-0   CLASS-C-16   SERIES-268
NARROW GAUGE

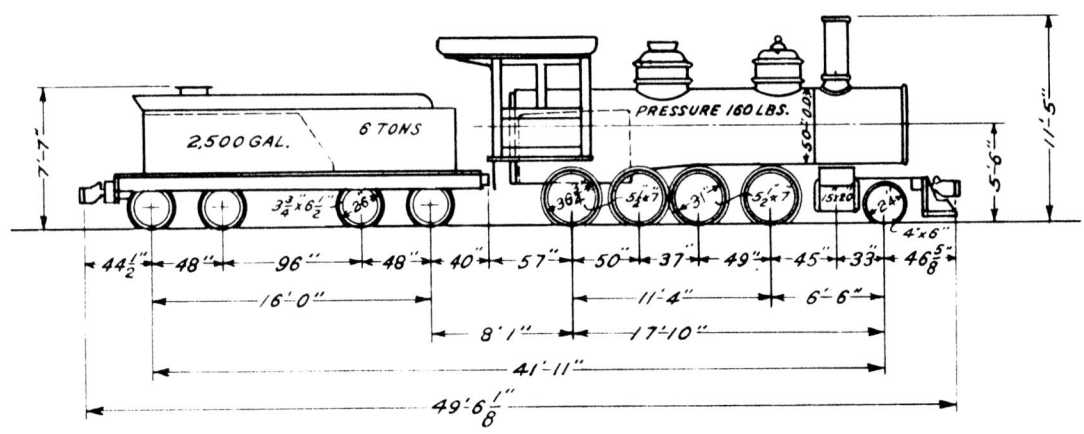

GAUGE _____ 3'-0"	
VALVE GEAR _____ STEPHENSON	
WHEELS _____ SPOKE	FIREBOX SIZE, INSIDE _____ $83\frac{5}{8}$ x $23\frac{3}{4}$"
	TUBES, 2" DIA., NO. _____ 148
GRATES _____ ROSEBUD	FLUES, LENGTH OVER SHEETS _____ $9'-7\frac{5}{8}$
	GRATE SURFACE, SQ. FT. _____ 14
	WIDTH OVER RUNNING BOARDS _____ 8'-7"
	WIDTH OVER CYLINDERS _____ 6'-10"
	WIDTH OVER FRAMES _____ 2'-7"

	TRACTIVE POWER _____ LBS. 16,540
	WT. ON ENGINE TRUCK _____ " 9,775
	WT. ON FIRST DRIVERS _____ " 14,295
H.S., FIREBOX _____ SQ.FT. 72	WT. ON SECOND DRIVERS _____ " 16,885
H.S., TUBES _____ " " 745	WT. ON THIRD DRIVERS-MAIN _____ " 14,365
	WT. ON FOURTH DRIVERS _____ " 13,790
H.S., TOTAL _____ " " 817	WT. ON DRIVERS-TOTAL _____ " 59,335
	WT. OF ENGINE _____ " 69,110
	WT. OF TENDER-LOADED _____ " 53,000
	WT. OF ENGINE & TENDER-LOADED " 122,110
BUILDERS-BALDWIN LOCO. WORKS	
DATE IN SERVICE _____ 1882.	

DENVER & RIO GRANDE WESTERN R.R.
TYPE-2-8-0   CLASS-C-18   ENGINE No. 318
NARROW GAUGE

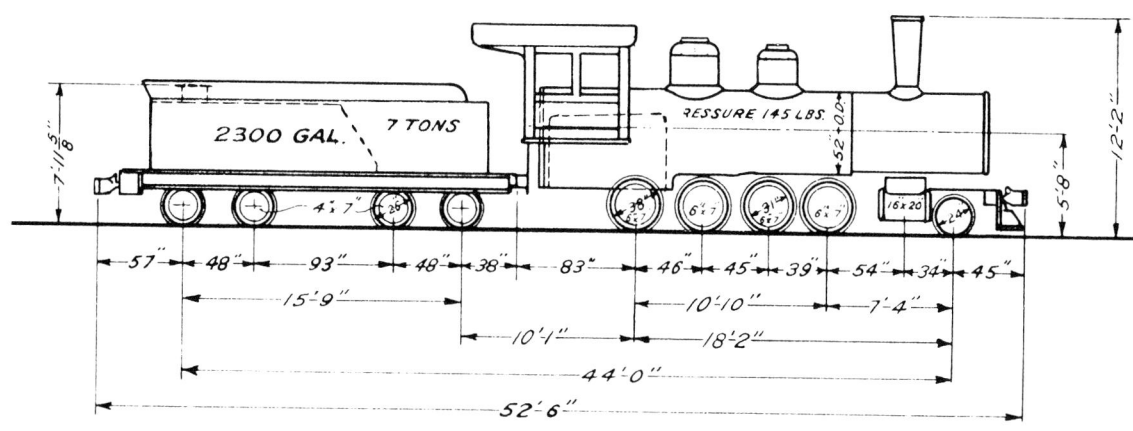

GAUGE ___ 3'-0"	
VALVE GEAR ___ STEPHENSON	
WHEELS ___ SPOKE	FIREBOX SIZE, INSIDE ___ $83\frac{7}{8} \times 24"$
	TUBES, 2" DIA., NO. ___ 154
GRATES ___ ROSEBUD	FLUES, LENGTH OVER SHEETS ___ $11'-7\frac{3}{4}"$
	GRATE SURFACE, SQ.FT. ___ 14
	WIDTH OVER RUNNING BOARDS ___ 8'-3"
	WIDTH OVER CYLINDERS ___ 7'-0"
	WIDTH OVER FRAMES ___ 2'-7"

	TRACTIVE POWER ___ LBS. 16,606
	WT. ON ENGINE TRUCK ___ " 8,000
	WT. ON FIRST DRIVERS, APPROX. ___ " 16,000
H.S. FIREBOX ___ SQ.FT. 86.98	WT. ON SECOND DRIVERS, APPROX. ___ " 16,000
H.S. TUBES ___ " " 934.02	WT. ON THIRD DRIVERS-MAIN, APPROX. 16,000
	WT. ON FOURTH DRIVERS, APPROX. ___ " 16,000
H.S. TOTAL ___ " " 1,021.00	WT. ON DRIVERS-TOTAL ___ " **64,000**
	WT. OF ENGINE ___ " 72,000
BUILDERS - BALDWIN LOCO. WORKS.	WT. OF TENDER-LOADED ___ " 57,000
DATE IN SERVICE ___ 1896	WT. OF ENGINE & TENDER-LOADED ___ " 129,000
REBUILT ___ JULY, AUG., 1917	

DENVER & RIO GRANDE WESTERN R.R.
TYPE-2-8-0 CLASS-C-19 ENGINE No. 340
NARROW GAUGE

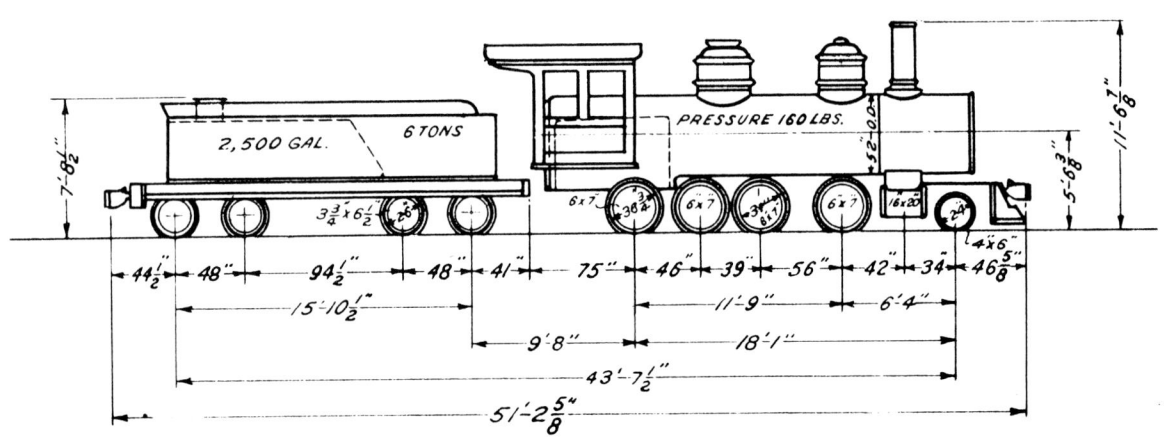

GAUGE _____ 3'-0"	
VALVE GEAR _____ STEPHENSON	
WHEELS _____ SPOKE	FIREBOX SIZE, INSIDE _____ 90 3/8" x 23 3/4"
	TUBES, 2" DIA., NO. _____ 151
GRATES _____ ROSEBUD	FLUES, LENGTH OVER SHEETS _____ 10'-6"
	GRATE SURFACE, SQ. FT. _____ 15
	WIDTH OVER RUNNING BOARDS _____ 8'-7"
	WIDTH OVER CYLINDERS _____ 7'-0"
	WIDTH OVER FRAMES _____ 2'-7"

	TRACTIVE POWER _____ LBS. 18,947
	WT. ON ENGINE TRUCK _____ " 10,260
	WT. ON FIRST DRIVERS _____ " 13,790
H.S., FIREBOX _____ SQ. FT. _____ 81.2	WT. ON SECOND DRIVERS-MAIN _____ " 16,940
H.S., TUBES _____ " " 830.1	WT. ON THIRD DRIVERS _____ " 17,810
	WT. ON FOURTH DRIVERS _____ " 15,460
H.S., TOTAL _____ " " 911.3	WT. ON DRIVERS-TOTAL _____ " 64,000
	WT. OF ENGINE _____ " 74,260
	WT. OF TENDER-LOADED _____ " 53,000
BUILDERS _ _ BALDWIN LOCO. WORKS.	WT. OF ENGINE & TENDER-LOADED _ " 127,260
DATE IN SERVICE _ JULY, 1881.	

DENVER & RIO GRANDE WESTERN R.R.
TYPE 2-8-0   CLASS C-21   ENGINE No. 361
NARROW GAUGE

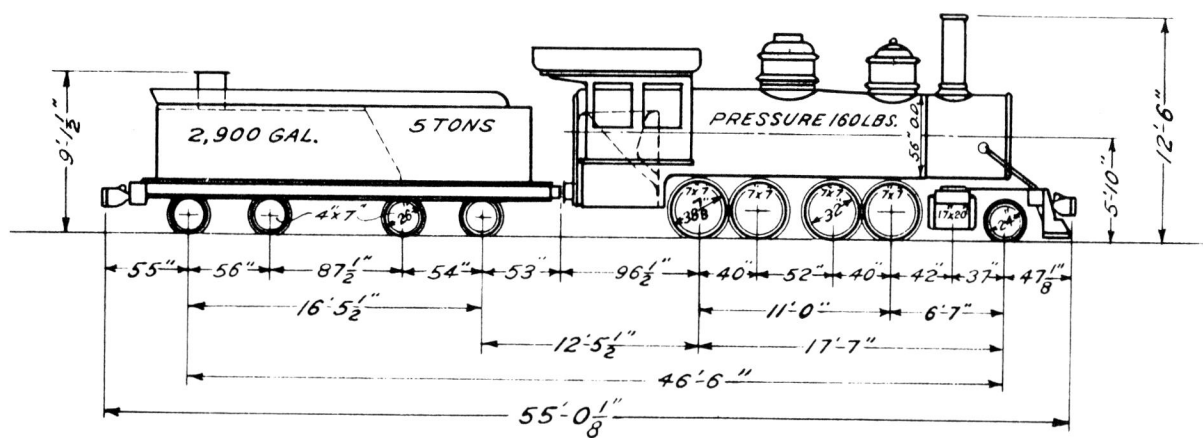

GAUGE _____ 3'-0"	
VALVE GEAR _____ STEPHENSON	
WHEELS _____ SPOKE	FIREBOX SIZE, INSIDE _____ 54 3/16" x 44 7/8"
	TUBES, 2 1/4" DIA., NO. _____ 111
GRATES _____ ROSEBUD	FLUES, LENGTH OVER SHEETS __ 14'-10 1/2"
	GRATE SURFACE, SQ.FT. _____ 16.8
	WIDTH OVER RUNNING BOARDS __ 7'-2 1/2"
	WIDTH OVER CYLINDERS _____ 8'-10 1/2"
	WIDTH OVER FRAMES _____ 4'-6 1/8"

	TRACTIVE POWER _____ LBS. 20,686
H.S., SYPHONS _____ SQ.FT. ___ 11	WT. ON ENGINE TRUCK ____ " 10,000
	WT. ON FIRST DRIVERS ____ " 17,700
H.S., FIREBOX _____ " " 83.5	WT. ON SECOND DRIVERS ___ " 21,450
H.S., TUBES _____ " " 1,074	WT. ON THIRD DRIVERS-MAIN _ " 20,400
	WT. ON FOURTH DRIVERS ___ " 26,100
H.S., TOTAL _____ " " 1,168.5	WT. ON DRIVERS-TOTAL ____ " 85,650
	WT. OF ENGINE _____ " 95,650
	WT. OF TENDER-LOADED ___ " 65,300
BUILDERS – BALDWIN LOCO. WORKS	WT. OF ENGINE & TENDER-LOADED _ " 160,950
DATE IN SERVICE – MAY, 1900.	

DENVER & RIO GRANDE WESTERN R.R.
TYPE-2-8-0 CLASS-C-25 ENGINE-NO.375
NARROW GAUGE

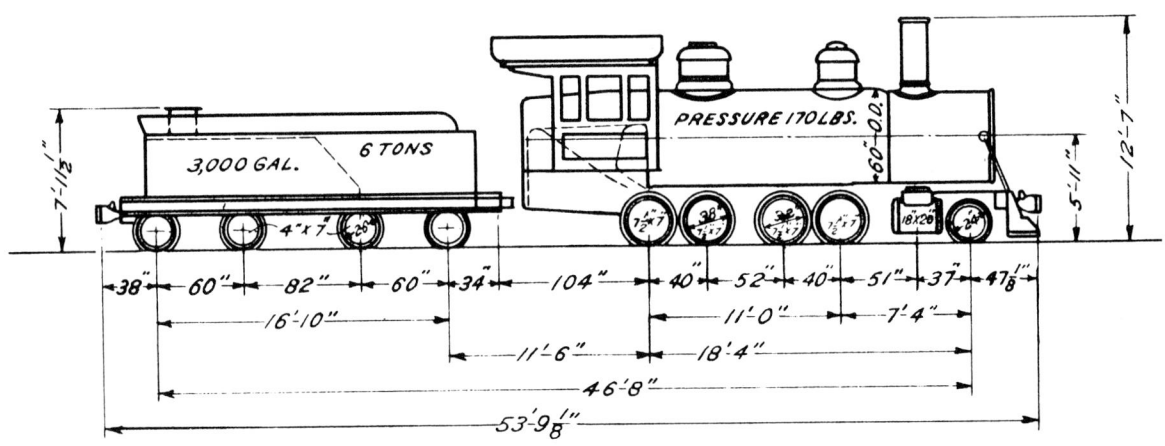

GAUGE	3'-0"
VALVE GEAR	STEPHENSON
WHEELS	SPOKE
GRATES	ROSEBUD

FIREBOX SIZE, INSIDE	54 3/16" x 50"
TUBES, 2" DIA., NO.	199
FLUES, LENGTH OVER SHEETS	15'-7"
GRATE SURFACE, SQ. FT.	18.7
WIDTH OVER RUNNING BOARDS	9'-3"
WIDTH OVER CYLINDERS	9'-1"
WIDTH OVER FRAMES	4'-7"

H.S., SYPHON SQ. FT.	12
H.S., FIREBOX " "	86
H.S., TUBES " "	1,623
H.S., TOTAL " "	1,721

BUILDERS-BALDWIN LOCO. WORKS
DATE IN SERVICE — MARCH, 1903.

TRACTIVE POWER LBS.	24,641
WT. ON ENGINE TRUCK "	10,000
WT. ON FIRST DRIVERS "	24,100
WT. ON SECOND DRIVERS "	26,400
WT. ON THIRD DRIVERS-MAIN "	28,700
WT. ON FOURTH DRIVERS "	28,200
WT. ON DRIVERS-TOTAL "	107,400
WT. OF ENGINE "	117,400
WT. OF TENDER-LOADED "	64,000
WT. OF ENGINE & TENDER-LOADED "	181,400

DENVER & RIO GRANDE WESTERN R.R.
TYPE-2-8-2 CLASS-K-27 ENGINE NO. 462
NARROW GAUGE

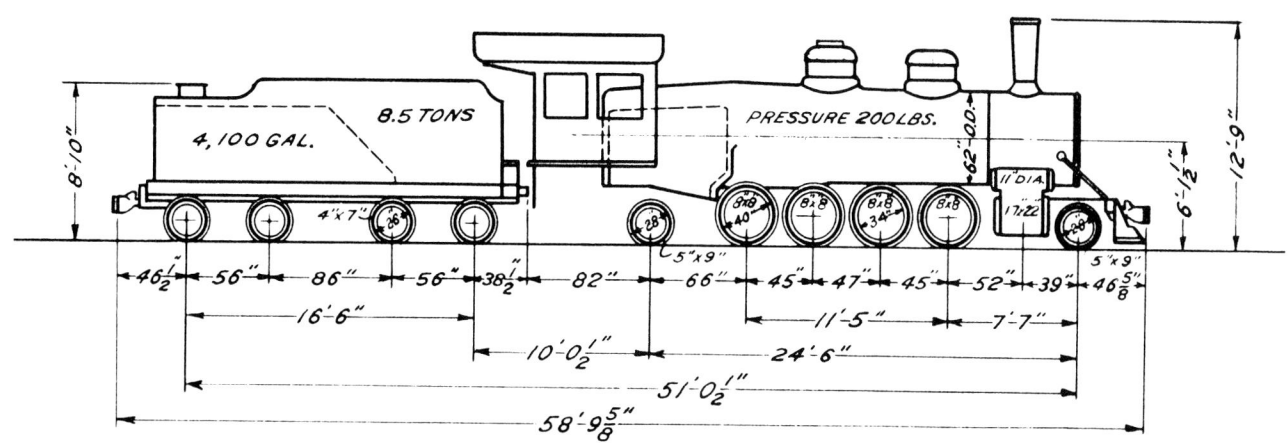

GAUGE _____ 3'-0"	
VALVE GEAR _____ WALSCHAERT	
WHEELS _____ SPOKE	FIREBOX SIZE, INSIDE _____ 72⅛"×60¼"
	TUBES, 2¼" DIA., NO. _____ 205
GRATES _____ ROSEBUD	FLUES, LENGTH OVER SHEETS ___ 16'-0"
	GRATE SURFACE, SQ. FT. _____ 30.17
	WIDTH OVER RUNNING BOARDS ____ 8'-11"
	WIDTH OVER CYLINDERS _____ 9'-5¾"
	WIDTH OVER FRAMES _____ 4'-8"

	TRACTIVE POWER _____ LBS. 27,000
	WT. ON ENGINE TRUCK _____ " 11,300
H.S., ARCH TUBES ____ SQ.FT. ____ 11	WT. ON FIRST DRIVERS _____ " 26,600
H.S., FIREBOX _____ " " ___ 102	WT. ON SECOND DRIVERS _____ " 27,475
H.S., TUBES _____ " " __ 1,932	WT. ON THIRD DRIVERS-MAIN __ " 27,250
	WT. ON FOURTH DRIVERS _____ " 24,100
H.S., TOTAL _____ " " __ 2,045	WT. ON TRAILER AXLE _____ " 19,925
	WT. ON DRIVERS-TOTAL _____ " 105,425
	WT. OF ENGINE _____ " 136,650
BUILDERS-BALDWIN LOCO. WORKS	WT. OF TENDER-LOADED _____ " 83,300
DATE IN SERVICE _____ 1903.	WT. OF ENGINE & TENDER-LOADED " 219,950

DENVER & RIO GRANDE WESTERN R.R.
TYPE-2-8-2   CLASS-K-27   ENGINES No. 463, 464
NARROW GAUGE

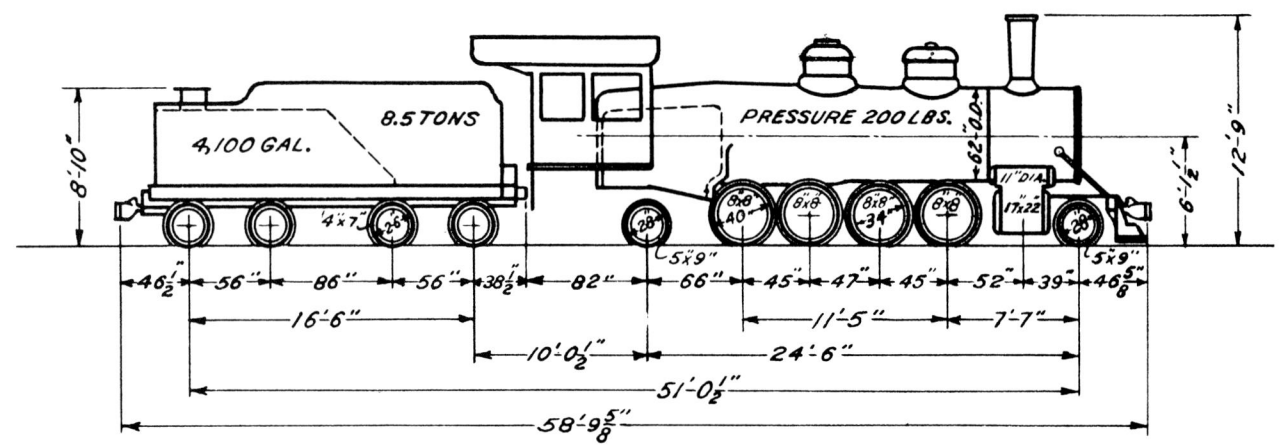

GAUGE _____ 3'-0"	SUPERHEATER _____ SCHMIDT TYPE A
VALVE GEAR _____ WALSCHAERT	
WHEELS _____ SPOKE	FIREBOX SIZE, INSIDE _____ 72⅛"x60¼"
	TUBES, 2¼" DIA., NO. _____ 97
	FLUES, 5½" DIA., NO. _____ 22
GRATES _____ ROSEBUD	FLUES, LENGTH OVER SHEETS _____ 16'-0"
	GRATE SURFACE, SQ.FT. _____ 30.17
	WIDTH OVER RUNNING BOARDS _____ 8'-11"
	WIDTH OVER CYLINDERS _____ 9'-5¾"
	WIDTH OVER FRAMES _____ 4'-8"

	TRACTIVE POWER _____ LBS. 27,000
	WT. ON ENGINE TRUCK _____ " 11,700
H.S., ARCH TUBES _____ SQ.FT. __ 11	WT. ON FIRST DRIVERS _____ " 27,319
H.S., FIREBOX _____ " " 102	WT. ON SECOND DRIVERS _____ " 28,194
H.S., TUBES _____ " " 909	WT. ON THIRD DRIVERS-MAIN _____ " 27,969
H.S., FLUES _____ " " 504	WT. ON FOURTH DRIVERS _____ " 24,818
H.S., TOTAL _____ " " 1,526	WT. ON TRAILER AXLE _____ " 20,250
	WT. ON DRIVERS-TOTAL _____ " 108,300
SUPERHEATER SURFACE _ " " 407	WT. OF ENGINE _____ " 140,250
	WT. OF TENDER-LOADED _____ " 83,300
BUILDERS — BALDWIN LOCO. WORKS.	WT. OF ENGINE & TENDER-LOADED " 223,550
DATE IN SERVICE — COMPOUND — 1903.	
DATE IN SERVICE — SIMPLE — 1909.	

DENVER & RIO GRANDE WESTERN R.R.
TYPE-2-8-2 CLASS-K-28 SERIES-473, 476, 478
NARROW GAUGE

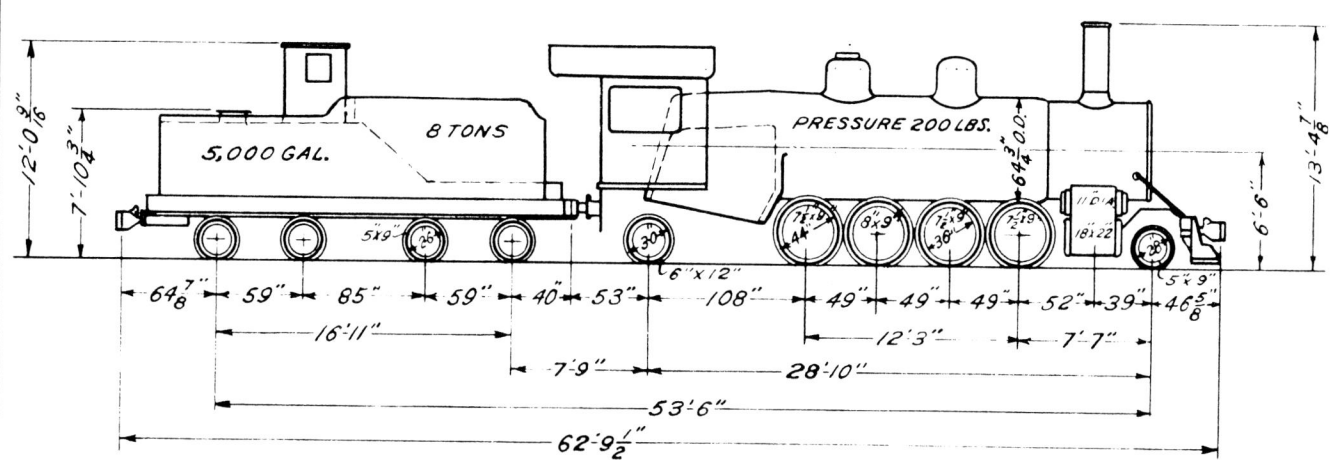

GAUGE — 3'-0"	SUPERHEATER — SCHMIDT TYPE A
VALVE GEAR — WALSCHAERT	
WHEELS — SPOKE	FIREBOX SIZE, INSIDE — $72\frac{1}{8}" \times 60\frac{1}{4}"$
	TUBES, $2\frac{1}{4}"$ DIA., NO. — 106
	FLUES, $5\frac{1}{2}"$ DIA., NO. — 22
GRATES — ROSEBUD	FLUES, LENGTH OVER SHEETS — 16'-0"
	GRATE SURFACE, SQ.FT. — 30.17
	WIDTH OVER RUNNING BOARDS — 9'-5"
	WIDTH OVER CYLINDERS — $10'-5\frac{1}{2}"$
	WIDTH OVER FRAMES — 4'-9"

	TRACTIVE POWER — LBS. 27,540
	WT. ON ENGINE TRUCK — " 20,500
	WT. ON FIRST DRIVERS — " 29,200
H.S., FIREBOX — SQ.FT. 102	WT. ON SECOND DRIVERS — " 29,200
H.S., TUBES — " " 994	WT. ON THIRD DRIVERS-MAIN — " 27,600
H.S., FLUES — " " 504	WT. ON FOURTH DRIVERS — " 27,500
H.S., TOTAL — " " 1,600	WT. ON TRAILER AXLE — " 22,000
	WT. ON DRIVERS-TOTAL — " 113,500
SUPERHEATER SURFACE — " " 396	WT. OF ENGINE — " 156,000
	WT. OF TENDER-LOADED — " 98,500
BUILDERS - AMERICAN LOCO. CO.	WT. OF ENGINE & TENDER-LOADED " 254,500
DATE IN SERVICE — OCT., 1923.	

DENVER & RIO GRANDE WESTERN R.R.
TYPE-2-8-2   CLASS-K-36   SERIES-480 TO 489
NARROW GAUGE

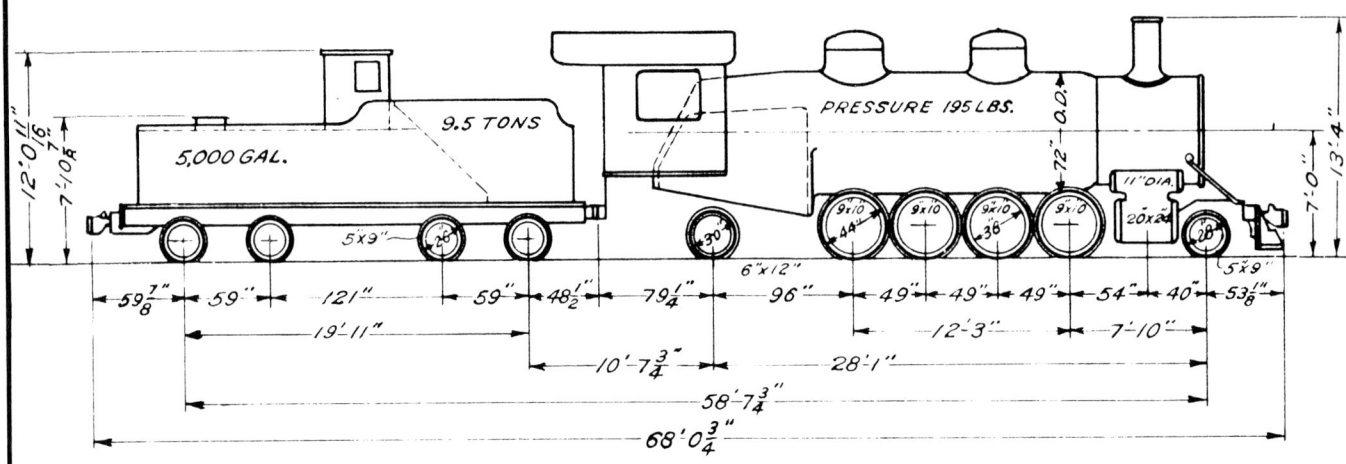

GAUGE _____ 3'-0"	SUPERHEATER _____ SCHMIDT TYPE A
VALVE GEAR _____ WALSCHAERT	
WHEELS _____ SPOKE	FIREBOX SIZE, INSIDE _____ 96 1/8" x 60 1/4"
	TUBES, 2 1/4" DIA., NO. _____ 137
	FLUES, 5 1/2" DIA., NO. _____ 30
GRATES _____ ROSEBUD	FLUES, LENGTH OVER SHEETS _____ 16'-0"
	GRATE SURFACE, SQ.FT. _____ 40.2
	WIDTH OVER RUNNING BOARDS _____ 9'-9"
	WIDTH OVER CYLINDERS _____ 10'-5"
	WIDTH OVER FRAMES _____ 4'-11 1/2"
CYCLONE FRONT END	

	TRACTIVE POWER _____ LBS. 36,200
	WT. ON ENGINE TRUCK _____ " 16,250
	WT. ON FIRST DRIVERS _____ " 32,800
H.S., FIREBOX _____ SQ.FT. _____ 145	WT. ON SECOND DRIVERS _____ " 36,900
H.S., TUBES _____ " " _____ 1,285	WT. ON THIRD DRIVERS-MAIN _____ " 40,150
H.S., FLUES _____ " " _____ 688	WT. ON FOURTH DRIVERS _____ " 34,000
H.S., TOTAL _____ " " _____ 2,118	WT. ON TRAILER AXLE _____ " 27,000
	WT. ON DRIVERS-TOTAL _____ " 143,850
SUPERHEATER SURFACE _____ " " _____ 575	WT. OF ENGINE _____ " 187,100
	WT. OF TENDER-LOADED _____ " 99,500
BUILDERS-BALDWIN LOCO. WORKS	WT. OF ENGINE & TENDER-LOADED " 286,600
DATE IN SERVICE _____ SEPT., 1925.	

DENVER & RIO GRANDE WESTERN R.R.
TYPE-2-8-2 CLASS-K-37 SERIES-490 to 499
NARROW GAUGE

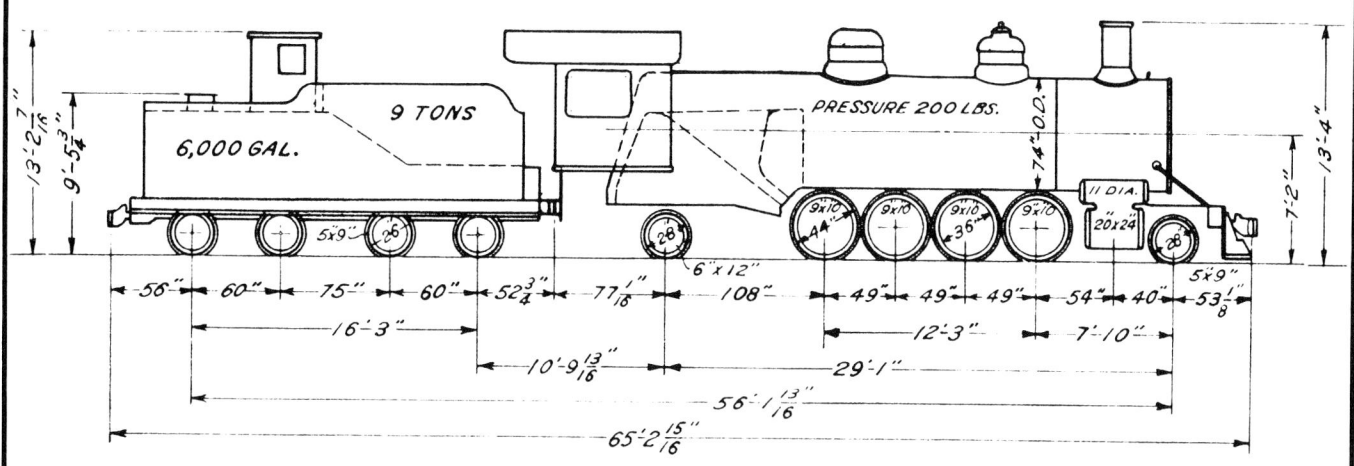

GAUGE ___ 3'-0"	SUPERHEATER ___ SCHMIDT TYPE A
VALVE GEAR ___ WALSCHAERT	
WHEELS ___ SPOKE	FIREBOX SIZE, INSIDE ___ 102 1/8" x 65 3/4"
	TUBES, 2" DIA., NO. {ENGINES WITH SYPHONS -- 173 / ENGINES WITHOUT SYPHONS - 183}
	FLUES, 5 1/2" DIA., NO. ___ 30
GRATES ___ ROSEBUD	FLUES, LENGTH OVER SHEETS ___ 14'-2"
	GRATE SURFACE, SQ. FT. ___ 46.6
ENGINES WITH SYPHONS ___ NO. 491	WIDTH OVER RUNNING BOARDS ___ 9'-9"
	WIDTH OVER CYLINDERS ___ 10'-5"
	WIDTH OVER FRAMES ___ 4'-11 1/2"
CYCLONE FRONT END - NO. 490, 491, 493-499	

	TRACTIVE POWER ___ LBS. 37,100
H.S., SYPHONS ___ SQ.FT. 46	WT. ON ENGINE TRUCK ___ " 15,020
H.S., ARCH TUBES ___ " " 30	WT. ON FIRST DRIVERS ___ " 33,470
H.S., FIREBOX ___ " " 173	WT. ON SECOND DRIVERS ___ " 36,460
H.S., TUBES {ENGINES WITH SYPHONS " " 1,275 / ENGINES WITHOUT SYPHONS " " 1,348}	WT. ON THIRD DRIVERS-MAIN ___ " 39,700
H.S., FLUES ___ " " 608	WT. ON FOURTH DRIVERS ___ " 38,650
H.S., TOTAL, ENG. WITH SYPHONS " " 2,102	WT. ON TRAILER AXLE ___ " 23,950
H.S., TOTAL, ENG. WITOUT SYPHONS " " 2,159	WT. ON DRIVERS-TOTAL ___ " 148,280
SUPERHEATER SURFACE ___ " " 495	WT. OF ENGINE ___ " 187,250
BUILDERS - BALDWIN LOCO. WORKS	WT. OF TENDER - LOADED ___ " 120,000
DATE IN SERVICE - 490-495, 1928	WT. OF ENGINE & TENDER - LOADED " 307,250
- 496-499, 1930.	
REBUILT-D.& R.G.W.-FROM C-41 CLASS, NO. 1003	
-1005, 1009, 1014, 1020, 1021, 1023, 1025, 1026.	

Acknowledgements

The period of time involved in gathering the material and preparing it for publication has stretched from year to year and so many people have encouraged me to continue with the task (and helped in the preparation and the furnishing of material), it is impossible to list them all. If anyone is not mentioned by name it does not mean that I am not duly appreciative of any assistance you gave. I do want to thank each and everyone, and acknowledge that without all the help and encouragement received, this book would not have finally been published.

The past and present personnel of the Rio Grande have gone well beyond the call of duty in helping me. From the top executives, G.B. Aydelott and W.J. Holtman, to the newest employee, I have received wholehearted support and help. The following have been especially helpful:

Jeanne Gustafsen
A.H. (Bob) Nance
E.H. (Ed) Waring
Ed Clarke
Patricia (Pat) Fick
H.W. (Ward) Bushacher

Leonard Bernstein
Joe Harris
Mike Kenyon
Shirley Thornley
J.S. Walker
Bob Buffalo

As always, the Colorado State Historical Society went all the way in finding and supplying material. To them my thanks.

Charles Felstead graciously allowed use of many fine locomotive roster photos I had thought would be unobtainable. Thanks, Charlie, for helping out.

And, thanks also to Cubar Associates of Golden, Colorado, for granting permission to use some material from their 1966 reprint of *Crofutt's Grip Sack Guide of Colorado - 1885*.

I also wish to acknowledge my gratitude for time given me, and the furnishing of some superb photos and illustrations of the Narrow Gauge, that were taken and preserved for today's railfans by these great photographers, historians and artists:

Chris Burritt
Richard H. Kindig
John Krause
A.M. (Andy) Payne
Mike Pearsall
Robert (Bob) W. Richardson,
    Colorado Railroad Museum
Dr. Richard Severance
Clayton Tanner

In the language of the Narrow Gauge country, *Mi gratitud y un mil gracias* to all.

Bibliography

Robert G. Athearn
   Rebel of the Rockies
   Railroad Renaissance in the Rockies
William J. Baker
   Charles Kingsley in Little London
William Blackmore
   Early Financing of the Denver & Rio Grande Railway
William Brandon
   The Men and the Mountain
George A. Crofutt
   Crofutt's Grip-Sack Guide of Colorado
   (As reprinted, 1969, Cubar Associates, Golden, Colorado)
Josie Moore Crum
   The D&RG in the San Juan
Colorado Railroad Museum — Annual 1965
   The Santa Fe's D&RG War No. 2
   Special Chili Line Issue
S. Kip Farrington
   Railroading from the Head End
Vardis Fisher and Opal Laurel Holmes
   Gold Rushes and Mining Claims of the Early American West
Fortune, 1949
   The Denver & Rio Grande
Curt Gentry
   The Madams of San Francisco
Geologic Survey, U.S.
   Minerals of Colorado — A 100-Year Record
John A. Gjevre, M.D.
   The Chili Line
LeRoy R. Hafen, PhD LittD
   Colorado and Its People
John B. Hungerford
   Narrow Gauge to Silverton
Interior Department, U.S.
   Professional Paper No. 138 - 1926
Interstate Commerce Commission —
   Transcripts, Briefs, and Decision of the Abandonment Proceedings, Alamosa-Durango-Farmington Denver and Rio Grande Western Railroad Company's Narrow Gauge
Rossiter Johnson
   Campfires and Battlefields (Civil War)
Northwestern University
   The Denver and Rio Grande Railroad — A Geographic Analysis
Welsh Nossman
   Unpublished memoirs
Mary Ann Olsen
   The Silverton Story
J.W. Powell
   The Exploration of the Colorado River and its Canyons
M.M. Quaife
   Kit Carson's Autobiography
Robert Edgar Riegel
   The Story of the Western Railroads
Thomas Ripley
   They Died With Their Boots On
Wilson Rockwell
   Memoirs of a Lawman
H.A. Rogers
   Unpublished manuscripts and memoirs
Marshall Sprague
   The Great Gates
Irving Stone
   Men to Match My Mountains
Britt Allen Storey
   William Jackson Palmer — Promoter
State of Colorado
   Colorado Geologic Survey, Annual Reports
R.B. Townshend
   A Tenderfoot in Colorado
Carl Ubbelohde
   A Colorado History
G.E. and B.R. Untermann
   Geology of Dinosaur National Monument, Utah-Colorado
Stanley Vestal
   Joe Meek — The Merry Mountain Man
William Walters
   A Gallery of Western Badmen
Stanley W. Zamonski and Teddy Keller
   The Fifty-Niners

And the notes and memories of hundreds of hours spent with Narrow Gauge railroaders while riding the caboose of an unforgettable number of trains, the *San Juan* and *Colorado-New Mexico Express*, on work trains and snow trains, in telegraph offices, sand-drying houses, coal chutes, roundhouses, railroaders' rooming and boarding houses, in Divisional and General Headquarters — with old-time miners, stockmen and lumbermen — and with the many Nuevo Mejicano friends I made and cherished (and some I still dream of).

Index

Index: Marilyn M. Heimburger

A
Abiquiu, 138
Achlesinger, Sebastian B., 24
Alamosa, 8, 9, 21, 25, 26, 34, 38, 41, 44, 45, 47, 50, 59, 62, 64, 78, 79, 83, 94-97, 99, 103, 105, 108-110, 114, 115, 119-124, 127, 154, 157, 158, 164, 178, 179, 202, 203, 205, 208, 210-212, 218, 222, 226, 230, 231, 232, 235, 236, 238-240, 242-244, 252
Alamosa Railway Company, 25
Alamosa Valley Courier, 238
Albuquerque, 22, 78, 79
Alcalde, 110, 114
Allison, 114
Altura, 115
Amargo, 47, 55, 57, 111, 114, 161, 216
American Smelting and Refining Company, 106, 133
Animas, 19, 23, 47, 58, 59, 62, 68, 71, 74, 75, 92, 94, 98-102, 107, 114, 115, 130, 131, 133, 134, 138, 141-143, 222, 223, 233
Antonito, 8, 9, 12, 13, 23, 26, 28, 34, 39, 41, 44, 45, 47-49, 58, 59, 70, 78, 79, 85, 88, 90, 105, 110, 114, 117, 119, 121-123, 125-128, 205, 211, 212, 223, 230-232, 235, 237
Anvil Mountain, 74, 136, 143
Apaches, 13, 44, 57, 129, 161, 216
Arboles, 111, 114
Archuleta, 111, 163, 238
Archuleta, Juan, 13
Arizona and Colorado Railroad, 92, 94
Arkansas River, 6, 13, 21, 23, 80, 135
Armijo, Governor Don Manuel, 121
Arrastra Gulch, 100, 141
Aspen, 16
Astor, 75
At The Old Depot, 248
Atchison, Topeka and Santa Fe, 16, 23-26, 79, 85-87, 127
Autrey, Gene, 70
Azotea, 59, 111, 114, 131, 152, 162, 216
Aztec, 92, 94, 96, 102, 114, 115
Aztecs, 88
Aydelott, G.B., 237

B
Baker, Charles, 74, 99, 100, 130, 136, 138, 141
Baker's Park, 62, 68, 74, 99, 100, 136, 138, 141, 142, 207
Balboa, 12
Ball Machine Shops, 133
Barlow and Sanderson, 121
Barranca, 78, 79, 110, 114, 223
Bass, L.K., 85
Beebe, Lucius, 202
Bell, Dr. William A., 18, 28, 30, 58, 62, 130, 131
Bent, Charles, 122
Bernalillo, 78
Big Horn, 39, 44, 48, 49, 111, 114, 215, 230
Biggs, 114, 152, 161, 162
Black Canyon, 19, 26
Black Hawk, Colorado, 100, 104, 106
Black Hills Central, 236
Blake Street, Denver, 24
Blair Street, Silverton, 76, 143
Blind Beaver Creek, 57
Bloomfield, New Mexico, 101, 102
Blue River Extension, 26
Bocea, 111, 114
Bolivar, J. Pluto, 248
Bondad, 114, 115
Bonita, 108
Borst, W.W., 30
Boston and Colorado Smelter, 106
Boston Treaty, 24, 25, 26, 34, 41, 79, 82, 85-88, 127
Boulder Lake, 162
Boulder Mountain, 74
Bountiful, 114
Bourke, John Gregory, 205, 216
Bowman, 115
Boydsville, 111
Boyle, Herbert M., 238, 241
Brady, 114
Bravo, 119
Brazos, New Mexico, 152, 162
Brewster, J.K., 32
Brigham's Monument, 215
Broad, 114
Broadwell Hotel, 119

Brooks, D.C., 30
Brunot Treaty, 74, 99, 100, 141
Buckman, 114
Burchmore, Robert N., 241, 243
Burnham Shops, 178
Byers, William Newton, 141

C
Calico Cut, 215
Caliente, 79, 88
California Gulch, 23
Calumet, 26
Canon City, 22-24, 26, 178
Canones Creek, 41
Capulin, 122
Carbon Junction, 114, 115
Carracas, 111, 114, 212
Carson, 114
Carson, Kit, 75
Cascade, 49, 62, 71, 115, 142
Cat Creek, 57, 111, 162
Cedar Creek, 236
Cedar Hill, 94, 115
Central City, 14
Central Pacific, 16, 18
Cerillos, New Mexico, 22
Chama, 12, 21, 26, 34, 41, 43, 44, 47-50, 52, 55, 57, 58, 64, 78, 79, 82, 83, 95, 103, 105, 109, 111, 114, 115, 117, 128-131, 149, 150, 152, 153, 156, 157, 161, 162, 164, 180, 205, 212, 215, 216, 226, 231, 235, 237, 239, 241, 252
Chama Lumber, 152
Chamita, 82, 114
Chapman, E.R. and Company, 86
Chattanooga, 143
Cherry Creek, 10, 14, 21, 24, 32, 74, 88
Cheyenne, Wyoming, 16
Chicago World's Fair, 178
Chihuahua, 14, 129
Childress, James, 241, 243
Chili Line, 8, 9, 13, 19, 28, 41, 78, 79, 82, 88, 90, 105, 110, 164, 205, 223, 226, 232, 236, 241
Christ of the Mines Shrine, 136
Chromo, 161, 162
Cinnamon Pass, 136
City of Holy Faith, 85, 88, 128
Civil War, 6, 7, 14, 18, 19, 128, 141
Clark, E.N., 150
Cliff Dwellers, 102
Cliff Ruins, 101
Clipper Theater, Durango, 100
Cochetopa, 136, 149
Colisium Theater, Durango, 100
Colmex, 115
Colorado City, 21
Colorado College, 16
Colorado Coal/Fuel and Iron, 18, 19, 62, 79, 86, 142
Colorado Eastern, 178
Colorado-New Mexico Better Transportation Association, 240
Colorado-New Mexico Express, 205, 208, 211
Colorado Railroad Museum, 85, 189, 191, 247
Colorado River, 108
Colorado Springs, 16, 18, 19, 21, 22, 30, 32, 149, 178
Colston House, 125
Columbus, Christopher, 12
Comanche Canyon, 79
Conejos, 23, 24, 34, 47, 58, 59, 85, 111, 119, 121-123, 125, 126, 215, 220
Connell Tank, 114
Continental Divide, 41, 47, 55, 57, 111, 131, 152, 162, 191, 216
Corlett, J.J., 125
Coronado, 6, 10, 12, 13, 25
Cortez, 12
Costilla, 13, 78, 85, 119, 121
Coxo, 111, 114
Coyote Park, 162
Crazy Woman Creek, 68, 71
Creede, 76, 110, 119, 143, 235
Cresco, 38, 111, 114
Crested Butte, 25, 26, 108, 169, 236
Cretaceous period, 10
Cripple Creek, 16
Crofutts Grip-Sack Guide, 35, 48, 49
Cross, Floyd, 241

Crystal River Railroad, 164, 169, 180
Cucharas, 23, 78
Culebra River, 13, 121
Cumbres, 189
Cumbres, 8, 9, 19, 21, 22, 26, 28, 34, 40, 41, 43, 44, 47-50, 52, 55, 60, 68, 95, 96, 111, 114, 116, 117, 119, 122, 127, 154, 157, 163, 191, 210, 211, 215, 219, 222, 223, 224, 226, 229, 230, 232, 233, 235-237, 240
Cumbres and Toltec Scenic Railroad, 197
Cunningham Pass, 41
Curecanti Needle, 19

D
Daily Record, Durango, 59
Daily Sentinel, Grand Junction, 238
Dalton, 114, 216
Darlington, 114
Davidson, James, 241
Dawson, Clyde, 150
De Escalante, Fray Silvestre Velez, 57, 130, 138
De Leon, Ponce, 12
De Niza, Marcus, 12
De Onate, Juan, 12, 25
De Ulibarri, Juan, 13
De Vaca, Cabeza, 12
De Vargas, Don Diego, 13
Del Norte, 142
Delores, 134, 162
Denver, 8, 14, 16, 18, 21, 22, 24-26, 28, 30, 32, 41, 55, 68, 75, 78, 79, 88, 99, 103, 104, 106, 114, 133, 138, 141-143, 149, 169, 203, 205, 208, 235, 242
Denver Circle Railway, 178
Denver and New Mexico Southern Railway, 21
Denver and South Park, 21
Denver and Southern, 30
Denver Pacific, 16
Denver Post, 237
Department of Agriculture, 149
Depression of 1929, 8, 143, 149, 163, 205, 235, 236
De Remer, J.R., 32
Diablo Canyon, 88
Diamonte Canyon, 161, 162
Diaz, Porfirio, 25
Dodge, D.C., 30
Dominguez, Fray Francisco, 57, 130
Drake, Sir Francis, 12
Dulce, 54, 57, 111, 114, 161, 163, 216
Durango, 8, 9, 13, 19, 23, 26, 28, 34, 41, 44, 45, 47, 55, 57-60, 62-64, 68-71, 75, 78, 90, 92, 94, 98-107, 114, 115, 129, 130-135, 138, 142, 143, 150, 153, 160, 164, 180, 191, 202, 203, 205, 208, 212, 214, 228, 233, 236-240, 242, 244
Durango and Silverton Railroad, 102, 241
Durango Land and Coal Company, 58, 131
Durango Herald, 238, 239
Durango Record, 99
Dyke, 115

E
Eberhart, Perry, 143
Edith, Colorado, 136, 162
Eilers, 106
El Cuartelejo, 13
El Magre, 111
El Mopre, 111
El Moro, 23
El Paso, 13, 21, 25, 28, 78, 88
El Vado, 82, 115, 151, 152, 161, 162
Eldorado, 141
Elk Creek, 71, 142
Elk Park, 71, 115, 142
Elwood Pass, 41
Embargo Creek, 44
Embudo, 19, 85, 110, 114
Ensenada, 152
Ephraim, 122
Espanola, New Mexico, 22, 26, 34, 41, 48, 78, 79, 82, 85-88, 114, 121, 127, 128
Espejo, 12, 25
Estrella, 114
Eureka, 141, 143
Evans, John, 59

F
Falfa, 111, 114

Farmington, New Mexico, 90, 92, 95, 96, 101, 102, 115, 181, 230, 235, 236, 238-241, 245, 249
Farmington Branch, 8, 90-92, 94, 95, 97, 114, 134
Farmington Daily Times, 238
Feather, M. Carl, 241
Feltwich, S.M., 30
Festiniog Railroad, Wales, 18
Field, T.M., 32
Field and Hill Company, 121
Fischer, Emil, 135
Flaugh, Colorado, 162
Flora Vista, 114, 115
Florence, Colorado, 22-24
Florence and Cripple Creek Railroad, 76, 169
Florida River, 57, 101, 114, 130
Fort Garland, 14, 78, 249
Fort Marcy, 78
Foss, Sam Walter, 9, 251
Fountain City, 30
Fountain River, 19, 21
Four Corners Regional Commission, 242
Franciscans, 12
Francisco's Plaza, 23
Francisco's Ranch, 23
Fremont, John Charles, 27, 44, 224
Fremont County, 32
Frisbie, Howard L., 241
Fruita, 149
Furness and Company, 169

G
Galisteo, 30, 78, 79
Gallegos, Julian, 122
Gallina Junction, 115
Gallinas, 161, 162
Gallup, New Mexico, 92
Garfield, President James, 111
Garfield Monument, 111, 114, 215
Garland City, 23, 25, 119
Gato, 57, 111, 130, 161, 162, 249, 250
General Meily, 88
Geronimo, 57, 129
Gildersleeve, Charles H. 85
Gilpin, William, 59
Gladstone, 75, 143
Glenwood Springs, 143
Globe Smelter, Denver, 106
Gold King Mining Company, 143
Gould, George, 91, 92, 94, 95
Gould, Jay, 25, 28, 91
Grand Junction, 26, 75, 238
Grand View Smelter, Rico, 103
Grant Smelter, Leadville, 106
Grant, Ulysses S., 129
Great Salt Lake, 8, 16, 25
Great Salt Lake Valley, 14
Green Mountain, 75
Green River, Utah, 26
Greene and Company, 100
Greenwood, William H., 30
Gregory, John H., 14
Gregory Lode, 14
Grenadier Mountain, 134
Grubbs, 115
Guadalupe, 122
Guggenheim, 106
Gunnison, 19, 26, 34, 55, 96, 106, 108, 136, 143, 149, 178, 205, 209, 236

H
Hall, 115
Halleck and Howard Lumber Company, 88
Hamilton, Edward, 241
Harlan, Ralph B., 241
Harriman, Edward H., 91, 92, 94
Hartner, 47
Hauser, 115
Hayden, F.V., 41
Head, Lafayette, 122
Hecla Iron Mine, 26
Hendrix, 115
Henry, 110, 114
Herald, Silverton, 62, 64, 143
Hercules, 115
Hermosa, 68, 107, 114, 115, 141, 142
Hesperus, Colorado, 92, 134
High Line, 62, 64, 69, 70, 74, 76, 142
Hillcrest, 114, 162
Hinman, Thomas T., 239, 242
Hobart, 114
Hoge, Rev. C.M., 131
Holbrook, H.R., 32
Holladay Street, Denver, 25
Home Ranch, 68, 115, 142
Hood, 115
Hooper, 236
Hopewell, New Mexico, 41
Horse Lake, 22, 41, 57, 115, 130, 138, 141, 152, 162
Hot Springs Iron Mine, 26
Howardsville, 75, 143
Howe, Jack, 108

Howeville, 110
House by the Side of the Road, 251
Hunt, A.C., 21, 30, 59, 79
Huntington, Collis P., 91
Hutchins, S.A., 32

I
Icke, Phillip F., 241
Ignacio, 111, 114, 130
Imperial Pacific Railroad, 21
Inca, 115
Interstate Commerce Commission, 88, 238-241, 243
Ireland, 115
Ironton, 136
Irvin, Charles H., 85, 87

J
Jack's Cabin, 110
Jackson, William S., 30
Jacona, 115, 114
Jacques, Jose Maria, 122
Jefferson, Pres. Thomas, 6
Jicarillas, 44, 57, 129, 161
Johnson, Senator Edward, 88
Joker Tunnel, 136, 143
Juanita, 57, 111, 114, 235
Jumping Jenny, 74, 143

K
Kansas Pacific Railroad, 14, 16, 18, 21, 30, 32, 249
Kearney, General, 128
Kearns, 115
Keightley, W.M., 131
Kendall Mountain, 74, 138
Kernas, Dr. Benjamin, 44
Kessler, Robert Lee, 241
Kettle Mountain, 212
King, Harry, 32
King Mine, 115
Knull, Ralph H., 241

L
La Boca, 111, 114
La Jara, 110, 114, 122, 162
La Madera, 88, 114, 151
La Madera Branch, 82, 88, 90, 111, 236
La Plata County, 99, 101, 102, 238
La Plata Miner, Silverton, 62, 64, 143
La Plata River, 92
La Veta, 23, 25
La Veta Pass, 16, 19, 22, 23, 26, 34, 169
Labran, Colorado, 22
Lago, 115, 162
Lake City, 136, 143, 236
Lake San Cristobal, 136
Lake Shalano, 70, 72
Lamborn, Robert H., 30
Laredo, Texas, 25
Larimer, General William, 7
Larimar Street, Denver, 21, 24
Las Sauces, 122
Lathrop, Gilbert, 180
Latter Day Saints, 14, 122
Lawrence, Kansas, 18
Law's Mill, 152
Lawton, 114
Lava, 48, 111, 114, 212
Leadville, 16, 23, 24, 34, 76, 104, 106, 133, 138, 143, 149
Lewis, Robert E., 150
Lewis and Clark, 6
Leyden, 114
Lightner Creek, 92
Little Giant, 100, 141
Little Navajo River, 162
Lobato, 38, 49, 52, 114, 216
Lodo, 114, 115
Lone Tree, 115
Loring Military Road, 136
Los Mogotes, 215
Los Piedras, 79
Los Pinos, 44, 47, 48, 57, 111, 114, 130, 215, 222
Louisiana Purchase, 6, 13, 16
Lowry, C.J., 85
Lumberton, New Mexico, 57, 114, 152, 161, 162
Lyden, Supt. Cole, 230, 231
Lyons, Alva, 211

M
Magoffin, Susan Shelby, 127
Manassa, 122
Mancos Station, 102
Market Street, Denver, 25
Marshall Pass, 8, 19, 22, 25, 26, 108, 119, 180, 191
Masterson, Bat, 143
Maxwell Land Grant, 21
May Day Canyon, 216
Maysville, 26
McCarthy, Judge Wilson, 18, 19
McKelvey, R. Franklin, 238, 241
McKelvey, Laverne, 241
McMullen, H.L., 125
McMurtrie, J.A., 25, 32, 34, 44, 55, 78, 79, 85

McNeill, John L., 241
Mears, Otto, 70, 74-76, 107, 108, 136, 143, 180, 236
Mears Junction, 8, 9, 26, 108, 236
Meily, Luther M., 86-88
Mellen, Mary Lincoln, "Queen," 8, 18, 21
Mercereau, J.P., 30, 32
Mexican National Railways, 18
Mexico City, 6, 12, 14, 18, 21, 24, 25, 88
Middleton, 143
Midland Terminal Railroad, 169
Miera, Don Bernardo, 130
Miller Coal Mine, 162
Million Dollar Special Wreck, 220
Mineral Point, 143
Mississippi River, 16
Missouri Pacific, 91, 235
Missouri River, 16
Moffet Tunnel, 180, 235
Mogotes, 122
Molas Pass, 138
Monarch Pass, 235
Monero, 55, 106, 111, 114, 161, 216
Monte Vista, 110
Montezuma, 31
Montezuma, 12, 88
Montezuma Lumber Company, 189, 191
Montezuma's Revenge, 126
Montrose, Colorado, 8, 9, 26, 28, 76, 108, 178, 236
Monument Creek, 21
Moore, 111, 114
Moore and Carlile, 32
Moreno Valley Railway, 30
Mormons, 14, 25, 26, 88, 121-123
Mount Blanca, 49, 212
Mountaineer, 169
Mud Tunnel, 219
Mudhens, 164, 180, 192, 193
Mundo, 114
Murname, 142
Murray, R.S., 161

N
National Association of General Passenger and Ticket Agents, 111
National Land and Improvement Company, 32
Navajo, 75, 90, 94, 96, 97, 111, 114
Navajo Canyon, 55, 57, 59, 216
Navajo Creek, 47
Navajo Indians, 13, 75, 132
Navajo River, 19, 57, 62, 130, 161, 162, 216, 232
Needle Creek, 71
Needle Mountain, 134
Needleton, 44, 71, 115, 142, 221, 223
New Mexico Express, 205
New Mexico Lumber Company, 149, 150
New Mexico State Corporation Commission, 241
New York World's Fair, 178
Newcomen Society, 18
Newton Lumber, 162
No Agua, 110, 114
North Pueblo, 30
North Star Mill, 115
Nossman, Welsh, 150
Nuevo Mejicanos, 25, 41, 86, 216
Nutria, 115

O
Occidental Hotel, 119
Ogden, Utah, 16, 18, 22, 25, 26, 75, 96
Ogden Gateway, 91, 235
Ojo Caliente, 111, 114
Omaha, 18
Orient Branch, 26, 236
Orman and Crook, 85, 86
Ortiz, 122
Osier, 12, 40, 49, 111, 114, 215, 231, 232, 237
Osier Mountain, 44
Ouray, 8, 25, 70, 75, 76, 143, 149, 236
Ouray, Chief, 70
Oxford, 111, 114

P
Padres, 41
Pagosa Junction, 57, 114, 115, 161, 162, 248, 249
Pagosa Lumber Company, 161-163
Pagosa Springs, 115, 152, 153, 161-163, 235, 250
Pagosa Springs Branch, 115, 162, 236
Pajarita, 110, 114
Palmer, General William Jackson, 8, 10, 13, 16, 18, 19, 21-30, 34, 41, 44, 47, 55, 57-60, 62, 64, 68, 74, 75, 79, 82, 85, 88, 90, 99, 103, 107, 108, 110, 111, 114, 119, 121, 123, 130, 131, 133, 134, 136, 142, 143, 169, 215, 235, 236, 243
Palmer Lake, 16, 30
Palmilla, 110, 114
Panic of 1873, 22, 149
Panic of 1893, 16, 106, 133, 152
Park Range, 149
Parlin, 236
Pearson, John, Ella, and Mary Isabelle, 131
Pennington, J.L., 60

311

Pennsylvania Railroad, 18
Perry, 115
Phantom Curve, 49, 215
Piedra, 47, 57, 130
Pike, Lt. Zebulon, 6, 9
Pikes Peak, 14
Pile, Governor of New Mexico, 100, 141
Pine River, 114
Pinkerton Springs, 102, 220
Pinos Altos, New Mexico, 22
Pitkin, Governor Frederick W., 59, 60
Platte River, 6, 10, 24, 88
Plum Creek, 19
Plum Station, 149
Poage, C.D., 248, 249
Poncha, 26
Poncha Pass, 21, 28, 108, 119, 121, 136
Porter, Ernest, 241
Posta, 114, 115
Potts, James D., 24
Pounds Brothers Planing Mill, 150
Prell, Linville, I., 241
Price, William, 162
Prince, 114
Public Utilities Commission of Colorado, 241
Pueblo, 13, 14, 21-24, 26, 32, 41, 87, 88, 103, 104, 106, 133, 142, 143, 205, 244
Pueblo Cheiftan, 238
Pueblo Indians, 13

Q
Quartz, 236

R
Raton Pass, 16, 21-23
Red Cliff, 26
Red Mountain, 75, 136
Reidel, George, 125
Reynolds, N.P., 31, 32
Richardson, Robert, 189
Rico, 70, 75, 103, 134, 143
Ridges Basin, 92
Ridgway Colorado, 75, 107, 236
Ridgway, Arthur, 19
Ridgway, Robert M., 19
Rincones, 122
Rio Arriba County, 152
Rio Bravo, 21
Rio Grande (film), 223
Rio Grande Rail Road and Telegraph Company, 21, 78
Rio Grande River, 6, 13, 21, 23, 25, 34, 41, 48, 78, 79, 86, 88, 110, 119, 121, 122
Rio Grande Southern, 70, 75, 76, 102, 104, 107, 134, 162, 236
Rio Grande Valley, 21, 25, 79, 119, 235
Rio Grande Western, 22, 26, 82, 91, 149, 169
Rio Grande and Pagosa Springs Railroad, 161, 162
Rio Grande and San Juan Railroad, 239, 242
Rio Grande and Southwestern, 114, 162, 163
Rio Grande, Pagosa and Northern Railroad, 162, 163
Rito Gato, 111
Rito Santa Fe, 88, 128
Rockwood, 62, 68-72, 115, 142, 220
Rocky Mountain News, 141
Rocky Mountain Railroad Club, 210
Rocky Mountain Railway Company, 21
Rodriguez, Father, 12, 25
Rogers, H. Austin "Auz", 248-250
Romeo, 45, 110, 114, 121
Romero, 110
Romney, Mrs., 99, 100
Roosevelt, Theodore, 149
Ross, 115
Royal Gorge, 19, 21, 23, 24, 80, 99
Royal Gorge War, 23, 24
Russell, Colorado, 23

S
Salida, 9, 26, 27, 28, 55, 96, 108, 164, 169, 178, 205, 236
Salt Lake City, 8, 16, 25, 26, 82, 92, 178
San Antone, 13, 47-49, 79, 212
San Antonio River, 41, 79, 110, 122
San Francisco, 18, 92
San Ildefonso, 78, 110, 114
San Isabel Forest, 149
San Jose, 122
San Juan, 45, 98, 159, 178, 202-217, 220, 239
San Juan, 13, 23, 25, 44, 70, 74, 79, 85, 90-92, 94, 96, 102, 103, 119, 122, 141, 149, 235
San Juan Basin, 91, 98, 99, 235, 236, 238, 242
San Juan Extension, 26, 34, 41, 44, 47, 48, 55, 82, 88, 108, 111, 123
San Juan Lumber Company, 241
San Juan Railway, 30
San Juan Range, 41, 100, 121, 122, 136, 138, 226
San Juan River, 9, 16, 19, 34, 41, 47, 57, 58, 62, 92, 99, 111, 130, 216, 232, 249
San Juan and New York Smelter, 104
San Luis Valley, 6, 13, 14, 21, 23, 24, 27, 28, 34, 49, 50, 58, 85, 88, 110, 119, 121, 122, 126, 136, 180, 211, 212, 226, 240, 242, 243

San Miguel, 122
San Pete Valley, 169
San Rafael, 122
Sanford, 122
Sangre de Cristo, 21, 23, 49, 78, 99, 121, 212
Sante Clara, 78, 110, 114
Santa Fe, 6, 8, 9, 13, 14, 16, 23, 25, 28, 34, 41, 78, 79, 82, 85-88, 105, 108, 114, 119, 123, 127, 128, 130, 141, 149, 205, 223, 242
Santa Fe Trail, 6
Santa Rita Railway, 30
Sawmill Mesa, 152, 162
Schuyler, Howard, 30, 31
Scott, Thomas A., 30
Sea of Cortez, 55
Seligman, Bernardo, 86
Seven Cities of Cibolla, 6, 12
Servilleta, 110, 114
Shavona, 126, 205
Shawano, 108
Sheridan, Kansas, 16
Sickels, T.E., 79
Silver City, New Mexico, 22
Silver Vista, 105, 207
Silverton, 8, 16, 19, 26, 28, 34, 41, 47, 58, 62-64, 66, 68-72, 74-76, 99, 100, 102-105, 108, 115, 121, 130, 134, 136-143, 172, 203, 207, 223, 228, 237, 242
Silverton Branch, 26, 62, 64, 90, 104, 114, 134, 138, 140, 142, 164, 180, 185, 220, 222, 232, 233, 236, 238
Silverton, Gladstone and Northern, 75, 143
Silverton Northern, 75, 143
Silverton Smelter, 115
Silverton Railway, 75, 143
Silverton Standard, 240
Smelter Hill, Durango, 135
Smith, 115
Solo, 111, 114
South Arkansas River, 21, 26
South Fork, 41, 122, 235
South Park Railway, 30
South Platte River, 14
Southern Colorado Coal and Town Company, 23
Southern Pacific, 90, 91, 235
Southern Union Gas Company, 95, 96
Southwest, Animas City, 59
Sprague, Marshall, 28
Spring Creek Divide, 161, 162
St. Louis, 18
State Corporation Commission of New Mexico, 88, 243
Steward, R.W. and Company, 88
Stinking Lake, 162
Stolsteimer Creek, 162
Stoney Pass, 41, 142
Struby, F.S. and Company, 121
Sublette, 39, 48, 111, 114, 215
Sullenberger, Alexander T., 152, 161-163
Sultan, 74
Summitville, 143
Sunnyside, 115, 143
Sunetha, 115
Swoop, Willis, 229, 230
Symes, Judge Foster J., 88

T
Tacoma, 68, 69, 115, 142, 222
Talian, 115
Tanglefoot Curve, 210, 215, 229, 240
Taos, 13, 14, 44, 79, 82, 88, 100, 114, 119, 121
Tefft, 115, 142
Telluride, 75, 134, 143
Tennessee Pass, 21, 26
Tenochtitlan, 88
Texas, Santa Fe and Northern Railroad Company, 85-88, 127, 128, 178
Thompson Mesa, 162
Thomson, John Edgar, 18, 30
Tierra Amarilla, 129, 152
Tierra Amarilla Southern Railway, 152, 162, 163
Tiffany, 111, 114
Toltec, 49, 111, 114, 215, 220
Toltec Scenic Railway, 39
Tombstone, 76
Tres Piedras, New Mexico, 79, 88, 110, 114
Trimble Hot Springs, 68, 102, 142
Trinchera River, 121
Trinidad, 13, 14, 22, 23, 106, 133
Tripartite Agreement, 24, 28
Tweed, Conductor, 229, 230

U
Uncompahgre River, 76
Uncompahgre Valley, 108
Union Contract Company, 32
Union Pacific, 16, 18, 26, 79, 149, 178
Union Station, Denver, 16, 19
Union Station, Salt Lake City, 18
United States Army, 60, 92, 107
Upper Arkansas River, 23
Utah and Pleasant Valley Railroad, 169
Ute Indians, 13, 44, 57, 58, 70, 72, 74, 99, 111, 129, 141, 250
Ute Mountain, 212

V
Vallecito River, 22
Valley Courier, Alamosa, 239
Veaver, John, 149, 150
Velarde, 85, 114
Villa Grove, 122
Volcano, 114, 232

W
Waddingham, Wilson, 21
Wagon Creek, 23
Wagon Wheel, 26, 121
Walker, John S., 241
Walsenburg, 13, 14, 23
Webb Canyon, 162
Weitbrec, R.F., 34, 41, 44, 47, 55, 78, 79
Westcliffe, 26
Western Colorado Railway, 30
Western Pacific, 91, 235
Wet Mountains, 149
White Rock Canyon, 78, 79
Whitecross Mountain, 136
Whitter, 133
Williams, Bill, 44
Willow Creek, 55, 114, 152, 162
Windy Point, 49, 215
Wirt, Emmet, 57
Wissmath, 115
Wolf Creek, 41, 48, 49, 52, 111, 216
Woods, John C., 180
Wotjas, Stanley J., 236
WWI, 88, 107, 121, 149, 235, 243
WWII, 9, 94, 134, 164, 194, 195, 210

Y
Young, Brigham, 14, 121
Young, William S. (Red), 223

Locomotives

Locomotive Number	Page Number
1	7
5 (Galloping Goose)	104
50 (diesel)	185
95	166
101	234
169	124
268	182, 183
318	186
340	187
343	188
345	181
346	189, 190, 191
453	192
461	193
463	206
471	164, 194
473	98, 207, 221
475	178
476	172, 195, 203, 204, 220
477	202
478	91, 207
481	196
482	197, 226
483	127, 210
484	117, 144, 145, 154, 157, 237
485	205, 240
486	107, 116, 169, 176, 177, 178, 179, 212
487	130, 158, 169, 170, 171, 179, 181, 204, 251
488	117, 127, 172, 178
490	115, 178, 234
491	129, 176, 177, 198, 224, 234
492	86, 117, 118, 130, 146, 154, 155, 157, 178, 180, 239, 241
493	83, 94, 116, 153, 156, 169, 181, 199, 249
494	103, 108, 110, 115, 170, 171, 232, 234
495	109, 174, 176, 177, 227, 238
496	108, 167, 200, 201
497	87
498	130, 227, 238, 240
499	83, 89, 169, 219, 252, 253
3000 (US Army diesel)	92, 93, 107
4700N (US Army diesel)	184

Maps

Page 82 — Rio Grande RR, circa 1920
100 — Durango, June 3, 1963
101 — System map
139 — Silverton Mining District, circa 1885-1890
150 — System map, 1925
236 — Rio Grande map, 1914
243 — D&RGW map, November 1978